To Improve the Academy

To Improve the Academy

Resources for Faculty, Instructional, and Organizational Development

Volume 19

Devorah Lieberman, Editor
Portland State University

Catherine Wehlburg, Associate Editor
Stephens College

ANKER PUBLISHING COMPANY, INC.
Bolton, Massachusetts

To Improve the Academy
Resources for Faculty, Instructional, and Organizational Development

Volume 19

ISBN 1-882982-43-6

Composition by Sherican Books, Inc.
Cover design by Boynton Hue Studio

Anker Publishing Company, Inc.
176 Ballville Road
P.O. Box 249
Bolton, MA 01740-0249

www.ankerpub.com

To Improve the Academy

To Improve the Academy is published annually by the Professional and Organizational Development Network in Higher Education (POD) through Anker Publishing Company, and is abstracted in ERIC documents and in Higher Education Abstracts.

ORDERING INFORMATION

The annual volume of *To Improve the Academy* is distributed to members at the POD conference in the autumn of each year. To order or to obtain ordering information, contact:

Anker Publishing Company, Inc.
P.O. Box 249
Bolton, MA 01740-0249
voice   (978) 779-6190
fax   (978) 779-6366
email   ankerpub@aol.com
web   www.ankerpub.com

PERMISSION TO COPY

The contents of *To Improve the Academy* are copyrighted to protect the authors. Nevertheless, consistent with the networking and resource-sharing functions of POD, readers are encouraged to reproduce articles and cases from *To Improve the Academy* for educational use, as long as the source is identified.

INSTRUCTIONS TO CONTRIBUTORS FOR THE NEXT VOLUME

Anyone interested in the issues related to instructional, faculty, and organizational development in higher education may submit manuscripts. Manuscripts are submitted to the current editors in December of each year and sent through a blind review process. Correspondence, including requests for information about guidelines and submission of manuscripts for Volume 20, should be directed to:

Devorah Lieberman
Vice Provost and Assistant to the President
Center for Academic Excellence
Portland State University
Portland, OR 97207-0751
voice   (503) 725-5642
fax   (503) 725-5262
email   liebermand@pdx.edu

Professional and Organizational Development Network in Higher Education (POD)

Mission Statement

Approved by the Core Committee on March 24, 1991:

The Professional and Organizational Development Network in Higher Education (POD) fosters human development in higher education through faculty, instructional, and organizational development.

POD believes that people have value, as individuals and as members of groups. The development of students is a fundamental purpose of higher education and requires for its success effective advising, teaching, leadership, and management. Central to POD's philosophy is lifelong, holistic, personal, and professional learning growth, and change for the higher education community.

The three purposes of POD are:

1)   To provide support and services for its members through publications, conferences, consulting, and networking.

2)   To offer services and resources to others interested in faculty development.

3)   To fulfill an advocacy role, nationally, seeking to inform and persuade educational leaders of the value of faculty, instructional, and organizational development in institutions of higher education.

Membership, Conference, and Programs Information

For information contact:

David Graf
POD Network
Nova Southeastern University/FGSEHS
1750 NE 167th Street
N. Miami Beach, FL 33162
phone (954) 262-8786
email   Grafd@nova.edu

Table of Contents

Preface

The theme of this year's *To Improve the Academy* is reflective of the POD conference 2000: "The Brave New Millennium." The chapters in this year's volume speak to the best in current and new trends in the field of faculty development. We have thoughtfully constructed this year's volume so that each of the three sections addresses areas in which the field of faculty development is greatly invested. Furthermore, the articles contained within this volume are balanced between application and practice and theory. All articles were selected through a rigorous blind review process. Section I is devoted to five of the areas that will be of primary concern to faculty developers as we enter the 21ˢᵗ century. Section II is devoted to how students learn and what roles faculty developers play in this process. Section III is devoted to the faculty developer's role in delivering support to faculty in their efforts to achieve professional development.

To Improve the Academy (Volume 19) required the efforts of many individuals who contributed to the outstanding quality of this volume. First and foremost, the contributing authors must be recognized. As you read through this volume, you will find yourself underlining the concepts put forth in many of the articles as well as copying the articles for colleagues at your institution with the intent of replicating ideas and programs on your own campuses. This would not be possible without the commitment of these authors to produce scholarship of faculty development. In a period when we each have little time to reflect on our own practice, conduct action research, study our own works, and contribute to a larger body of knowledge, these authors have met the scholarly challenge and have taken the time and effort to advance the field of faculty development. The authors in this volume deserve our praise, thanks, and recognition for their efforts to advance the field.

In particular, I wish to thank my associate editor, Catherine Wehlburg, for supporting me throughout the process of delivering this volume. The role of associate editor is critical in delivering a product such as *To Improve the Academy*. Also, the quality of this volume speaks to all the reviewers who took the time and effort to read, comment on, and give feedback to each person who submitted an article. Their contributions were immense. The reviewers for this volume are William Cashin, Julie Furst-Bowe, Madelyn Healy, Edmund Hansen, William Timpson, Ben Ward, Leslie Cafarelli, Nancy Diamond, Tricia Kalivoda, Ann Kovalchick, Sabrina Marschall, Judith Miller, Ed Nuhfer, Daniel Pratt, Laurel Willingham-McLain, Dina Wills, Kenneth Baldwin, and Douglas Robertson.

It takes hundreds of hours for an editor to produce a publication such as *To Improve the Academy*. Without the support of upper-level administrators at my home institution, I would not have been able to edit this volume. I would like to recognize the following individuals for the support they offered me: President Dan Bernstine, Provost Mary Kathryn Tetreault, and Vice Provost Sherwin Davidson. When leaders in the university recognize the importance of faculty development to the success of the university, they validate the time and effort it takes to assume editorial responsibilities for work such as *To Improve the Academy*. Under their leadership, my scholarly work in faculty development has been validated and rewarded.

I also wish to thank individuals on my campus who helped me with the process of completing this volume. Dawn Roznovsky, Office Specialist, Center for Academic Excellence, kept me organized, interacted with reviewers, and kept my editorial compass pointed in the right direction. Ann Rivinus, my assistant for campus initiatives, reviewed articles for APA style and citation veracity. Donna Bergh, Executive Assistant to the Provost, helped with editing and organizing this volume. Without these three individuals, I surely would have become mired and overwhelmed by process details. Also, I would like to recognize the importance of working with a publisher who is supportive of its editors. Anker Publishing was there when I needed them. They answered questions, offered encouragement, and when met with obstacles, suggested alternative strategies for completing this volume. I have never worked with an easier, more responsive, or more collaborative publisher.

I would be remiss if I did not thank my husband (Roger) and children (Alicea and Emery Rose) for the encouragement they gave me to work many hours and days on *To Improve the Academy* (Volume 19). Not often is a wife and mother as fortunate as I to have such endless familial support.

Devorah Lieberman
Vice Provost and Assistant to the President, Campus Initiatives
Director, Teaching and Learning Excellence
Portland State University
May 2000

Introduction

The articles brought together in this volume of *To Improve the Academy* reflect current research in faculty development and trends for the future of faculty development. POD's mission has three foci: to provide services and support, to offer services and support, and to inform and persuade educational leaders of the value of faculty development in higher education. The articles in this volume were selected based on the following three criteria: 1) the quality of the submission, 2) the insight that it brings to the future of faculty development nationally and internationally, and 3) the alignment with the POD mission statement. As a result, the articles represent the highest quality in terms of content and application to those who benefit from being among POD's membership and those who avail themselves of POD's resources.

We have also included POD's "Ethical Guidelines for Educational Developers." A POD committee constructed these guidelines which were then adopted by the POD Core (Core Meeting, Spring 2000). These guidelines will serve us well as the number of faculty developers increases and their responsibilities become even more pervasive in the academy.

Section I: Focus on Trends in Faculty Development contains five articles. These articles were selected and/or invited because they each address trends that are critical to the roles of faculty developers in institutions of higher education. Cambridge speaks to the National Conversation on scholarship of teaching and the importance of the faculty developer's role in the AAHE/Carnegie campus conversations. She invites readers of the articles to encourage their campuses to actively participate in this national conversation. Hecht offers readers the current state of chair development and the faculty developer's role in supporting and working with department chairs as leaders within their organizations. Ehrlich tackles service learning and offers a historical perspective on the movement, suggesting strategic directions in which faculty developers can move their own institutions. Bonilla and Palmerton contribute an article addressing diversity issues, which are central to the vision of POD. The diversity theory and application are a must-read and must-do for

POD members and affiliates. Section I closes with an article by Cox that brings the learning community concept to faculty of the 21st century. The model application for campus-wide learning communities offered in this article can serve to launch new learning communities or direct existing ones.

Section II: Focus on Faculty Development and Student Learning provides articles which ask us to think critically about the student as learner. There are times that student learning is forgotten as the central focus for what we do and why we entered higher education. The chapters in this section serve as a reminder that, as educators, student learning serves as our primary goal. Angelo, in his usual wisdom, reminds us of our own practice and our dearest values. He offers us lessons that bring us to answer his question: "Why is it that the vast majority of well-intentioned efforts in American higher education seem to result in little or no long-term improvement in student learning?" Fink encourages us to think differently about student learning and offers a new taxonomy to address students' higher-level learning. Hativa takes us into the classroom and suggests very specific strategies, grounded in data, that professors could incorporate into classroom interactions that lead both to increased student learning and to increased student satisfaction. Nellis, Clarke, DiMartino, and Hosman describe an outstanding program for faculty at Valencia Community College that focuses on faculty interaction and student learning, incorporating outcomes, content, processes, resources, structures, and assessment. There are lessons to be learned from this program that may serve as a model for any institution of higher education. Paulsen brings us from the undergraduate student to the graduate teaching assistant. His discussion of the program that he has developed for over a decade offers insight into graduate student learning and, in particular, teaching assistant development. Smith reminds us that research universities often overlook learning opportunities that are available to their undergraduate students when faculty and graduate students partner with the intent of enhancing the undergraduate experience. She describes a successful program that partners faculty, graduate students, and undergraduate students in learning the research process. Strada's chapter focuses the reader on the importance of designing a syllabus that brings professor and student to a point where the professor uses the syllabus as a roadmap and the student uses it to enhance learning. Cook's chapter takes us from the focus on individual development for faculty to professional development for departments as a whole. She clearly addresses how a faculty developer can move a department to think about professional development for the faculty within their own unit. She illuminates the importance of engaging all faculty within a department rather than randomly encouraging faculty from across a campus. Finally, Courtney reminds us that higher education today compels us to address the uses of technology in online learning and that the technology used in learning must serve as value-added rather than merely an add-on to course delivery.

Section III: Focus on Faculty Development and Professional Support brings the reader to the role that faculty developers play in supporting faculty and administrators in their professional development efforts. As faculty strive to become better teachers and scholars, faculty developers can provide essential support along these paths. The chapters in this section offer excellent examples of practice, grounded in theory, that can further faculty professional growth. Pierce describes an outstanding program for new faculty that integrates mentoring, survival skills, teaching skills, and establishing research agendas. Gray and Birch describe another related program. In their chapter, they compare and contrast faculty writing and scholarship programs at two institutions. The lessons learned from each program will benefit faculty developers attempting to implement a faculty scholarship program on their campus. Kreber takes us past the process of scholarly writing to documenting scholarly teaching for promotion and tenure purposes. Her chapter clearly delineates how scholarly teaching can be documented and peer reviewed in a teaching portfolio. Akerlind and Quinlan keep us focused on scholarship but introduce it in light of collegiality. They reinforce the roles colleagues play in enhancing each other's scholarship. They reinforce the notion that faculty interaction is important for scholarly growth and needs to be reinforced. Atkins, Brinko, Butts, Claxton, and Hubbard move us even further into the discussion of professional growth, scholarly growth, and personal growth. This chapter addresses faculty pressures and their impact on faculty satisfaction. Their suggestions for improving faculty quality of life should be heeded by all faculty developers and institutional administrators. Middendorf rounds out this volume, addressing the reality of faculty development and administrative support. With the support of administrators, faculty developers can have a much more pervasive and long-term impact on their campuses. She offers specific strategies for engaging administrators in the goals of faculty development.

As the field of faculty development gains greater institutionalization in higher education, nationally and internationally, it is imperative that faculty development scholars continue to study their work, offer it for peer review, and share it with larger audiences. The work within this year's *To Improve the Academy* offers examples of this scholarship.

> Devorah Lieberman
> Center for Academic Excellence
> Vice Provost and Assistant to the President, Campus Initiatives
> Portland State University
> May 2000

Ethical Guidelines for Educational Developers

PREAMBLE

Educational developers, as professionals, have a unique opportunity and a special responsibility to contribute to improving the quality of teaching and learning in higher education. As members of the academic community, we are subject to all the codes of conduct and ethical guidelines that already exist for those who work or study on our campuses and in our respective disciplinary associations. In addition, we have special ethical responsibilities because of the unique and privileged access we have to people and information, often sensitive information. This document provides general guidelines that can and should inform the practice of everyone working in these development roles.

Individuals who work as educational developers come from many different disciplinary areas. Some of us work in this field on a part-time basis, or for a short time; for others, this is our full-time career. The nature of our responsibilities and prerogatives as developers varies with our position in the organization, our experience, and our interests and talents, as well as with the special characteristics of our institutions. This document attempts to provide general ethical guidelines that should apply to most developers across a variety of settings.

Ethical guidelines indicate a consensus among practitioners about the ideals that should inform our practice as professionals, as well as those behaviors that we would identify as misconduct. Between ideals and misconduct is an area of dilemmas: where each of our choices seems equally right or wrong; or where our different roles and/or responsibilities place competing—if not incompatible—demands on us; or where certain behaviors may seem questionable, but there is no consensus that those behaviors are misconduct.

It is our hope that these guidelines will complement individual statements of philosophy and mission and that they will be useful to educational developers in the following ways:

- in promoting ethical practice by describing the ideals of our practice

- in providing a model for thinking through situations which contain conflicting choices or questionable behavior

- in identifying those specific behaviors which we agree represent professional misconduct

RESPONSIBILITIES TO CLIENTS

- Provide services to everyone within our mandate, provided that we are able to serve them responsibly

- Treat clients fairly, respecting their uniqueness, their fundamental rights, dignity, worth, and their right to set objectives and make decisions

- Continue services only as long as the client is benefiting, discontinuing service by mutual consent; suggest other resources to meet needs we cannot or should not address

- Maintain appropriate boundaries in the relationship; avoid exploiting the relationship in any way; and be clear with ourself and our client about our role

- Protect all privileged information and get informed consent of our client before using or referring publicly to his/her case in such a way that the person could possibly be identified

COMPETENCE AND INTEGRITY

Behavior

- Clarify professional roles and obligations

- Accept appropriate responsibility for our behavior

- Don't make false or intentionally misleading statements

- Avoid the distortion and misuse of our work

- When providing services at the behest of a third party, clarify our roles and responsibilities with each party from the outset

- Model ethical behavior with coworkers and supervisees and in the larger community

- Accept appropriate responsibility for the behavior of those we supervise

Skills and Boundaries

- Be reflective and self-critical in our practice; strive to be aware of our own belief system, values, biases, needs, and the effect of these on our work

- Incorporate diverse points of view

- Know and act in consonance with our purpose, mandate, and philosophy, integrating them insofar as possible

- Ensure that we have the institutional freedom to do our job ethically

- Don't allow personal or private interests to conflict or appear to conflict with professional duties, or client's needs

- Continually seek out knowledge, skills, and resources to undergird and expand our practice

- Consult with other professionals when we lack the experience or training for a particular case or endeavor and in order to prevent and avoid unethical conduct

- Know and work within the boundaries of our competence and time limitations

- Take care of our personal welfare so we can take care of others

Others' Rights

- Be receptive to different styles and approaches to teaching and learning, and to others' professional roles and functions

- Respect the rights of others to hold values, attitudes, and opinions different from our own

- Respect the right of the client to refuse our services, or to ask for the services of another

- Work against harassment and discrimination of any kind, including race, gender, class, religion, sexual orientation, age, nationality, etc.

- Be aware of various power relationships with clients; e.g., power based on position or on information; don't abuse our power

CONFIDENTIALITY

- Keep confidential the identity of our clients, as well as our observations, interactions, or conclusions related to specific individuals or cases

- Know the legal requirements regarding appropriate and inappropriate professional confidentiality (e.g., for cases of murder, suicide, or gross misconduct)

- Store and dispose of records in a safe way; comply with institutional, state, and federal regulations about storing and ownership of records

- Conduct discreet conversations among professional colleagues; don't discuss clients in public places

RESPONSIBILITIES TO THE PROFESSION

- Attribute materials and ideas to their authors or creators

- Contribute ideas, experience, and knowledge to colleagues

- Respond promptly to requests from colleagues

- Respect your colleagues, and acknowledge their differences

- Work positively for the development of individuals and the profession

- Cooperate with other units and professionals involved in development efforts

- Be an advocate for our institutional and professional mission

- Take responsibility when you become aware of gross unethical conduct in the profession

CONFLICTS ARISING FROM MULTIPLE RESPONSIBILITIES, CONSTITUENTS, RELATIONSHIPS, LOYALTIES

We are responsible to the institution, faculty, graduate students, undergraduate students, and our own ethical values.

These multiple responsibilities and relationships to various constituencies, together with competing loyalties, can lead to conflicting ethical responsibilities, for example, when:

- An instructor is teaching extremely poorly, and the students are suffering seriously as a result

  Conflict: responsibility of confidentiality to client teacher versus responsibility to students and institution to take some immediate action

- A faculty member wants to know how a TA, with whom we are working, is doing in his/her work with us or in the classroom

  Conflict: responding to faculty's legitimate concern versus confidentiality with TA

- We know firsthand that a professor is making racist, sexist remarks or is sexually harassing a student

  Conflict: confidentiality with professor versus institutional and personal ethical responsibilities, along with responsibility to students

- A fine teacher is coming up for tenure, has worked with our center or program for two years, and asks for a letter to the tenure committee

  Conflict: confidentiality rules versus our commitment to advocate for good teaching on campus and in tenure decisions

In such instances, we need to practice sensitive and sensible confidentiality:

- Consult in confidence with other professionals when we have conflicting or confusing ethical choices

- Break confidentiality in cases of potential suicide, murder, or gross misconduct. In such cases, to do nothing is to do something

- Inform the other person or persons when we have to break confidentiality, unless to do so would be to jeopardize our safety or the safety of someone else

- Decide cases of questionable practice individually, after first informing ourselves, to the best of our ability, of all the ramifications of our actions. Work to determine when we will act or not act, while being mindful of the rules and regulations of the institution and the relevant legal requirements

Conflicts Arising from Multiple Roles

As educational developers, we often assume or are assigned roles which might be characterized as, for example, teaching police, doctor, coach, teacher, or advocate, among others. We endeavor to provide a safe place for our clients; we are at the same time an institutional model and a guardian or a conscience for good teaching. These multiple roles can also lead to ethical conflicts.

Some educational developers, for example, serve both as faculty developers and as faculty members. As faculty we are on review committees, but through our faculty development work have access to information that probably is not public, but is important to the cases involved. Given these multiple roles, it is important always to clarify our role for ourselves, and for those with whom and for whom we are working. When necessary, recuse ourselves.

Summative Evaluation

A particular case of multiple roles needing guidelines is the summative evaluation of teaching. Faculty and administrators (chairs, deans, etc.) have the responsibility for the assessment of teaching for personnel decisions.

In general, educational developers do not make summative judgments about an individual's teaching. In particular, we should never perform the role of developer and summative evaluator concurrently for the same individual, other than with that person's explicit consent and with proper declaration to any panel or committee. However, we may provide assessment tools, collect student evaluations, help individuals prepare dossiers, educate those who make summative decisions, and critique evaluation systems.

Conclusion

These guidelines are an attempt to define ethical behaviors for the current practice of our profession. The core committee welcomes comments and suggestions as we continue to refine this document in light of the changes and issues confronting us as educational developers in higher education. The guidelines will be updated on a periodic basis.

We would like to thank our many colleagues who offered their thoughtful comments on earlier drafts.

In creating this document, we have referred to and borrowed from the ethical guidelines of the following organizations: American Psychological Association, American Association for Marriage and Family Therapy, Guidance Counselors, Society for Teaching and Learning in Higher Education, and The Staff and Educational Development Association.

Prepared by Mintz, Smith, & Warren, January 1999. Revised March 1999, September 1999, and March 2000.

Section I

Focus on Trends in Faculty Development

1

Fostering the Scholarship of Teaching and Learning: Communities of Practice

Barbara L. Cambridge
American Association for Higher Education

As part of the scholarship of teaching and learning, faculty members study the ways in which they teach and students learn in their disciplines, and how campuses foster this scholarship at an institutional level. A national initiative called the Carnegie Academy for the Scholarship of Teaching and Learning constitutes three programs to engage and support individuals, campuses, and disciplinary associations in this form of scholarly work. In To Improve the Academy *(Volume 18) this program was discussed. The article this year offers examples of individual faculty and campus initiatives centered on the scholarship of teaching and learning.*

INTRODUCTION

Dennis Jacobs has introduced cooperative learning into a large lecture course of general chemistry at the University of Notre Dame. The retention rates, test performance, and interest level of students in the cooperative learning course have exceeded those for students of similar ability enrolled in a more traditional general chemistry course on the same campus. Dennis is interested now in answers to the following questions: 1) Which features of the new course (pairing students in lecture to analyze and predict chemical behavior, small group problem solving activities, weekly graded homework, online quizzes, increased socialization) have had the greatest impact on student learning? 2) What design elements of cooperative learning activities are most successful in stimulating meaningful discussion, promoting deeper conceptual understanding, and developing individual problem solving skills? and 3) What is the long-term impact of such a course? Are students more successful in advanced courses if they have had a collaborative problem solving experience in a foundation course?

Like Dennis, most faculty have questions about the impact of their pedagogical decisions on student learning. And more and more faculty are doing something about finding answers to those questions through designing projects that build on what is known about learning, specifically about learning in their disciplines. This exciting work occurs in pockets on campuses of all kinds throughout the country, but often it remains local, improving teaching and learning within the investigator's own classroom but not adding to the knowledge base of the discipline, partly because of traditions about teaching that thwart its identification as scholarly work. Teaching has been regarded as private, difficult to study and critique, and less worthy than traditional research of serious regard and valuing.

Fortunately, faculty who pose, study, and begin to answer intriguing questions about their teaching can enter a newly emerging community of scholars. These scholars apply to their scholarship of teaching criteria pertinent to all scholarship: clear goals, adequate preparation, appropriate methods, significant results, effective presentation, and reflective critique (Glassick, Huber, & Maeroff, 1997). They expect to go public with their findings, to receive the kind of peer review that interrogates their methods and conclusions, and to change their teaching and scholarly investigations of teaching based on that review. They also expect that their institution's reward system will acknowledge and value their scholarship of teaching and learning.

You may be asking at this point what planet I am writing about. But I did say "an emerging community of scholars." Communities must be built, and there are multiple individuals and groups committed to the building of this new community of scholars of teaching and learning. In this chapter, I will describe one effort to enlarge this new community through support of individuals, campuses, and associations devoted to the work. Dennis is a member of that effort, and you with your campus are welcome to join this growing community.

THE CARNEGIE ACADEMY FOR THE SCHOLARSHIP OF TEACHING AND LEARNING

The Carnegie Academy for the Scholarship of Teaching and Learning (CASTL), with funding from The Pew Charitable Trusts and in collaboration with the American Association for Higher Education, is designed to foster the practice of scholarly inquiry about teaching and learning. Its three parts attend to three ways in which faculty members enter their professional worlds: as individuals, as members of a campus faculty, and as members of disciplinary groups.

Pew Scholar Fellowship Program

The Pew Scholar Fellowship Program selects scholars from designated disciplines to pursue their work in a concentrated way through funding, opportunities for interactions with other scholars, and, all importantly, time for carrying out a scholarly project.

Pew Scholars are contributing to the emergent definition of the scholarship of teaching and learning. Pat Hutchings, senior scholar at the Carnegie Foundation for the Advancement of Teaching and leader of its CASTL higher education work, suggests that the definition can begin with what the scholarship of teaching and learning is not.

1) The scholarship of teaching and learning is not new. Faculty members have generated important work—from many academic levels and disciplines—for many years upon which new scholars can build. Traditionally, however, faculty members have not become familiar with this literature through their graduate programs.

2) The scholarship of teaching is not for everyone for all time. Faculty members do different kinds of scholarly inquiry and pose different questions at different times in their professional lives. Some scholars will choose to focus on teaching and learning; others will not. Some will choose to do this work throughout their careers; others may move in and out of the work.

3) The scholarship of teaching and learning does not replace other kinds of scholarship. The scholarships of discovery, application, and integration join with the scholarship of teaching as one way to look at an array of scholarly possibilities.

4) Each discipline offers different ways to approach this work. For example, rhetoric and composition warrant narrative as a way to investigate and disseminate learning; chemistry values a more empirical approach.

5) The scholarship of teaching and learning is not aimed exclusively at publication. Scholars of teaching and learning are exploring multiple ways of making their work public, including the web, faculty development activities, and public presentations.

6) The scholarship of teaching is not simply for a faculty member's own improvement. It contributes to the practice of others.

7) No one has this kind of work all figured out (Hutchings, 1999).

In fact, the work of helping to figure it out is one challenge for Pew Scholars. Ansel Adams once said that there is nothing worse than a clear image of a fuzzy concept. Knowing that a definitive definition would be premature at this time, the Pew Scholars will over time increase knowledge about the concept of the scholarship of teaching and learning. The kinds of projects contributing to this development are as various as the scholars doing them. Here is just a glimpse of the range of work undertaken:

- In business, Anthony Catanach, accounting at Villanova University, is developing strategies for long-term assessment of students' use of competencies from his intermediate financial accounting course, a two-semester course considered the core of the accountancy major. He wants to determine the effects of innovative pedagogies used in his course on students' performance in subsequent classes and professional work.

- In English, Mariolina Salvatori, the University of Pittsburgh, is theorizing an approach to teaching that develops a teacher's attentiveness to her students' "moments of difficulty" for their hidden potential to produce understanding. Naming something "difficult" demonstrates a form of knowledge that is both profitable and responsible to tap. She is studying the stumbling blocks in learning in different disciplines to understand how other disciplines confront this aspect of teaching.

- T. Mills Kelly, in history at Texas Tech University, is focusing on the ways in which student learning changes in response to the medium used to present essential source materials. Running parallel sections of the same Western Civilization course offering materials in multimedia format and in print only, he is particularly interested in the influence of the web.

- Peter Alexander's "Math and Social Justice" capstone course for undergraduate mathematicians at Heritage College has the key goal of enhancing students' quantitative worldview while they work on projects that meet each student's definition of social justice and which benefit local communities. Beginning from Dubinsksy et al.'s Action, Process, Object, Schema model of undergraduates' mathematics understanding, Peter is developing ways to assess students' growth in quantitative worldview.

- Stephen Chew, a psychologist at Samford University, is examining the effect of surface and structural components of examples used by teachers. Teachers often give surface components, which strongly influence student understanding and ability to generalize from the example. Stephen aims to help faculty in multiple disciplines structure examples and problems to optimize student understanding.

- As editor of *Teaching Sociology*, Jeffrey Chin of Le Moyne College is studying the evolution of the scholarship of teaching in sociology from 1983-1998, using papers published in the journal as a database. He will compare his results with a 1983 study that extended back to 1973 to determine if progress has been made in cumulative scholarship and in a convergence of teaching-learning strategies.

- Deborah Vess, at Georgia College and State University, is examining the effects of interactive, online modules in an interdisciplinary global issues course by developing an assessment instrument to determine the development of students' critical abilities in the modules and interviewing students to ascertain intellectual problems faced in constructing their solutions and integrating resources. She wants to understand how students apply abstract theory to actual world situations and to document the relationship of interdisciplinary work to growth in critical abilities.

This sample of the range of projects illustrates the interesting intellectual problems that are challenging scholars in multiple fields. The Pew Scholars Fellowship Program promotes synergy among these scholars.

Campus Program

The second component of CASTL also offers synergy, this time among campuses. The Campus Program is designed for institutions of all types that are prepared to make a public commitment to new models of teaching as scholarly work and is implemented through the American Association for Higher Education. Any interested campus is encouraged to organize its efforts and then to register its process and goals so that all campuses can learn from one another.

DEVELOPING A DISCOURSE

Whenever a new community of scholars forms, the community develops language that it collectively uses to talk about what it wants to talk about. Because the term "scholarship of teaching" is so new, the Campus Program begins with a campus-wide focus on a draft definition of the scholarship of teaching, and is offered as a conversation starter. In fact, the first phase of Campus Program participation is named "campus conversations" to emphasize the need for dialogue and for developing discourse about teaching and learning. Campuses are invited to take apart and revise the draft definition so that the campus has a clearer sense of what it means by doing the scholarship of teaching and learning. The draft definition is, "The scholarship of teaching is problem posing about an issue of teaching or learning, study of the problem through methods appropriate to the disciplinary epistemologies, application of results to practice, communication of results, self-reflection, and peer review."

Several campuses have reported their negotiated versions of a definition. These examples illustrate the thinking at three quite different campuses, two of which have generated a definition and one of which has a process in motion that suits the size and type of campus that it is.

Abilene Christian University

Following a series of departmental and college meetings and discussion on an interactive web page, Abilene Christian University decided on major changes in the definition because they feared that the language emphasized a research methodology that would exclude some practices such as curriculum revision or teaching portfolios that they believed are appropriately classified as scholarship of teaching and that the language of the draft definition emphasized the process more than the definition. Their definition reads, "The scholarship of teaching is public discourse conceptualizing teaching." "Public" is making our work accessible to others for critical review and use. "Discourse" includes oral and written discourse in such varied contexts as curriculum committees; faculty development presentations; and publications on the web, teaching portfolios, or journal articles. While both informal and formal opportunities to present findings are considered scholarship of teaching, they are weighted differently in faculty evaluations such as tenure and promotion. "Conceptualizing" teaching is more than good teaching: It requires careful thought, analysis, and self-reflection about teaching. "Teaching" cultivates the exchange of ideas among teachers, students, and others in and out of the classroom.

Elon College

Elon College frames a different definition:

> The scholarship of learning/teaching a) seeks to develop new
> knowledge (through discovery, integration, application) in the

field of inquiry and to share what is learned widely so that insights can be built upon and oversights corrected; b) invites collaboration throughout the process; c) sets a direction of inquiry and commits to shared standards as to how results will be measured; d) remains alert to the most exciting thinking in the disciplines that bear on the task; e) invites constructive critique from the academic community (colleagues, students, and like-minded peers).

We choose to speak of the learning-teaching enterprise. This shift emphasizes that what is examined must be a partnership of students and teachers in which both partners learn and both partners, in different ways, teach. We wanted to make learning central and also to highlight educational content in the various fields.

The Ohio State University

To root the discussion in concrete, disciplinary contexts, each member of the executive council of the Academy of Teaching convened a conversation in her or his own academic unit (involving similar units if desired). The proposed topic for discussion was "Learning Pitfalls in Introductory Classes." The conversations addressed such questions as: What are some common concepts that are especially confusing for students in our introductory courses? What skills are especially hard for them to master? How do we know when students are really stuck? How do we explore the nature of the problem? What do we do with the information we obtain? Are there systematic ways in which our faculty and discipline could address these issues and share our findings? Based on the answers to these questions, how do we define the scholarship of teaching for our context? Is this definition applicable to nonintroductory courses as well?

A forum is now planned at which different groups will compare their results and look for commonalties across disciplines. The goal is to arrive at a university definition of the scholarship of teaching, identification of the ways in which it is supported and constrained, and a plan of action for cultivating such scholarship in the future.

IDENTIFYING CONDITIONS FOR DOING THE SCHOLARSHIP OF TEACHING AND LEARNING

In the next part of campus conversations, campuses identify ways in which they support or inhibit the scholarship of teaching and learning. Campus groups take up such questions as who does the scholarship of teaching and learning on our campus? Do hiring and orienting practices locate and support faculty members committed to the scholarship of teaching? What are the most central teaching issues on our campus, and how is the campus addressing those issues? Are faculty members rewarded for doing the scholarship of teaching? How does our campus culture discourage, and how does our campus culture affirm the scholarship of teaching and learning? What specific steps can the campus take to create conditions generative of the scholarship of teaching and learning? This environmental scan enables a campus to identify an area for study and actions that will enhance its support for this kind of work.

Campuses that have completed their campus audit and have determined or are deciding on a focus for future campus-wide work are inevitably considering a range of work. Several examples signal that range.

Western Washington University

Western Washington University has drafted an action plan to profile the scholarship of teaching and learning in a way that elevates the status of teaching on its campus. With commitment from its president, who provided a summer stipend for a faculty leader to work with colleagues for planning, the campus will focus on a theme during each of three quarters of the academic year: *recognizing* the scholarship of teaching, *reflecting* on that work, and *rewarding* it. These 3-R's discussions will begin first term with main events such as a presidential luncheon for all faculty and a series of campus lectures and breakfast meetings followed by workshops.

In addition, 35 faculty members from each of the campus's 35 departments and programs are being selected to examine the effectiveness of a case study and peer review model to develop and advance faculty skills intended to enhance student learning in critical thinking, writing in the disciplines, symbolic reasoning, and affective development. They will try to answer the following questions: Can a faculty-based case study grounded in a peer review and self-reflective approach improve student learning in noncontent domains? Will this process significantly improve instructional competence and cross-disciplinary dialogues about teaching and learning and enhance the scholarship of teaching at WWU? Faculty will generate case studies from their own teaching as exemplars of student learning problems and themes in noncontent domain. These case studies will be used as springboards for faculty using a variety of methodologies. The campus plans to use electronic threaded discussions, inclassroom peer review, self-reflective writing, and the identification and development of student learning and faculty development assessment tools.

Augustana College

Augustana College faculty have identified five general areas on which they would like to focus. The participating faculty (45 of the college's 150 full-time faculty members) have affiliated themselves with one of five question groups. The five groups and some of the questions under consideration include:

The student. How can an instructor tap students' internal motivation? How do various modes of learning and teaching interact with differing styles and abilities? Is students' motivation subject to change through strategies we can employ?

The classroom. What is the interaction between content and teaching strategy? How do gestures facilitate learning? How can teaching techniques be matched to outcomes and audience?

The engaging text. What happens to students when they are assigned readings? What happens during highlighting? Is there a difference in reading comprehension from hard copy versus screen text? Can we teach students to "talk back" to textbooks? What prereading approaches facilitate the reading process?

Impact of technology. How does technology impact learning? Do course webpages and chat groups facilitate learning? Does requiring that writing assignments be on disk improve the quality of writing and feedback?

Foreign study. How does foreign study impact students? What intellectual and social growth occurs during these experiences? What classroom experiences best facilitate learning in this context?

Resident campus experts on quantitative and qualitative research approaches have met with the participants to discuss options for structuring the inquires. Members of each group read common texts to provide a starting point for refining their research questions. By the end of summer 1999, each group will have developed a strategy for investigating a specific question.

Rockhurst College

The two central questions for Rockhurst College are 1) How do we make our inquiries about teaching and learning issues public in ways useful to our campus colleagues and to our disciplines? and 2) Can we make this new area of scholarly discussion highly interdisciplinary to promote wider dialogue and new perspectives?

A seminar group of 15 faculty from a variety of disciplines and levels of teaching experience will follow four steps in this process. Along the

way each seminar member will have access to an on-campus consultant—a faculty or administrative volunteer from a different discipline
that has special expertise (teaching and research). These consultants will
provide suggestions on resources and methods, serve as sounding boards
for ideas, and occasionally join seminar discussions or make special presentations. Thus the "broadcast area" and potential impact of the seminar
will be immediately increased. The action plan for the seminar includes
four steps:

Step 1) To develop a common language, seminar members will read
a core set of materials on learning theory, the scholarship of teaching and
learning, college teaching, assessment, and higher education. Each seminar member will select a course they teach to serve as a practical context
for exercises and discussions related to teaching as a scholarly act.

Step 2) Each seminar member will "deconstruct" the course they
have selected—reexamining its component parts (objectives, assignments, assessments) in light of the readings, discussions, seminar presentations, and advice from consultants. The primary goal will be to identify
discipline-based and interdisciplinary areas of research within a course
framework. Participants will present their findings to the seminar for further discussion and refinement. They will also engage in scholarly projects suggested by this process.

Step 3) Building on Step 2, the seminar will attempt to identify and
answer key questions about teaching as a scholarly act, including appropriate research methods, types of evidence for such scholarship, standards and criteria for peer review, elements unique to a discipline, and interdisciplinary connections.

Step 4) Seminar members will prepare articles and presentations on
the seminar experience and their course research. The workshop leader
will construct a seminar workbook as a model device for subsequent faculty development activity.

Occasions for sharing processes and products of campus work are
part of the second phase of the Campus Program. Beginning with a colloquium prior to the 1999 American Association for Higher Education
National Conference on Higher Education, two-day colloquia will be
held each year to enable cross-campus interaction and reports of progress
both by Pew Scholars and by Campus Program participants. Meetings of
campuses of similar type or working on similar issues are being held as interest and need arise.

Campuses are supported in their work also by a WebCenter that offers resources, places to post drafts or finished products, sites of conversation around specific themes, and information about the work of all registered campuses and of individuals on those campuses. Faculty and staff on a Campus Program campus can sign on to make full use of all the features of the WebCenter.

Work with Scholarly Societies
Faculty members often derive their primary professional identify through their disciplines, reinforced by the current form of graduate education and by the ways in which their work is acclaimed. The third arena of activity in CASTL acknowledges the centrality of the disciplinary and professional societies in promoting the scholarship of teaching and learning. Some associations have actively and publicly supported the work. For example, the American Sociological Association has published a book on peer review in sociology, building on work done by sociologists and others in the AAHE Peer Review project. The American Historical Association is working with Pew Scholar William Cutler from Temple University in providing examples of course portfolios on the web for response and use by other historians. The National Council of Teachers of English, the Academy of Management, and the American Chemical Society are featuring the topic of the scholarship of teaching and learning at upcoming conferences. Pew Scholar Randy Bass is leading a major project for the American Studies Association focusing on the ways in which the web opens new opportunities for both creation of and interaction about scholarship of teaching and learning. These examples illustrate the ways in which scholarly societies can play a central role in fostering the scholarship of teaching and learning. At the 1999 Colloquium on Campus Conversations at AAHE, Carla Howery of the American Sociological Association challenged her colleagues who provide leadership in associations to do an association audit. In that audit, associations ask themselves how they contribute not only to the professional identity but also to the full range of professional work of their members, including the scholarship of teaching and learning. CASTL and AAHE have convened over 20 associations, primarily in disciplines represented in its Pew Scholar cohorts, to discuss strategies for supporting their members in this professional work and to devise their own projects for seed funding. The work of Pew Scholars like Jeff Chin and Donna Duffy offer essential information to associations about the impact of their work in this area.

WHAT'S NEXT?

At the 1999 Pew Scholar Institute, Peter Alexander, a mathematician from Heritage College, sparked thinking with the application of some principles of architecture to the scholarship of teaching and learning. Peter described as essential to architectural projects commodity, firmness, and delight. Commodity implies utility: the structure must serve the purposes for which it is built. Firmness includes substantiality or significance. And delight brings pleasure, joy, and satisfaction into the equation. In a later session at that same Institute, Lee Shulman picked up that language in advocating for distributed awareness, practice, and valuing of the scholarship of teaching and learning. He suggested that the standard of value for the scholarship of teaching and learning would certainly include at least utility (commodity) and delight. How will we know if this scholarship has utility and delight? Shulman answers that the work will be useful and interesting to more and more people in higher education if it is 1) generative, 2) longitudinal, and 3) collaborative.

Shulman referred to Aristotle's distinction between a face and a bag of coins. If any part of a face is removed or added to, the face changes, becoming something essentially different. If, on the other hand, a bag of coins has a few coins removed or added, the bag is recognizable as the same bag of coins. Shulman hopes that the scholarship of teaching and learning will change the face of higher education, not just alter the same old bag.

To make this change, the scholarship must first be generative, demonstrating clearly why doing the work is worth the trouble, that is, demonstrating that it is worth changing habits of mind and processes of teaching and learning that have been deeply engrained and are deeply familiar.

Secondly, the view of scholarship of teaching and learning must be longitudinal. Just as pool players think of the next shot as one in a strategic series, we must see individual projects as part of efforts unfolding over time. Because new questions, occasions, and circumstances will evolve, new hypotheses, projects to test those hypotheses and ways to share conclusions will need to be developed. Along this line, Pew Scholar Randy Bass calls for a new way of viewing problems in teaching and learning, that is, as interesting and complex problems not to be solved once and for all but to be continuously explored as they emerge in different contexts (Bass, 1998).

Thirdly, the scholarship of teaching and learning is collaborative. Our rich tradition of building on the research of scholars before us or beside us holds in the scholarship of teaching and learning. "It takes a village," said Shulman about the need for collaborative efforts in addressing the wonderfully complex problems that engage our intellectual and emotional abilities. This collaborative work will add to the critical mass that will serve as "an existence proof" for our colleagues who are just beginning to understand the nature of the scholarship of teaching and learning (Shulman, 1999).

In his book *The Fifth Discipline*, Peter Senge advises that transformative change can occur when genuine openness is present. He calls for "reflective openness," which "looks inward and starts with the willingness to challenge our own thinking, to recognize that any certainty we ever have is, at best, a hypothesis about the world. It involves not just examining our own ideas, but mutually examining others' thinking" (Senge, 1990). The Pew Scholars Fellowship Program, the Campus Program, and the work with scholarly societies efforts all embrace the need to challenge our own deepest thinking and to do so in the company of others engaged in the same work. Teaching and learning will become central in the definition of a professor's role, the identification of a campus's function, and the heart of disciplinary association existence only when we accept the challenge of exploring with commodity, firmness, and delight the complex and exciting sites of learning in higher education.

REFERENCES

Bass, R. (1998). *Inventio*. www.georgemason.com.

Cambridge, B. L. (2000). The scholarship of teaching and learning: A national initiative. In M. Kaplan & D. Lieberman (Eds.), *To improve the academy, 18,* 55–68. Bolton, MA: Anker.

Glassick, C., Huber, M., & Maeroff, G. (1997). *Scholarship assessed: Evaluation of the professoriate.* San Francisco, CA: Jossey-Bass.

Hutchings, P. (1999). *1999 Pew Scholars Institute.* Menlo Park, CA.

Senge, P. (1990). *The fifth discipline.* London: Century, Business.

Shulman, L. (1999). *1999 Pew Scholars Institute.* Menlo Park, CA.

Contact:

Barbara L. Cambridge
American Association for Higher Education
One Dupont Circle, Suite 360
Washington, DC 20036
(202) 293-6440
Email: bcambridge@aahe.org

Barbara L. Cambridge is director of teaching initiatives at the American Association for Higher Education. She is on leave from Indiana University Purdue University, Indianapolis where she is professor of English and associate dean of the faculties. At AAHE, Cambridge coordinates the Campus Program, one of the three activities of the higher education program at the Carnegie Foundation for the Advancement of Teaching.

AN INVITATION

Videotape
A videotape titled *Fostering a Scholarship of Teaching* is now available to introduce key concepts behind the Pew Scholars Fellowship Program and the Campus Program. The video, which features, among others, Lee Shulman and selected Pew Scholars, can be used effectively to help groups of faculty understand the concept of the scholarship of teaching and learning, prompt consideration of involvement in the Campus Program, and explain CASTL to educational leaders and others interested in the quality of education.

Any campus registered for the Campus Program is welcome to a copy of the video by contacting Teresa Antonucci at American Association for Higher Education. She may be reached at tantonucci@aahe.org or (202) 293-6440.

Anyone else interested in the video may order a copy by contacting Terri Coats in the publications department of the Carnegie Foundation for Teaching at (650) 566-5102. The cost for the video is $9.00, including shipping with sales tax if applicable.

Booklets
Booklets about the Campus Program and about the Pew Scholars Fellowship Program are available from AAHE and from the Carnegie Foundation. Contact either site for single or multiple copies.

2

Transitions and Transformations: The Making of Department Chairs

Irene W. D. Hecht
American Council on Education
Center for Institutional and International Initiatives

When we talk about a need for leadership in higher education, we are in fact demanding that chairs be leaders. Is there then another level of transition that is required today of those who become chairs? Is task mastery a guarantee of being a leader? If there are other adaptations needed, what might they be? That is the focus of this exploration. This chapter examines the theory behind leadership and applies to it models that are aligned with the leadership skills needed for successful chair leadership. This article specifically addresses the role of faculty developers in supporting department chairs in their roles as institutional leaders and visionaries.

INTRODUCTION

No one would question that there is an important shift in responsibility for the person who moves from being a faculty member to being a department chair. In fact, anyone contemplating that transition will find valuable two descriptions of the process, one offered by John Bennett (1983), the other by Walter H. Gmelch (1993). After reviewing those two astute snapshots of the transition process, my purpose will be to explore yet one more layer, asking the question: wherein lies the transition or transformation into a leader? My premise is that mastering tasks does not ipso facto attest to the transmutation into a leader. That process is embodied in important changes in perspective combined with the ability of managing important adjustments in human relationships.

Referring to department chairs as leaders does not always seem apt terminology. Within institutions at the level of central administration, there is still an overhang of the concept of chairs being the information conduit between administration and faculty. Deans want to be secure in the assumption that they are providing chairs with complete information and that in turn chairs are delivering clear messages with implicit agendas from central administration. And they rely on chairs to be effective in implementing institutional decisions. As for chairs, particularly new chairs, we know from questionnaires administered to participants in the America Council on Education's national workshops for chairs that they most frequently describe their role as that of facilitator for and supporter of their faculty (Hecht, 1999).

As with any caricature, both pictures—administrative agent or faculty—supporter is simplistic. However, conversations with chairs also indicate that the attitudes embedded in the caricature still retain validity. Meanwhile, the issues being faced by higher education institutions— changes in pedagogy; the distance learning revolution; the teaching-learning revolution; issues of productivity; the reconfiguration of faculty work conditions, including the addition of nontraditional and part-time faculty—are requiring visionary leadership and deft management. And unlike the bricks and mortar phase of campus building in the 1960s, these issues have to be solved if not exclusively at the department level, at least with the active engagement of department faculty. Thus, when we talk about a need for leadership in higher education, we are in fact demanding that chairs be leaders. Is there then another level of transition that is required today of those who become chairs? Is task mastery a guarantee of being a leader? If there are other adaptations needed, what might they be? That is the focus of this exploration.

TWO MODELS

John Bennett: A Transition Model

The first transition model we have is that offered by John Bennett in 1983. Bennett suggested that there were three major transformations that would face anyone upon becoming a department chair. One was the transition from specialist to generalist. As academicians we are trained to be expert in what may be a very restricted and even esoteric area of knowledge. Upon becoming a department chair, the incumbent needs to be equally interested in the range of specialties represented by the total faculty of the department. The second transition Bennett suggests is moving from being an individualist to being a person running a collective. That transition parallels the move from specialist to generalist. As a faculty member, one is responsible for one's individual actions and decisions; as a chair one is responsible for decisions that affect other individuals. But note that Bennett goes beyond suggesting that the chair is responsible for other individuals to being responsible for the combined work of the faculty as a group. This is an important point because it suggests a shift from serial, one-on-one relations with various individuals to the ability to create a unified purpose among individuals.

The last transition Bennett points to is the refocusing of loyalty from one's discipline to the institution. This is perhaps Bennett's most challenging observation. Academic training is so discipline-focused that it is more natural to think that what a chair needs to do is see the discipline within the context of the institution. Bennett, however, pushes beyond that point to suggest that it may be necessary to set the disciplinary focus to one side and look at the needs and goals of the institution independent of department interests. That is certainly a challenging standard to set before any chair.

Walter H. Gmelch: From Professor to Chair

The second model is one which Gmelch has presented on a number of occasions at the American Council on Education workshops for department/division chairs and deans. The model also appears in his text *Leadership Skills for Department Chairs* (Gmelch, 1993). The Gmelch model identifies a series of what one might call lifestyle changes when one becomes a chair. The once solitary life becomes a socially oriented one: chairs must now focus attention on the needs and wants of others. Scholarship is often a chair's major sacrifice as s/he writes fewer manuscripts and instead churns out memoranda (or today, email). The stable, rather predictable life of a faculty member becomes the mobile, unpredictable life of a chair. Although new chairs are less apt to perceive the transition from austerity to prosperity, that, too, is a lifestyle change. In some departments, there is a physical aspect to that change if the position of chair comes with larger office space. It is unusual if the position does not bring the chair greater access to secretarial and student-aid assistance. There is also the "prosperity" of being able to call upon college/university staff to provide information and support.

Another transformation is from client to custodian. As a faculty member, one is in the position of asking for support up the line. As chair, one becomes the custodian of those requests, and in fact the chair may influence the fate of those client requests. On the other hand, there is a loss of individual power as one finds that instead of professing to one's colleagues, one needs to devote hours to persuading them of the need to

FIGURE 2.1
The Transformation from Professor to Chair

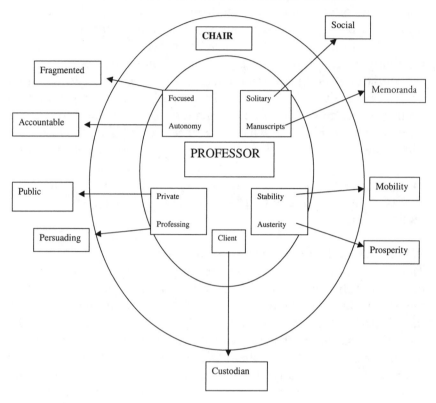

adopt a particular (rational) policy or take on (necessary) implementation tasks. And there is a loss of privacy as one becomes a public person. As one of the regular ACE presenters, Mary Lou Higgerson, puts it, as chair "you are never off duty." In small town settings, particularly, that can be a burden. Chairs are also burdened with the need to be accountable rather than autonomous. Distressing today is the range of audiences to which one finds oneself accountable! Lastly, chairs have to adapt to a life where focus is fragmented, and time is cut into minute slices. Attention may need to shift from working with a faculty member who has a home crisis, to the secretary whose computer has broken down, to the student who needs a waiver, and the dean who is desperate for your section of a board report, to say nothing of the random, unannounced visits, requests, admonitions enlivened by protests and ultimata that blow all one's carefully laid time-management strategies to the winds.

The transitions and transformations described by Bennett and Gmelch are real. All chairs experience them with varying degrees of comfort or distress. But is there yet another dimension? Is there anything different about approaching the tasks enumerated as a leader rather than a manager? I am using the term "manager" to indicate the performance of designated tasks that are the responsibility of a chair. Is there something more than the performance of the required tasks that differentiates the leader? That is the issue I will now explore.

THE CHAIR AS ACADEMIC LEADER

There is a familiar adage which says "Where you stand depends upon where you sit." Like all aphorisms, it both embodies a commonsense truth while simultaneously ignoring the complexity of reality. The truth in the statement lies in the acknowledgment that specific jobs or positions or roles carry with them recognized obligations. These exist independent of the particular person inserted into that position. Furthermore, that obligation is acknowledged both by the responsible person and the general citizen, player, participant, etc. who forms the other half of the equation. That pattern can be extrapolated across an infinite array of human relationships from parent and child, to policeman and citizen, boss and employee, professor and student. Each set has a recognized pattern of relationships of which the parties are aware. As long as the parties to the definition respect the rules, relationships remain workable and, ideally, can be highly productive and creative. If either side waffles on the basic understandings, tensions develop that can undermine the productivity of a relationship and, at worst, can create social breakdown and even armed confrontation.

However, this is only the surface layer of the aphorism which suffers from two serious limitations. Its first oversimplification is that it assumes that the parties are located indefinitely in particular defined positions. But as we all know, throughout life our positions change. Children grow up and themselves become parents. The citizen stopped by the policeman may be the proprietor of a business with dozens of employees. The boss may be afflicted with a serious illness and become a dependent patient. The student will one day become an expert in something unfamiliar to current professors. Time pushes us continually into new roles. That being the case, we are continually making transitions to new identities.

The second limitation is the unspoken assumption that knowledge lies within the position and that as soon as someone takes on a positional responsibility, changes in behavior will take place automatically. There is certainly a measure of truth in that conviction. The clearer the obligations of a position, the more likely a new incumbent will pick up the appropriate behaviors. But if the positional identity is itself ambiguous, the incumbent will have much more difficulty in adapting. That is in fact the case with the role of department chair. It is a position boasting a closet-full of contradictions. Chairs remain faculty members. So, they are still subject to the same institutional requirements imposed on all other faculty. With rare exception, they continue to teach, even if with reduced load. They continue to work physically in the same confines as when they were faculty only (though in some large departments the chair may move to more spacious quarters). They have review obligations for their faculty colleagues, but those review powers are exercised within informal bonds of friendship and association that can be difficult to ignore. Institutional structures and mores add to the ambiguity. Our colleges and universities persist in using command pyramids to depict their operations. In that model, chairs reside at the bottom of the pyramid as recipients of information, exhortations, and requests from the middle and upper reaches of the pyramid. And yet current circumstance has awakened deans and provosts of the need for proactive leadership at the department level—leadership that needs to be integrated with the larger goals of the institution.

If leadership is now required from department chairs, it must be acknowledged that there is much in current practice, customs, and conceptual vision that stands in the way. At the same time, the need for leadership at that level of the institution is now compelling. What adjustments may chairs need to make if they are to answer that institutional call for leadership? There are three aspects of the chair role that chairs themselves will need to adjust. One is chairs' understanding of their roles and responsibilities, the second is perspective on time, and third is a recalibration of human relationships. In addition, two adjustments will be needed at the institutional level. First, institutions will need to revamp their view of chairs and acknowledge their leadership contribution, and second, the dialog between chairs and deans will need to be rewritten.

ROLES AND RESPONSIBILITIES OF CHAIRS

Gaining the positional title is the easy first step. For department chairs, the responsibility is often thrust upon them. Perhaps the previous chair has had enough and steps down. Or a long-sitting chair decides to retire from faculty life. Or the current chair is ready for a sabbatical. Or maybe the department has defined terms of tenure, and someone else must take up the reins. Or perhaps the would-be chair has seen an opportunity to help the department and feels ready to test a new role. A little judicious lobbying may then put the individual in line to be offered the position. Somewhere in the process there will be the ego boost. Either faculty colleagues will elect you; or they will lobby you to take the position; or the dean may approach you soliciting your assistance. However it happens, for a brief moment new chairs will feel wanted and appreciated. It is even possible to feel a bit of a hero for stepping in where no one else wished to tread.

But it is foolish to expect the moment of appointment euphoria to last very long. The descent into the details of department reality may come not only swiftly, but brutally. Whether it is the need to hire adjuncts for the next term, or the obligation to make a tough tenure recommendation, or the need to staunch a bleeding budget, new chairs can expect something to burst the bubble of innocence long before they are comfortable in the position.

Whatever the details of appointment, inherent ambiguity abounds. To whom are you responsible? Do you serve at the pleasure of a dean? The probability is that the dean will have played at least a symbolic role, a bit like the Pope anointing the Holy Roman Emperor in centuries past. It is more likely that the dean will have had more than a ceremonial role. In current practice the dean may in fact hold final control over chair appointments. That will likely be the case if the chair is recruited from outside the institution. On the other hand, chairs and deans know that no chair can operate without a decent level of support from the department faculty. Does that mean that faculty colleagues are the chair's main constituency? Faculty are very likely to make that assumption. Proximity of contact and commonality of interest may induce a chair to pursue responsibilities with the complimentary conviction that faculty colleagues are and should be the main focus for concern.

From the start, chairs find themselves operating in a murky landscape of either ill-defined or conflicting expectations. A natural response may then be to concentrate on the tangible tasks that must be managed and mastered. Even new chairs have a sense of what a number of those tasks will be. The challenge in this domain lies in getting a grasp of the total package of tasks and learning to organize their handling efficiently and in a timely manner. It may initially be bewildering, because these task lists are fed not only by departmental routines, but also by institutional requirements. During the first cycle, some of these tasks will certainly come up seemingly from nowhere with a deadline of yesterday.

Let us assume for a moment that as a new chair you are able to make the adjustment to juggling multiple tasks within the same time frame and that you have developed your own tricks and strategies for managing your time effectively. Does that make one a leader, or are there are other characteristics a leader will manifest even in the domain of task management? I suggest there are deeper layers. Task mastery alone will not lift a chair above the level of super clerk. To organize tasks into an effective sequence is best described as clerical-level management. And indeed, many chairs complain that the job is more suited to a super clerk than it is to the skills of a faculty member. What would transform a tedious sequence of tasks into work fit for a leader?

One bridge lies in the articulation of purpose. If tasks are performed by rote without supporting a larger purpose, task activity becomes boring, wasteful, a drain of energy, and a source of frustration. On the other hand, when tasks are carried out because there is an important purpose to be served, even routine activity becomes important. A chair who is effective as a leader will be adept at demonstrating the larger purpose of a tedious task. For example, faced by a state requirement to review productivity in the department, the chair has the choice of offering the task as an unnecessary activity mandated by someone over whom the department (and institution) has little controlling influence, or of explaining how completing this task externally required can be handled in such a way as to support department interests. For example, how can the department use the data gathered for an outside review to leverage the department's interests? Chairs will manifest themselves as leaders to the extent that they are able to transmute the tasks demanded of the department into tasks that will support the goals of the department. The key leadership role for chairs is grasping the larger picture, demonstrating the connection between external audiences and the department, and keeping the department aware of its own vision.

The ability to keep track of the larger purpose (which I believe to be critical to thinking as a leader) also can reduce pressure on chairs. For example, faculty review is a stressful task. Chairs may focus on that task only in those moments when institutional policy demands that they make judgments for retention, promotion, and tenure. As chairs become leaders, they will see the review process as the practical mechanism and final step in a process of building a topflight departmental faculty. The chair-leader sees the creation of an outstanding department as an unending and continual process. It means encouraging the professional development of pretenure faculty, encouraging the teaching experiments of all faculty, recognizing the professional achievements of all members of the department, supporting a department culture of mutual support and collaborative achievement. With an important, comprehensive purpose in mind of building a quality department, the stress elicited by the need to make judgments about colleagues falls into a less threatening perspective. Reviews are the summative tool that follows all the formative work a chair has exerted throughout the academic year. If the formative work has been done with care and consistency, the summative last step should not embody surprises on either side.

Time

There is another facet of task completion that will distinguish the super clerk from the leader. In a leadership discussion with several chairs at an American Council on Education workshop, one participant offered this insight, "As a leader, I need to think about time in a different dimension." What this person meant was that he had found it important to think about decisions in a long rather than a short time frame. Any manager makes dozens of decisions in every workday. Part of being an efficient manager is being able to sift information rapidly and arrive at a conclusion (decision) quickly. There is even a measure of exhilaration and a sense of accomplishment in being able to make those decisions swiftly. But leadership is manifest when one can differentiate between those decisions which are simple or routine and those which have the potential of impact beyond the immediate moment. For example, a proposal from a faculty member for a sabbatical could be described as a routine request. Chairs and departments, however, are aware that any sabbatical leave affects the department curriculum, the graduation progress of students, the teaching loads of colleagues, etc. Hence, departments may have policies that require sabbatical requests to be filed by a specific date, with decisions being made in the context of all the requests and the collective impact on the department, curriculum, and enrolled students. The same may be true for any number of decisions. Decisions which grant a privilege to one member have implications for all members of the department. A learned leadership skill is the ability to place a single event or request into a longer time frame and broader context. The closest some people are able to come to a leadership frame of mind is to simply say "no" to any request, operating on the assumption that any decision will have consequences—and at best will create new problems and demand new energy. Unfortunately that reaction on the part of a so-called leader simply freezes an organization into a state of immobility.

A facet of the art of thinking in extended time is the ability to anticipate those unanticipated consequences. Unanticipated consequences are just that: unanticipated. In the early days of the automotive revolution, it did not require great genius to see that we would need paved as opposed to gravel roads and that we would need to have lots of fuel stations available for the care and feeding of the horseless carriage. But how many anticipated that the automobile would destroy air quality? Had we done so, would we have halted the development of the automobile? Or would we have worked harder at developing an electric car? And had we pursued the latter course, what unanticipated consequences would have followed that decision? Perhaps the best one can do is expect the unexpected. That at least permits a leader to see the unexpected as a part of the routine of leading.

However, for chairs, especially new chairs, the most stressful change they face is the sheer volume of tasks they are expected to execute. We know this from questionnaires administered at the American Council on Education chair workshops. The expanded task list which all chairs struggle with makes time-management seem like the key to peace and sanity. And there is no doubt that on becoming a chair the incumbent will need to organize time differently. Perhaps the most uncomfortable transition is reconciling oneself to the fact that you need to be as disciplined in the use of time as the weight-watcher needs to be with the ingestion of food. The fact that one's effort to control time will frequently be derailed by the ad hoc arrival of people and problems needing attention, only makes expert time-management more important. One of the luxuries that is denied chairs is that of simply "going with the flow." Chairs adopting that tactic will soon find themselves drowning in a river of uncompleted tasks which unfortunately will often affect the lives of others who will soon lose patience with free-form practices.

One of the prices of good time-management is a loss of spontaneity. It becomes imperative to remain conscious of time as a finite commodity—the only commodity that can never be replaced. The time spent talking to "A" means time away from task "C". Time spent completing task "G" means you could not attend to the needs of faculty member "F". Effective time-management means being constantly aware of anything to which you devote attention in terms of its importance in the context of the other tasks and people you know are clamoring for your attention. It means actively prioritizing each thing, request, problem, person that comes forward. Good time management even means prioritizing time for yourself and for a measure of spontaneous activity. It means building in time-buffers to deal with the unexpected!

Human Relationships

Perhaps the most shocking change for any department chair is the alteration that takes place in human relationships. A powerful plaint on the part of chairs concerns the shift that takes place in their relationships with department colleagues. This may be the greatest source of stress for new chairs. I have heard a variety of comments on this matter. Some chairs find themselves ostracized from their favorite lunch group. Graced with a positional title, those you thought were your "pals" are no longer comfortable having you sit with them as they grouse, laugh, chide about their daily routine. Chairs who persist in maintaining friendly contact with old friends are apt to find that they are fostering suspicion among the rest of the faculty. They may even find that the old friends are themselves uncomfortable with the old intimacy. John Bennett (1983) pinpointed this transition particularly well when he stated that in moving from a faculty position to that of chair, you move from being responsible for yourself as an individual to being responsible for the welfare of a group. As a chair you are responsible in equal measure for each and every member of the department and the exercise of that responsibility is more complex than it was 25 years ago. Departments are far less homogeneous than they were say in 1970. Even though the percentage of women faculty nowhere near parallels the percentage of women students in our institutions (which now exceeds 50%), nor does the representation of racial and ethnic minorities. Nonetheless, most department are no longer exclusively white, male bastions. If, as chair, you come from the venerable WASP category you have the challenge of being the leader for faculty who are different from you and who may harbor rancor and suspicion about your ability to be evenhanded, to say nothing about your instincts for being supportive of those who are different. If you are a chair who is from either a racial or ethnic minority or a woman, you may be even more taxed as you work to be "fair" to all members of the department. You may have to buck unspoken convictions that you cannot be up to the task. Or if you attempt to lead in an unexpected direction or insist on using unfamiliar principles in decision-making, you may find yourself thwarted by passive-aggressive behavior, procrastination, or even open hostility.

Specific responses will certainly vary from department to department and from institution to institution and will be affected by past history of both the department and the institution. What you can expect is that you will no longer be treated as an ordinary colleague. There will be a measure of distance or formality that will be observed, if not on your side, certainly on the part of your colleagues. To buck that seismic shift will undermine your success as a leader. You can put this distancing down as one of the prices of positional leadership.

This change in relationships can be a source of great dismay and discomfort. What perhaps is left unsaid is the frightening prospect that one has lost all one's friends! Gone is the luxury of dropping down to a favorite colleague's office to unburden oneself of the day's distresses. This is true for one's personal anxieties and is categorically true for most worries you have about the department, particularly if those concerns focus on the performance of particular individuals. Knowing that this adjustment will need to take place can give you leverage on the problem. Realizing that collegial friendship within the department will be constricted, a new chair can be proactive in encouraging an alternative network of friends. Rather than seeing the leadership transition as one that is going to reduce one's social range, use the situation as a platform to expand the reach of friendship. Inside the institution other chairs may be a source for new friendships. Within the community, this can be an ideal moment to cultivate work-related contacts into friendships, or it may be a moment to build contacts around your personal interests and hobbies. One door may indeed be closed, but it may be the very moment to realize that the room has a number of unexplored portals that only need to be pushed open.

Professional relationships will also change between the chair and other players in the institution. Among those, none will be more important than the dean or provost to whom a chair reports. A chair who sees no other relationship to a dean than that of subordinate to superior will be severely constrained as a leader. Effective leadership in a chair does not mean being a prima donna who must have everything her way. Nor does it mean being a humble lackey following the master's orders. Leadership in a department chair means being proactive, having a shared vision with department colleagues, and connecting that departmental vision with the goals of the institution. It means being aware of the needs and stresses experienced by other leader-colleagues. In a recent chair/dean workshop, I had the opportunity to hear a chair announce with some amazement that as a result of working together with deans, he had come to the realization that deans were people, too! That may seem remarkably naive, but I suspect that deans would be appalled to hear how often chairs do not see them as human at all. Deans and chairs need to put effort into creating a collegial level of discourse. After all, most institutional problems cannot be effectively ameliorated without a coordinated (and cooperative) effort by both deans and chairs. Here again is an instance where chairs can exert leadership in helping build linkages that support common goals. Leadership is denigrated when it is practiced as a sport of winner-take-all.

INSTITUTIONAL ADJUSTMENTS

Chair Leadership within the Institution

If chairs are to become leaders rather than super clerks, chairs will need to think more broadly about their roles; they need to be disciplined in their use of time; and they need to be prepared to reorganize their personal associations with their faculty colleagues. But leadership takes place within a context, and the institution is that context. Working under current definitions of university structure, there are impediments to the acceptance of chairs as leaders. Unlike the position of dean, provost, or president which are positions that share a broad framework of responsibilities that range across all varieties of institutions, the position of chair lacks such clarity. The terminology itself is remarkable, ranging from chair to chairperson, to coordinator, to head to lead faculty. Even when the same term is used, do not expect the same principles of definition to apply. Institutions that are looking to chairs to be proactive leaders need to look at their terminology—and the assumptions that inhere to that terminology. Are their leadership expectations compatible with the title assigned? And chairs need to understand the institutional context as they endeavor to meet the leadership expectations of their departments.

Chairs and Deans

Lastly, the process of dialog between deans and chairs needs to be reformulated. In reviewing questionnaires from participants at the American Council on Education chair workshops, it is evident that chairs and deans usually meet with regularity. What I find interesting is that when asked who presides and who sets the agenda, the common response to both questions is: the dean. While that response does not reflect the dynamic of conversation at such meetings, it does suggest that in practice, it is the dean who forms the agenda and retains control of the dialog. There are examples of chairs who report either that chairs meet independently or who indicate that there is an elected chair who presides at chair/dean meetings. But those responses are the exception.

For chairs to exert their full potential as leaders, this process of dialog needs to change. Deans are not reluctant in stating that they cannot achieve their goals without the support of chairs. If such is the case, then deans need to engage chairs as partners in the discussion. It also means that deans need to foster a collegial discussion among chairs rather than fostering a position of rivalry between them. Institutions cannot afford the luxury of warfare between departments—one department's win being another department's loss. Deans need to help chairs find their points of common interest.

CONCLUSION

Functioning as a leader assumes specific adjustments in behavior. These adjustments are common to leaders in general. However, the transformation process is particularly fraught for those who become department chairs. This is true in part because of the ambiguities of the position and the lack of clarity about its scope at the institutional level. While new chairs are particularly concerned about task-mastery, the truth is that the attitudinal adjustments are the ones most important for chairs to make if they are to become effective leaders. One perspective that needs adjustment is that concerning tasks. Unless a chair intends to operate as super clerk, s/he must see tasks within the context of department and institutional goals. Routine tasks are important when they are carried out as part of broad goals. A second adjustment that makes for an effective leader is a revised understanding of time. Chairs feel overwhelmed by the scope of responsibility thrust upon them. Hence, managing time becomes a prime problem. A key step in mastering the time challenge is constantly to prioritize, making time for those things that truly matter and setting aside those that fall on a lower level of priority. The last and most trying adjustment is in human relationships, which will have to be handled more objectively than subjectively.

Chairs will not attain their maximum effectiveness as leaders without adjustments across the institutional context. Upper administration needs to define and make publicly explicit its expectations of chairs. Having done that, institutions must make the necessary adjustments to policy documents. However, the most important adjustments may be the behavioral ones that will be required of deans who need to find the means to include chairs individually and as a category in the leadership processes of the institution. For those who succeed, the payoff for our institutions will be high in terms of more effective leadership in meeting the challenges of an uncertain future.

REFERENCES

Bennett, J. (1983). *Managing the academic department.* Phoenix, AZ: Oryx.

Gmelch, W. H., & Miskin, V. D. (1993). *Leadership skills for department chairs.* Bolton, MA: Anker.

Hecht, I. W. D. (1999, Fall). Transitions from faculty member to department chair. *The Department Chair: A Newsletter for Academic Administrators, 10* (2), p. 5.

Contact:

Irene W. D. Hecht
Senior Associate
American Council on Education
Center for Institutional and International Initiatives
Washington, DC 20036

President
Higher Education Associates
3432 NE Schuyler St.
Portland, OR 97212
(503) 249-8392 (telephone and fax)
Email: d9ih@odin.cc.pdx.edu

Irene W. D. Hecht is a consultant to and a Senior Associate with the American Council on Education (ACE). Since 1992, Hecht has directed the ACE Department Leadership Program, applying her broad experience in both private and public higher education to lead the expansion of ACE's national seminar program for department chairs. In addition to her scholarly publications as an historian, Hecht has written for the *The Department Chair* newsletter and contributed to the volume edited by Peter Seldin, *Improving College Teaching.* Her new book with Mary Lou Higgerson and Walter H. Gmelch, *The Department Chair as Academic Leader,* is available from Oryx Press.

3

Education for Responsible Citizenship: A Challenge for Faculty Developers

Thomas Ehrlich
San Francisco State University
The Carnegie Foundation for the Advancement of Teaching

Higher education professionals need clearer, stronger frameworks for the integration of both civic and moral learning and the more common cognitive learning that occurs in traditional classrooms. This article addresses when and why this author chose to focus on community service-learning as a way to reengage in direct work with students and other civic responsibilities. His discussion focuses on student acquisition of academic knowledge and skills through service-learning and the study of ethical dilemmas facing professionals in different fields. He proffers in-depth discussion on service-learning programs championed by the Carnegie Foundation and addresses how these programs working with faculty across the country ground their philosophy in moral and civic responsibility. Finally, and in some ways most importantly, he discusses how all of us in higher education need clearer, stronger frameworks for the integration of both civic and moral learning and the more common cognitive learning that occurs in traditional classrooms.

INTRODUCTION

I was eight years old in 1942 when my family moved to Washington, DC, where my father served in the Office of Price Administration. My major civic involvement during World War II was contributing my mother's iron to a scrap drive being held by a local movie house, which promised free admission in exchange for a ten-pound contribution. My mother was not thrilled at losing her only means of pressing clothes, but I felt very patriotic.

Twenty years later, I moved back to Washington with my family to serve in the Kennedy administration. I took seriously the charge to "ask what you can do for your country," and my experience confirmed what my father had taught me—the opportunity to engage in public service is one of life's true privileges. It gives purpose to one's life as well as pleasure. Public service can take many different forms, but it is a common calling in every sense.

During my first tour in Washington, I worked for George W. Ball as he sought to persuade President Johnson that the war in Vietnam was a mistake. That effort failed, but I left government service to teach with a profound sense that every citizen has an obligation to strive for a better America, and that whether my vocation was civil servant or teacher, my avocation had to be some form of civic involvement.

As a law school professor and then dean at Stanford University, I became increasingly troubled that the public profession of law—and law schools such as mine—ignored poor people, those most in need of using the legal system, those most abused by the system. And I found that lawyers were generally unwilling—really, I think, they were emotionally unable—to provide their time and talent pro bono to do public work with poor people. Over and over I heard attorneys say that "They just wouldn't be comfortable with me," meaning that the speaker wouldn't be comfortable with them. Public service, I came to learn, is an acquired taste, and while one is never too old to begin, it certainly helps to start at an early age.

When I left Stanford to head the Legal Services Corporation, which funds civil legal help for the poor, I learned again and again what a privilege it is to do public work. And when I had the good fortune to try to run the foreign aid program for President Carter—"run" is hardly the right verb—I had more lessons in that same course of study.

I departed from my foreign aid position on the day President Reagan was inaugurated, and, as when I left Washington during the Vietnam War, I was disappointed by much that was government policy. But I never lost my commitment to public work, or public service as I still call it. In various ways since then, I have been engaged in encouraging young people to make that commitment and to act on it. The University of Pennsylvania, where I was provost, and Indiana University, where I served as president, both offered super opportunities to put commitment into practice. I have been particularly pleased by the remarkable growth of the national organization, Campus Compact, in which I have been much involved. It began with a small group of presidents in 1985, and includes about 650 presidents today.

I am deeply troubled, however, by clear evidence of what Wendy Rahn (1998) of the University of Minnesota terms "the steep erosion in support for the American political community among younger generations. Americans socialized in more recent decades have less positive and more negative feelings when thinking about the country than older generations, attach less personal importance to their American identity, [and] are less likely to value citizenship as an important attribute of American identity . . . " (p. 3).

PEDAGOGIES OF ENGAGEMENT FOR CIVIC RESPONSIBILITY

When I decided to leave university administration and return to teaching at San Francisco State University and writing at the Carnegie Foundation for the Advancement of Teaching, I focused on community service-learning as a way to reengage in direct work with students and their civic responsibilities. Over the previous decade, I taught a number of undergraduate courses that linked community service and academic study through structured reflection—at Indiana University and Duke University. In each of those community service-learning courses, I sought four interrelated clusters of learning goals: academic learning, social learning, moral learning, and civic learning.

Academic learning was the starting point for most of those courses. Community service is an integral part of my course on "Ethics and Professions," for example, primarily because I am convinced that the students gain more academic knowledge and skills than they would without that service, as we consider ethical dilemmas facing professionals in different fields. This is no less true of a course, "Law and Society," in which we examine the impact of law and lawyers in shaping American society from Puritan days to the time of O. J. Simpson and the impact of American society in shaping the legal system. The primary reason students in that course engage in community service, usually related to juvenile justice, is that they gain a deeper understanding of the interactions of law and society, in both personal and policy terms.

At the same time, I believe that students in these courses gain social, moral, and civic learning as well. By social learning I mean interpersonal skills such as careful listening, sympathy for others, and the ability to lead, to compromise, to change one's mind, and so forth, as well as personal traits such as self-esteem—skills that are important to personal interactions in any social setting and vital to success in most careers.

Moral learning, on the other hand, refers to helping students think about themselves in relation to others—who are their neighbors and what are their obligations to their neighbors? Service connects thought and feeling in a deliberate way, creating a context in which students can explore how they feel about what they are thinking and what they think about how they feel. The interaction of academic study and community service, guided by reflection, offers students opportunities to consider what is important to them—and why—in ways they too rarely experience otherwise. This dimension of learning was primary in a seminar that I offered on "Altruism, Philanthropy, and Public Service." It was designed particularly to enhance students' moral character by challenging their personal reactions to moral situations in both their readings and their community service, and by reflecting on those reactions in class discussions, papers, and personal journals.

In each class I tried to evaluate the results through surveys of attitudes and by considering the portfolios of students' work taken as a whole. Measured by what students reported, and by some rudimentary reviews of student attitudes, the results were encouraging in terms of academic, social, and moral learning, though in different degrees for different courses. When I tried to assess impact of these courses on civic learning, however, they seemed to fall short. By civic learning I mean coming to understand how a community functions, what problems it faces, the richness of its diversity, the need for individual commitments of time and energy to enhance community life, and most of all, the importance of working as a community to resolve community concerns.

Benjamin Barber (1992) of Rutgers, Robert Putnam (1995) at Harvard, and many others have stressed that community service is one of the most important ways, often the most important, to counter a seeming trend of civic disengagement among students. Civic learning—in the sense of how a community works and how to help it work better—and academic learning should be mutually reinforcing, as John Dewey (1916, 1938) emphasized. But I found it hard to confirm to myself, let alone to others, that my courses were having much impact on the civic learning of my students, in ways that I could regard as academic, social, and moral learning, though I stress that all four dimensions are closely related and reinforcing.

I found myself increasingly speaking out about the importance of community service-learning as an antidote for the decline of social capital and the fractionation of community that Putnam has chronicled. But how did I know, I kept asking myself? How sure was I that as a result of my courses, the civic learning quotient of my students was really enhanced? And, in all events, couldn't I do better if I were to focus squarely on civic learning, against the background of what I had learned through other courses and by reading of the work of other faculty? That is exactly what I did over the past year.

I began by reflecting on my own courses and by reading about others that seek explicitly to "experience citizenship," in the fine phrase that is the title of the AAHE service-learning monograph on political science. Taken as a whole, that volume; other publications, particularly from Campus Compact; and my own experiences suggested that service-learning should be linked to two other powerful pedagogies: problem-based learning and collaborative learning. Taken together, these three pedagogies reflect the three key elements that John Dewey stressed in the democratic learning process:

1) Process should engage students in reaching outside the walls of the school and into the surrounding community, as is the aim of community service-learning, as opposed to closed classroom learning.

2) It should focus on problems to be solved, as is the basis of problem-based learning, as opposed to discipline-based learning.

3) It should be collaborative, both among students and between students and faculty, as is the aim of collaborative learning, as opposed to individual learning.

Problem-based learning has been emphasized by some higher education faculty for a long time, but has received increased attention in recent years. The essential element is not simply that problem-based courses are interdisciplinary or multidisciplinary, but rather that a problem is the starting point in designing a course. As students advance, they tackle increasingly difficult problems using increasingly sophisticated techniques and increasingly complex knowledge bases. The problem approach, as Dewey taught us, is a key in preparing students for active participation in the ongoing renewal of democracy. That renewal involves much more than attention to the minimum responsibilities of a citizen—to vote and to participate in various civic organizations—though these responsibilities are certainly both important and ignored by most citizens today. But democracy also calls for citizens to identify community problems and to work communally to resolve those problems. At its best, the problem-based learning can further this key objective of civic learning.

Collaborative learning also has a long history and is increasingly part of undergraduate education. As president of Indiana University, the most common criticism I heard from employers was that our graduates were ill-trained to work as members of a team. Although most of the tasks these graduates would be called upon to perform in the workplace would be done as team members, most of their undergraduate work was done alone. Collaborative learning is a pedagogy particularly targeted toward enhancing the skills and abilities required to be a productive team member. It is also integral to a democratic society in which citizens interact with each other, learn from each other, grow with each other, and together make their communities more than the sum of their parts. Dewey urged that a community of learners is the primary mechanism through which this democratizing process can best occur. Collaborative learning, at its best, offers an opportunity to put this exhortation into practice.

Dewey's vision and his cautions about a democratic society underscore the importance of both these pedagogies. The vision was of an interactive, collaborative society in which the processes of decision on how to solve a problem are more important than the problem itself. It was balanced by cautions that uncertainty surrounds every decision about a problem, and every fact on which a decision is based. Those pedagogies are important for their potential to strengthen civic learning, and they are particularly powerful when combined with community service-learning. Community service-learning is their natural pedagogical partner. Community service-learning enables students to put into practice what they gain in academic study and to bring insights from service directly to their consideration of academic analysis. In my grazing through the fields of higher education in recent years, seeking tutorials about community service-learning courses, this troika repeatedly appears as a powerful combination.

PRACTICING WHAT I PREACH

On this basis, I sought to shape a new course at San Francisco State University that would employ all three pedagogies. The next step was to sit down with a group of civic leaders in San Francisco to discuss the elements they thought were important in civic leadership and the design of a project to enhance those elements in our students. Fortunately, the Urban Institute of San Francisco State University was a ready ally in reaching this group. The institute serves to link the university and its strengths with the city, its opportunities, and its needs. The institute sponsors a series of projects that promote student and faculty learning and research on the one hand and the resolution or amelioration of city concerns on the other. The institute is both an academic and an administrative unit, reporting directly to the university president, Robert Corrigan, himself a champion of preparing students for lives of engaged citizenship. The institute is also the home of the office of community service-learning, which supports faculty and students in a wide range of community service-learning courses.

The Urban Institute recently joined with a nonprofit civic group to form the San Francisco Policy Center. The center is a gathering of civic leaders from various sectors of the City—including community-based organizations, business, labor, and education—who came together to design programs that could use the resources of the university to assist the city. A number of those programs are underway, particularly in the arena of job training. Over the course of numerous sessions I sought the counsel of this group in shaping the pilot project. The leaders had different perspectives on almost every issue we considered, but they were united in their concern that a new generation of civic leaders was not apparent in San Francisco, and in a desire to share in the education of their successors. We discussed at some length what cluster of issues would work best as a focus for the project. Like most urban centers, San Francisco faces no end of tough problems. Among those we considered were municipal transportation; employment strategies; juvenile crime; a controversy about a major freeway running through the city; health issues, particularly AIDS; environmental concerns; and San Francisco neighborhoods in the wake of federal and state welfare reform. In the end we chose the last of those topics. I am now convinced, however, that any of them could have worked well for the civic education goals we established, because all of them related to disadvantaged groups in the city and broad issues of social justice. This meant we excluded such controversial questions in the city as the chaos caused by cyclists who demanded more attention on the bridges coming into the city and on the city streets. This is a tough cluster of issues, but not one that affects many poor or low-income people.

From the outset, based on advice from the members of the policy center, we planned that a centerpiece of the project would be a forum of civic leaders from a range of perspectives who would discuss the topic chosen and to try to reach common ground. This meant that the topic would have to have real importance, and ideally, so would the forum in terms of other places in which civic leaders argue their case in San Francisco. There had to be a clear sense that the issue was worth discussing on its own merits—the pedagogical program must be attached to something real. If, for example, all significant concerns regarding municipal transportation were going to be decided through collective bargaining, then a forum on that topic would not be appropriate. In the worse sense, it would have been an academic exercise.

We also concluded that care was needed in defining the issue so that it was broad enough to be of center stage importance and specific enough to be resolvable. Crime was too big. What caliber guns should be carried by police was too small. Juvenile crime, or the proper role of citizen review boards, and the question of civilian control over the police, might be just right. We also concluded that to be successful, the project needed to enable students to:

- read and discuss relevant materials

- interact with civic leaders who are working on a real city problem

- work themselves on that problem

- reflect on what they have learned in the realms of theory and practice and how/whether the two connect

In the end, we concluded that the impact of welfare reform on San Francisco neighborhoods would be ideal, primarily because the civic leaders thought it a central concern on which discussion among two different groups of civic leaders was needed. One group was those familiar with issues of public housing; the other group was those familiar with welfare and welfare reform. Neither group had spent much time talking to the other. The forum would provide a useful opportunity to do that, and the work of the students could be of direct benefit to both groups. At the same time, I stress my conviction that we could have chosen, for example, employment strategies, and engaged in an equally productive project from the perspective of civic education. In the years ahead, I hope to test that belief.

The choice of San Francisco neighborhoods in the wake of welfare reform was also made easier because my co-teacher, Lori Bamberger, has a wealth of knowledge about urban housing issues. Although the primary course goals were centered on civic learning, not learning about housing or welfare, the one could not occur without the other, and Ms. Bamberger brought particular strengths in the housing field. From the outset, we designed and taught the course together, she bringing strengths relating to urban development and I ones having experience relating to civic responsibility.

We chose two complementary sets of materials for the course—one on civic responsibility—primarily readings from Barber and Battistoni (1993), "Education and Democracy,"—and one on issues of urban poverty—primarily readings from Danzinger, Sandefur, and Weinberg (1994), "Confronting Poverty: Prescriptions for Change." Each class was designed to move back and forth among questions raised in these materials so that the issues of civic responsibility were handled in terms of their impact on concerns about urban poverty, and problems of urban poverty were viewed as matters of civic concern.

In one class session, for example, the focus was immigration, citizenship, and welfare reform. We considered the implications of welfare reform for immigrant households, children, the elderly, and the disabled. We asked whether place of birth was a fair way to discriminate in the allocation of government benefits; whether place of birth should be the primary criterion for citizenship; whether citizenship should be a primary criterion in the distribution of welfare. What should be the citizenship test for immigrants? We also focused specifically on the implications of the welfare reform legislation in targeting elderly and disabled immigrants for benefit reductions; e.g., the effect of restricting eligibility for food stamps, and so forth.

We built the course around the forum, which met during the third week of classes. In preparation for that session, students read a sufficient amount of material to have a basic understanding of both current housing and welfare rules in San Francisco, and particularly how the new federal and state legislation was creating massive shifts in eligibility for public benefits among poor people. The forum brought together 22 civic leaders from city government, nonprofit organizations, the Chamber of Commerce, and private business concerns. It was the first time that the group as a whole had come together, though many of them knew and had worked with each other. Students were mainly observers, but they had an opportunity to ask questions and to mingle with the civic leaders before and after the forum. During the three-hour forum, Ms. Bamberger led a structured discussion and debate on the options available to the city and the organizations present, and how best to take advantage of the least painful paths in support of poor people. Students said they came away inspired by the leaders, sobered by the challenges that had been raised, and committed to work on those challenges.

All the members of the forum agreed to assist the students in their work. Apart from readings and class discussions focused on those read-ings, the students had two other closely related clusters of responsibilities. The first was to spend at least five hours per week in a community service agency that helps welfare recipients. Ms. Bamberger and I had identified seven community agencies that met this criterion and had offered to as-sist in the course. The leaders of those agencies were also participants in the forum. Arriba Juntos, for example, is a Latino, community-based or-ganization that helps families achieve self-sufficiency, with a particular emphasis on job-training. Chinatown Community Development Center, on the other hand, is a neighborhood-based housing and community de-velopment organization that provides services to low-income tenants.

The only agency not directly related to welfare or housing was a group called Students Helping in the Naturalization of Elders (SHINE). This is a program to train and enable students to be citizen coaches for immi-grants who are studying for the naturalization examination. The students working at SHINE helped immigrants gain citizenship knowledge and skills and in the process strengthened those skills themselves. The course easily could have been developed around a substantive focus on poor im-migrants and their problems in San Francisco, with all the students serv-ing in SHINE, and also working on substantive issues similar to those we considered, but with a particular concentration on immigrants.

We made significant efforts throughout the course to link the stu-dents' community service to the readings on both civic responsibility and poverty through class discussions and a brief paper that each student wrote as a publicity brochure for her or his agency. A number of these pa-pers were good enough to be used by the agencies involved. The other main link between academic study and community service was an exten-sive field project that students worked on in teams of four or five in the four San Francisco neighborhoods that include most welfare recipients: Mission, Bayview/Hunters Point, Visitacion Valley, and Chinatown. In most cases, the students in each team were also working in a community service agency in the neighborhood where they were also doing their field study. We gave them a substantial set of background materials full of data about demographics, housing, and poverty, as well as studies that had pre-viously been done on San Francisco public housing and welfare issues. None of the prior studies had examined the impact of welfare reform on these four neighborhoods, and the students did not need to do any library research. Rather, each team prepared a "Neighborhood Study on the Im-pact of Welfare Reform" consisting of demographic data particular to the neighborhood, including the prevalence of welfare recipiency, average income levels, and so forth; an objective summary of the welfare-related needs of the neighborhood arising out of welfare reform—how many households will need jobs, child-care, transportation, and other projected impacts; housing stock information; summaries of residents' concerns, and the concerns of businesses, about welfare reform; summaries of welfare-related services, such as job-training and child-care, available to neighborhood residents; options and recommendations for giving priority in housing assistance; commentary on how the recommendations of a housing task force established by the San Francisco mayor would affect the neighborhood; neighborhood analysis of one of the numerous city-wide proposals for helping poor people; and finally an action plan for the neighborhood.

This is an ambitious agenda, but the students were assisted by a detailed protocol for the report, and we spent half of a three-hour class engaged in roleplaying about the ways that students would learn the information they needed from talking with welfare recipients and others. Looking back, there are important ways that the course can be improved, particularly by better integrating community service, class discussions, readings, and field surveys. But this initial effort was a true success in terms of fostering civic learning, in the views of both the students and agencies involved. Ms. Bamberger and I did extensive surveys of attitudes, interests, and involvement in civic affairs both at the start and end of the course. Those surveys indicate that most of the participating students expected to remain active and engaged citizen leaders of San Francisco—or another community—for the rest of their lives, regardless of career choice, and that the course had a real effect on that expectation. The differences between before and after were not great, but they were positive. The first survey question, for example, asked how strongly students agreed or disagreed with the statement, "Adults should give some time for the good of their community." In the initial survey, half agreed, and half agreed strongly. By the second survey, all but two agreed strongly. At the beginning of the semester, a slight majority said that they neither agreed nor disagreed that "It is important to me to become a community leader," and the rest agreed with the statement. By the end, a strong majority agreed, and several agreed strongly. Finally, at the start of the course many students were ambivalent about the statement that "Volunteer service will/would be valuable in my career," but by the end, all of the students agreed, and most students agreed strongly.

I do not want to overstate the importance of the survey results, but the increase in students' commitment to political engagement and civic leadership was supported by other assessments. Discussions with the students over the course of the semester confirmed that the shifts were significant. We also conducted a general course evaluation at the end of the semester, which revealed strong student support for the course and the need for more efforts to integrate the course readings, discussions, community service, and projects. Of course, 15 is a small number of students and there may have been a selection bias as most of the students probably came to the class with a higher level of civic engagement than the average student. The surveys and other evaluations suggest, however, that even those students who joined the class with what may have been higher-than-average levels of civic engagement probably came away from the course with an even stronger commitment to active political participation and community involvement.

LESSONS LEARNED

Experiences such as this one persuade me that civic responsibility is not a dimension of learning that can be pasted on a student's character while she or he learns calculus. Rather, it is a complex combination of cognitive and emotional learning. To gain clearer insight into what works in this realm, my colleague at the Carnegie Foundation for the Advancement of Teaching, Anne Colby, and I have a major project underway. The focus of our project is undergraduate education and the development of moral and civic responsibility. We are examining current efforts at colleges and universities to enhance moral and civic responsibility, and also helping to strengthen those efforts. We are identifying programs that are well-grounded in a thoughtful conceptual framework, that engage strong student and faculty interest, and that provide experiences which challenge students both intellectually and morally. We also plan to make detailed information about those programs easily accessible. Most important, we want to encourage and support serious concern about the development of undergraduates' moral and civic responsibility among faculty and administrative leaders. The overall aim of the project is to aid colleges and universities in better preparing their students to be informed, committed, socially responsible, and ethically conscientious citizens.

We are not seeking to isolate moral and civic learning from intellectual learning. To the contrary, we believe that intellectual learning is inadequate unless it is infused with moral and civic learning, and that moral and civic learning is ineffective unless it is integrated with rigorous intellectual learning. Nothing is more important to enhancing civic responsibility than this integration. We are exploring the tensions in finding sound balance between an educational experience that is rooted in a strong values-based campus, with its dangers of indoctrination and political correctness, and a campus that promotes open and objective inquiry to the exclusion of preparing students to make their own moral and civic judgments.

Our project is identifying policies and practices that promote the capacities of undergraduates to make reasoned judgments that are infused with moral and civic concerns. We do not expect to provide rigorous assessments of those policies and practices, although that may be attempted in subsequent stages. But we do expect to provide evidence that particular efforts are intended to help students develop the capacities needed to reach judgments that include moral and ethical considerations, and that those efforts have the intended effects.

Our project is consciously and closely tied to the other work of the Carnegie Foundation for the Advancement of Teaching. One is the Carnegie Academy, which is a project on the scholarship of teaching. The project has three components. The first is a program to help a group of faculty in a variety of fields (chemistry, English, management, and psychology in our first year) engage in that scholarship through two ten-day summer periods together, and through further interactions over the academic year. The second is a network of associated campuses, each of which is working to foster and support faculty work on the scholarship of teaching. And the third is collaboration with a number of disciplinary and professional organizations that are also interested in promoting the scholarship of teaching. The other main program at the Carnegie Foundation is focused on preparation for the professions; and will examine that preparation over a five-year period, with particular attention to law, engineering, medicine, social work, the clergy, and education. We are encouraging faculty at the campuses we are studying to participate in the Carnegie Teaching Academy and their campuses to affiliate with the Academy. We are also focusing significant attention in the professions program on issues of moral and civic responsibility, and we expect that those issues will also be central in the design of the project on preparing future college and university teachers.

The project began only last year, but already we have learned some lessons. Five seem to me particularly relevant here:

1) Moral and civic learning are interconnected. This may seem obvious to some, but it is certainly resisted by others. To us, however, the ev-

idence is overwhelming that a strong moral compass is needed as a predicate to civic engagement.

2) The development of moral and civic character is not on the radar screens of most colleges and universities except as a matter of public relations rhetoric. Almost all institutions do refer to these goals for students in their mission statements. At most colleges and universities, however, the mission statement is ignored, indeed unknown, by administrators, faculty, and students. Our Carnegie colleague, William M. Sullivan (2000), has persuasively argued that "much of higher education has come to operate on a sort of default program of instrumental individualism. This is the familiar notion that the academy exists to research and disseminate knowledge and skills as tools for economic development and the upward mobility of individuals" (p. 4). Sullivan laments that a consequence of this default program of instrumental individualism is that leadership in both the private and public sectors is increasingly dominated by "narrow careerism and private self-interest" (p. 5).

3) Our initial explorations indicate that the most effective strengthening of moral and civic character occurs on campuses where curricular and extracurricular learning experiences are consciously woven into a larger, integrated whole. The campus culture at these institutions is key in their shaping of civic and moral learning. At this stage, it may be more accurate to term this judgment a premise rather than a lesson learned. It is the basis for our choices, for in-depth studies, of a small group of colleges and universities that exhibit a high degree of intentionality about the education of their students.

4) We believe that important contributions to moral and civic learning can be made by a variety of different curricular and extracurricular approaches, among the overwhelming majority of campuses that do not have any degree of institutional intentionality about enhancing the civic and moral character of their students. Curricular approaches include required courses in ethics, freshman seminars, capstone experiences, faculty seminars to encourage faculty to bring moral and civic issues into their discussions of course material, and curricular sequences that aim to help students shape their lives and work in civically and morally committed directions. In addition, many campuses emphasize the three pedagogies I mentioned that hold great potential for civic engagement: service-learning, collaborative

learning, and problem-based learning. A fourth, one that can be especially exploited at research universities, is linking undergraduate research to current community concerns.

Numerous colleges and universities also have centers or institutes that focus on civic responsibility, social change, and various aspects of ethics. The missions of these centers vary, but most include both curricular and extracurricular activities, such as student leadership development programs, programs of university/community partnerships around pressing social issues, and special residence hall experiences.

We are examining the efforts of a wide range of institutions under various categories, including freshman seminars, capstone programs, ethics across the campus, academic centers, student leadership programs, and faculty leadership programs. Within each category, we are trying to identify good practices.

5) In some ways most important, all of us in higher education need clearer, stronger frameworks for the integration of both civic and moral learning and the more common cognitive learning that occurs in traditional classrooms. I suspect we all have a tendency to separate the civic and moral from the intellectual in our teaching, to worry that we are not being professional if we bring our normative judgments about moral or civic issues into the classroom. And certainly there are real tensions in helping students both in developing their own civic and moral stands and in translating those stands into action, while at the same time avoiding inculcation. But the moral and intellectual relativism that comes from setting forth competing theories of urban decay, for example, without helping students reach their own moral and civic judgments on which theory or combination of theories is most compelling, is an abdication of faculty responsibility.

CONCLUSION

Time and again over the past months, I have heard faculty members in fields such as political science, philosophy, psychology, and economics say that their only role is to report, to analyze, to criticize. Whether and how their students develop moral and civic judgments—let alone translate those judgments in action—is not their business. This approach is dangerous for our democracy. Our students need to integrate and balance intellectual virtues and moral and civic virtues that together will enable them to make judgments and to act on those judgments.

In the end, higher education should be devoted not just to the spread of knowledge, but to the pursuit of virtuous action. It should have an impact on how students make the important choices that shape their lives. That goal cannot be achieved, of course, without faculty who are not only dedicated to enhancing the civic responsibility of their students, but also prepared to do so through programs of faculty development. The combinations of knowledge, skills, and values that together can enable students to become active participants in their communities must be learned first by faculty. The faculty, in turn, need assistance in transmitting those combinations to students in ways that do not inculcate but rather enable them to make their own civic judgments and to act on those judgments. This is a vital role for faculty development, one that has been too long neglected.

ACKNOWLEDGMENTS

My thanks to Lori Bamberger and to Elizabeth Beaumont for assistance in preparing this essay. Portions of this essay, in somewhat different form, were published in *PS: Political Science & Politics, 32* (2), pp. 245–250, and 1999, September/October *About Campus, 4* (4), pp. 5–9.

REFERENCES

Barber, B. (1992). *An aristocracy of everyone: The politics of education and the future of America.* New York, NY: Ballantine.

Barber, B., & Battistoni, R. (Eds.). (1993). *Education for democracy.* Dubuque, IA: Kendall/Hunt.

Barber, B., & Battistoni, R. (1993). A season of service: Introducing service-learning into the liberal arts curriculum. *PS: Political Science and Politics, 26* (pp. 235–262). Dubuque, IA: Kendall/Hunt.

Battistoni, R., & Hudson, W. (Eds.). (1997). *Experiencing citizenship: Concepts and models for service-learning in political science.* Washington, DC: American Association for Higher Education.

Boyte, H, & Kari, N. (1996). *Building America: The democratic promise of public work.* Philadelphia, PA: Temple University Press.

Danzinger, S. H., Sandefur, G. D., & Weinberg D. H. (Eds.). (1994). *Confronting poverty: Prescriptions for change.* Cambridge, MA: Harvard University Press.

Dewey, J. (1916). *Democracy and education.* New York, NY: Macmillan.

Dewey, J. (1938). *Experience and education*. New York, NY: Collier Books.

Jackson, K. (Ed). (1994). *Redesigning curricula*. Providence, RI: Campus Compact.

Putnam, R. (1995, January). Bowling alone. *Journal of Democracy*, 6, pp. 65–78.

Rahn, W. (1998, May 8–9). *Generations and American national identity: A data essay*. Presentation at the Communication in the Future of Democracy Workshop. Washington, DC: Annenberg Center.

Rothman, M. (Ed.). (1998). *Service matters*. Providence, RI: Campus Compact.

Sullivan, W. M. (2000). Institutional identity and social responsibility. In T. Ehrlich (Ed.), *Civic responsibility and higher education* (pp. 19–36). Phoenix, AZ: Oryx Press.

Contact:

Thomas Ehrlich
Distinguished University Scholar
San Francisco State University
Senior Scholar, The Carnegie Foundation for the Advancement of Teaching
555 Middlefield Rd.
Menlo Park, CA 94025
(650) 566-5137
Email: ehrlich@carnegiefoundation.org

Thomas Ehrlich is Senior Scholar at the Carnegie Foundation for the Advancement of Teaching and distinguished University Scholar at San Francisco State University. He was formerly president of Indiana University, provost of the University of Pennsylvania, and dean of Stanford Law School. He was also the first president of the Legal Services Corporation and the first head of the International Development Cooperation Agency, reporting to President Carter. He serves on many boards, including Bennett College, the Corporation for National Service, and the Public Welfare Foundation, and is chair of the board of the American Association for Higher Education. He is author or coauthor of eight books, many articles and reviews, and has received four honorary degrees.

4

A Prophet in Your Own Land? Using Faculty and Student Focus Groups to Address Issues of Race, Ethnicity, and Gender in the Classroom

James Francisco Bonilla and Patricia R. Palmerton
Hamline University, St. Paul, Minnesota

In this study, six focus groups of faculty and students addressed issues of how race, ethnicity, and gender affected their classroom experiences. Consistent themes emerged across all groups, including feeling unsafe and vulnerable, concerns about equity, power, and role modeling. As importantly, the research process itself became a vehicle for growth and change in the community at large, both inside and outside the classroom. Six recommendations are offered for those who seek innovative approaches to addressing race and gender in the classroom.

INTRODUCTION

One of the most difficult aspects of faculty and organizational development work is gaining the full commitment of all to the development effort. One of the larger obstacles for faculty developers addressing sensitive issues such as race, ethnicity, and gender is the perception that peers cannot be prophets in their own land. Because of embeddedness in the institution, colleagues are often skeptical of an insider's ability to be neutral or well informed enough to provide new or different insights. This can be especially true for people of color and for women. Often termed "buy-in," the success of a development effort depends upon the willingness of members of the organization to accept the legitimacy of the findings, to engage in discussion and problem solving, and then be willing to do the work necessary for growth.

When we began our series of focus groups in the spring of 1997, our purpose was to hear from faculty and students what would help them in addressing the enlivening yet often contentious issues of race, ethnicity, and gender in the Hamline classroom. Our goal at the outset was quite simple: We wanted to know if race and gender were indeed real issues in the classroom for faculty and students. We hoped to discover insights that would help us plan faculty development. What we discovered, however, was that the research process itself resulted in significant growth: for our respondents, for members of the campus community, and for us. In this essay, we will describe the process we used in order to show how attempts to gain insight into the problems faced became a vehicle for change in the community at large. Serendipitously, we became in-house prophets, by legitimizing the voices of those who needed to be heard.

In this essay, we will describe the process used to gain insight into our own institution and its members, and we will touch upon the illuminating, occasionally painful, but always rich texture of experiences revealed through the course of our conversations. With few exceptions, we found that a clear majority of our participants believe race and gender are significant issues both outside and inside the classroom. As the sessions progressed, we asked participants to detail for us how race and gender manifested in their classroom and finally, what would be helpful, from a faculty development perspective, in addressing the issues described.

METHODS

As a qualitative method for data collection, focus groups bring together several participants to discuss topics of mutual interest to them and the researchers (Morgan & Spanish, 1984). Focus groups have become increasingly popular as a method of applied research as well as for gathering in-depth information about the experiences, ideas, and expectations of specific populations (Kreps, 1995). To quote Kreps, "In the final analysis, although focus groups are not necessarily the best method to use in every applied research context, they are a powerful group facilitation technique that can be used to stimulate group discussion" (p. 199). It was very much our intention that a report to the Hamline community would stimulate discussion about good teaching and the role diversity plays in the classroom. What we did not anticipate was that the focus groups themselves would begin that process.

Our rationale for choosing the focus group approach is rooted in the qualitative literature and the idea that knowledge based on discovery, insight, and understanding from the perspective of those being studied offers great promise (Krieger, 1985; Lincoln & Guba, 1985; Merriam, 1988; Orbe, 1998). In particular, understanding the experiences of Hamline faculty and students offered us the greatest promise for contributing to our collective knowledge base as faculty developers, and more importantly, to the understanding of the needs of faculty and students in the classroom. Hence, the overarching purpose of this study was to use an inductive process to discover the resources needed by faculty to help them provide the best educational experiences for all students. One of the disadvantages of focus groups is concern over the generalizability of the data gathered given the small sample size. To overcome this limitation, we intentionally designed a process that was as participative as possible.

The project used three faculty and three student focus groups to address issues of race, ethnicity, and gender in the college classroom. The groups lasted approximately one and one-half hours each. Each group was cofacilitated by both researchers, who were Hamline faculty members: one Caucasian female and one Latino male. In this way we could also serve, in part, as peer debriefers (Rossman & Marshal, 1989). All group sessions were audiotaped and transcribed for later analysis. As researchers, we came to these data with a variety of lenses, male and female, Caucasian and Latino, and as communications studies, education, and organizational behavior scholars. The following summary represents several hundred hours of data gathering and analysis.

Our sample consisted of members of the undergraduate Hamline community. Hamline University is an urban, Methodist-affiliated university with an undergraduate College of Liberal Arts, a law school, and graduate programs in public administration, education, and liberal studies. We focused our attention on the undergraduate College of Liberal Arts. In the College of Liberal Arts, Hamline has approximately 1600 full-time undergraduate students, 65% female. The students of color population is currently 11%. Many ethnicities are represented, primarily African-American, Hmong, Vietnamese, Cambodian, Native American/American Indian, Hispanic, and Middle Eastern. Our full-time faculty of color population in the College of Liberal Arts stands at 6%, and 45% of full-time faculty members are female.

Our sample was self-selecting to the extent that participants answered our letter of invitation. We were fortunate to have CLA faculty volunteer from 13 departments in all five divisions. Our pool of focus group participants intentionally constituted a diverse racial and gender representation (16 Caucasian faculty and six faculty of color, 10 males and 12 females). Our student groups were composed of 12 seniors and juniors invited from leadership positions on campus and represented four divisions of the college (fine arts, humanities, social science, and natural science). They included five Caucasian students and seven students of color, four males and eight females. To facilitate the most candid discussions possible, we organized students into separate focus groups, one Caucasian and two groups of color. We did not segregate faculty groups by color.

Our focus group interviews followed a consistent format. All participants received the questions prior to arriving for the interview session (see Figure 4.1). Faculty and students were asked the same questions. We were particularly interested in stories that individuals could tell to illustrate their experiences, and we encouraged participants to expand upon their initial remarks with examples and stories that would help us understand what they meant. There were at least two reasons for the focus on stories. One, narrative accounts include nuances and context that more linear explanations often fail to include. Second, storytelling has been shown to provide means by which other participants can connect their experiences. The stories begun by one person often encourage embellishment by others who add their own stories. A chaining phenomenon can occur, which may signal the existence of a larger interpretive framework functioning across a social grouping (Bormann, 1972; Bormann, Cragan, & Shields 1994; Bormann, Cragan, and Shields, 1996; Cragan & Shields, 1981).

Our analysis occurred in several stages. All interviews were transcribed and subjected to analysis by each of the researchers individually. We then met and discussed our analyses. In all cases, we discussed how we had arrived at our interpretations, finding at times that even when we agreed we had different reasons and different perspectives informing our conclusions. These peer analysis sessions were crucial to our design. Before beginning, we made an explicit decision to rely upon our multiple identities—a Caucasian, female Minnesota/South Dakota, Protestant; and a Latino, male New York, Catholic—instead of attempting to somehow overcome them (Merriam, 1988). We did not believe it was possible to overcome them. In fact, we did not believe it would be a positive thing to do so, even if we could. Rather, we attempted to use our lenses as resources, by working to be aware explicitly of the ways in which we were linking with our participants in order to understand them and their

FIGURE 4.1
Memo to Focus Group Participants

MEMO

To: Focus Group Participants
From: James Francisco Bonilla, Visiting Sanders Chair in Education
        Patricia Palmerton, Director of Oral Communication
Date: March 6, 1997

Thank you again for your willingness to participate in the upcoming focus group session. Please read the following information carefully. If you have any questions, please feel free to call either Professor Bonilla or Professor Palmerton.

Statement of Confidentiality and Permission
As part of the assessment efforts to support both the oral communication program and cultural diversity at Hamline, we are conducting this study looking at race, ethnicity, and gender as they relate to the experience of faculty and students in the classroom. These discussions will be audio-taped for transcription purposes in order to facilitate analysis of the data. All discussion will be confidential, and any names mentioned in the course of discussion will be deleted from the transcripts. Audiotapes will be destroyed at the end of this research.

By your participation we assume your permission to summarize in a report (in a confidential manner) the points and concerns raised in this discussion.

Focus Group Agenda
I.   Introductions and Overview
II.   Goals and Ground Rules
III.   Questions

    A. Some people say race, ethnicity, and gender don't affect what happens in the classroom. Some people say they necessarily affect what happens in the classroom. If you had to take a stand on this, what stand would you take?
    B. What kinds of things have happened to you, or to others, that seem related to race, ethnicity or gender?
    C. What are the implications of this discussion at the university level? For example, how do you see these experiences related to the way that cultural breadth is working at Hamline?

IV.   Closure

perspectives better. In essence, we attempted to use conscious partiality as a resource rather than as a confounding bias (Mies, 1983).

When we had an initial draft of our findings, we enacted the second stage: member checking. This occurred in two different ways. First, we met with a group of faculty who had been meeting for several months on issues of diversity on campus. Not all members of this group had been participants in our study, but some had. We met with this group first in order to help us see potential problems in the presentation of the data, and, to be frank, to gain moral support. On the basis of feedback provided by this group, we revised the draft. We then sent copies of the revised draft report to all faculty who had participated in the study and invited them to luncheon meetings to discuss the draft, identify concerns they had with the presentation of the data, or concerns about confidentiality. At this point, we were prepared to revise the draft again to address concerns raised, should it become evident we had breached our promises of confidentiality or that we had significantly misinterpreted or missed points that had been expressed.

The third stage consisted of releasing the final draft to the faculty at large, and providing luncheon meetings for any faculty members who wanted to meet to discuss the report. At the fourth stage, we distributed the final draft to the student participants and to student services staff. We specifically did not distribute the draft to this group until faculty had had a chance to review it and discuss it, since the topic of the initial research was classroom interaction. As such, we felt that faculty were potentially vulnerable and deserved to see the report before hearing about it from a student or student services staff member. As a result of distributing the document to student services staff, we were asked to hold another luncheon with those staff members to discuss the implications of the report, so this meeting was added to our process.

What follows are excerpts from the report distributed to faculty, administration, students, and student services staff. Since the focus of this essay is faculty organizational development, we have not included the primary body of the report detailing all the quotations and stories upon which we based our conclusions. In many ways, the findings presented here do not break new ground. Many of these dilemmas have previously been reported elsewhere in the literature on multicultural teaching in the academy (Adams, 1997; Border & Chism, 1992; Morey & Kitano, 1997; Schoem, Frankel, Zuniga, & Lewis, 1995). What does set this effort apart in our estimation was the extent to which our faculty identified with these findings. These were not perceived as judgments made by some "external experts" from the "outside." Rather, the process of searching out Hamline faculty and student voices gave the community ownership over the findings, and as we will see later, at developing follow-up recommendations and calls to action and participation.

SELECTED FINDINGS

One of the things we found is that Hamline is blessed with a wealth of faculty who care deeply about good teaching and the needs of students, all students. In our interviews, we were struck time and again by the responses from faculty and students that made it clear this is a community that is concerned with doing the right thing. There is a tendency among those interested in social issues like race and gender to catch people doing things wrong. This tendency would do the faculty and students of the Hamline community a serious injustice. In the process of reviewing this report it will be obvious at times that we are not always succeeding to the degree we should or to the degree we want to. Indeed, some of the reports of the painful experiences of students and faculty in our community gave us pause. However, even as we catch ourselves making mistakes, we also must endeavor to catch one another doing things right.

Among the things that we heard faculty members were doing well were stories describing high expectations that encourage students' performance. Often faculty members were perceived as approachable and open, and we heard about heated dialogues or exchanges initiated by faculty on race that resulted in lasting multiracial friendships and understanding. As faculty developers, we emphasize that these positive experiences need to be recognized and emulated: The faculty member that models for others how to deal positively with racist or sexist remarks; the faculty member that assumes capability, despite difficulty with course material. Students mentioned faculty fairness, open-mindedness, and support. "The power of the professor to affect students because of their expectations is phenomenal," said one student in discussing the way in which encouragement from a faculty member helped her overcome previous "horrible" experiences. Students discussed with great appreciation the willingness shown by some faculty members to address issues of race, ethnicity, and gender rather than avoid them.

Nevertheless, both faculty and students identified troubling issues. The next part of this essay highlights some of these concerns.

Themes Across All Groups

Five themes were identified which spanned all the focus groups. They were:

1) A pervasive sense of uneasiness. Most faculty and students of color reported feeling uneasy, unsafe, and vulnerable addressing issues of race and gender in the classroom. The pervasive question seemed to be: "Is this a psychologically and emotionally safe place?" Feelings ranged from discomfort to literally feeling psychologically unsafe. Our informants approached the concern about safety differently. Some reported having experienced sanctions that make them feel unsafe. These are most often subtle, for example, "If I bring my ethnicity into something . . . you can hear people breathe out of their noses really hard." Said another student, "[Y]ou can hear them laugh or make snide comments . . . I can feel the tension. It's hard to describe the tension when it does happen, but I can feel it—like needles." Others just feared experiencing sanctions. In general, Caucasian students and Caucasian male faculty were least likely to report having experienced situations that contributed to feelings of dis-ease.

2) Issues of equity in the classroom. Many faculty members were unclear as to how/should/do faculty make special efforts for certain students. Issues raised within this theme included questions about the levels of academic preparedness of students of color, social expectations of Caucasian students and faculty, and whether diverse learning styles in the classroom were being acknowledged.

3) The role of faculty. Faculty were perceived as being powerful and as role models. Yet they were also seen as keepers of the grade, having the ability to punish or protect and to facilitate or deny issues in the classroom. Many of the participants agreed that some faculty members are hesitant to confront issues of race in the classroom.

4) Different needs and at different stages of learning. Faculty and students alike observed that different students bring different understandings of and experiences with issues of race and gender. Many questions were raised about the teaching implications when students at different stages of learning collide. Another concern raised was the teaching implications of having one or two students of color in a class with all Caucasian students when it came to content related issues of race and ethnicity.

5) Institutional commitment. A final theme across all groups was the questioning of institutional commitment. Many sensed a greater concern for image than for substance. For example, some groups questioned whether the cultural breadth (CB) requirement was too diffuse, allowing students to avoid issues of race and gender in the United States. Another example was limited CB course offerings that were not sufficiently discipline specific, particularly in math and the sciences. There were concerns about the lack of support for faculty in developing expanded cultural breadth course offerings. This was related to a larger concern questioning the willingness of the institution to address problems related to diversity when they are brought to the attention of institutional decision-makers. Finally, important questions were asked about the adequacy of campus supports that make it likely all students can meet high academic standards.

Selected Themes within Groups

To further analyze our data we broke down the findings into subthemes by focus group population.

1) What faculty members said were the hardest issues for them. Many faculty felt caught in a cycle of a) not being sure of student preparedness, b) wondering about their own expectations of student performance, and c) wanting to set appropriate expectations. A related dilemma was that when students didn't meet expectations, faculty were unsure how to give feedback without it being be perceived as racist, given differing cultural backgrounds and the expectations carried by the student about the faculty member. There was considerable fear of being seen as a racist or as having a political agenda. All three faculty groups reported confusion about knowing if, or when, or how, to be helpful while simultaneously stressing academic standards.

2) What Caucasian students said are the hardest issues for them. This group unanimously discussed feeling silenced about race, a form of self-censorship. For example, Caucasian students reported being afraid of offending and being thought to be racist. "I'm very careful about what I say because I don't want to be thought of that way [i.e., as racist]." Another student said, "I have not spoken up just because . . . I don't want to be viewed as racist or something . . . so I've just kept my views to myself."

On the one hand, they were aware of their lack of exposure, yet on the other hand they felt expected to be aware of how to interact with students of other races or ethnicities. Like the faculty, they were also dealing with a fear of offending, of being misinterpreted, or seen as racist or sexist. Several told stories regarding their struggle to bridge or connect with students of color.

3) What students of color said were the hardest issues for them. Nearly all sensed discomfort from Caucasian students and faculty, which was often expressed nonverbally. When confronting subtle responses by Caucasian faculty and students, students of color were at risk of being perceived as "overly sensitive" or "paranoid," fulfilling the confrontational racial/ethnic stereotype, or being misinterpreted. Many students complained about the added expectation that they will educate the campus on issues of race and ethnicity without help from the faculty. Like their Caucasian peers, many students of color felt silenced. Unlike their Caucasian peers, many also reported feeling isolated.

4) Gender matters. The question of needing to protect male students in intense classroom discussions related to gender was widely raised. For example, one faculty member explained "I have to be sensitive to not shut out the males." Some faculty discussed male students as not being ready to confront gender as a social construct. There were also clear differences among faculty regarding levels of comfort with self-disclosure in interactions with students. Some male faculty reported discomfort with relational teaching styles apparently expected by some female students. Female faculty members discussed the difficulty of establishing their authority in the classroom. Women students of color reported difficulty identifying primarily with their gender because they were so strongly identified in terms of race.

5) Identity. Several female faculty and students as well as a number of students of color reported that one strategy for coping with their experiences of discrimination or discomfort was to assimilate themselves with a Caucasian male norm on campus by becoming genderless or invisible racially. While not physically possible, participants described behaving in ways whereby their obvious physical difference was downplayed, ignored, or rendered as irrelevant as possible.

6) Classroom authority. Many faculty members expressed concerns with establishing their authority and legitimacy in the classroom. These issues manifested differently depending on the gender or racial identity of the faculty member. A number of female faculty and faculty of color reported experiencing classroom challenges to their authority, often unrelated to the topics of race and gender. Several also cited examples of lower evaluation scores for teaching a race or gender related course while a Caucasian/male colleague would be evaluated more favorably for the same course and perceived as less biased. A few Caucasian/male faculty members reported challenges to their legitimacy in addressing issues related to race and gender.

Participants' Calls to Action

In closing each focus group, we asked, "Given the issues raised here today, what would be helpful, from your perspective?" What follows is our summary of participants' responses, organized by population.

1) What faculty said would be helpful to them.

- help in untangling issues of fairness, favoritism, and equity in the classroom
- help in addressing needs of students with different levels of awareness regarding race and gender
- suggestions for supporting students of color without seeming intrusive
- creation of a more supportive environment rather than a change in academic standards
- refinement of the cultural breadth requirement and expansion of opportunities for additional course creation

2) What Caucasian students said would be helpful to them.

- greater exposure to racial diversity as a means of learning and developing increased awareness
- in a safe environment, more opportunities to speak and risk making mistakes without fear of being labeled a racist
- Caucasian faculty serving as role models by dealing effectively with racist behaviors in the classroom
- refinement of the cultural breadth requirement and expansion of course options, especially ones that are discipline specific

3) What students of color said would be helpful to them.

- faculty explicitly admitting their limitations, i.e., "I am still l learning and won't get it right," so we all can feel we are in this together
- more space in the classroom to express themselves without fear of intimidating Caucasian students or faculty, a place where a multiplicity of voices can be heard

- more involvement with the faculty in the classroom and faculty participation in events to educate the broader campus community, to "help shoulder the load"

- refinement of the cultural breadth requirement and expansion of course options

SUMMARY OF FINDINGS

Across all six groups, it became clear that many of the participants struggled to connect with others. We heard a stream of stories that indicated, to varying degrees, that issues of safety and vulnerability made meaningful engagement with others, both in and out of the classroom, a challenge. Students described a sense of isolation from and lack of connection to diverse communities (including US racial minorities and international students). A majority of students and faculty expressed a discomfort or uneasiness with issues of race when they arose in the classroom.

Throughout all the themes there was a consistent thread: Cultural differences (race, ethnicity, and gender) influence perceptions of behaviors and attributions about the meaning of behavior. In turn, these perceptions and attributions influence choices about how to respond to behavior. Regardless of status as faculty member or as student, all expressed concerns, at times, about ambiguity of meaning and not knowing exactly how to interpret the behaviors they were encountering. It appeared in faculty concerns about how their well-intentioned behaviors would be received, in students' of color frustration about responses to their voices, and in Caucasian students' fears about offending others simply because of their ignorance about what might be offensive. The desire to understand the other better and to be understood by the other was repeated time and again.

We see a snapshot of a campus composed of many diverse voices, perceptions, and behaviors; students and faculty whose preferred ways of communicating differ from the boisterous and animated to the reserved and cautious; many males having been trained in one form of classroom interaction confronting a sometimes new reality of less hierarchical, more relational communication patterns; students who learn through more field-sensitive teaching and those who are more field independent. Sometimes the mix is electric and learning spikes; other times students and faculty felt confused, angry, and/or disappointed.

Hamline reflects a larger American drama of making one community out of the many. To be successful, it seems we will have to resolve the dynamic tensions of those who want more contact and interaction and those who are more comfortable with distance.

In the words of one of our faculty of color describing what it means to come here when one is a student of color and one's experience has not been in a predominantly Caucasian institution:

> I describe it as there's this really great house. It's really beautiful, and it's really neat, and it's been built by people who are all 5'6" or under. They want you to come because they think it's great that you're a little different from them and they would really like you to come and be in their house, but you're six feet tall. Everything in the house is set up for people 5'6" and under. You spend all your time bending over, hitting your head on ceilings and things, and you can't quite figure out why you're really uncomfortable, but you notice that your back starts to hurt, and you notice that you don't quite fit, and you notice that everybody else seems really happy but you're feeling kind of miserable. Sometimes they figure out that maybe you're not the right height so they build one room where you can go and stand up. You will have to still operate in the whole rest of the house bent over; it's not comfortable . . . [T]o me as a person of color, that's my experience . . . This is not my cultural world. People relate to me as if I were white. They don't know anything about my culture. So I'm always adapting to them. And having to operate in their world. That's exactly how the students of color talk to me . . . It's more this vague sense of dis-ease.

RECOMMENDATIONS MADE TO THE CAMPUS COMMUNITY

A draft of the following recommendations emerged as we wrote our report to the Hamline community. We developed the final recommendations building on the comments, observations, and recommendations of faculty and students made in the "member-check" luncheon meetings. These provided us with a series of possible next steps. We organized these under the relevant themes outlined earlier in this article.

Faculty and Student Exposure

1) Faculty and students of all colors expressed a need for strategies that can help us confront some of the fears and concerns related to issues

of race and gender. These include exploring the difference between the intent of our behaviors and the sometimes unintended effect they may have on others. Not unlike undertaking an exercise program after some months of inactivity, addressing these issues inevitably involves some level of discomfort and pain for students. Therefore, it seems equally important that we share processes for ensuring, to the best of our abilities, that students feel safe enough in the classroom to risk exploring these topics with some level of assurance that they will not suffer irreparable harm. However, it must be made clear to them that a safe environment is not necessarily always a comfortable one.

2) Several faculty members asked the question, "How can we be sure our gestures are welcoming gestures?" There was an expressed need for faculty development strategies that enlarge faculty radar for sensing when issues of classroom culture(s) are in conflict (i.e., in communications styles or learning style differences) and when they are not the issues.

3) We heard from students of color, Caucasian students, and a number of faculty that often the classroom environment is not conducive to a multiplicity of voices. For several faculty members, this translates into help in creating an environment in class where it is seen as a safe place to express oneself, particularly on sensitive topics such as race, gender, and ethnicity.

4) The responsibility for tackling discomfort and uneasiness through exposure cannot be relegated entirely to the classroom. Student affairs programming can/must help complement the academic experience as much as possible. To that end, new student orientation can begin to establish as normative the discussion of issues of race, ethnicity, and gender so students are less surprised when they engage these topics in the classroom. These must be continued in hall and campus programming throughout the year.

5) Also under the banner of exposure must come examination of the cultural breadth requirement. A discussion needs to be undertaken on the identified phenomenon of students getting by cultural breadth without the necessity of being exposed to or confronting issues of racial and gender discrimination in the United States. Students are not trying to skirt difficult topics. In several instances, students informed us that it was difficult finding courses that were

discipline specific to put into their schedules. Efforts can and should be made to expand course options for certain underrepresented majors. This should include institutional support (time and resources) so that faculty can develop course offerings that meet majors' needs. Perhaps a pilot grants program can be developed in-house, or larger grants can be written to outside funders that dovetail and help initiate such curriculum development. One suggestion could be to seek funders that are interested in curriculum innovations that help students prepare for the exigencies of dealing with the dynamics of the changing culture of the workplace or survival skills for students in the next millennium.

6) As part of the new faculty orientation series, at least one session should be devoted exclusively to teaching, learning, and diversity in the classroom. The session should include the challenges of having only one or two students of color in the classroom and dealing with gender dynamics.

Fairness, Favoritism, and Equity

Many faculty and students expressed varying degrees of ambivalence and confusion over what constitutes fairness, favoritism and equity. Faculty expressed concerns that by reaching out to certain students and not others they might be perceived as not treating all students equally. The two recommendations in this area are as follows:

1) A discussion is needed among faculty addressing what constitutes effective teaching in a classroom with diverse learners. Questions of whether some students learn differently and the implication to the teaching and learning process could shed needed light on these themes. These questions go beyond race and gender and have considerable legal importance when exploring issues of disability in the classroom as well.

2) None of the faculty or students we interviewed was in favor of lowering academic standards. However, a number of faculty members expressed the belief that the key was not in lowering academic standards, but in creating a supportive environment to help students meet those standards. Many faculty and students of color felt the institutional environment had much ground to cover before it could be categorized as supportive. Work on this needs to go forward.

Addressing Racial and Gender Identity Development
We heard from faculty and students that they deal with a wide variety of peers who range from the minimally exposed and naive to those in denial or resistant to the angry and confrontational to those who are open and committed to exploring issues of oppression and difference.

1) Classroom dynamics are profoundly influenced by students and faculty at various stages of racial and gender identity development (Adams, Bell, & Griffin, 1997; Tatum, 1997; Schoem, Frankl, Zuniga, & Lewis, 1995). Teaching and learning are intertwined with the level of developmental readiness of the learner and teacher. Faculty and staff could benefit from a greater understanding of the stages of racial identity development and their implications to pedagogy. Similar models also pertain to the development of gender identity.

2) One key to helping students of all colors negotiate the transition between stages of racial and gender awareness is the importance of role models and mentors (Adams, Bell, & Griffin, 1997). Students are heavily influenced by what they see respected faculty and staff doing. We can either engage with these issues (and thus send one message) or avoid issues (thus sending an entirely different message). Discussions need to be undertaken as to how faculty and staff can best influence the campus climate away from uneasiness and toward productive engagement. Students of color were very clear that they sought greater contact with faculty and were especially appreciative of efforts at making a connection. To paraphrase one student, it's okay if faculty admit they may make mistakes . . . that way we're all in it together.

CONCLUSION

We found that race and gender were indeed real issues in the classroom. We developed insights into what faculty and students felt would be helpful in addressing these concerns. A serendipitous discovery was that the research process itself yielded tangible faculty development benefits; namely, it engendered campus-wide discussion among half the faculty and a significant number of students about the role diversity plays in the classroom.

On the heels of the release of our report, we have been able to build support for several initiatives related to multicultural teaching. One success was that the faculty unanimously passed a resolution that clarified

and significantly strengthened the college's cultural breadth requirement. It resulted in institutionalizing a teaching for diversity session into
the annual new faculty orientation. In addition, support for faculty development in the area of teaching for diversity became formally incorporated into the newly drafted strategic vision for the College of Liberal
Arts.

Finally, we used the study as a basis for grant writing to area foundations in order to support curriculum development for teaching for diversity. Hamline University was recently awarded a $75,000 challenge grant
from the Otto Bremer Foundation for our Race, Gender, and Beyond
Project. This will support the development of nine revised or new
courses. In the parlance of organizational development, we impacted the
system on several levels. We influenced student awareness and student affairs programming and impacted faculty awareness and administrative
support for faculty development efforts.

RECOMMENDATIONS FOR FACULTY DEVELOPERS ADDRESSING RACE AND GENDER IN THE CLASSROOM

Based on our experiences, we make the following recommendations to
faculty developers who would be prophets in their own land:

1) Get your community talking about race and gender. Listen. They
   have much to share.

2) Although you will hear things that are truly discouraging, they need
   to be heard and given legitimacy.

3) Assume people are doing the best they know how, and wherever possible, catch them doing things right. Focus on trying to understand,
   not on judging.

4) Use a multiracial, multiethnic, male-female faculty development research team wherever possible. The more lenses you bring the better
   you see (Bonilla, 1992).

5) Use "the choir." In preparation for presenting our findings campus-
   wide, we intentionally asked for assistance from faculty experienced
   and committed to multicultural teaching. This was a critical step in
   helping to tailor our report to a potentially less supportive and more
   skeptical audience. While it is often said to be a waste of time to
   preach to the choir, we found that this process allowed experienced

faculty to see others benefit from their hard-won lessons. There is no more empowering experience for a teacher, and no better means for affirming the choir.

6) Hitchhike on a current administrative concern. For example, we benefited by being able to capitalize on the current interest in assessment and evaluation by tying excellence in teaching to teaching for diversity.

In the end, what set this effort apart was the extent to which our faculty identified with these findings. These were not perceived as judgments by some external experts from the outside. Rather, the process of searching out Hamline faculty and student voices representing as many perspectives as possible gave the community ownership over the findings as well as investment in pursuing solutions. In using a faculty development process that gave voice to faculty and student concerns, we legitimized those voices. This empowered rather than disempowered us as faculty developers by recognizing members of the community as agents for change. Contrary to conventional wisdom, you *can* be a prophet in your own land.

REFERENCES

Adams, A., Bell, L., & Griffin, P. (Eds.). (1997). *Teaching for diversity and social justice: A sourcebook*. New York, NY: Routledge.

Bonilla, J. (1992). *Walking the walk: Towards creating more racially diverse institutions of higher education*. Unpublished doctoral dissertation, University of Massachusetts at Amherst.

Border, L. B., & Chism, N. V. N. (Eds.). (1992). *Teaching for diversity*. San Francisco, CA: Jossey-Bass.

Bormann, E.G. (1972). Fantasy and rhetorical vision: The rhetorical criticism of social reality. *Quarterly Journal of Speech, 58*, 396–407.

Bormann, E. G., Cragan, J. F., & Shields, D. C. (1994). In defense of symbolic convergence theory: A look at the theory and its criticisms after two decades. *Communication Theory, 4*, 259–294.

Bormann, E. G., Cragan, J. F., and Shields, D. C. (1996). An expansion of the rhetorical vision component of the symbolic convergence theory: The cold war paradigm case. *Communication Monographs 63*, 1–28.

Cragan, J. F., & Shields, D. C. (Eds.). (1981). *Applied communication theory and research*. Prospect Heights, IL: Waveland.

Kreps, G. (1995). Using focus group discussion to promote organizational reflexivity: Two applied communication field studies. In L. R. Frey (Ed.), *Innovations in group facilitation: Applications in natural settings* (pp. 177–199). Cresskill, NJ: Hampton Press, Inc.

Krieger, S. (1985). Beyond "subjectivity": The use of the self in social science. *Qualitative Sociology, 9* (4), 309–324.

Lincoln, Y., & Guba, E. (1985). *Naturalistic inquiry.* Newbury Park, CA: Sage.

Merriam, S. B. (1988). *Case study research in education: A qualitative approach.* San Francisco, CA: Jossey-Bass.

Mies, M. (1983). Toward a methodology for feminist research. In G. Bowles & R. Klein (Eds.), *Theories of women's studies* (pp. 117–139). New York, NY: Routledge.

Morey, A., & Kitano, M. (Eds.). (1997). *Multicultural course transformation in higher education: A broader truth.* Boston, MA: Allyn & Bacon.

Morgan, D., & Spanish, L. (1984). Focus groups: A new tool for qualitative research. *Qualitative Sociology, 7,* 253–270.

Orbe, M. P. (1998). *Constructing co-cultural theory: An explication of culture, power, and communication.* Thousand Oaks, CA: Sage.

Rossman, G., & Marshal, C. (1989). *Designing qualitative research.* Newbury Park, CA: Sage.

Schoem, D., Frankel, L., Zuniga, X., & Lewis, E. (Eds.). (1995). *Multicultural teaching in the university.* Westport, CT: Praeger.

Tatum, B. D. (1997). *Why are all the Black kids sitting together in the cafeteria? And other conversations about race.* New York, NY: Basic Books.

Contact:

James Bonilla
Assistant Professor
Education and Graduate Public Administration & Management
Hamline University
1536 Hewitt Avenue
St. Paul, MN 55104

Patricia R. Palmerton
Department of Theatre Arts and Communication Studies
Hamline University
1536 Hewitt Avenue
St. Paul, MN 55104

James Bonnilla has a joint appointment to the College of Liberal Arts and the Graduate School of Public Administration & Management. His primary duties are teaching courses on Education and Cultural Diversity; Organizational Behavior; and Race, Gender, and the Workplace at the undergraduate and graduate levels. He is also Director, the Bremer Race, Gender, and Beyond Project and serves as an in-house consultant to the faculty on issues of teaching for diversity via grant making and programming. His current research interests include multicultural organizational change in the academy, teaching for diversity and leadership in diverse settings. He lives on a 124-year-old farm just outside St. Peter, Minnesota.

Patricia Palmerton is Professor of Communication Studies at Hamline University. She has worked extensively nationally with faculty across disciplines on integrating oral communication activities into the classroom. In addition to her work on curriculum development, she teaches courses in rhetorical theory, gender and communication, and interpersonal communication. She has published work on oral communication processes in post-secondary education and the relationship between rhetoric and social change.

5

Faculty Learning Communities: Change Agents for Transforming Institutions into Learning Organizations

Milton D. Cox
Miami University

In my 20 years of faculty development, I have found faculty learning communities to be the most effective programs for achieving faculty learning and development. In addition, these communities build communication across disciplines, increase faculty interest in teaching and learning, initiate excursions into the scholarship of teaching, and foster civic responsibility. They provide a multifaceted, flexible, and holistic approach to faculty development. They change individuals, and, over time, they change institutional culture. Faculty learning communities and their "graduates" are change agents who can enable an institution to become a learning organization. In this article I introduce faculty learning communities and discuss ways that they can transform our colleges and universities.

In higher education, this is a time of increasing interest in learning communities. Palmer (1998) searches for "an image of teaching that has challenged me for years, one that has an essential but seldom-named form of community at its core: to teach is to create a space in which the community of truth is practiced" (p. 90). Cross (1998) addresses the question, "Why Learning Communities? Why Now?" She gives three reasons: "philosophical (because learning communities fit into a changing philosophy of knowledge), research based (because learning communities fit with what research tells us about learning), and pragmatic (because learning communities work)" (p. 4). Learning communities also play an important role in helping individuals and institutions experience a structure that is part of the learning paradigm (Barr & Tagg, 1995; Barr, 1998). Furthermore, Shapiro and Levine (1999) observe that "When campuses begin to implement learning communities, whether they know it or not they are embarking on a road that leads to a profound change in culture" (front cover).

Students who have participated in learning communities develop an educational citizenship, "an understanding of the nature and importance of mutual interdependence in shared learning endeavors" (Tinto, 1995, p. 12). Tinto also reports that students "learned more, found academic and social support for their learning among their peers, and they became actively involved in their learning" (p. 12). Learning communities give students a sense of belonging; thus, they persist rather than retreat. These students "made a significant and unusual leap in intellectual development during their learning community experience" (Gabelnick, MacGregor, Matthews, & Smith, 1990, p. 66). According to Perry (1970), "once students embrace complexity and begin to build the habits and skills of making meaning within that complexity, there is no turning back" (pp. 107–108, as quoted in Gablenick et al., 1990, p. 71).

Although the above comments are about student learning communities, they are also true for faculty learning communities. Faculty are students when they are members of a faculty learning community—an active, collaborative, year-long learning environment. Fulton and Licklider (1998) claim that "New visions of professional development suggest that the practices needed to support faculty learning are analogous to those needed to support student learning" (p. 55). It is no surprise, then, that learning and development outcomes for faculty in learning communities are similar to those for students who are members of student learning communities.

Thus, faculty who are graduates of faculty learning communities have a perspective that goes beyond their disciplines and includes a broader view of their institution and higher education. With respect to intellectual development in this arena, participants may move through multiplicity, interested in and trying many new approaches to teaching, to relativity (Perry, 1970), assessing various approaches against their learning objectives, and applying the scholarship of teaching. They, too, embrace and make meaning within the complexity of teaching and learning beyond their disciplines. They are likely to take responsibility for involvement in setting institutional goals, pursuing difficult campus issues, and contributing to the common good. And they persist in their efforts because they belong to a community of support.

LEARNING COMMUNITIES

Student Learning Communities

In the 1920s and '30s, Alexander Meiklejohn and John Dewey developed the concept of a student learning community in higher education. Increasing specialization and fragmentation caused Meiklejohn (1932) to call for a community of study and a unity and coherence of curriculum across disciplines. Dewey (1933) advocated learning that was active, student centered, and involved shared inquiry. A combination of these approaches generated a few promising but short-lived programs, for example, at the University of California, Berkeley (Tussman, 1969). However, after success with student learning communities at The Evergreen State College in the 1970s (Jones, 1981), several institutions initiated learning communities that have produced a pedagogy and structure that has led, among other things, to students' increased grade point averages and retention (Gabelnick et al., 1990). Learning community models include linked courses, clusters, freshman interest groups, federated learning communities, and coordinated studies. These structures vary in complexity from linked courses, in which a cohort of students enrolls in two courses and the degree of faculty cooperation varies, to coordinated studies, in which a cohort of students and faculty participate in a multidisciplinary program taught in block mode around a central theme (Gabelnick et al., 1990). The term learning community traditionally has been applied to programs that involve first- and second-year undergraduates, along with faculty who design the curriculum and teach the courses. I call these student learning communities, although "The modeling, mentoring, and learning in this situation are invaluable in faculty development" (Gabelnick et al., 1990, p. 80).

Faculty Learning Communities

I define a faculty learning community to be a cross-disciplinary faculty group of eight to 14 members engaged in a year-long program with a curriculum about enhancing teaching and learning and with frequent seminars and activities that provide learning, development, and community building. In the literature about student learning communities, the word student usually can be replaced by faculty and still make the same point;

for example, "As students develop ownership of 'their' learning community, a sort of civic pride arises and students want to do well" (Gabelnick et al., 1990, p. 59). I have found that faculty develop a similar civic pride, for example, as each faculty community prepares and delivers its annual campus-wide seminar on participants' individual and joint innovations in teaching and learning (Cox, 1999b).

The term faculty learning community is new, although a few such faculty development programs have been around since the mid-1970s, for example, the Lilly Endowment's Post-Doctoral Teaching Fellows Program that enabled small communities of junior faculty to include a focus on teaching during one of their pretenure years (Austin, 1992). However, faculty learning communities have been overlooked as an effective avenue for faculty development. For example, Kurfiss and Boice (1990) surveyed members of the Professional and Organizational Development Network in Higher Education (POD) to determine existing and desired faculty development practices. The faculty learning community approach was not included in the 26 practices reported, although 18 of the 26 are involved in faculty learning community activities. Wright and O'Neil (1995) surveyed key instructional role players at institutions in the US, Canada, the UK, and Australia to determine the potential of 36 faculty development practices that could improve teaching on their campuses. Again, faculty learning communities or their equivalent are not included on this list, although 30 of the 36 practices take place in, or are connected to, communities. This data suggests the absence of a holistic, connected approach to faculty development.

Examples of Faculty Learning Communities

For over 20 years, we have been designing and directing faculty learning communities at Miami University, a state-supported Doctoral I institution with 14,500 undergraduates, 1500 graduate students, and 750 full time faculty on the Oxford campus, plus two regional, urban, commuter campuses, each with 2000 students and 50 faculty. I define two types of faculty learning communities: cohort-focused and issue-focused. I have developed and worked with two or more examples of each type, which are components of Miami's teaching effectiveness programs. In addition to faculty learning communities, these programs include a wide variety of teaching grants that support the development of teaching innovations by individuals and departments, plus the usual assortment of faculty development activities such as campus workshops, consultations, and new faculty orientation. These programs are funded by contributions from Miami alumni.

Cohort-focused communities. Cohort-focused faculty learning communities address the teaching, learning, and developmental needs of an important cohort of faculty that has been particularly affected by the isolation, fragmentation, or chilly climate in the academy. The curriculum of this year-long community is shaped by the participants to include a broad range of teaching and learning areas and topics of interest to them. Two examples of cohort-focused communities at Miami are the Teaching Scholars Community for junior faculty (Cox, 1995), in place for 22 years, and the Senior Faculty Community for Teaching Excellence for mid-career and senior faculty (Cox & Blaisdell, 1995), in place for 10 years.

The junior faculty community provides a safe place for pretenure folks in their second through fifth years to meet and work on teaching opportunities with peers from other disciplines. Most participants develop into quick starters (Boice, 1992). The outcomes noted in Figure 5.1 indicate that they also become very interested in the teaching process and gain a perspective of teaching, learning, and higher education beyond their disciplines. They become comfortable in the university community, overcoming the great stress often felt by junior faculty (Sorcinelli, 1992). Figure 5.2 shows that the faculty partner—an experienced faculty mentor—has a strong impact on the development of junior faculty members (Cox, 1997). At Miami, participants are tenured at a significantly higher rate than junior faculty who do not participate in this community (Cox, 1995). Junior faculty communities will make a positive impact on the culture of an institution over the years if given multi-year support (Cox, 1995; List, 1997).

The senior faculty community offers participants time, safety, funds, and colleagueship across different disciplines in order to reflect on past teaching and life experiences and investigate and chart new directions. Figure 5.2 indicates that this community values most the colleagueship and learning from the other participants, the release time of one course for one semester for the year, and the retreats and conferences. Figure 5.1 reports outcomes similar to those for junior faculty community members. The senior community fulfills many of Karpiak's (1997) recommendations of what the university administration should do for professors at midlife: provide opportunities for them to be members of a team, to help each other grow as intellectuals, to develop support networks, and to counsel each other on career matters. The institution is humanized through the recognition and support of the different contributions that these experienced professors bring.

These two cohort-focused communities provide faculty development

FIGURE 5.1
RATINGS OF COMMON PROGRAM OUTCOMES
Miami University
PROGRAM EVALUATION
FACULTY LEARNING COMMUNITIES

Results from the question, "Estimate the impact of the community on you with respect to each of the following program components. '1' indicates a very weak impact and '10' indicates a very strong impact." Number in parentheses is the ranking of this outcome over the years the question has been asked. Number on second line is mean for that outcome over the years the question has been asked.

Outcomes	Junior Faculty Community	Senior Faculty Community	Difference Community	Cooperative Learning Community
1. Your interest in the teaching process	(1) 8.5	(1) 8.6	(4) 8.8	(3) 9.6
2. Your view of teaching as an intellectual pursuit	(3) 8.1	(4) 7.9	(1) 9.8	(3) 9.6
3. Your understanding of and interest in the scholarship of teaching	(5) 7.8	(7) 7.5	(2) 9.4	(1) 9.7
4. Your comfort level as a member of the Miami University Community	(4) 8.0	(3) 8.0	(9) 7.5	(1) 9.7
5. Your perspective of teaching, learning, and other aspects of higher education beyond the perspective of your discipline	(2) 8.3	(2) 8.3	(6) 8.3	(10) 7.7
6. Your total effectiveness as a teacher	(6) 7.7	(6) 7.6	(7) 8.2	(9) 8.3
7. Your awareness and understanding of how difference may influence & enhance teaching and learning	(11) 6.4	(8) 7.4	(5) 8.4	(5) 8.7
8. Your understanding of the role of a faculty member at Miami University	(8) 7.1	(4) 7.9	(7) 8.2	(11) 6.9
9. Your research and scholarly interest with respect to your discipline	(10) 6.7	(11) 6.4	(3) 9.2	(7) 8.6
10. Your awareness of ways to integrate the teaching/research experience	(8) 7.1	(9) 7.2	(10) 6.8	(5) 8.7
11. Your technical skill as a teacher	(7) 7.2	(10) 6.9	(10) 6.8	(8) 8.4
OVERALL MEAN FOR COHORT	7.6	7.4	8.3	8.7

Other items specific to a particular community were also rated; they are available from the author.

FIGURE 5.2
RATINGS OF COMMON PROGRAM COMPONENTS
Miami University
FACULTY LEARNING COMMUNITIES
PROGRAM EVALUATION
Results from the question, "Estimate the impact of the community on you with respect to each of the following program components. '1' indicates a very weak impact and '10' indicates a very strong impact." Includes reports from those who engaged in a particular component and rated it. Number in parentheses is the ranking of this component over the years the question has been asked. Number on second line is mean for that component over the years the question has been asked.

Components	Junior Faculty Community	Senior Faculty Community	Difference Community	Cooperative Learning Community
1. The colleagueship and learning from other participants	(1) 8.9	(1) 8.7	(1) 8.8	(1) 9.9
2. The retreats and conferences	(2) 8.2	(3) 7.7	(3) 8.3	(2) 8.9
3. Release time (Junior, Senior) or substantial funds for professional expenses (Difference, Cooperative)	(2) 8.1	(1) 8.7	(5) 7.3	(5) 7.7
4. The teaching project	(4) 8.0	(3) 7.7	(2) 8.5	(4) 8.1
5. Seminars	(6) 7.6	(6) 7.4	(4) 7.8	(3) 8.5
6. Student associates	(8) 5.4	(3) 7.7	N/A	(6) 7.6
7. A one-to-one faculty partnership (Junior: senior faculty mentor; Senior: faculty partners in learning)	(5) 7.9	(8) 6.0	N/A	N/A
8. Observation of a faculty partner's and others' classes	(7) 6.8	(7) 6.3	(6) 7.0	(7) 3.0
OVERALL MEAN FOR COHORT	7.9	7.5	8.0	7.7

Other items specific to a particular community were also rated; they are available from the author.

that prepares "staff at each stage of their career so they take on new roles and responsibilities" (Brew & Boud, 1996, p. 20).

Issue-focused communities. Each issue-focused learning community has a curriculum designed to address a special campus teaching and learning issue, for example, diversity, cooperative learning, or development of teaching portfolios. These communities offer membership to a variety of faculty ranks and cohorts, but with a focus on a particular theme. A particular issue-focused faculty learning community is no longer offered when the campus-wide teaching opportunity or issue of concern has been satisfactorily addressed. Three examples of issue-focused communities at Miami are the Faculty Community Using Difference to Enhance Teaching and Learning, in place for three years (Stevens & Cox, 1999); the Community Using Cooperative Learning to Enhance Teaching and Learning (Cox, 1999a), in place for one year; and the Teaching Portfolio Project (Cox, 1996), in place from 1993–1996.

We created the Faculty Community Using Difference to Enhance Teaching and Learning in order to involve faculty in addressing serious diversity issues on campus. The strategy hinged on the belief that if faculty could connect diversity issues with ways to increase the learning of their students, instructors would get involved. The safety offered by this faculty learning community has been important in opening a constructive dialogue and fostering risk taking. "Learning communities have features that feminist literature suggests are important, such as cooperation and shared power, development of a personal connection to the material being studied, and emphasis on the affective aspects of learning" (Gabelnick et al., 1990, p. 79). Figure 5.1 notes that members in this community have a level of comfort in the university community below those in other groups. This is a result of concerns raised by their investigations about their campus climate. They rate highly the impact of pedagogical scholarship and their view of teaching as an intellectual pursuit. This is a result of their readings, seminars, and conversations.

The teaching portfolio project was developed to meet faculty interest in investigating and constructing teaching portfolios. Rather than take a campus-wide approach, we chose to let participating departments design and develop uses and procedures particular to their disciplinary and departmental cultures. The teaching portfolio project involved communities at two levels. First, a learning community team was formed by each participating department, with membership across departmental subdisciplines, ranks, and interests. The learning community at the campus-wide level was made up of the faculty who coordinated the communities in their departments or divisions. This community of team coordinators provided an invaluable support group with which to share ideas, frustrations, and successes (Cox, 1996).

The Faculty Community Using Cooperative Learning to Enhance Teaching and Learning provides a safe place for faculty who wish to try this aspect of active learning. According to Millis (1990), "Faculty developers can speed the dissemination process by helping faculty understand a) the nature of cooperative learning; b) its documented, well-researched impact on student achievement, self-esteem, social skills, and interracial harmony; and c) its liberating effects on college-level teaching and learning" (p. 44). A faculty learning community provides an excellent place to accomplish these goals. This community also rates highly the impact of the scholarship of teaching (Figure 5.1). In sharp contrast to the Difference Community, this group is comfortable in the university community.

New issue-focused faculty communities under consideration for 2000–01 include ones on technology, problem-based learning, service-learning, team teaching, and student learning communities.

Aspects of Faculty Communities

The following items are common to all of the faculty learning communities described above.

Long-Term Goals
The long-term goals of faculty learning communities for the university are to

- build university-wide community through teaching and learning
- increase faculty interest in undergraduate teaching and learning
- nourish the scholarship of teaching and its application to student learning
- broaden the evaluation of teaching and the assessment of learning
- increase faculty collaboration across disciplines
- encourage reflection about general education and coherence of learning across disciplines
- create an awareness of the complexity of teaching and learning increase the rewards for and prestige of excellent teaching

- increase financial support for teaching and learning initiatives
- investigate and incorporate ways that difference can enhance teaching and learning.

Each faculty learning community has its own additional specific objectives (Cox, 1999a). For example, an objective of the Junior Faculty Community is the development of syllabi that articulate clear learning objectives, and an objective of the Community Using Difference is to increase the use of pedagogies and behaviors that create inclusive classroom cultures.

Activities

According to Fulton and Licklider, "Faculty, like their students, learn by reading, experiencing, reflecting, and collaborating with others" (1998, p. 55). Each year the activities for these communities vary somewhat but are likely to include the following.

Biweekly seminars on teaching and learning. Seminars in a faculty learning community go "beyond the individual ponderings of good teachers to a community of conversation where teachers cannot only express their conceptions of teaching in discussion and reflection with others, but go beyond mere technical elements or classroom practice to the richer dimensions of human understanding" (Harper, 1996, p. 263). Recent topics include assessing student learning, enhancing the teaching/learning experience through awareness of developmental stages (for example, student intellectual development or the inclusiveness of one's course curriculum), sharing student and faculty views of teaching and learning (the community members and their student associates meet) (Cox & Sorenson, 1999), and having all participants of a community read topics selected from articles or books (See Appendix 5.1). Some seminars are led by guest faculty; others are conducted by the participants themselves. In the second semester, individuals or the group present a seminar to the entire campus. As on other campuses, this reading group facet of a community has contributed to campus organizational and curriculum change (Eckel, Kezar, & Lieberman, 1999), for example, on the Cox campus, the establishment of a liberal education program. Communities of conversation are established in faculty learning communities because these communities are not evaluatory, trust and respect is established, and participants are open to the concerns of the others (Harper, 1996).

National conferences and retreats. Retreats and conferences provide a developmental approach that unfolds chronologically to enable

- introduction of new members to the community culture and its expectations
- bonding
- learning from nationally recognized teacher scholars
- learning from the other community members
- learning about national issues and polices in higher education beyond one's discipline
- the opportunity to present a paper on teaching and learning
- passing the torch to new members

An opening/closing retreat is held in May, with the graduating members of the community sharing information and experiences with the new participants about various aspects of the program, such as helpful seminar topics, faculty partner and student associate selection, teaching projects, and national conferences. In the early fall, a bonding retreat occurs at another campus or national teaching conference; it is also the setting for seminars with faculty from other universities. In late fall, each community participates in the annual Lilly Conference on College Teaching at Miami University, a meeting of nationally known teacher-scholars and faculty from other campuses. During the second semester, each group attends a national conference on higher education, such as Lilly-West or American Association of Colleges and Universities. Members are encouraged to make presentations at the Lilly conferences. Our office pays all travel expenses.

Teaching projects. Members of all communities individually pursue self-designed learning programs, including a teaching project, for which they receive financial support. Past projects have included developing expertise and courseware for computer-assisted instruction, redesigning an ongoing course for distance learning, and investigating, learning, and trying a new teaching method. Most of these projects are shared with the university at a campus-wide seminar.

Faculty partners. Each community member selects a colleague to work with during the year. In the case of junior faculty, the person is an experienced faculty member from outside that community who serves as a mentor. Senior faculty community members pair up with someone inside that community, as in the New Jersey Partners in Learning model (Katz & Henry, 1993).

Student associates. Each participant selects one or two students who provide perspectives for that participant's teaching and learning project, as well as about seminar topics discussed in that community. Strategies for student selection, engagement, and rewards are provided in Cox and Sorenson (1999).

The Scholarship of Teaching

Each community engages in a sequence of activities designed to introduce its members to a discipline that is new to most of them: the scholarship of teaching. Our faculty development office has an extensive library and subscribes to the few newsletters and multidisciplinary journals that publish the scholarship of teaching. Seminars early in the program address topics from the community's focus book (Appendix 5.1) or articles that provide introductions to key topics such as student intellectual development (Thomas, 1992; Kloss, 1994). As members begin their teaching project, they are expected to place it in context (Richlin, in press). We encourage projects that are relatively straightforward, perhaps involving classroom assessment techniques (Angelo & Cross, 1993) and classroom research (Cross & Steadman, 1996). This requires reading the appropriate scholarship of teaching. Participants share their project development with each other during the first semester. In the latter part of the second semester, they present their projects to the campus, including handouts with references. At first some feel uncomfortable with this. They react with surprise to the possibility of becoming an expert in a new discipline so quickly—after all, it took them years to master their disciplines. However, except for junior faculty, these are seasoned practitioners of teaching. Once the participants—even the junior faculty—become familiar with the scholarship of teaching needed for their projects, gain support from their community, and experience the helpful perspectives of the multidisciplinary audience to whom they present, they become interested partners in the scholarship of teaching.

Compensation and Rewards

Participation in a faculty learning community takes a lot of time and work: attendance at weekend retreats, national conferences, and biweekly seminars; interaction with a student associate and a faculty partner; reading the new literature of the scholarship of teaching; development of and work on a teaching project; and preparation of a seminar presentation for the campus and, perhaps, a national conference.

We have two ways of compensating faculty participants. First, and best, is to provide release time from one course for one semester. This is done at the rate for adjuncts. If a department chair can create the release time in another manner, then the department receives the funds and usually allocates them to the faculty member, for example, to purchase technology or international travel. This compensation is available only in the cohort-focused communities. Also, each member receives funds to enable his or her learning plan or teaching project. Junior faculty participants each have $125 available, and senior faculty have $500.

Unfortunately, we do not have the budget to provide release time for members of the issue-focused communities. There, each participant receives an honorarium to use for professional expenses. Members of the Community Using Difference each receive $1500, and members of the Cooperative Learning Community receive $1000. In the teaching portfolio project, each participating department received $5000.

Each community coordinator receives one course release time for both semesters plus the honorarium available for his or her particular community. Service as a coordinator must be approved by his or her department chair.

Applications for Community Membership

Before applying for membership in a faculty learning community, faculty must obtain approval from their chair, dean, and, if applicable, their regional campus executive director. Chairs are encouraged to write a letter of support. Applications for participation in the next year's community are due in late March.

Requests for information that are common to the application forms for each community are as follows:

- Briefly describe the nature of your current teaching responsibilities. Include the learning objectives from one of your courses as stated in your syllabus.

- Describe innovative teaching activities in which you have been involved (efforts to improve teaching, development of curricular materials, etc.).

- Indicate two or three of your most pressing needs regarding teaching and learning.

- Describe your reasons for wanting to participate in this community.

- Part of this program is an individual teaching project pursued by each participant. At this time, what area of interest do you wish to pursue? Of course, this may change as you engage your community.

- This community involves working with a faculty partner and student associate of your choice. Although you need not have particular persons in mind at this time, in what ways would you take advantage of this opportunity, and how do you see this aspect of the program as being helpful to you?

- What do you think you can contribute to this community (for example, particular teaching experience)?

- Briefly state your philosophy of teaching.

Selection Procedure and Criteria
Different subcommittees of Miami's Committee for the Enhancement of Learning and Teaching (CELT) select the membership of each community. Each subcommittee is chaired by the coordinator of that community, and members include former community participants, a student associate, and a member of CELT who has not been a part of the community. Selections for the new year are recommended to the provost. New participants are announced in mid-April.

The selection criteria used to evaluate applications are commitment to quality teaching, level of interest in the community, need, openness to new ideas, potential for contributions to the community, and plans for use of the award year. Participants are chosen to create a diverse group representing a variety of disciplines, experiences, and needs.

Assessment
Participants of all communities agree to prepare mid-year and final reports indicating the impact of the community on outcomes related to program goals and objectives (Figure 5.1) and the impact of the various components of the community on their teaching and learning (Figure 5.2). The results of this assessment relative to the objectives particular to a certain community and not common to all communities are reported elsewhere in the literature (for junior faculty, in Cox, 1995, for senior faculty, in Cox & Blaisdell, 1995, and for the Community Using Difference, in Stevens & Cox, 1999). In an open-ended section of the report, each participant also details the results and status of his or her teaching project and interaction with faculty partner and student associate.

The selection subcommittee for a community reviews the mid-year and final reports and serves in an advisory role to the coordinator of the community.

Leadership

As we form new communities, we select as coordinators former faculty participants who have been exemplary members in one or more of the communities. They are usually successful seminar presenters or members of past junior faculty groups who have later served as mentors. Some have led effectively as committee chairs of CELT. All exhibit a talent for and interest in faculty development and have experience in the topic of the community they lead. Among faculty, they are positive opinion leaders (Middendorf, 1999). However, contrary to Middendorf's recommendations, we do not involve them sparingly. Instead, these coordinators make generous commitments of time and effort to their communities. They also share the results of their communities locally and nationally; all have presented at national faculty development or teaching conferences. Thus, each community coordinator makes a civic contribution to the common good of students, faculty, the university, and teaching and learning.

Recommendations for Start-Up

An overview of the aspects of and recommendations for initiating and continuing faculty learning communities is in Cox (1999). Materials for practice in each community are in Cox, Cottell, & Stevens (1999). I recommend that developers begin with just one community in order to gain experience, fit the community approach into their campus culture, and build support by providing assessment results. When administrators are given choices, they tend to invest first in faculty development for junior faculty and in diversity or technology issues; these may be the best places to start on the campus. For more detailed recommendations for starting a junior faculty community, see Cox (1995, 1997).

Overcoming Obstacles

Some obstacles must be addressed in order to start and continue faculty learning communities. One obstacle is the length of time needed for an institution to show a cultural change as a result of the community approach—at least five years. Other obstacles include cost, participants' time commitment, and the isolated nature of faculty life—the group structure of the community experience is not for everyone. These obstacles are similar to some of those that challenge student learning communities, as Barr (1998) observes: "Faculty experimenting with learning communities are finding themselves hard-pressed to keep them going" (p. 22).

The annual cost for each community of eight to ten members plus coordinator varies from $20,000 to $30,000. The top expense items are release time (or honorarium) and travel. However, providing first-class treatment for participants earns their generous time commitment, appreciation, and support.

Communities do not appeal to everyone. For example, an excellent teacher, who had served successfully as a mentor in our junior faculty community and also followed a colleague's participation in the senior faculty community, approached me with an enthusiastic suggestion: Perhaps just one meeting of a community at the start of the year would suffice, enabling full concentration on one's individual teaching project the rest of the year. Another faculty member suggested that we bring in an expert at the start and avoid the amateurish discussions of the group. With this in mind, developers initiating communities should continue other support for individuals: grants, consultations, and "one-time-only" seminars.

Nevertheless, once one successful faculty learning community is up and running, and barring an unexpected university-wide budget shortfall, the positive outcomes for participants and the institution should convince administrators to continue and expand funding. Enthusiastic participants will convince reticent colleagues to join.

If the developers' campus looks favorably upon the outcomes of student learning communities, then they can argue that faculty learning communities can produce similar outcomes for faculty.

The Role of Faculty Developer

Faculty developers play a key role in managing the operations of faculty learning communities. As part of my role as director of teaching effectiveness programs, I coordinate the junior faculty community and oversee the other three. This consists of working closely with each faculty coordinator. Our office handles room scheduling, meals, travel, publicity, and budget items.

As developers within our institutions, "we need to promote an understanding of the process of faculty development over time, leading to a full integration of the fragments of academic work" (Kreber & Cranton, 1999, p. 225). Providing a variety of faculty learning communities over the years enables faculty to concentrate on specific issues or developmental needs at various times during their careers.

FACULTY LEARNING COMMUNITIES AS CHANGE AGENTS

Including faculty learning communities in your institution's repertoire of faculty development practices answers the need for more holistic, connected, and flexible approaches to faculty development and thoughtful institutional change. Faculty learning communities answer the question posed by Hubbard, Atkins, & Brinko (1998): "how to address the larger issue of institutional, professional, and personal change as a whole, inter-relational and interacting, multifaceted system" (p. 39). Faculty learning communities address the paradigm shift in educational development and institutional change in the manner Chism (1998) encourages, by incorporating faculty study and the redress of "hitches" in the system: "As educational developers, we are also in an ideal situation to create communities of inquiry related to the changes that could be made: for example, a special interest group exploring multicultural teaching or service learning" (p. 143). Issue-focused faculty learning communities are just such an example, providing a way to embrace hitches in order to accomplish change.

Becoming a Learning Organization

Senge (1990) describes a learning organization as one that connects its members closely to the mission, goals, and challenges of the organization. These close connections are necessary for the organization to meet the demands of rapid change. While faculty often have such connections within their departments and disciplinary organizations, faculty usually do not have the broad interests of their institutions at heart. There are few rewards for doing so—most are department- and discipline-based. Rarely has a turf battle in a university senate meeting (when a quorum could be mustered) been resolved by the opponents offering to consult and consider the university's and students' best interests. As a result, faculty remain isolated from colleagues in other disciplines, and the curriculum remains fragmented. Thus, both faculty and students miss out on connections across disciplines. Campus-wide action on issues (except, perhaps, parking and salaries) flounders from lack of interest, involvement, and support.

Senge (1990) describes the five components of a learning organization, components that foster close connections among the people within an institution. Patrick and Fletcher (1998) translate these components into behavior for the academy. Figure 5.3 describes both perspectives and shows how faculty learning communities foster the reflection, learning, and action needed to establish these components in our colleges and universities.

Evidence of Success

Figure 5.2 provides evidence that faculty learning communities produce team learning and community for their members: The program impact of "colleagueship and learning from other participants" is ranked first by

FIGURE 5.3
Senge's Five Components of a Learning Organization and Ways That Faculty Learning Communities Enable Them

General Description Senge (1990)	Transforming Colleges and Universities Into Learning Organizations Patrick & Fletcher (1998)	Ways That Faculty Learning Communities Enable Senge's Five Components of a Learning Organization
Systems Thinking View of the system as a whole, a conceptual framework providing connections between units and members; the shared process of reflection, reevaluation, action, and reward	Creation and recovery of a common language and processes across departments and divisions; setting and honoring institutional missions, goals, actions, and rewards	Time, funding, safety, teams, and rewards to enable multidisciplinary participants to discover, reflect on, and assess pedagogical and institutional systems; members' discovery and appreciation of the synergy of connected campus units
Personal Mastery Support for individuals to achieve their maximum potential as experts in their fields and to address opportunities and problems in new and creative ways	Support for faculty to continue as experts in their disciplines yet broaden their scholarship beyond discovery to include integration, application, and teaching, particularly multidisciplinary perspectives	Development of individual teaching projects to address opportunities or shortcomings in one's teaching and learning; a developmental introduction to and practice of the scholarship of teaching with multidisciplinary perspectives; becoming an expert teacher inside and outside one's discipline
Mental Models Culture and assumptions that shape how an organization's members approach their work and its relationship to society; relationship of employees to the organization, peers, and clients	Change from a culture of autonomy and rewards for individual work to one of community building; rewards for faculty contributions to institutional goals and solutions of problems	Members' opposition to the isolation and fragmentation of the academy; high value of colleagueship across disciplines; participation an honor with financial rewards; discovery and appreciation of differences among students and their development; value of students as associates and sojourners
Building a Shared Vision Collaborative creation of organizational goals, identity, visions, and actions shared by members; outcomes a result of teamwork, with each individual's contribution an integral part	Sharing of departmental and disciplinary visions across disciplines; identifying joint approaches to issues such as implementing student learning communities, improving student learning, integration of technology, creation of an intellectual community	Development of pedagogical goals and joint approaches in each community and sharing these with the campus; e.g., using technology in teaching, inclusiveness of classroom and curriculum, active learning, assessment of learning; discussion of campus-wide issues; taking positions and action
Team Learning Creation of opportunities for individuals to work and learn together in a community where it is safe to innovate, learn, and try anew	Colleges and universities with "learning communities for teaching and research with colleagues and students" (p. 162)	Team learning—the heart and purpose of a faculty learning community

those in each community. With respect to outcomes (Figure 5.1), the greatest impact of the cohort communities is on the participants' interest in the teaching process. The greatest impact of the issue-focused communities is on the participants' interest in the scholarship of teaching and view of teaching as an intellectual pursuit.

Another measure of success is the support received from administrators. This is evident in that Miami's provosts have tripled funding over the last 15 years to enable the initiation of new communities.

Evidence that communities foster civic pride is found in participants' contributions to leadership of the university. Currently two of Miami's six deans are graduates of faculty learning communities, as well as seven of 44 department chairs. Of the 146 faculty still at Miami who have served as mentors in the junior faculty community, over one-third (50/146) are former learning community participants. Of the 46 faculty members currently on the university senate, 16 (35%) are current or former members of faculty learning communities. Finally, of the 175 Miami faculty who volunteered to be on the 1998–99 faculty teaching resource list, 116 (66%) are former or current members.

Although effective faculty leaning communities alone will not transform an institution into a learning organization, over time they can produce a critical mass of key individuals and leaders plus the network necessary to connect campus units. Gabelnick et al. (1990) implore, "We need to create programs that bring us together structurally in some cases, intellectually and emotionally in others. . . . Learning communities are one way that we may build the commonalties and connections so essential to our education and our society" (p. 92). Harper (1996) contends that "Creating such opportunities for conversation and community among faculty is imperative, not only to the personal and professional growth and reflection of individual faculty, but also for the growth of the higher education community at large" (p. 265).

Learning communities, both faculty and student, can provide individuals, colleges, and universities with a means for achieving success in a rapidly changing world.

ACKNOWLEDGMENTS

I thank the Miami faculty members who have coordinated faculty learning communities: Muriel Blaisdell, Interdisciplinary Studies—The Senior Faculty Community for Teaching Excellence; Phillip Cottell, Accountancy—The Faculty Community Using Cooperative Learning to

Enhance Teaching and Learning; Mel Cohen, Political Science, and
Martha Stevens, Communication—The Faculty Community Using Difference to Enhance Teaching and Learning. All of these colleagues have
made terrific contributions to the common good.

REFERENCES

Angelo, T. A., & Cross, K. P. (1993). *Classroom assessment techniques: A handbook for college teachers* (2nd ed.). San Francisco, CA: Jossey-Bass.

Austin, A. E. (1992). Supporting junior faculty through a teaching fellows program. In M. D. Sorcinelli & A. E. Austin (Eds.), *Developing new and junior faculty* (pp. 73–86). New Directions for Teaching and Learning, No. 50. San
Francisco, CA: Jossey-Bass.

Barr, R. B. (1998, September-October). Obstacles to implementing the learning
paradigm. *About Campus, 3* (4), 18–25.

Barr, R. B., & Tagg, J. (1995, November/December). From teaching to learning—A new paradigm for undergraduate education. *Change, 27* (6), 13–25.

Boice, R. (1992). *The new faculty member: Supporting and fostering professional development.* San Francisco, CA: Jossey-Bass.

Brew, A., & Boud, D. (1996). Preparing for new academic roles. *The International
Journal for Academic Development, 1* (2), 17–26.

Chism, N. V. N. (1998). The role of educational developers in institutional
change: From basement office to front office. *To improve the academy, 17,*
141–154. Stillwater, OK: New Forums.

Cox, M. D. (1995). The development of new and junior faculty. In W. A. Wright
& Associates (Eds.), *Teaching improvement practices: Successful strategies for higher
education* (pp. 283–310). Bolton, MA: Anker.

Cox, M. D. (1996). A department-based approach to developing teaching portfolios: Perspectives for faculty developers. *To improve the academy, 15,*
275–302. Stillwater, OK: New Forums.

Cox, M. D. (1997). Long-term patterns in a mentoring program for junior faculty: Recommendations for practice. *To improve the academy, 16,* 225–268.
Stillwater, OK: New Forums.

Cox, M. D. (1999a). *Teaching communities, grants, resources, and events, 1999–00.*
Oxford, OH: Miami University.

Cox, M. D. (1999b). Peer consultation and faculty learning communities. In
C. Knapper & S. Piccinin (Eds.), *Using consultation to improve teaching* (pp.

39–49). New Directions for Teaching and Learning, No. 79. San Francisco, CA: Jossey-Bass.

Cox, M. D., & Blaisdell, M. (1995, October). *Teaching development for senior faculty: Searching for fresh solutions in a salty sea.* Paper presented at the 20th annual Conference of the Professional and Organizational Development Network in Higher Education, North Falmouth, MA.

Cox, M. D., Cottell, P. G., & Stevens, M. P. (1999, October). *Developing and coordinating faculty learning communities: Procedures and materials for practice.* Workshop presented at the 24th annual conference of the Professional and Organizational Development Network in Higher Education, Lake Harmony, PA.

Cox, M. D., & Sorenson, D. L. (2000). Student collaboration in faculty development: Connecting directly to the learning revolution. *To improve the academy, 18,* 97–127. Bolton, MA: Anker.

Cross, K. P. (1998, July-August). Why learning communities? Why now? *About Campus,* 4–11.

Cross, K. P., & Steadman, M. H. (1996). *Classroom research: Implementing the scholarship of teaching.* San Francisco: Jossey-Bass.

Dewey, J. (1933). *How we think.* Lexington, MA: Heath.

Eckel, P., Kezar, A., & Lieberman, D. (1999, November). Learning for organizing: Institutional reading groups as a strategy for change. *AAHE Bulletin, 52* (3), 6–8.

Fulton, C., & Licklider, B. L. (1998). Supporting faculty development in an era of change. *To improve the academy, 19,* 51–66. Stillwater, OK: New Forums.

Gabelnick, F., MacGregor, J., Matthews, R. S., & Smith, B. L. (1990). *Learning communities: Creating connections among students, faculty, and disciplines.* New Directions for Teaching and Learning, No. 41. San Francisco, CA: Jossey-Bass.

Harper, V. (1996). Establishing a community of conversation: Creating a context for self-reflection among teacher-scholars. *To improve the academy, 15,* 251–266. Stillwater, OK: New Forums.

Hubbard, G. T., Atkins, S. S., & Brinko, K. T. (1998). Holistic faculty development: Supporting personal, professional, and organizational well-being. *To improve the academy, 17,* 35–50. Stillwater, OK: New Forums.

Jones, R. (1981). *Experiment at Evergreen.* Cambridge, MA: Shenkman.

Karpiak, I. E. (1997). University professors at mid-life: Being a part of . . . but feeling apart. *To improve the academy, 16,* 21–40. Stillwater, OK: New Forums.

Katz, J., & Henry, M. (1993). *Turning professors into teachers: A new approach to faculty development and student learning.* Phoenix, AZ: Oryx.

Kloss, R. J. (1994). A nudge is best: Helping students through the Perry Scheme of intellectual development. *College Teaching, 42* (4), 151–158.

Kreber, C., & Cranton, P. (2000). Fragmentation versus integration of faculty work. *To improve the academy, 18,* 217–231. Bolton, MA: Anker.

Kurfiss, J., & Boice, R. (1990). Current and desired faculty development practices among POD members. *To improve the academy, 9,* 73–82. Stillwater, OK: New Forums.

List, K. (1997). A continuing conversation on teaching: An evaluation of a decade-long Lilly Teaching Fellows Program, 1986–1996. *To improve the academy, 16,* 201–224. Stillwater, OK: New Forums.

Meiklejohn, A. (1932). *The experimental college.* New York, NY: HarperCollins.

Middendorf, J. K. (1999). Finding key faculty to influence change. *To improve the academy, 18,* 83–93. Bolton, MA: Anker.

Millis, B. J. (1990). Helping faculty build learning communities through cooperative groups. *To improve the academy, 9,* 43–58. Stillwater, OK: New Forums.

Palmer, P. J. (1998). *The courage to teach: Exploring the inner landscape of a teacher's life.* San Francisco, CA: Jossey-Bass.

Patrick, S. K., & Fletcher, J. J. (1998). Faculty developers as change agents: Transforming colleges and universities into learning organizations. *To improve the academy, 17,* 155–170. Stillwater, OK: New Forums.

Perry, W. J. (1970). *Forms of intellectual and ethical development in the college years.* New York, NY: Holt, Rinehart, and Winston.

Richlin, L. (in press). *Teaching excellence, scholarly teaching, and the scholarship of teaching.* New Directions for Teaching and Learning. San Francisco, CA: Jossey-Bass.

Senge, P. M. (1990). *The fifth discipline.* New York, NY: Doubleday.

Shapiro, N. S., & Levine, J. H. (1999, November-December). Introducing learning communities to your campus. *About Campus, 4* (5), 2–10.

Sorcinelli, M. D. (1992). New and junior faculty stress: Research and responses. In M. D. Sorcinelli & A. E. Austin (Eds.), *Developing new and junior faculty* (pp. 27–37). New Directions for Teaching and Learning, No. 50. San Francisco: Jossey-Bass.

Stevens, M. P., & Cox, M. D. (1999, October). *Faculty development and the inclusion of diversity in the classroom: A faculty learning community approach.* Paper presented at the 24th annual Conference of the Professional and Organizational Development Network in Higher Education, Lake Harmony, PA.

Taylor, P. G. (1997). Creating environments which nurture development: Messages from research into academics' experiences. *The International Journal for Academic Development, 2* (2), 42–49.

Thomas, T. (1992). Connected teaching: An exploration of the classroom enterprise. *Journal on Excellence in College Teaching, 3,* 101–119.

Tinto, V. (1995, March). Learning communities, collaborative learning, and the pedagogy of educational citizenship. *AAHE Bulletin, 47* (7), 11–13.

Tussman, J. (1969). *Experiment at Berkeley.* London: Oxford University Press.

Wright, W. A., & O'Neil, M. C. (1995). Teaching improvement practices: International perspectives. In W. A. Wright & Associates (Eds.), *Teaching improvement practices: Successful strategies for higher education* (pp. 1–57). Bolton, MA: Anker.

Contact:

Milton D. Cox
University Director
Teaching Effectiveness Programs
Miami University
Oxford, OH 45056
(513) 529-6648
cixmd@muohio
www.muohio.edu/lillyconference

Milton D. Cox is university director for teaching effectiveness programs at Miami University, where he founded and directs the annual Lilly Conference on college teaching. He also is founder and editor-in-chief of the *Journal on Excellence in College Teaching.* He directs the 1994 Hesburg Award–winning teaching scholars' community for junior faculty and oversees the other faculty learning communities at Miami. For the past 30 years he has taught mathematics, designing, and teaching courses that celebrate and share with students the beauty of mathematics. He incorporates the use of student learning portfolios and Howard Gardner's concept of multiple intelligences in his mathematics classes. Cox has developed programs to enable the presentation of undergraduate student papers at national profession meetings. In 1988 he received the C. C. MacDuffee award for distinguished service to Pi Mu Epsilon, the national mathematics honorary society.

APPENDIX 5.1
FOCUS BOOKS FOR FACULTY LEARNING COMMUNITIES

These books are given to the community members at their opening retreat in May. They read them over the summer, and beginning seminars involve discussion of themes and issues raised in the reading.

**Community Using Cooperative Learning
to Enhance Teaching and Learning**

(99–00)   Johnson, D. W., Johnson, R. T., & Smith, K. A. (1998). *Active learning: Cooperation in the college classroom.* Edina, MN: Interaction.

Senior Faculty Community for Teaching Excellence

(99–00)   Palmer, P. J. (1998). *The courage to teach: Exploring the inner landscape of a teacher's life.* San Francisco, CA: Jossey-Bass.

(98–99)   Levine, A., & Cureton, J. S. (1998). *When hope and fear collide: A portrait of today's college student.* San Francisco, CA: Jossey-Bass.

(97–98)   Schön, D. A. (1988). *Educating the reflective practitioner: Toward a new design for teaching and learning in the professions.* San Francisco, CA: Jossey-Bass.

(96–97)   Elbow, P. (1986). *Embracing contraries: Explorations in teaching and learning.* New York, NY: Oxford University Press.

Junior Faculty Learning Community

(several years)   McKeachie, W. J. (1999). *McKeachie's teaching tips: Strategies, research, and theory for college and university teachers* (10th ed.). Boston, MA: Houghton Mifflin.

(several years)   Grunert, J. (1997). *The course syllabus: A learning-centered approach.* Bolton, MA: Anker.

(several years)   Angelo, T. A., & Cross, K. P. (1993). *Classroom assessment techniques: A handbook for college teachers* (2nd ed.). San Francisco, CA: Jossey-Bass.

Community Using Difference to Enhance Teaching and Learning

(99–00)   Tatum, B. D. (1997). *"Why are all the black kids sitting together in the cafeteria?" and other conversations about race.* New York, NY: Basic Books.

Miscellaneous Information

"There is a deep hunger among faculty members for more meaningful, collegial relationships and more 'conversational structures' in our institutions" (Gabelnick, MacGregor, Matthews, & Smith, 1990, p. 86).

Engelkemeyer, S. W., & Brown, S. C. (1998, October). Powerful partnerships: A shared responsibility for learning. *AAHE Bulletin, 51* (2), 10–12.

Tosey, P., & Gregory, J. (1998). The peer learning community in higher education: Reflections on practice. *Innovations in Education and Training International, 35* (1), 74–81.

Palmer, P. J. (1997, December). Teaching & learning in community. *About Campus, 2* (5), 4–12.

Section II

Focus on Faculty Development and Student Learning

6

Doing Faculty Development as if We Value Learning Most: Transformative Guidelines from Research to Practice

Thomas A. Angelo
DePaul University

If producing high-quality student learning is American higher education's defining goal, how can faculty development best contribute to its realization? In response to that question, this essay synthesizes theories, findings, and strategies from a variety of literatures into seven transformative ideas which, taken together, have the potential to make our mental models of and approaches to faculty development more effective. It also offers seven guidelines based on these ideas, as well as related, practical strategies for doing faculty development as if student learning matters most.

INTRODUCTION

Caveat lector. References to transformation in the title and throughout this paper are not casually made. Transformation denotes significant, qualitative change, not merely tinkering with, adding on, or moving bits about. Given its transformative perspective, this essay will be of little use to readers looking for simple, quick, or easy solutions. Instead, it is written for those convinced that their institutions can and, indeed, must provide more effective teaching, produce more and better learning, foster more meaningful scholarship, and operate in a more collaborative fashion. At the same time, it is written for faculty developers with high but realistic expectations, those who recognize that meaningful, transformative change typically requires years of well-conceived, well-led, sustained effort.

Why Haven't We Made More Progress?

Since the beginnings of the current higher education reform movement in the mid-1980s, thousands of American faculty developers, administrators, and faculty leaders have promoted change under the banners of assessment, continuous quality improvement, active learning, strategic planning, distance education, and other related movements. Much has changed as a result of their efforts and much has improved, of course. Nonetheless, there are still surprisingly few well-documented examples of significant, lasting gains in student learning at the department or institutional level. More broadly, nearly 30 years of organized faculty development efforts in the US have reaped rather modest rewards, if evidence of improved student learning is the relevant indicator.

Five Possible Reasons

Why is it that the vast majority of well-intentioned change efforts in American higher education seem to result in little or no long-term improvement in student learning? Peter Ewell offers two compelling reasons: "They [the change efforts] have been implemented without a deep understanding of what 'collegiate learning' really means and the specific circumstances and strategies that are likely to promote it. [and] They have for the most part been attempted piecemeal both within and across institutions" (1997, p.3). This essay suggests three additional, related reasons. A third reason is that most faculty development models in the past have stressed changing what the teacher does, rather than understanding and changing what the students do. As Biggs notes: "Aligning practice on the basis of what students should be doing is likely to be more fruitful than focusing only on what teachers and administrators do (1999, p. 74). Fourth, most American academic change efforts have not acknowledged or addressed the legitimate reasons faculty have for resisting change. Simply put, many faculty fear that attempts to increase productivity and promote learning-centered practice will undermine scholarship and academic freedom, two deeply held values in academic culture; at the same time, few believe that more attention to teaching and learning will lead to more rewards or recognition. And, fifth, academic change efforts in the US are too often peripheral to the institution's core strategic plans and, therefore, unsupported or undersupported by top management.

If the above diagnosis is correct, then faculty developers who simply rededicate themselves to working harder—doing more of the same—are unlikely to reap better outcomes than their predecessors. Instead, if we are to move from tinkering to transformation, it may be time to rethink and perhaps even replace some of our traditional ideas about academic change and improvement and the strategies that flow from them. If we value learning most, then transformation is clearly required.

KEY ASSUMPTIONS

The remainder of this essay rests on six key assumptions. First, it assumes that a central, if not the primary goal of faculty development is to promote high-quality, deep learning by helping faculty help their students learn more effectively and efficiently than they would on their own. Second, it assumes that shared purpose matters, that an academic unit will more likely succeed in providing high-quality teaching and producing high-quality learning if its students, faculty, and the relevant administrators explicitly agree on that goal and work together toward realizing it. Third, it assumes that effective collaboration toward shared goals is still far from the norm in most universities. To make it so would require a transformation in the ways academic administrators, staff, and students think about and carry out their daily work. Fourth, it views academic departments as the most promising units of instructional reform and heads of departments as the natural leaders in transforming departmental cultures. Fifth, it asserts that the academic profession collectively knows a great deal about promoting effective teaching, learning, collaboration, and change in higher education, and that guidelines based on this knowledge from research and practice can orient our efforts toward success. And lastly, the essay assumes that faculty developers, in their roles as "metaprofessionals" (Candy, 1996, p. 17), are best placed and prepared to help department chairs and faculty identify shared goals, learn to collaborate effectively toward those goals, and apply existing knowledge to specific disciplines and contexts in order to improve student learning.

SEVEN TRANSFORMATIVE IDEAS

This essay draws together a diversity of perspectives, theories, concepts, terms, and strategies from a range of literatures—among them cognitive science, higher education, psychology, and management. Referred to below as transformative ideas, they are the social construction of knowledge, mental models, the learning paradigm, learning productivity, learning communities, the scholarship of teaching, and assessment. These seven ideas, taken seriously and together, have the potential to help us transform our mental models and standard practices. They can help us construct a new and transformative vision, or metaphor, of academic departments (and institutions) as productive, scholarly learning communities. A productive department, in this vision, is one that helps students and faculty to produce demonstrably high-quality learning. The scholarly aspect of the vision is well-expressed by Boyer: "What we urgently need today is a more inclusive view of what it means to be a scholar—a recognition that knowledge is acquired through research, through synthesis, through practice, and through teaching" (1990, p. 24). And in a learning community, students and faculty collaborate to achieve shared, significant learning goals (Angelo, 1997, p. 3). This vision is very similar to that expressed by Candy in his discussion of "the university as a learning organization" (1996, p. 10).

The Social Construction of Knowledge

Simply put, the constructivist view of learning is that humans learn not primarily by receiving and copying impressions and information *from* the world, but rather by constructing and reconstructing our own mental conceptions *of* the world. As Piaget (1975) and many others have noted, we often force and distort new information and experience to fit our existing conceptions—or reject them outright if they do not fit. Social constructivists agree that meaning is largely internally constructed, but they stress that shared meanings—socially constructed and negotiated—are necessary for human communication and society. An academic discipline, with its (largely) shared concepts, dialect, and culture is a paramount example of socially constructed and continually reconstructed knowledge.

Constructivism is arguably the dominant model of human learning in educational psychology today. The transformative power of social constructivism inheres both in its rejection of the traditional transmission of knowledge and banking metaphors, and in its assertion that learners must construct knowledge, understanding, and meaning for themselves. This construction is accomplished largely through interaction and negotiation with the world and other humans—including faculty, other students, and authors living and dead. (See Chapter 7 in Belenky, Clinchy, Goldberger, & Tarule, 1986.) For faculty, this means that students, in order to learn deeply, must become active partners in the construction of their learning. Similarly, faculty developers intent on change must engage their colleagues in constructing or adapting new, shared, contextually relevant concepts, rather than presenting faculty with imported prefabricated mental models for adoption.

Mental Models

In *The Fifth Discipline*, Peter Senge defines mental models as ". . . deeply ingrained assumptions, generalizations, or even pictures or images that influence how we change the world and how we take action" (1990, p. 8). Senge argues that building a learning organization requires us to reflect on, make explicit, reconsider, and sometimes redesign these implicit mental models (1990, pp. xiv & xv). The transformative implication here is that our existing mental models must often be socially deconstructed before change can occur. In relation to the corporate world, Senge notes, "Many insights into new markets or outmoded organizational practices fail to get put into practice because they conflict with powerful, tacit mental models" (1990, p.8). For the academic developer, as for the lecturer, acknowledging and making explicit those implicit mental models is a necessary first step toward new learning. For example, many teachers and students still tacitly believe that learning occurs by transmission; thus, the continuing appeal of the noninteractive lecture to both groups. Before these students and teachers can see the value of alternate, highly interactive approaches, they must be open to questioning their preexisting model of learning.

The Learning Paradigm

In a widely read and discussed article, Robert Barr and John Tagg (1995) argued that American higher education is undergoing an industry-wide paradigm shift, a transformation from a faculty- and teaching-centered to a student- and learning-centered model. As Barr and Tagg see it, the primary purpose of higher education—and, by extension, of academic departments—in this new paradigm will be producing learning, not providing instruction. By shifting the focus from a means (teaching) to the intended end (learning), Barr and Tagg redefine classroom teaching as only one of several possible means for producing learning. Inherent in the learning paradigm is a radical shift from the usual quantitative, credit hour- and headcount-based models of undergraduate education to a more qualitative, competency, and mastery based view. If institutions can be thought of as producing learning, then raising questions about their levels of learning productivity—and not just about numbers of graduates or credit units generated—begins to make sense.

Learning Productivity

This phrase has multiple and overlapping meanings (Poulsen, 1995), starting with the dreaded doing more with less. In this essay, however, learning productivity means promoting more, deeper, and better learning with the resources available. It requires that we work more cost- and time-efficiently to the extent we can do so without sacrificing learning quality. To be useful, a model of learning productivity requires that we develop clear goals, criteria, and standards for learning production, as well as means to assess and measure outputs. (See also Johnstone, 1993.)

Learning Communities
While various definitions exist, most center around a vision of faculty and students working together systematically toward shared, significant academic goals. Collaboration is stressed, competition deemphasized, and both faculty and students must take on new, often unfamiliar roles. The faculty member's primary role shifts from delivering content to designing learning environments and experiences, and to serving as coach, expert guide, and role model for learners. In a learning community, the student's role changes as well, from relatively passive observer of teaching and consumer of information to active co-constructor of knowledge and understanding (See Gablenick, MacGregor, Matthews, & Smith, 1990; Angelo, 1997; Tinto, 1997; and Cross, 1998.)

The Scholarship of Teaching
While this phrase originally referred to only one of the four categories Ernest Boyer promoted in *Scholarship Reconsidered* (1990)—the other three being the scholarships of discovery, of integration, and of application—the scholarship of teaching soon became shorthand for expanded and more diverse visions of faculty roles. The transformative thrust of this idea comes in valuing a broader range of scholarly activity (Rice, 1991), and in finding ways to make those activities public, accessible to others, and open to evaluation by peers—as the products of the traditional scholarship of discovery, publications and grants, already are (Glassick, et al., 1997).

Assessment
Palomba and Banta define assessment as ". . . the systematic collection, review, and use of information about educational programs for the purpose of improving student learning and development" (1999, p. 4). Central to this model is the belief that our assumptions about learning outcomes should be empirically tested and that our claims should be based in evidence. Even a quick look at the unsupported claims made in

almost any university's public relations materials will show how distant this goal remains.

Drawing on the ideas discussed above, the next section offers faculty developers seven practical guidelines for transforming academic units into more productive, scholarly learning communities. Following each of these broad guidelines are specific suggestions for promoting scholarly collaboration among students and faculty in order to improve learning.

SEVEN GUIDELINES FOR DEVELOPING PRODUCTIVE AND SCHOLARLY LEARNING COMMUNITIES: SUGGESTIONS AND RESOURCES

1) Build Shared Trust: Begin by Lowering Social and Interpersonal Barriers to Change

Most of us learn little of positive or lasting value from people we do not trust. To form a productive departmental learning community, then, faculty must come to trust each other, their head, and their academic developer. The same is true of student-student and student-faculty relations. As Ramsden argues: "Genuine learning requires an atmosphere of trust and an absence of fear; in these circumstances academics, like their students, take risks, improve, and do remarkable things" (1998, p. 268). There are many academic units, no doubt, where such an atmosphere does not currently exist. Nonetheless, it is possible, with time and effort, to create a positive climate for improvement in most departments. And helpful resources exist. For example, in Chapters Eight and Nine of *Strengthening Departmental Leadership,* Lucas (1994) provides many practical suggestions for team building and conflict management with faculty. In Chapters 3 and 22 of *Teaching Tips* (1999), McKeachie provides analogous ideas for building classroom community with students.

As a simple first step in trust—before turning to problems, tasks, and issues to be resolved—faculty developers might take time to highlight what faculty are already doing well, and to share successful strategies. Encouraging staff to provide examples of successful teaching and learning experiences allows them to present their best face, and demonstrates that each is an intelligent, capable person with ideas to contribute to the good of the whole.

After faculty have jotted down answers to the questions above, they break into five- to seven-person groups. Each person has no more than three minutes to tell his or her story, and all are encouraged to look for common themes among the examples. Those common themes can then

FIGURE 6.1

Sharing Lessons Learned from Successful Teaching

Directions: Focus on a specific unit, lesson, concept, or skill that you teach particularly well. With that successful experience in mind, take the next five minutes to jot down answers to the six questions below. As you write, prepare to explain your example to your colleagues in the small group in no more than three minutes.

1) What course is your example taken from?

2) What exactly were you trying to teach? (What was your main teaching goal or objective?)

3) How did you teach it? (What, specifically, did you do that promoted success?)

4) How did you know your students had learned it? (How did you assess/evaluate their achievement of your goal?)

5) What did you learn, as a teacher, from that experience?

6) What is the big lesson (general principle) about effective teaching and learning that your example illustrates? Put another way, why did what you did work so well? (How would you explain this to a beginning teacher?)

---

be mined for transferable lessons in a subsequent whole group discussion. With attention to time limits, this exercise can easily be completed in three-quarters of an hour. More ambitious faculty developers may want to capture and document the good examples to share more widely. Whatever the means, the big point here is to start, not with problems and debate, but by attending to faculty members' needs to feel respected, valued, safe, and in the company of worthy, smart, well-intentioned peers.

2) Build Shared Motivation: Collectively Determine Goals Worth Working toward and Problems Worth Solving—and Consider the Likely Costs and Benefits

Once a working level of shared trust has been established, the academic developer can begin to develop a shared learning improvement agenda. Most of us work more productively if we have clear, personally meaningful, reasonable goals to work toward. Students in courses and faculty in departments accomplish more when they share some learning goals in common. While students and faculty typically do have goals, they rarely can articulate clearly what those goals are, rarely know how well they match their peers' goals, and rarely focus their goals on learning. Faculty goals often focus on what they will teach, rather than what students will learn and how, and students goals often focus on getting through and getting on. Thus, since goals powerfully motivate and direct our behavior (Stark, et al., 1989, p. iii), developing a set of shared learning goals is a logical next step in building a productive learning community.

There are many techniques for determining goals (see, for example, Palomba & Banta, 1999, Chapter 2), but the key is to discover or develop learning-related goals in common. The "Teaching Goals Inventory," developed by K. Patricia Cross and me, is a noncopyrighted, quick, self-scorable questionnaire to help faculty identify their most important instructional goals (Angelo & Cross, 1993, pp. 393–397.) An even simpler approach is to ask faculty to list two or three things they would like to learn in the coming year or that they would like to make certain the department's students learn well before graduating—and then to look for common goals across the lists. Whatever the shared goals are, in order to be useful they must be clear, specific, linked to a time frame, feasible, and most important, significant.

Goals are not always sufficient to motivate us to learn. After all, if the status quo is not problematic, why change? But neither do all problems provide useful starting points. As Ewell notes, "Maximum learning tends to occur when people are confronted with specific, identifiable problems that they want to solve and that are within their capacity to do so" (1997, p. 4). It is critical, in any case, to connect and frame problems within a larger vision of shared goals, so that energies and resources are not dissipated in myriad efforts that add up to little or no improvement.

Once shared goals have been established, identifying related problems can be more fruitful. The following is a three-step exercise for use with faculty and students to identify promising problems. First, once you have a problem in mind, write down what you think the best solution would be. Second, assuming that were the solution, *could* the group actually implement it? And third, even if it could be implemented, would the group choose to do so? If the answer to either of the latter questions is "no," it is probably not a problem worth taking on. If the answers are "yes," on the other hand, then it is time for a cost-benefit analysis—however informal—of the proposed solution. I recommend trying to guesstimate the following types of costs before committing to a problem:

human time and effort, financial resources, costs in political capital, and opportunity costs. That is, what other important problems will you be unable to deal with if you follow this course?

3) Build a Shared Language: Develop a Collective Understanding of New Concepts (Mental Models) Needed for Transformation

Given that most of us assume we are speaking Standard English, it is surprising how often we fail to understand one another. In fact, however, even those of us who are native English speakers regularly use disciplinary dialects—environmental biology, literary studies, social psychology—as well as unique, personal idiolects in the classroom. Building a shared vision for transformative change requires shared mental models and shared language for describing and manipulating those models. That often requires building a shared group dialect, or at least some shared vocabulary. In other words, before we can collaborate productively to build learning communities, we must establish what we mean by key terms such as learning, community, improvement, productivity, or assessment. Taking this step will allow us to make explicit any implicit conflicts among our mental models.

A simple strategy for uncovering different mental models is to ask faculty to describe or define in writing what they mean by one of the terms that is central to departmental goals. Let us say the term is assessment. Then collect those responses and discuss them or create a concept map from them, making visually apparent the areas of agreement and difference. You may find that assessment means, variously, standardized testing, student ratings of faculty, marking, institutional research, or time wasted to the various individuals. Rather than contesting these preexisting definitions, you might suggest the adoption of an additional, shared working definition, much like adding another meaning after a word listed in a dictionary. This add-on strategy does not require that individuals give up their existing mental models, something many will resist. Instead it only requires that they acknowledge differences between their models/meanings and the group's and that they use the group model when collaborating.

4) Design Backward and Work Forward: Work Backward from the Shared Vision and Long-Term Goals to Determine Outcomes, Strategies, and Activities

Backward design simply means starting with the desired end, goal, or overall vision, then determining the related outcomes and the best means to reach them. Typical departmental curricula, as a counterexample, have been designed forward—or more accurately, not designed, but built forward. That is, the faculty usually decide which courses we want to teach and how we want to teach them, then we pile all our courses up and try to construct a curricular rationale for the pile. As an alternative, Wiggins and McTighe (1998) propose a three-stage backward design process: 1) "identify desired results, 2) determine acceptable evidence, and 3) plan learning experiences and instruction" (p. 9). Backward design—which is basically the same model underlying the assessment process and strategic planning—presupposes shared trust, goals, and mental models.

5) Think and Act Systematically: Understand the Advantages and Limitations of the Larger System(s) within which We Operate and Seek Connections and Applications to Those Larger Worlds

Senge writes "Systems thinking is a discipline for seeing wholes. It is a framework for seeing interrelationships rather than things, for seeing patterns of change rather than static snapshots" (1990, p. 68). The main point here is that all of us operate within larger contexts, which affect and are often affected by our actions. It is relatively common in academic life for individuals or departments to make decisions and changes independently that end up causing ripples, or even crises, throughout the larger organization. Many of us have found our daily working lives unexpectedly and negatively affected by decisions made by the campus's information technology managers. For example, a simple, cost-efficient central administration decision not to continue supporting a particular software package or operating system can have devastating impacts on the research of a few faculty.

Academic departments, of course, are systems within systems. Consequently, there are some limits to the amount and type of change an individual department can initiate or maintain. For example, few departments could, on their own, move to a totally qualitative, competency-based curriculum without dramatically compromising their students' likelihood of graduating. Ewell notes that systems thinking ". . . first demands a comprehensive audit of current and contemplated policies, practices, and behaviors. It also requires a detailed analysis of current values and rewards and how these will inhibit or support desired changes" (1997, p. 6). One simple way to begin this systems audit process is to draw a diagram of all those within, and perhaps outside, the university with whom the department engages and to determine the likely impact of proposed changes on each entity. It is usually sufficient to estimate the likely impact on each person or office using a scale that runs from -3 (large negative impact) to 0 (no impact) to $+3$ (large positive impact). A quick look at the score distributions and totals will help you gauge in advance the wisdom of proceeding and your likelihood of succeeding.

6) Practice What We Preach: Use What We Have Learned about Individual and Organizational Learning to Inform and Explain Our Efforts and Strategies

Those who teach by example and who live their own lessons have the most lasting impact on learners. In a list of six big-ticket items that promote learning, Ewell includes "approaches in which the faculty constructively model the learning process" (1997, p. 5), such as apprenticeships and guided practice. He also notes that "Change requires people to relearn their own roles" (Ewell, 1997, p. 6), suggesting that we cannot hope to transform the teaching and learning process for our students unless we can learn to transform our own mental models and behavior.

Given the research on effective collegiate learning, a fruitful endeavor for many departments would be to develop the faculty member's own skills at working cooperatively toward shared aims. In other words, train faculty in groupwork. Research findings on cooperative learning show that it is one of the most demonstrably effective learning approaches available. As faculty grow more skilled at effective teamwork ourselves, we not only increase our likelihood of success in transforming departments, but also enhance our ability to help our students learn to collaborate effectively.

7) Don't Assume, Ask: Make the Implicit Explicit. Use Assessment to Focus on What Matters Most

At heart, assessment is not about measurement tools and analytical techniques; it is first and foremost about asking the right questions. Whatever we assess—evaluate, measure, judge, mark—is what those being assessed will likely pay more attention to and do more of. Making the assessment process transparent and aligning it with goals and learning activities are critical steps in promoting improved learning outcomes. As Ramsden notes, "From our students' point of view, the assessment always defines the actual curriculum" (1992, p. 187). Thus, assessment is a powerful tool for focusing our attention and efforts. Since attention and effort, like time and energy, are limited resources, we must be very mindful to focus assessment efforts only on what matters most, or we risk wasting those same precious resources.

At the same time, the ways we assess faculty and students can pro-mote or preclude change by affecting their motivation and fortunes. Recognizing the key role of assessment in change efforts, the Carnegie Foundation for the Advancement of Teaching realized that departments and institutions interested in implementing the recommendations in Boyer's (1990) *Scholarship Reconsidered* would need a workable framework for assessing the scholarship of teaching. That framework, presented in *Scholarship Assessed* (Glassick, Huber, & Maeroff, 1997) will be of use to all change-minded faculty developers. Since grading is the most common form of assessment faculty engage in, and probably the most important to students, making our grading more fair and valid can have far-reaching positive effects. Walvoord and Anderson's *Effective Grading* (1998) is a comprehensive handbook for those interested in improving this dimen-sion of assessment.

This takes us back to the second and fourth guidelines. We must first decide what our key shared goals are, then determine how we will know if we have achieved them well enough, and only then decide on the in-structional and assessment methods and techniques to be used. Through-out the process, of course, we can use assessment methods to uncover tacit differences or misunderstandings by asking questions that will make the implicit explicit. Once a department has developed its tranformative, learning-centered vision and goals, there are several general assessment resources that may be of use, including books by Angelo and Cross (1993), Gardiner, Anderson, and Cambridge (1997), Nichols (1995), and Palomba and Banta (1999).

In Summary: Five Modest First Steps

All long journeys begin with a single step, the proverb reminds us. Let me sum up by offering not one but five first steps in the journey toward de-partmental transformation. These five steps mirror Peter Senge's (1990) five disciplines: personal mastery, mental models, shared vision, team learning, and systems thinking.

As a first step toward personal mastery, we must resist the under-standable urge to rush the change process. It rarely works. Experience shows that most successful academic innovations take years to bear fruit. We are likely to save time and grief later in the process by taking time at the front end to develop shared trust, shared language, and a small num-ber of shared goals. Second, to explore mental models, in addition to building trust, we can begin by sharing examples of successful teaching experiences, definitions of meaningful learning, and examples of exemplary student work. In other words, we can start with a focus on success. Third, building on the first two steps, we can work with faculty to develop a shared vision of what students should know and be able to do at the end of a course, a sequence, or the major—and thus make possible backward design. Fourth, from the beginning, we can promote group-work and team learning in our departments and units. Since the quality of group process largely determines the productivity of the group, we may need to engage an expert facilitator to teach faculty how to work together effectively as a departmental learning community before they can do the same with students. And fifth, we can apply systems thinking to departmental planning. We might begin by asking how well what we are envisioning fits within the institutional structure and agenda, as well as how it fits into the existing systems of faculty roles and rewards and of students' academic careers.

ACKNOWLEDGMENT

The author wishes to thank the scholarly academic developers of the Higher Education Research and Development Society of Australasia (HERDSA), whose ideas and examples have enriched this paper and my professional practice.

REFERENCES

Angelo, T.A. (1997). The campus as learning community: Seven promising shifts and seven powerful levers." *AAHE Bulletin, 49* (9), 3–6.

Angelo, T.A., & Cross, K.P. (1993). *Classroom assessment techniques: A handbook for college teachers* (2nd ed.). San Francisco, CA: Jossey-Bass.

Barr, R. B., & Tagg, J. (1995). From teaching to learning: A new paradigm for undergraduate education. *Change, 27* (6), 12–25.

Belenky, M. F., Clinchy, B. M., Goldberger, N. R., & Tarule, J. M. (1986). *Women's ways of knowing: The development of self, voice, and mind.* New York, NY: Basic Books.

Biggs, J. (1999). What the student does: Teaching for enhanced learning. *Higher Education Research and Development, 18* (1), 55–76.

Boyer, E. L. (1990). *Scholarship reconsidered: Priorities of the professoriate.* Princeton, NJ: The Carnegie Foundation for the Advancement of Teaching.

Candy, P. C. (1996). Promoting lifelong learning: Faculty developers and the university as a learning organization. *The International Journal for Faculty development, 1* (1), 7–18.

Cross, K. P. (1998). Why learning communities? Why now? *About Campus, 3* (3), 4–11.

Ewell, P. T. (1997). Organizing for learning: A new imperative. *AAHE Bulletin, 50* (4), 10–12.

Gabelnick, F., MacGregor, J., Matthews, R., & Smith, B.L. (Eds.). (1990). *Learning communities: Creating connections among students, faculty, and disciplines.* New Directions for Teaching and Learning, No. 41. San Francisco, CA: Jossey-Bass.

Gardiner, L. F., Anderson, C., & Cambridge, B. L. (1997). *Learning through assessment: A resource guide for higher education.* Washington, DC: American Association for Higher Education.

Glassick, C. E., Huber, M. T., & Maeroff, G. I. (1997). *Scholarship assessed: Evaluation of the professoriate.* San Francisco, CA: Jossey-Bass.

Johnstone, D. B. (1993). Enhancing the productivity of learning. *AAHE Bulletin, 46* (4), 3–5.

Lucas, A. F. (1994). *Strengthening departmental leadership: A team-building guide for chairs in colleges and universities.* San Francisco, CA: Jossey-Bass.

McKeachie, W. J. (1999). *Teaching tips: Strategies, research, and theory for college and university teachers* (10th ed.). Boston, MA: Houghton Mifflin.

Millis, B. J. & Cottell, P.G. (1998). *Cooperative learning for higher education faculty.* Phoenix, AZ: Oryx.

Nichols, J. O. (1995). *A practitioner's handbook for institutional effectiveness and student outcomes assessment implementation.* New York, NY: Agathon.

Palomba, C. A., & Banta, T. W. (1999). Assessment essentials: Planning, implementing, and improving assessment in higher education. San Francisco, CA: Jossey-Bass.

Piaget. (1975). *The development of thought: Equilibration of cognitive structures.* New York, NY: Viking.

Poulsen, S. J. (1995). Describing an elephant: Specialists explore the meaning of learning productivity. *Wingspread Journal, 17* (2), 4–6.

Ramsden, P. (1992). *Learning to teach in higher education.* London, England: Routledge.

Ramsden, P. (1998). *Learning to lead in higher education* (2nd. ed.). London, England: Routledge.

Rice, E. (1991). The new american scholar: Scholarship and the purposes of the university. *Metropolitan Universities, 1* (4), 7–18.

Senge, P. M. (1990). *The fifth discipline.* New York, NY: Doubleday.

Stark, J. S., Shaw, K. M., & Lowther, M. A. (1989). *Student goals for college and courses.* Report No. 6. Washington DC: School of Education and Human Development, The George Washington University.

Tinto, V. (1997). Universities as learning organizations. *About Campus, 1* (6), 2–4.

Walvoord, B. E., & Anderson, V. J. (1998). *Effective grading: A tool for learning and assessment.* San Francisco, CA: Jossey-Bass.

Wiggins, G., & McTighe, J. (1998). *Understanding by design.* Alexandria, VA: Association for Supervision and Curriculum Development.

Contact:

Thomas A. Angelo, Associate Professor and
Director, the SNL Assessment Center
School for New Learning–DePaul University
25 East Jackson Blvd., 2nd Floor
Chicago, IL 60604-2305
(312) 362-5135
(312) 362-8809 (Fax)
Email: Tangelo@wppost.depaul.edu
URL: http://www.depaul.edu/~tangelo/assessment

Thomas Anthony Angelo is Associate Professor and founding Director of the Assessment Center at DePaul University's School for New Learning, a competency-based liberal arts college for adults.

7

Higher-Level Learning: The First Step toward More Significant Learning

L. Dee Fink
University of Oklahoma

In order to design significant learning experiences for students, teachers first need to be able to formulate powerful and challenging goals for their courses. This essay describes a taxonomy of higher-level learning that consists of six kinds of learning: foundational knowledge, application, integration, the human dimension, motivation, and learning how to learn. The argument is made that this taxonomy goes beyond the familiar taxonomy of Benjamin Bloom and encompasses a wide range of goals that are currently advocated by many national organizations and scholars in higher education. The taxonomy can be used to design better courses, choose among alternative teaching strategies, and evaluate teaching.

INTRODUCTION

For the past 20 years, I have been working as an instructional consultant with faculty members at my institution to help them find ways to improve their teaching. One consequence of this activity is that I have found myself on a personal journey that seems to parallel a national effort: searching for better ways of providing significant learning experiences for students in higher education. One of my conclusions is that this search would be greatly facilitated if we could find ways of describing our educational goals in terms that would be appealing to the major constituencies in higher education; e.g., faculty members, students, administrators, disciplinary associations, employer groups.

One distinction that needs to be made at the outset is the difference between higher-level learning and active learning. The idea of active learning is one of the most important ideas to take hold in American higher education in recent years (Bonwell & Eison, 1991). The central argument of this movement is that active learning (i.e., having students do something and think about what they are doing) is more powerful in terms of creating significant, lasting learning than is passive learning (e.g., listening, reading). In my view, this argument is totally correct.

However, as important as the concept of active learning is, it is ultimately a concept that is focused on how people learn, not on what they learn. I propose that the higher education community needs a parallel concept that is focused on what students learn, and that an appropriate name for this concept is higher-level learning.

I also need to clarify what I mean by significant learning experiences. When using this term, I am simply referring to what any caring and thoughtful teacher wants for his/her students: a learning experience that will be significant to the students in some meaningful way. One of the goals of this essay is to offer the language of higher-level learning as one way of giving greater focus and direction to this general desire to provide significant learning experiences for students in higher education.

In this essay, I will a) offer some comments on why higher education needs a new way of identifying what constitutes significant learning, b) describe the construction and characteristics of a new taxonomy of higher-level learning that seems to meet this need, and c) point out some of the possible uses of such a taxonomy.

NEED FOR A NEW WAY OF IDENTIFYING SIGNIFICANT LEARNING

As mentioned earlier, I have found myself on a personal journey, searching for a better way of identifying significant learning. My journey seems to parallel a national effort to formulate more significant learning experiences for students.

My Personal Journey

My own search for better ideas on this topic was jump-started several years ago when someone on campus asked me: "Given all your experience of observing other people's courses, what do you think makes a good course good?" After recovering from the realization that I did not have a ready answer for one of those innocent but profound questions, I began working on an answer and eventually developed a list that I capriciously called "Fink's Five Principles of Fine Courses."

1) Challenge students to higher-level learning

2) Use active forms of learning

3) Have teachers who interact and communicate well with student

4) Give students frequent and immediate feedback on their learning

5) Have a fair system for assessing and grading students

This list simply reflects my view that, if someone's teaching successfully meets these criteria, their teaching is good, no matter what else is bad about it, e.g., even if a teacher is not enthusiastic or organized. Conversely, if someone's teaching does not meet these five criteria, their teaching is poor, no matter what else is good about it. And for me, the single most important item on this list has always been the first item. If the students are indeed being challenged to, and achieving, something that can meaningfully be called higher-level learning, then the learning experience has been good, no matter what else is bad about the course. The bottom line is that important learning has been achieved.

Events on the National Scene
In the mid-1980s the National Institute of Education (NIE) urged universities to produce demonstrable improvements, not only in student knowledge, but also in students' "capacities, skills and attitudes" (NIE, 1984). The following year the Association of American Colleges (AAC) suggested a minimum required curriculum, followed by the statement that "we have clearly placed our emphasis on how to learn" (AAC, 1985). A few years later a number of disciplinary associations began issuing calls for similar change. A national study of business management education identified a need for more of the following: leadership and interpersonal skills; ethics; integration across functional areas; and linkages between national spheres, corporations, and local communities, and theory and practice (Porter & McKibbin, 1988). The engineering profession has modified its accreditation criteria, effective in the year 2000, to require evidence that students develop, among other things, the ability to function on a multidisciplinary team, communicate effectively, recognize the need for lifelong learning, and understand the ethical character of the engineering profession (ABET, 1998). A commission of the National Association of State Universities and Land Grant Colleges (NASULGC) called on colleges to develop instructional programs that focus on values: "The biggest educational challenge we face revolves around developing character, conscience, citizenship, tolerance, civility, and individual and social responsibility in our students" (NASULGC, 1997).

Individually authored publications have offered similar statements. For example, after completing a major study on redesigning higher education, Lion Gardiner (1994) noted that society's leaders in business, industry, and government have identified several important kinds of learning needed by citizens and workers in the years ahead. Labeling these as critical competencies, Gardiner's list included a) a variety of personal characteristics (e.g., conscientiousness, ethics, respect for people different from oneself), b) skills (e.g., communication, interpersonal team skills, critical thinking, and problem solving), c) the ability to adapt to change, and d) knowing how to keep on learning.

These several statements are calling on the higher education community to produce a new kind of learning. This new kind of learning will be exciting, but it will challenge faculty members to find new ways of teaching and will challenge students to find new ways of learning.

THE SEARCH FOR A LANGUAGE TO DESCRIBE SIGNIFICANT LEARNING

As faculty members begin the process of searching for new ways of teaching, we first need a language that will allow us to describe important or significant kinds of learning that make sense across disciplines. Where can we find such a language?

When teachers have pondered this question in the past, they have frequently turned to the well-known taxonomy of educational objectives formulated by Benjamin Bloom and his associates in the 1950s. Although there were in fact three taxonomies (cognitive, affective, and psychomotor), teachers referred to the one in the cognitive domain most often (Bloom, 1956). The cognitive taxonomy consisted of a hierarchy of six levels of learning. These were, from the highest to the lowest:

- evaluation

- synthesis

- analysis

- application

- comprehension

- knowledge (meaning recall knowledge)

This taxonomy has been used both as a framework for formulating course objectives and as a basis for testing student learning. Today, when teachers look for ways to go a little further in their courses, they often refer to the taxonomy of higher-level learning offered by Bloom's taxonomy.

There is no question about the value of the accomplishments of Bloom and his associates. Any model that commands this kind of respect half a century later is extraordinary. However, as noted above, individuals and organizations involved in higher education have been expressing a need for important kinds of learning that do not emerge easily from the Bloom taxonomy; e.g., learning how to learn, leadership and interpersonal skills, ethics, communication skills, character, tolerance, the ability to adapt to change, etc.

My interpretation of the aforementioned statements is that they are expressing a need for new kinds of learning, kinds that go well beyond the cognitive domain of Bloom's taxonomy. While the statements call for cognitive learning that is more than knowing and even thinking, there also seems to be a felt need to go beyond the limits of "cognitive" learning itself.

CREATING A NEW TAXONOMY

In order to create a new taxonomy, one that goes further than the Bloom taxonomy, I had to take a different approach than he did. Bloom interviewed teachers about what they thought students ought to know or be able to do, and then created a language that allowed him to categorize and distinguish their responses. But his taxonomy was not related to any model of learning.

I decided it would be important first to create a model of learning that identified distinctive kinds of important learning, and then create a taxonomy based on this model. After reading many statements about what various writers see as significant kinds of learning and interviewing many students about what they found to be significant in their own educational experience, I concluded that there are two distinct dimensions of learning that need to be understood: kinds of change in the learner and the foci of learning. All learning results in some kind of *change* in the learner, and yet all learning is *about* something, i.e., is focused on something. I have identified five kinds of change in the learner and five foci of learning that I call the components of learning (See Table 7.1). Understanding these two dimensions of learning can be of great value in explaining why any particular learning might be significant or important for learners.

TABLE 7.1
A Model of the Components of Learning

Learning: A Change in . . .	Learning about . . .
• Caring	• Learning (i.e., the process of learning)
• Acting	• Self
• Connecting	• Others
• Thinking	• Ideas
• Knowing	• Phenomena

The First Dimension of Learning: Kinds of Change in the Learner
The first dimension of significant learning begins with our view of learning itself. If we view the concept of learning as referring to some kind of lasting change in a learner, then we can ask the question: What kinds *of* change might constitute significant change, i.e., significant learning? There seem to be five kinds of change that need to be recognized: caring, acting, connecting, thinking, and knowing.

Caring. Sometimes as the result of a course or other informal learning experience, people change in the degree to which they care about something. When this happens, the learner acquires new feelings, interests, and/or values about something.

Acting. A student may also develop new abilities to act, meaning a readiness to engage in an action. This may involve learning a new skill (e.g., playing the violin, giving a public speech, or learning how to manage a complex project).

Connecting. At times people learn how to make new connections as the result of their learning. This may come in the form of recognizing similarities among phenomena, ideas, or processes, or noting the interaction among various events or objects.

Thinking. One of the more important changes people report is learning how to think more effectively about some subject. I am using this term as a large umbrella concept that subsumes other more specific kinds of thinking. I like the triarchic view of Robert Sternberg (1989) who recognizes three major kinds of thinking:

- critical thinking, in which people analyze and evaluate something

- creative thinking, in which people imagine and create something new

- practical thinking, in which people apply and use information and ideas; e.g., problem solving and decision-making.

Knowing. The most familiar change in a learner is coming to know something. By this I am simply referring to what happens when students understand and remember information, ideas, terms, etc.

The Second Dimension of Learning: The Foci of the Learning

Sometimes, when we learn something significant, it is not because of a change in ourselves as learners, but because of the significance of what we learn about. When we learn, we learn about different things. What are the different kinds of things we can learn about that give significance to our learning? I call these the foci of learning, and have identified five different foci: learning, others, self, ideas, and phenomena (see Table 7.1).

Learning. In some really powerful learning experiences, people learn about learning itself. They may acquire a new understanding of how one learns about a particular subject (e.g., learning about the scientific method), how to be a better student (e.g., regulating one's study time), or how to become a self-directed learner (e.g., setting a learning agenda and developing a plan for achieving it).

Others. Sometimes, either because of the subject matter or because of the way the course is taught (e.g., extensive use of small group interaction), people learn about others. Students can acquire a better understanding of and/or learn how to more effectively interact with important others in one's life. Usually this refers to other people, but it could include other kinds of life as well; e.g., animals, plants, etc.

Self. Students may also learn about their own self. This happens when they develop a new understanding of or feeling about what kind of person they are (a new self-image), or when they acquire a new image of the kind of person they could be and want to be (a new self-ideal).

Ideas. A powerful kind of learning also occurs when students learn about new ideas. By ideas, I am referring to interpretive perspectives that enable a person to construct explanations and/or predictions about objects, events, people, etc. Marxism and evolution are examples of well-known and important interpretive perspectives.

Phenomena. The most familiar form of learning is when we learn about a particular phenomenon or phenomena in the realm of the natural sciences (bird, rocks, and weather), the social sciences (individuals, societies, organizations), or the humanities (music, literature, art).

Using the Components to Create a Taxonomy

Now that we have a clear picture of the components of significant learning, we can use them to construct a taxonomy of higher-level learning.

TABLE 7.2
Six Important Kinds of Learning

Key Component(s) of Learning Involved	Special Value	General Label
LEARNING	Provides capability for long-term continuation of learning.	LEARNING HOW TO LEARN
CARING	Provides the energy (short term or long term) for learning; without this, nothing significant happens.	MOTIVATION
SELF, OTHERS	Connects one's self to oneself and to others; gives human significance to the learning.	HUMAN DIMENSION
CONNECTING	Adds power by connecting different ideas, disciplinary perspectives, people, and/or realms of life.	INTEGRATION
THINKING, ACTING	Allows other learning to become useful.	APPLICATION
KNOWING (esp. about PHENOMENA and IDEAS)	Provides necessary understanding for other kinds of learning.	FOUNDATIONAL KNOWLEDGE

By grouping a few of the components that seem to be related, we can identify six general kinds of significant learning in a way that makes it easy to recognize the special educational value of each category. Table 7.2 shows the six general groupings that I constructed, and the label that I put on each category. These six categories represent six distinct kinds of significant learning, and as such, give us a new taxonomy of higher level learning.

THE TAXONOMY OF HIGHER-LEVEL LEARNING

These six kinds of learning offer faculty members and instructional consultants a powerful road map for ways of providing significant learning experiences for students in higher education. The resulting taxonomy of higher-level learning (see Figure 7.1) allows us to identify important kinds of learning that most of us would like for students to achieve in our courses and curricula.

FIGURE 7.1
A Taxonomy of Higher-Level Learning

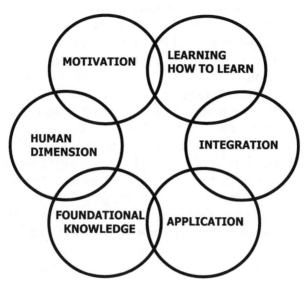

Distinctive Characteristics of the Present Taxonomy
This taxonomy of higher-level learning is different from the Bloom taxonomy in two important ways.

Scope of the taxonomy. First, this one goes well beyond the Bloom taxonomy in the kinds of learning described. The first three types of learning in this taxonomy (foundation, application, and integration) have different labels but in fact are similar to the kinds of learning Bloom described: remembering, understanding, analytical thinking, critical thinking, creative thinking, applying information and ideas, etc. However, the other three categories in the present taxonomy point to new kinds of learning not easily described by Bloom's taxonomy: ethics, leadership, dealing with cultural diversity, self-directed learning, etc. Hence the present taxonomy seems to be better adapted to the expressed educational needs of contemporary society.

Interactive nature. The second significant difference is that the present taxonomy is interactive, not hierarchical. The Bloom taxonomy was always presented as and perceived to be a vertical set: The bottom items were a prerequisite for learning the higher items, and the higher items had greater educational value. I do not disagree with the validity of these relationships in the Bloom taxonomy. However, the present taxonomy has a different character. The six kinds of learning in this taxonomy seem to be interactive rather than hierarchical in nature. When viewed this way, all are equal in terms of their general educational value.

This interactive characteristic is very important for teachers because it means the various kinds of learning are synergistic. And this in turn means that teaching is no longer a zero sum game! Teachers don't automatically have to give up one kind of learning to achieve another. Instead, when a teacher finds a way to help students achieve a new kind of learning, this can in fact enhance, not decrease, student achievement in the other kinds of learning. For example, if a teacher finds a way to help students learn how to effectively use the information and concepts in a course to solve certain kinds of problems (application), it is easier for them to get excited about the value of the subject (motivation). Or, when students learn how to effectively relate this subject to other ideas and subjects (integration), it is easier for students to see the significance of the course material for themselves and for others (human dimension).

EDUCATIONAL GOALS THAT ILLUSTRATE THE TAXONOMY

Another way of understanding the meaning of the taxonomy is to examine some specific goals associated with each category of learning in it. To do this, I will relate the taxonomy to educational goals advocated in the general literature on college teaching, and then show how the taxonomy can be used by teachers to construct goals for their own courses.

Higher-Level Learning and General Educational Goals

The literature on college teaching contains a large assortment of recommendations for what teachers should be teaching and what students should be learning in college. Each of the proposed educational goals is important, yet each is different from the others in terms of the kind of learning being recommended. Table 7.3 contains a list of several educational goals that various writers have put forth as desirable for college courses and curricula. In this table, I have sorted the goals into groups, according to the kind of higher-level learning that each seems best to express. In this case, the taxonomy seems to help one understand the distinct significance of many different kinds of learning as well as the relationships among them.

TABLE 7.3
Educational Goals and the Taxonomy of Higher-Level Learning

LEARNING HOW TO LEARN
- **How to be a better student** (e.g., self-regulated learning, deep learning)
- **How to ask and answer certain kinds of questions** (e.g., scientific method, historical method, inquiry learning)
- **How to be a self-directing or intentional learner** (e.g., self-directed learning, self-reflective practitioners, adult learning projects)

MOTIVATION
- **Wanting to be a good student** (in a given course and/or in general)
- **Excited about a particular activity or subject** (e.g., birdwatching, reading history, listening to music)
- **Excited about living right** (e.g., taking charge of one's life)

HUMAN DIMENSION
• **Character building**	• **Working as a member of a team**
• **Multicultural education**	• **Citizenship**
• **Leadership**	• **Serving others** (local, nat'l, world)
• **Ethics**	• **Environmental ethics**

INTEGRATION
- **Interdisciplinary learning** (e.g., connecting different disciplines, perspectives)
- **Learning communities** (e.g., connecting different people)
- **Learning and living/working** (e.g., connecting different realms of life)

APPLICATION
- **Critical thinking**
- **Creativity**
- **Practical thinking** (e.g., problem solving, decision-making)
- **Managing complex projects**
- **Performance skills** (e.g., foreign language, communication, operating technology, fine arts performances, sports)

FOUNDATIONAL KNOWLEDGE
- **Conceptual understanding:** a full understanding of the concepts associated with a subject, that allows explanations, predictions, etc.
- **Deep understanding:** an understanding that is anchored in a framework of meaning(s)

Higher-Level Learning and Specific Courses

It may be hard for an individual teacher to look at all these lofty educational goals and imagine how he or she could possibly incorporate them into everyday courses. But the taxonomy of higher-level learning can help teachers develop a set of goals for their courses that indeed go well beyond the familiar goal of covering the content.

To test this idea, I interviewed a number of teachers on my own campus. They all selected courses they frequently taught and then answered some questions about possible goals for that course. The questions focused on each category of higher-level learning. The questions and the responses of one teacher, a professor of microbiology, are shown in Table 7.4 in order to illustrate what their answers looked like.

What I learned from these interviews is that teachers can, with a little guidance, identify specific goals for almost any course that reflect all the categories in the taxonomy of higher-level learning. And in every case, these goal statements represented kinds of learning that the teacher truly valued and, in most cases, went well beyond what the teacher had been using in the past. In sum, the taxonomy was capable of giving direction and impetus to a latent desire of teachers to set more ambitious and yet clearly focused learning-centered goals for their courses.

USING THE TAXONOMY OF HIGHER-LEVEL LEARNING

There are several ways this taxonomy and its associated components can be of value to college teachers, administrators, and students.

Improved Course Design

The first and most obvious application is to help teachers design courses and curricula that will truly provide students with higher-level learning experiences. One of the first tasks teachers have to accomplish when designing a course is to decide what they want their students to learn or get out of the course. One approach to this task is to list the topics of the course or the powerful concepts introduced in the course. These are of course important. But listing the topics and concepts do not indicate what we want the students to learn about these topics and concepts. The alternative approach to this task is the design approach which begins by asking what it is we want students to learn and then by deciding what teaching/learning strategies would best achieve the desired kind of learning. The ideas and language of higher-level learning can give the teacher a set of tools to describe his/her course goals with more focus and direction. In addition to wanting our students to know something about the subject, do we also want them to also learn how to apply the ideas? Do we want them to learn how to integrate them with other ideas? And so forth.

Also, the model of the components of learning allows teachers to see two clear ways of increasing the significance of their course goals. One

TABLE 7.4

Higher-Level Learning Goals for a Specific Course

Questions for Formulating Higher-Level Learning Goals	Responses of a Microbiology Professor "A year after this course is over, I want and hope that students will . . ."
I. FOUNDATIONAL KNOWLEDGE • What key facts, terms, formula, concepts, relationships, etc., are important for students to understand and remember in the future?	• ". . . remember the terms associated with microbial anatomy, biochemistry, and disease." • ". . . understand 'orders of magnitude', i.e., what exists at different levels or scales, in relation to other objects." • ". . . remember the primary categories of organisms."
II. APPLICATION • What kinds of thinking are important for students to learn here: • Are there other important skills that students need to learn? • Do students need to learn how to manage complex projects?	• ". . . be able to critically evaluate bodies of literature in academic and popular outlets." (critical thinking) • ". . . be able to mathematically calculate the rate and extent of microbial growth." (skill)
III. INTEGRATION • Are there important connections (similarities and interactions) that students should recognize and make?	• ". . . integrate ideas about energy, from chemistry and microbiology." • ". . . relate ideas about microbial biology with processes in higher organisms, e.g., metabolism, disease."
IV. HUMAN DIMENSION • Is there anything you would like for students to learn about themselves? • Is there anything important that students could or should learn about understanding others and/or interacting with others?	• ". . . come to see themselves as people who are more educated about microbiology than the average lay person. • ". . . be able to inform and educate other intelligent citizens about the role of microbiology in personal and public life; e.g., educate their roommates about proper ways of cooking hamburger."
V. MOTIVATION • Are there any changes you would like to see, in what students care about, i.e., any changes in their feelings, interests, and/or values?	• ". . . be excited about microbiology as a broad, complex, multifaceted field of study; i.e., a subject that is concerned with more about organisms than just their role as causes of human diseases." • ". . . value the importance of precise language in this field of work, as part of professionalism."
VI. LEARNING HOW TO LEARN • Are there things you would like for students to learn about • how to be a good student in a course like this? • how knowledge is constructed for this particular kind of subject matter? • how to become a self-directing learner relative to this subject?	• ". . . be able to know how to read assigned material responsibly." (being an effective student.) • ". . . know how the scientific method works, especially the importance of identifying and testing the hypothesis." (a method of learning that is particular to this subject matter.) • ". . . be able to identify important resources for their own subsequent learning." (becoming a self-directing learner.)

way is by trying to promote more significant forms of change in the learner; i.e., more than just knowing. The second way is by increasing the foci of the course, learning about more than just the phenomena that constitute the subject of the course.

Better Basis for Choosing among Alternative Teaching Strategies
During the last few decades, the scholarship of teaching in higher education has generated a wonderful array of new and exciting ways of teaching: problem-based learning, writing across the curriculum, team learning, experiential learning, collaborative learning, computer-based learning, and so on. While this has created a wealth of choices, the very extent of the options can also be overwhelming. They all look good, yet one cannot do them all, at least not simultaneously. So how does a teacher choose among them? The answer I would give to that question is to use higher-level learning as a criterion. Which approach to teaching seems likely to promote the most kinds of higher-level learning, in the greatest depth? For example, if one approach seems to offer good foundational knowledge and good application learning, but a second approach offers both of these plus better learning about the human dimension and learning how to learn, then I would definitely choose the latter option over the former.

Bigger Perspective of the Literature on Teaching and Learning
The literature on teaching and learning in the last three decades or so has grown tremendously and truly has blossomed a "thousand lights." However, this very wealth of ideas creates the need for some kind of conceptual framework that will allow us to see the relationships among these different ideas more clearly. It would seem that the taxonomy of higher-level learning could be very helpful in this regard.

As shown in Table 7.3, the extended list of educational goals receiving much national attention at the present time can be sorted into different groups, based on the kind of higher-level learning that is the central feature of each particular goal. Having the bigger picture in mind when reading about any one of these allows us to appreciate its special value without being misled into believing that it is the whole of significant learning.

A New and Better Basis for Evaluating Teaching
Academic departments and teachers continuously face the unenviable task of having to evaluate teaching, without the benefit of a shared vision

and language for describing what constitutes good teaching and good learning. As a result, the default criterion has become: "How well do students like the teacher or the course, relative to other teachers and other courses?"

Although I strongly believe that student reaction to teaching is an essential component of a full evaluation of teaching, I think a significantly better criterion would be: "Was a particular course or teacher effective in terms of promoting higher-level learning?" When the answer to this is "yes," then the course or teacher was successful—regardless of whether the lecturing style was good or not, whether he or she lectured at all, or whatever. And conversely, when a course does not promote much higher level learning, then there is a problem that needs to be addressed by the teacher—again, regardless of how good the lectures were, how popular he or she was with students, etc.

The bottom line when evaluating teaching should be: Did significant learning occur or not? And the taxonomy of higher level learning gives us a language with which we can address this question, applicable across disciplines.

Guiding Student Reflections on Their Own Learning

One of the rapidly emerging lessons in the realm of active learning is that students need to periodically reflect on their own learning, asking such questions as, "What am I learning in this course? Of what value is it? How do I connect this learning to previous learning and to future activities? What else do I need to be learning in the near or distant future?" One-minute papers, student journaling, and learning portfolios all address the need for students to reflect on their own learning, in increasing levels of scope and extent.

However, as students reflect on these questions, they are likely to find significant value in a conceptual framework that will guide their reflective thinking. I have had a few experiences thus far suggesting that the model of the components of learning (Table 7.1) can in fact provide a very rich road map to this kind of reflection.

I recently had occasion to interview a pair of students who had participated in a summer internship in Washington, DC, and who were trying to prepare future interns. During the interview, I posed a series of questions focused on each of the components.

1) During the time you were working as an intern, how did you change, in terms of

- what you care about differently now, than you did before?

- what actions you are capable of performing now?

- what you can connect or integrate now, that you could not before?

- your ability to think about problems in political science?

- what you know?

2) What did you learn about

- the process of learning about politics?

- interacting with other people?

- yourself?

- some of the major ideas you studied in political science?

- the phenomena involved (in this case, politics)?

The answers from the two students were different from each other, very focused, and very rich.

I came away from this experience convinced that the components of learning can provide a good road map for helping learners acquire a better understanding of what they have learned in a rich learning experience. This in turn positions students well to work on the question of what they need and want to learn next. It also feeds well into the general effort of finding ways to help learners become more effective as self-directed, intentional learners.

CONCLUSION

In one of the most widely read articles on higher education in recent years, Barr and Tagg (1995) describe what they believe to be a major change taking place in American higher education. This change is a paradigm shift in which institutions are thinking less about providing instruction (the teaching paradigm) and more about producing learning (the learning paradigm). This paradigm shift, to the degree that it is in fact occurring, creates a new need. The real need, though, is not just to produce learning, but to produce significant learning.

My belief and hope is that the model of higher-level learning described here has the potential for giving us the critical first step toward more significant learning: a language and set of values for describing the goals of learning experiences that most people can accept as being truly significant. College and university faculty will still need to learn how to translate this general language into specific terms for particular courses and curricula. And they will need to learn how to use multiple forms of active learning and new forms of feedback and assessment, in order to make these new, more ambitious goals a reality. But if they can learn how to do all that, the result should be a significantly different and much more exciting form of education than is often the case at the present time.

REFERENCES

AAC (Association of American Colleges). (1985). *Integrity in the college curriculum: A report to the academic community.* Washington, DC: Association of American Colleges.

ABET (Accreditation Board for Engineering and Technology). (1998). *Criteria 2000,* (3rd). Baltimore, MD: Accreditation Board for Engineering and Technology.

Barr, R. B., & Tagg, J. (1995). From teaching to learning—A new paradigm for undergraduate education. *Change, 27* (6), 13–25.

Bloom, B. S. (Ed.). (1956). *Taxonomy of educational objectives. The classification of educational goals. Handbook I: Cognitive domain.* New York, NY: David McKay.

Bonwell, C. C., & Eison, J.A. (1991). *Active learning: Creating excitement in the classroom.* ASHE-ERIC Higher Education Report 1. Washington, DC: George Washington University.

Gardiner, L. (1994). *Redesigning higher education: Producing dramatic gains in student learning.* ASHE-ERIC Higher Education Report 7. Washington, DC: George Washington University.

NASULGC (National Association of State Universities and Land-Grant Colleges). (1997). *Returning to our roots: The student experience.* Washington, DC: National Association of State Universities and Land Grant Colleges.

NIE (National Institute of Education). (1984). *Involvement in learning: Realizing the potential of American higher education.* Washington, DC: National Institute of Education.

Porter, L. W., & McKibbin, L. E. (1988). *Management education and development: Drift or thrust into the 21st Century?* New York, NY: McGraw-Hill.

Sternberg, R. J. (1989). *The triarchic mind: A new theory of human intelligence.* New York, NY: Penguin.

Contact:

L. Dee Fink
Director, Instructional Development Program
Hester Hall, Room 203
University of Oklahoma
Norman, OK 73019
(405) 325-2323
(405) 325-7402 (Fax)
Email: dfink@ou.edu

Dee Fink has been Director of the Instructional Development Program at the University of Oklahoma since it was established in 1979. He has done work on student learning, new faculty members, the evaluation of college teaching, and instructional design. He has co-directed the workshop on getting started at the annual POD conference since 1992. During the past year or so, he has been leading campus workshops on how to design instruction for higher-level learning. In his own life, he is exploring the relationship among spirituality, leadership, and learning.

8

Clarity in Teaching in Higher Education: Dimensions and Classroom Strategies

Nira Hativa
Tel Aviv University

This essay presents research knowledge regarding the main dimensions of effective teaching in higher education, concentrating on clarity in teaching and its components—classroom behaviors and strategies that promote clear teaching. On this basis, I suggest arranging all dimensions and classroom strategies of effective teaching within a logical structure of interconnected teaching behaviors whose contribution to student learning is based on theory and research. The model organizes all dimensions and strategies of effective teaching in three hierarchical levels and is illustrated by successively breaking down clarity in teaching into intermediate dimensions and classroom behaviors and strategies. The model may help faculty understand how classroom strategies work—how they contribute to the higher dimensions of effective teaching, and eventually to student learning. In this way, understanding the model may promote faculty knowledge of and motivation for adopting and using effective strategies in teaching, and their perception of teaching as a scientific activity rather than a disorganized and random collection of isolated techniques with no scientific rationale and structure.

DIMENSIONS, BEHAVIORS, AND STRATEGIES OF EFFECTIVE TEACHING

Recent research has identifed the main dimensions of, and specific strategies and techniques for, effective college and university teaching. The four main dimensions of effective classroom teaching mostly agreed upon in research are 1) clarity/understableness, 2) organization/ structure, 3) interest/enthusiasm/expressiveness, and 4) interaction/

rapport with students (e.g., Feldman, 1989; Marsh & Dunkin, 1997; Murray, 1983; 1997). In addition, research and practice identified hundreds of classroom-specific teaching behaviors and strategies that contribute to effective teaching. They are listed in a variety of publications by teaching centers in universities and colleges, and in books on teaching tips/techniques (e.g., McKeachie, 1999). Knowledge of effective classroom teaching strategies bears several important practical applications. These behaviors serve as items in teacher evaluation forms and in observation tools in case study research on teaching. But their most important application is for instructional development—to guide teachers in using classroom strategies that improve their effectiveness.

Because of the large number of beneficial teaching strategies and techniques available, researchers tend to group them under categories of the occasion for use or on the basis of some general psychological principles. To illustrate, in McKeachie's book, they are grouped under headings such as "meeting a class for the first time," "organizing effective discussions," "lecturing," "peer learning, collaborative learning, cooperative learning," and "learning and cognition in the college classroom." However, although the main dimensions of effective teaching were identified primarily by using factor analysis of teacher behavior in the classroom in teacher evaluation forms, it is rare to find in the literature distinct links between classroom behaviors and the main dimensions of effective teaching, along with explanations of how these behaviors contribute to the main dimensions.

CLARITY IN TEACHING

I hereby offer a model that connects classroom teaching strategies to the main dimensions of effective teaching. To illustrate the suggested model, I concentrate on one of these dimensions—on teaching clarity. The term clarity is frequently mentioned in the context of teaching. Every so often we hear students complain of unclear teachers or instructors who state that they have explained a difficult concept clearly. Hativa and Raviv (1996) identified teacher ratings on clarity to be consistent across time and courses, suggesting that students have a good perception of the nature of clear teaching. Clarity is essential for effective teaching. A review summarizing almost two decades of research on teacher clarity concluded that:

> Although there is evidence to suggest that a number of teacher behaviors facilitate learning (e.g., enthusiasm, variability, task orientation), there also is growing evidence that clarity of explanation may be the requisite of effective teaching, at least effective expository teaching (Cruickshank & Kennedy, 1986, p. 43).

Moreover, studies found strong correlation between teaching clarity and student learning and their satisfaction from instruction. This was found for all school levels, and across all providers of measurement—observers, learners, and teachers through self-ratings (Evans & Guymon, 1978; Feldman, 1997; Hines, 1982; Hines, Cruickshank, & Kennedy, 1985; Rosenshine & Furst, 1971). Unclear instructors confuse students, diminish their understanding of the material and their self confidence as learners, increase their anxiety, and force them to invest extra time and effort in learning from sources, particularly the textbook, other than the teacher (Hativa, 1984). In spite of its importance to student learning, clarity in teaching received only little attention as compared with other dimensions of effective teaching, and most related research has concentrated primarily on the pre-college level.

What is the meaning of clarity in teaching? Most clarity studies did not define this notion. The few studies that did offer a definition related it to student understanding of the material taught during the lesson, as opposed to mere rote learning (e.g., Feldman, 1989; Hativa, 1998; Hines et al., 1985). For student understanding I hereby adopt the following definition:

> 'Understanding' refers to an individual's ability to use knowledge in novel situations, for example, to solve problems, fashion products, or create stories . . . Understanding is the ability to think with knowledge, according to the standards of good practice within a specific domain, such as math, history, ceramics, or dance (Boix, 1997, p. 382).

This essay focuses on classroom teaching strategies that promote clear teaching. Several dozens of these strategies have already been identified (e.g., Bush, Kennedy, & Cruickshank, 1977; Cruickshank, Kennedy, Bush, & Meyers, 1979; Hines, 1982), too many to be all included in teacher evaluation forms or in tools for rating classroom behavior by observers. Thus, we need to identify from this pool of strategies those that most strongly contribute to clear teaching.

WHICH CLASSROOM STRATEGIES MAKE THE STRONGEST CONTRIBUTION TO LESSON CLARITY?

Major attempts have already been made to arrange clarity-related classroom strategies in order of importance or of frequency of use. A group of researchers centered at Ohio State University (e.g., Cruickshank et al., 1979; Kennedy, Cruickshank, Bush, & Myers, 1979) started this work by asking pre-college-level students to describe relevant strategies of their most clear and most unclear teachers. Analyses of these descriptions identified over 100 clarity strategies. The researchers' next step was to give a list of these strategies to students to rate each on its extent of use by teachers who had high and low on clarity rating. On the basis of students' responses, researchers sorted these strategies on their level of contribution to clarity. Hines (1982) extended these studies to the university level. She listed 53 classroom clarity strategies identified either in these earlier studies or through observation and analysis of university teaching. She then assigned undergraduate students to rate the occurrence of each listed behavior twice—with reference to their highest-clarity teachers and to their lowest-clarity ones. Hines then used discriminate analysis of student responses to arrange the strategies in decreasing order of discriminating power between high- and low-clarity instructors. The first 28 prime discriminators on her list, in decreasing order of discriminating power, are:

1) Gives explanations students understand
2) Presents content in a logical manner
3) Explains things simply
4) Teaches at an appropriate pace
5) Answers students' questions
6) Asks questions to find out if students understand
7) Repeats things that are important in handouts
8) Repeats things when students do not understand
9) Points out what is important to learn
10) Stays with the topic until students understand
11) Summarizes the material presented in class
12) Asks students if they know what to do and how
13) Distributes time adequately over topics.
14) Explains the assignments and the materials students need to use
15) Explains and then stops for questions
16) Tells students what they are expected to do/know
17) Stresses difficult points
18) Describes the assignments and how to do them
19) Teaches step-by-step
20) Allows students time to ask questions
21) Writes important things on board or
22) Shows how to remember things
23) Uses examples when explaining
24) Shows similarities and differences between things
25) Compares new material with what students know
26) Goes over difficult problems in class
27) Explains meaning of unfamiliar words
28) Explains and stops for students to think about it

In another type of study, Murray (1985) used a factor analysis procedure to identify from observers' ratings of an initial list of 93 classroom strategies, those that load the highest on lesson clarity. In the following list of the items identified, * marks those that significantly correlate with students' ratings of the same teacher on overall performance. In parentheses are the corresponding items in Hines's study:

a) Uses concrete examples of concepts (23)

b) Stresses important points* (7, 9, 21)

c) Gives multiple examples* (23)

d) Points out practical applications

e) Repeats difficult ideas (8, 10, 17, 26)

Two additional items—on questions in the classroom—found by Murray as loading on another main dimension of effective teaching (interaction), appear in Hines's list as prime discriminators of clarity. These are:

f) Encourages questions and comments* (5, 15, 20)

g) Asks questions of class* (6)

Indeed, questions may belong in both categories—interaction and clarity—as they form the basis for any good teacher-student interaction and make an essential contribution to clear teaching. This contribution is based on posing questions to gauge students' understanding to then fill in the gaps, or encouraging students to ask questions when they do not understand and then answering these questions and continuing to explain until students understand. Unfortunately, there is no indication in Murray's list on the loading of these two items on clarity as a main dimension of effective teaching.

Smith (1978) used trained raters to rate the videotaped classroom teaching of 99 community college teachers' clarity. The ten strategies that were most highly related to overall teacher clarity were:

1) Uses examples with explicit referents
2) Lets students ask questions
3) Answers student questions
4) Asks questions related to material taught
5) Encourages students to ask questions
6) Shares overall structure of lecture with students
7) Teaches step-by-step
8) Prepares students for what is upcoming
9) Uses verbal markers of importance
10) Summarizes material at appropriate points in the presentation

A more recent study (Benz & Blatt, 1994) used qualitative methods to identify components of teaching effectiveness. University students were asked to explain in writing why they rated their teachers as they did on the standard rating questionnaire. The most frequent explanations for ratings of a teacher as very clear were:

a) Explains the subject matter well

b) Repeats explanations

c) Presents in an orderly manner

d) Uses examples

e) Personalizes examples

f) Uses frequent questioning

The substantial similarity of strategies identified as components of clarity in the different studies, conducted in different types of institutions, locations, and using different research methods provides validity to those clarity behaviors and strategies.

To summarize, the components—classroom strategies and behaviors—of clarity that are found repeatedly, in at least two of these four studies, are (in parentheses, the number of studies):

1) Using examples when explaining (4)

2) Posing questions to students (to find out if they understand) (4)

3) Enabling/encouraging students to ask questions (4)

4) Answering students' questions (3)

5) Repeating things when students do not understand (3)

6) Relating material/explanations to students' prior knowledge/experience (3)

7) Stressing important points (e.g., by writing on the board or in handouts, repeating them) (2)

8) Summarizing the material (at appropriate points in the presentation) (2)

9) Teaching step-by-step (2)

10) Presenting content in a logical/orderly manner (2)

The following are most of the rest of items found only once in those four studies:

11) Staying with the topic until students understand

12) Giving sufficient "wait time"—frequently stopping for students to think

13) Pointing out practical applications

14) Describing the assignments and how to do them

15) Going over difficult problems in class

16) Showing similarities and differences between things

17) Going over difficult problems in class

18) Teaching at an appropriate pace

Altogether, this list suggests the main classroom strategies to adopt for promoting their clarity in teaching.

A MODEL FOR DIMENSIONS OF CLARITY IN TEACHING

Rationale

Providing college and university faculty with a list of strategies may be very beneficial in promoting their teaching effectiveness. However, providing lists of do's and don'ts has some shortcomings. There is a growing tendency to promote the perception of teaching in higher education as scholarly work. According to this approach, teaching should be perceived as an act of intellectual invention, deserving faculty's time and attention, and its status, especially in research universities, should be raised to the same level as that of research (Shulman & Hutchings, 1997). In this approach, the current view of teaching by faculty as "simply a matter of methods and techniques" (p. 7) should change to that of a scientific activity. Providing faculty with a list of do's and don'ts promotes their perception of teaching as a disorganized and occasional collection of isolated techniques with no scientific rationale and structure.

I suggest arranging all dimensions and classroom strategies in a logical structure of interconnected teaching behaviors whose contribution to student learning is based on theory and research. An important strategy for effective teaching is using an advance organizer—providing students with a general framework of a lesson or a topic of study before going into detail. This framework serves as a basis for embedding the content of the lesson/topic (e.g., Ausubel, 1978). For the same reason we need to provide college and university faculty with a general framework of effective instructional dimensions and strategies before giving them lists of specific effective classroom teaching behaviors. The model I suggest provides a general framework of interconnections between dimensions and classroom strategies and thus may promote faculty's perception of teaching as having a scientific structure, rather than being simply a matter of methods and techniques, or an aggregation of unrelated teaching techniques.

Breaking Down Clarity into Categories and Subcategories

There are probably a variety of alternatives for breaking down clarity into categories, subcategories, and classroom behaviors. The following is my suggestion for the breakdown of clarity, using content analysis based on my experience working with faculty members on instructional development, on analysis of many dozens of hours of videotaped lessons, and on my previous studies (e.g., Hativa, 1983; 1985; 1995; 2000).

First, I have broken down the notion of 'clarity' into four components:

a) Simplifying the material presented

b) Avoiding "noise" in teaching

c) Adapting instruction and explanations to the students

d) Clarifying after completing instruction

I have further broken down each of these first-level components into subcategories:

a) Simplifying the material presented

   i) Teaching in two (or more) cycles

   ii) Teaching in small steps

   iii) Identifying the main points

   iv) Building explanations in a logical sequence

These are still not concrete classroom behaviors, so that each of them can be further broken down. Let us concentrate on (i) Teaching in two (or more) cycles. This teaching strategy starts with teaching a new topic by presenting its easier-to-comprehend aspects, or a simplified version of the topic, and teaching the more complex version only after the first version is sufficiently understood. Each subsequent teaching cycle is presented at a somewhat more complex and difficult level than the previous one. The cycles are not necessarily presented sequentially; they may be presented concurrently; in parallel; or in a spiral format, integrated with one another. Teaching in two or more cycles is based on a well-known pedagogical method named the spiral principle (Bruner, 1960) that rests on the same idea: Teach a topic in a few cycles—start with the simplest and build up the following ones so that each is somewhat more complicated and difficult than the previous ones. There are several techniques for presenting a simplified version of the new topic in the first cycle. For example:

i)   Teaching in two (or more) cycles.

   1) Presenting a concrete case before discussing an abstract notion

   2) Presenting a comparable case that is familiar to the students (an example, an analogy, a metaphor, a similar or a contradicting case)

   3) Presenting a visual or intuitive interpretation of the formal or abstract topic to be taught

   4) Presenting a rough notion of a concept or figure before going to the more complex but accurate one

   5) Presenting a plan for action, and only then performing the plan

   6) Presenting first the core notion before giving all the details

Similarly, the breakdown of the other categories of a) simplifying the material presented follow (Hativa, 2000):

ii) Teaching in small steps.

   1) Breaking down the topic into small chunks

   2) Arranging the chunks in a coherent logical sequence (see category (d))

   3) Teaching each chunk until students understand, before going to the next one

iii) Identifying the main points:

   1) Emphasizing/stressing main points by varying intonation, writing on the board or on transparencies, stressing points verbally—by marking and signaling

   2) Repeating important points

   3) Summarizing the main points

iv) Building explanations in a logical sequence.

    1) Concentrating on the main line of thought

    2) Going smoothly from one idea or step to the next without diverging into irrelevant material

    3) Coherently tying together the different ideas in the presentation

    4) Using properly transitions (transitional phrases)

    5) Avoiding skipping steps in a sequence, in proofs, developments, or explanations

    6) Avoiding leaving out pieces of information for students to fill in themselves, without clear guidance on how to do this

    7) Avoiding making frequent errors

    8) Avoiding "jumping around" in presentations

This was a short elaboration on a) Simplifying. I do not elaborate on all the subcategories of clarity in teaching because doing this in depth will be too long for the aim of this essay—to demonstrate the breakdown process of the main dimension of clarity. I only present hereby in short the breakdown of d) Clarifying after completing instruction. Gaining a full and meaningful understanding of the material taught is established only when students can apply this knowledge by demonstrating understanding performances—performing some thinking tasks that are based on that material. The tasks can be of a diverse nature such as explaining, providing illustrations and analogies, comparing and contrasting, providing evidence and justification, putting in context, generalizing, applying and transferring to new situations, and solving problems (Perkins, 1992; 1998). A full level of understanding is gained gradually during the lesson and after the lesson (e.g., through solving related problems or doing other homework assignments). To deepen students' understanding within the framework of the lesson and help them retain and apply the new material, teachers should add clarification procedures after students have supposedly gained basic comprehension of the material—upon completion of teaching a topic. The main clarification procedures that teachers use in this case are

d) Clarifying after completing instruction

    i) Looking back (i.e., laying the basis for "understanding performances")

    1) Recapitulating the core idea, or the end result

    2) Simulating the process or reviewing the steps

ii) Sharpening the meaning (i.e., demonstrating understanding performances)

    1) Providing additional examples and illustrations (additional to those presented while teaching the material in the first time)

    2) Providing additional analogies, metaphors, and visual or intuitive interpretations

    3) Showing similarities, and discriminating between similar cases

    4) Showing positive as well as negative examples

    5) Presenting cases of use and misuse of the new concepts, and cases of nonexamples

    6) Stressing main attributes

    7) Presenting special cases, limit/border cases

    8) Presenting applications

    9) Identifying the type/category; stating which cases would apply in what conditions/ occasions

iii) Helping students apply learned material (i.e., training students in understanding performances)

    1) Demonstrating solutions to problems

    2) Providing algorithms for procedures and processes

    3) Providing plans for action

All the behaviors and strategies identified in the four studies of clarity components are included in this structure, and moreover, the structure presents many more behaviors of this type. We can explain how these subcategories and behaviors contribute to lesson clarity, using the psychological information-processing model. For example, "avoiding noise" enables for the listener to take in the teacher input through the senses whereas simplifying the material presented, adapting instruction and explanations to the students, and clarifying after completing instruction facilitate the embedding of the new knowledge in the existing cognitive structure (Hativa, 2000).

A Conceptual Model for Dimensions of Effective Teaching

The aim is to arrange all these categories and subcategories of teaching clarity, and generally of effective teaching, within a hierarchical structure of levels and sublevels. Most publications that refer to effective teaching behaviors use only two levels of dimensions: main dimensions (e.g., lesson clarity and organization) and their components (classroom strategies). The proposed model adds an intermediate-level dimension that includes clarity behaviors that mediate between the main dimension clarity and its components—classroom strategies. The breakdown of clarity into components can be repeated several times so that more than one dimension belongs to the intermediate-level category.

Thus, the new model organizes all dimensions and strategies of effective teaching in three hierarchical levels. The upper level includes the main dimension of effective teaching, e.g.; organization and clarity. The lower level contains all classroom strategies. The middle level consists of one or more layers of intermediate-level teaching dimensions that mediate between the main dimensions and the specific classroom strategies. The intermediate-level dimensions are defined either from top-down—breaking down the main dimensions into major components—or from bottom-up, by clustering (using factor or content analysis) of classroom strategies. Figure 8.1 illustrates the structure of the model:

FIGURE 8.1
Dimensions of Effective Teaching

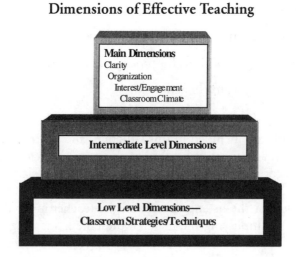

To illustrate for lesson clarity, Figure 8.2 shows the structure of the clarity dimensions in this model:

FIGURE 8.2
Structure of Clarity Dimensions

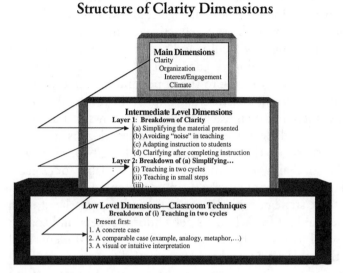

The intermediate dimension in Figure 8.2 is made up of several layers of general behaviors, and the lowest dimension consists of many classroom teaching strategies/ techniques that contribute to clarity.

IMPLICATIONS OF THE MODEL

Implications for Theory and Research

The model can be modified and improved, and similar structures (of intermediate and low-level dimensions) should be identified for the other dimensions of effective teaching, such as course and lesson organization, or interest and student engagement. The studies by Hines (1982; 1985), that sorted components of clarity in accordance with their discriminating power between clear and unclear teachers, can be replicated for these other main dimensions. Identifying the strength of contribution of teaching strategies for all main dimensions of effective teaching can promote research on effective teaching in higher education. When observing teachers in their daily work or analyzing videotaped lessons, researchers can use tools that list only those strategies identified as of the strongest contribution to the main dimensions of effective teaching.

Implications for Practice
The model suggests a framework of interconnected teaching dimensions
and strategies and explains how these strategies work—how they contribute to the main dimensions of effective teaching. The model can be
used to increase the general pedagogical knowledge of college and university teachers in workshops on effective teaching for faculty and in programs of educating new faculty and teaching assistants for their role as
teachers. Faculty developers can present this model with the list of
teacher behaviors belonging to the upper, intermediate, and lower-level
dimensions of effective instruction, explain how it works, and how faculty can adapt it into their teaching. Research shows that no teacher, however effective and clear, uses more than a few dozens specific effective
classroom strategies (Hativa, Barak, & Simhi, 1998). However, faculty
should be familiar with the many strategies available for effective teaching and the connections among them, as presented in the model. Knowledge of these strategies enables teachers to plan and select for classroom
use those that best fit each one's perceptions, beliefs, and goals in teaching; personal style and characteristics; the particular students in class; the
course; the subject area, and other contextual factors.

The model presented here can also guide the process of improving
instruction at the higher education level. Understanding this model can
support self-improvement efforts of teachers as well as guide the work of
instructional experts/developers with faculty members to increase the
teaching effectiveness. To illustrate, when instructional developers guide
teachers to start an explanation of a complex concept with a visual or intuitive interpretation (see Figure 8.2), they may explain the psychological
learning principles underlying this method. Then they can use the model
to explain how this method (of teaching in two or more cycles, with the
first one simpler than the second or third) simplifies the explanations for
the students, helps them understand, and thus promotes clarity of explanations and effective learning.

A third practical application of the model is for designing student
rating forms in a scientific manner. These forms usually include several
items to represent each main teaching dimension, and different forms
use different items to represent the same teaching dimension. The selection of items from the whole pool of possible items that represent that dimension has not been based to date on scientific methods. Knowledge of
the strength of contribution of teaching strategies to each main dimension of effective teaching enables one to select only those strategies that

most strongly contribute to that dimension. Designing the student rating forms on a scientific basis, as suggested here, will increase the validity of these ratings.

REFERENCES

Ausubel, D. P. (1978). In defense of advanced organizers: A reply to the critics. *Review of Educational Research, 48*, 251–258.

Benz, C. R., & Blatt, S. J. (1994, April). *Faculty effectiveness as perceived by both students and faculty: A qualitative and quantitative study.* Paper presented at the annual meeting of the American Educational Research Association, New Orleans, LA.

Boix, V. (1997). Of kinds of disciplines and kinds of understanding. *Phi Delta Kappa, 78* (5), 381–386.

Bruner, J. S. (1960). *The process of education.* Cambridge, MA: Harvard University Press.

Bush, A. J., Kennedy, J. J., & Cruickshank, D. R. (1977). An empirical investigation of teacher clarity. *Journal of Teacher Education, 28* (2), 53–58.

Cruickshank, D. R., & Kennedy, J. J. (1986). Teacher clarity. *Teaching and Teacher Education, 2* (1), 43–67.

Cruickshank, D. R., Kennedy, J. J., Bush, A. J., & Meyers, B. (1979). Clear teaching: What is it? *British Journal of Teacher Education, 5* (1), 27–33.

Evans, W. E., & Guymon, R. E. (1978, March). *Clarity of explanation: A powerful indicator of teacher effectiveness.* Paper presented at the annual meeting of the American Educational Research Association, Toronto, Ontario, Canada.

Feldman, K. A. (1989). The association between student ratings of specific instructional dimensions and student achievement: Refining and extending the synthesis of data from multisection validity studies. *Research in Higher Education, 30* (6), 583–645.

Feldman, K. A. (1997). Identifying exemplary teachers and teaching: Evidence from student ratings. In R. P. Perry & J. C. Smart (Eds.), *Effective teaching in higher education: Research and practice* (pp. 368–395). New York, NY: Agathon.

Hativa, N. (1983). What makes mathematics lessons easy to follow, understand, and remember? *Two Year College Mathematics Journal, 14* (5), 398–406.

Hativa, N. (1984). Sources for learning mathematics in undergraduate university courses. *International Journal of Mathematics Education in Science and Technology, 15* (3), 375–380.

Hativa, N. (1985). A study of the organization and clarity of mathematics lessons. *International Journal of Mathematics Education in Science and Technology, 16* (1), 89–99.

Hativa, N. (1995). The department-wide approach to improving faculty instruction in higher education: A qualitative evaluation. *Research in Higher Education, 36* (4), 377–413.

Hativa, N. (1998). Lack of clarity in university teaching: A case study. *Higher Education, 36* (3), 353–381.

Hativa, N. (2000). *Teaching for effective learning in higher education.* Dordrecht, Holland: Kluwer Academic Publishers.

Hativa, N., Barak, R., & Simhi, E. (1998). *Expert university teachers: Thinking, knowledge, and practice regarding effective teaching behaviors.* Paper presented at the conference of the EARLI-SIG on Higher Education, Leiden, Holland.

Hativa, N., & Raviv, A. (1996). University instructors' ratings profiles: Stability over time and disciplinary differences. *Research in Higher Education, 37* (3), 341–365.

Hines, C. V. (1982). *A further investigation of teacher clarity: The observation of teacher clarity and the relationship between clarity and student achievement and satisfaction.* (Doctoral dissertation, The Ohio State University, Dissertation Abstracts International, 42, 3122A.)

Hines, C. V., Cruickshank, D., & Kennedy, J. J. (1985). Teacher clarity and its relationship to student achievement and satisfaction. *American Educational Research Journal, 22* (1), 87–99.

Kennedy, J. J., Cruickshank, D. R., Bush, A. J., & Myers, B. (1978). Additional investigations into the nature of teacher clarity. *Journal of Educational Research, 72* (2), 3–10.

Marsh, H. W., & Dunkin, M. J. (1997). Students' evaluations of university teaching: A multidimensional perspective. In R. P. Perry & J. C. Smart (Eds.), *Effective teaching in higher education: Research and practice* (pp. 241–313). New York, NY: Agathon.

McKeachie, W. J. (1999). *Teaching tips: Strategies, research, and theory for college and university teachers* (10th ed.). Boston, MA: Houghton Mifflin.

Murray, H. G. (1983). Low-inference classroom teaching behaviors and student ratings of college teaching effectiveness. *Journal of Educational Psychology, 75* (1), 138–149.

Murray, H. G. (1985). Classroom teaching behaviors related to college teaching effectiveness (pp. 21–34). In J. G. Donald & Sullivan (Eds.), *Using teaching to improve*. New Directions for Teaching and Learning, No. 23. San Francisco, CA: Jossey-Bass.

Murray, H. G. (1997). Effective teaching behaviors in the college classroom. In R. P. Perry & J. C. Smart (Eds.), *Effective teaching in higher education: Research and practice* (pp. 171–203). New York, NY: Agathon.

Perkins, D. N. (1992). Understanding performances. In D. N. Perkins (Ed.), *Smart schools: From training memories to educating minds* (pp. 75–79). New York, NY: Free Press.

Perkins, D. N. (1998). What is understanding? In M. S. Wiske (Ed.), *Teaching for understanding: A practical framework*. San Francisco, CA: Jossey-Bass.

Rosenshine, B., & Furst, N. (1971). The use of direct observation to study teaching. In R. M. W. Travers (Ed.), *Second handbook of research on teaching* (pp. 122–217). Chicago, IL: Rand McNally.

Shulman, L., & Hutchings, P. (1997). *Fostering a scholarship of teaching and learning: The Carnegie Teaching Academy*. Menlo Park, CA: The Carnegie Foundation for the Advancement of Teaching.

Smith, S. (1978). *The identification of teaching behaviors descriptive of the construct: Clarity of presentation*. (Doctoral dissertation, Dissertation Abstracts International, 39(06), 3529A.)

Contact:

Nira Hativa
Chairperson, Center for Education Faculty Development
School of Education
Tel-Aviv University (TAU)
Tel Aviv 69978
Israel
972 3 640 8840
972 3 640 8157 (Fax)
Email: Nira@post.tau.ac.il

Nira Hativa holds a master's degree in mathematics from Israel and a Ph.D. in math education from Stanford University. She wears two hats: One is serving as a full-time university professor with teaching, research, and publications that focus on teaching in higher education-teaching processes; teaching effectiveness; teacher perceptions, beliefs, and thinking; and instructional development. The other hat is serving part time as faculty developer on special projects, working for several years with almost all faculty members in a single department or school. Her permanent position is at TAU, but she has also served in both roles at Stanford University, where she designed and produced—with the support of the Center for Teaching and Learning at Stanford—a sequence of nine videotape programs to promote effective teaching in the math/science/engineering areas.

9

Preparing Today's Faculty for Tomorrow's Students: One College's Faculty Development Solution

Patrick Nellis
Helen Clarke
Jackie DiMartino
David Hosman
Valencia Community College

Valencia Community College in Orlando, Florida, has created a faculty development program underwritten for the past five years by a US Department of Education Title III Strengthening Institutions Grant. Our program rose from a deliberate desire to build active, collaborative faculty teams that would, in turn, build active, collaborative classrooms; our results demonstrate that faculty development programs based on observable and measurable outcomes can positively affect student academic performance and persistence. This essay details this faculty development project.

OUR BEGINNINGS

Since its origin, the American community college movement has fought to keep the door open to students who have traditionally been refused admission into higher education. A major concern remains that the typical community college freshman does not possess the tools needed to succeed in college. Although we have afforded them access to higher education, we have often neglected to equip them with the essential tools for success in the academy. At Valencia Community College in Orlando, Florida, we have found that a dynamic and structured faculty development program can have a positive impact on student performance. We based our program on the wealth of current literature on learning and curriculum development theory. The most important component in the implementation of our program was using the principles of active and collaborative learning. We modeled the classroom techniques faculty participants later used in their own teaching practice.

Faculty development at Valencia has taken many directions. The college has made attempts at professional development over the past 30 years, from reimbursement for workshops and conferences to the occasional external consultant. Recently, the institution has established an ongoing series of brief seminars offered to a wide variety of faculty and staff about a myriad of topics, including campus safety, retirement planning, legal issues in hiring, and so on. A small number of seminars have been directly related to curriculum, teaching, or learning. However, at Valencia, a systematic faculty development effort has been underway for the past five years, underwritten by a US Department of Education Title III Strengthening Institutions Grant. Through this process, we learned much about designing and implementing a faculty development program. The program grew out of Valencia's need to redevelop its curriculum (Gianini and Todd, 1995); we saw this as an opportunity to establish a well-planned faculty development program. To meet our challenge, we created a symbiotic relationship between curriculum and faculty development. Our faculty participants expanded their teaching skills and abilities while collaboratively redesigning courses. A unique outcome of our pedagogical diversity is that we have created a comprehensive model for faculty development [see Figure 9.1]. This model should prove to be particularly useful since Valencia, a comprehensive community college serving students over a three-county metropolitan area, shares similar challenges with many in the higher education community.

We began designing our faculty development program with the daunting reality that 90% of our 5,000 annual FTIC (first time in college) students were mandated into developmental reading, writing, and/or mathematics courses as measured by the College Placement Test (CPT). Retention, persistence, and completion rates of those students were at or below the national averages according to data analysis conducted by Valencia's Office of Institutional Research conducted in 1998. We believed we could effect positive change in the performance of all students by enhancing the teaching skills of the faculty and the learning skills of the students. While much has been accomplished in terms of improved teaching through a focus on active learning, we also saw the need to tie

FIGURE 9.1
PROGRAM OUTLINE

OUTCOMES / PRODUCTS **What do you want faculty to** **be able to do as a result of this** **program?**	Performance-based course outcome summaries Specific learning and retention strategies (best practices) Course manuals for students Course manuals for adjunct professors
CONTENT **What do you want faculty to** **learn, to explore?**	Critical thinking Diversity/inclusion Developmental advising Assessment
PROCESSES **How do you want faculty to** **learn?**	Collaborative learning among peers Guided readings and seminars (face-to-face and online dialog) Consultant presentations and topical workshops Practice teaching, peer observation Design, test, publish results
RESOURCES **What will faculty need to sup-** **port learning?**	Faculty release times, faculty stipends Consultants, materials Management, staff (funded internally and by grants)
STRUCTURES **What organizational frame-** **work will the program need?**	Project-based (a course or a significant module) Team-based (not committee work; more than workshops) Managers, leaders, design team participants
ASSESSMENT **How do you know faculty has** **learned?**	Qualitative and quantitative Data on pilot test of course design: retention and achievement

classroom activities to the specific learning goals of a course, as well as to the overall competencies of a Valencia graduate [see Figure 9.2]. This approach to course design is sometimes referred to as "outcomes-based instruction" or "performance-based instruction" (PBI), the term we use at Valencia.

We have recently focused our course redesign efforts on the college preparatory (pre-college credit courses) area and expanded our impact by involving more faculty and staff, thereby increasing the number of students affected by the pilot sections college-wide. We remain serious about offering students real access to quality higher education, and our

FIGURE 9.2

VALENCIA'S STUDENT CORE COMPETENCIES

Valencia's student core competencies are complex abilities that are essential to lifelong success. These general competencies can be applied in many contexts and must be developed over a lifetime. They specify how learning can be expressed and assessed in practice. They enable students and faculty to set learning goals and assess within and across the many disciplines of human inquiry.

THINK

TO THINK, WHAT MUST YOU DO?
- Analyze data, ideas, patterns, principles, perspectives
- Employ the facts, formulas, procedures of the discipline
- Integrate ideas and values from different disciplines
- Draw well-supported conclusions
- Revise conclusions consistent with new observations, interpretations, or reasons

HOW AND WHERE MUST YOU THINK?
- With curiosity and consistency
- Individually and in groups

COMMUNICATE

TO COMMUNICATE, WHAT MUST YOU DO?
- Identify your own strengths and need for improvement as a communicator
- Employ methods of communication appropriate to your audience and purpose
- Evaluate the effectiveness of your own and others' communication

HOW AND WHERE MUST YOU COMMUNICATE?
- By speaking, listening, reading, and writing
- Verbally, nonverbally, and visually
- With honesty and civility
- In different disciplines and settings

VALUE

TO VALUE, WHAT MUST YOU DO?
- Recognize values as expressed in attitudes, choices, and commitments
- Distinguish among personal, ethical, aesthetic, cultural, and scientific values
- Employ values and standards of judgement from different disciplines
- Evaluate your own and others' values from individual, cultural, and global perspectives
- Articulate a considered and self-determined set of values

HOW AND WHERE MUST YOU VALUE?
- With empathy and fair-mindedness
- Individually and in groups

ACT

TO ACT, WHAT MUST YOU DO?
- Apply disciplinary knowledge, skills, and values to educational and career goals
- Implement effective problem solving, decision-making, and goal-setting strategies
- Act effectively and appropriately in various personal and professional settings
- Assess the effectiveness of personal behavior and choices
- Respond appropriately to changing circumstances

HOW AND WHERE MUST YOU ACT?
- With courage and perseverance
- Individually and in groups
- In your personal, professional, and community life

faculty development program is at the heart of our college-wide transformation into a more learning-centered college. The data on student performance, reported later in this article, are encouraging and give reason to believe that we now have the ability to keep our promise of educational access.

THE FRAMEWORK

Our efforts have focused on general education curriculum and have produced courses and teaching improvements resulting in improved student outcomes. The changes have begun to shift the entire college from teacher-centered to learner-centered where both teacher and student actively participate in learning. The program has enabled the faculty to do the following:

1) Renew connections to their disciplines

2) Participate in a campus academic culture that helps build connections between faculty members and across disciplines

3) Understand that underprepared students require developmental education prior to entering college-level courses

4) Evaluate and change curricula, including individual courses

5) Establish an inclusive learning environment that meets the needs of a diverse student body

6) Create a new paradigm where the students' learning potential and progress are maximized using active learning experiences

To meet these goals, Valencia's faculty development effort, managed by a program director, is supported by a full-time faculty development staff of four and two administrative assistants. Annually, 24 faculty members comprise the core of the curricular design team leadership. They, in turn, guide an additional 60 faculty and staff design team participants. Figure 9.3 depicts the structure of the program's personnel organization for one of four discipline areas.

The management team selects faculty leaders and co-leaders during the preceding summer. Faculty leaders are reassigned 50% of their time to faculty development activities and co-leaders receive a $2,200 stipend. During the fall term, faculty leaders and co-leaders with primary responsibility for the curricular and instructional innovations participate in

FIGURE 9.3
Personnel Organization

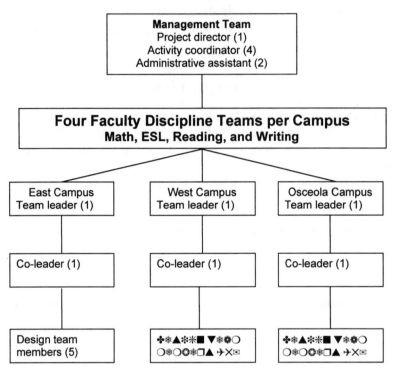

seminars, workshops, and online discussions facilitated by the management team. A variety of topics are addressed which pertain to enhancing student mastery of Valencia's competencies [see Figure 9.2]. Some of the reading list and consultants are selected by the management team, and some room for negotiating topics of interest is held for discussion with the new faculty leaders. Concurrently, the faculty leaders and co-leaders identify courses for redesign and related projects that they wish to pursue in the spring semester.

A group of additional faculty members is selected for the spring semester to work on discipline area design teams. Each faculty leader selects design team members. They then begin 60 hours of training, research, curriculum-development activities, workshops, and course revision/development. Design team members receive a $1,100 stipend for their work. The newly expanded design teams help bring the team's goals into reality. Each design team redesigns course(s), including teaching strategies, accompanying materials, and assessments for implementation in a pilot section in the following academic year. The summer term is devoted to faculty development participants producing final products for the fall and conducting workshops for the at-large faculty. Finally, during the following fall term, faculty pilot-test their courses and ideas. The management team orchestrates the collection of student and instructor performance data. Figure 9.4 depicts the cycle of Valencia's faculty development program.

FROM TELLING TO DOING: WORKING WITH FACULTY AS LEARNERS

The intention of our faculty development process has been to mirror desired outcomes. That is, we want our faculty to move from telling students about subjects to having the students doing a variety of things to demonstrate what they know and what they have learned. We have had to create a process for our faculty to do the projects that would show that they had internalized and could apply the best practices for improving student learning. Since we wanted our faculty to create performance-based instruction for their students, we have modeled our faculty development program on the principles of performance-based instruction (PBI).

Performance-based instruction asks the designer of learning experiences to consider two questions carefully:

1) What will the student be able to do?

2) How will we be able to know that they can actually do it?

The emphasis is not on knowledge recall or content per se, but on student performance. At the end of a learning experience, some level of competent or valuable student ability must be demonstrated. To facilitate PBI course design, we utilize the Wisconsin Instructional Development System (WIDS) [see Appendix 9.1], a software database management program. This program links student performance outcomes to the stated course competencies and to the overall competency goals of a Valencia graduate. Taking the PBI perspective seriously constitutes a shift in emphasis in higher education, with vast implications for everything we do as faculty and faculty developers, not the least of which is the design and delivery of instruction (O'Banion, 1997).

The management team has created a variety of engaging learning activities for our faculty, but in the spirit of PBI, each activity has been

FIGURE 9.4
Faculty Development Cycle

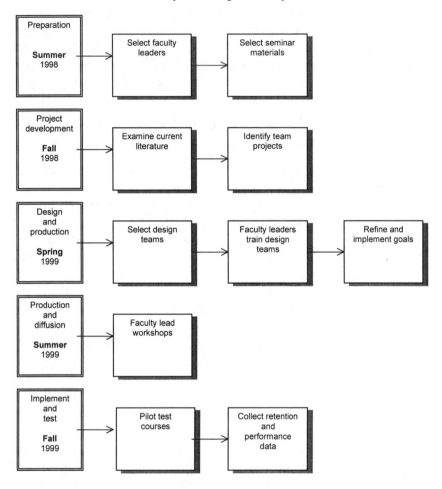

consciously employed to build toward the learning and performance outcomes of the faculty development program. Of course, we know the vital importance of practical, challenging, and interesting learning activities for faculty development workshops. The difference here has been, rather than offer isolated workshop activities, we have connected each learning experience to the desired and measurable outcomes of the faculty development program (as outlined in Figure 9.1).

Likewise, one major goal for faculty development is that participants create a course outline in which the learning activities for students are connected to measurable course outcomes. The management team establishes the conditions under which the faculty can apply their knowledge of PBI to this task. This is essentially a critical thinking process by which the faculty participants analyze what they do with students and why they do it. To write a PBI summary for their individual course designs, faculty participants construct activities around issues of pedagogy, discipline-specific content, and critical thinking itself, as both an outcome and as a method of instruction.

Early in the fall semester of each year, faculty engage in learning activities centered on critical thinking. Using the seminar method modeled after the Washington Center for Improving the Quality of Undergraduate Education, we structure seminars based on academic inquiry, often an all too rare experience outside the context of graduate school. Face-to-face seminars continue throughout the faculty development program based on a variety of texts. Each seminar is extended via an online conferencing system, CAUCUS, that permits team members to reflect on the seminar and return to the reading to post comments that further the group's understanding of the topic's complexities. A follow-up meeting typically has the structure of a workshop, rather than a seminar, where members apply the concepts to their project.

Following a seminar on a key text for course design, faculty participants then identify the core concepts of a particular course. This leads to a concept mapping exercise where participants visually explicate the concepts and processes associated with mastery of a specific core concept. Because this activity is often challenging, we use cooperative learning formats with the faculty as a source of support for the exercise. As an avenue to learning PBI, faculty members write course outcomes based on student performance. For example, the remedial reading team rewrote a course goal from "understand main idea," a comprehension-level skill to "critique literal meaning from reading passages," a student performance more congruent with synthesis-level college reading requirements. The content of courses must be reconceptualized in terms of the students thinking and doing something observable and measurable with the content.

Our approach to each outcome has centered on active and cooperative learning. We have consciously applied Kolb's (1984) experiential learning model by varying the activities and modes from concrete to reflective to abstract to application. Most important, these activities have been clearly tied to enhancing faculty participants' ability to create the

PBI course summary that guides the teaching and learning process during the pilot test of their redesigned courses. In our faculty development program, we have moved from topics like critical thinking or learning style theory to a variety of activities that foster the internalization of the content and its classroom application. We take assessment seriously for both the course design and the program itself. We incorporate formative and summative assessments throughout our program.

UNCOVERING THE CONTENT

While our program has not been driven by a set of topics to cover, our work does have a specific content, the core of which is captured by the four key concepts: 1) critical thinking, 2) diversity/inclusion, 3) developmental advising, and 4) assessment. Our identification of these four topics reflects both the needs and priorities of the college. The interrelation of these key concepts is clearly unavoidable. We have found that although analytically distinct, they frequently overlap in the practice of faculty development and by extension, teaching. Figure 9.5 identifies the curricular components of the faculty development program:

FIGURE 9.5
PROGRAM CONTENT

TOPIC	KEY CONCEPTS	KEY ISSUES/QUESTIONS
Critical thinking 1	Elements of thinking Intellectual standards Developmental stages	Content = thinking Recall is not knowledge Fostering growth
Diversity 2	Motivation Culture Construction of knowledge Learning styles	Establishing inclusion Developing attitude Seeking broader truths Responsive teaching
Developmental advising 3	Rapport building Life and career goals Learning styles Academic plan	Broad, classroom-based group strategies Focused, one-on-one advising meetings
Assessment 4	Classroom assessment techniques Course embedded assessment College core competencies	What are they learning? What can they do? Are we educating our students?

Performance-based instruction is not listed as a topic because it is the master concept for the whole set of content topics. All of our work is designed under the PBI model. Additionally, active and cooperative learning are more logically at the level of teaching strategies and are therefore not considered separate topics. While they are foundational and must be learned, they are actually methods which support the goals of critical thinking, diversity, developmental advising, and assessment rather than coequal topics in their own right. Technology, pictured as a watermark, overlays the chart because the use of technology is incorporated throughout our work, from PowerPoint, to Internet, to WIDS, to Valencia's customized advising software, Cyber Adviser.

OUTCOMES

The outcomes were in three major areas: 1) curricular designs and products created by faculty participants, 2) student academic performance in courses taught by faculty participants, and 3) persistence rates of students in pilot courses. Research databased on pilot courses taught by faculty participants show remarkable improvement in student performance.

Table 9.1 shows data from our most recent set of pilot courses taught during fall semester 1998. The student passing rates with a grade of C or better and the student retention rates (reenrollment for the next semester) are higher for the redesigned pilot courses than for the nonpilot courses, in both college preparatory and college level.

TABLE 9.1
Results of Pilot Courses

	Passing Rate (with A, B, or C)	Retention (re-enrollment Rate)
College preparatory (remedial) courses		
Pilot (N = 187)	68%	78%
Nonpilot (N = 4840)	56%	69%
College level general education courses		
Pilot (N = 648)	69%	75%
Nonpilot (N = 4617)	66%	66%

The college preparatory courses included reading level 2, writing level 2, and mathematics level 1. The college-level courses included English composition level 2, Spanish at all 3 levels, and a variety of humanities courses.

Our faculty development program for the 1998–99 year was exclusively focused on college preparatory courses in reading, writing, mathematics, and English as a Second Language. This was in response to a crisis in remedial education at our college and an acknowledgment of the successful pilot-tested designs that we have fostered over the past three years. Table 9.2 shows the pilot tests in several remedial areas that have increased student performance:

TABLE 9.2
Passing Rates in Pilot Courses

Pilot Courses in College Prep (Remedial)	Improved Passing Rate over non-pilot course
Reading 2 (N=286) fall 1996	**15%** higher than reading 2 previous semester
Writing 2 (N=162) fall 1996	**15%** higher than writing 2 previous semester
ESL 2 (N=31) fall 1996	**21%** higher than ESL previous semester
Math 1 (N=109) fall 1997	**7%** higher than math 1 previous semester
Math 2 (N=100) fall 1997	**26%** higher than math 2 previous semester

These measures of student performance in terms of passing rates and retention indicate the success of Valencia's faculty development program. We have also collected data on the faculty themselves. The following table is based on a sample of 12 faculty members who have been involved in the faculty development program over the past five years and shows the average improvement in their teaching performance after participating in the program:

TABLE 9.3
Teaching Performance

	Student Passing Rates	**Student Retention Rates**
12 faculty participants After at least one year of faculty development	15% increase on average	10% increase on average

We also conducted a survey on a random sample of all full-time, college-wide faculty and staff. The survey instrument was designed to measure, on a Likert scale, faculty awareness and use of various teaching, learning, and advising strategies such as active learning, cooperative learning, and developmental advising. The respondents were grouped into three categories: 1) no involvement in faculty development, 2) one year of involvement in faculty development, 3) more than one year in-volvement in faculty development. The results showed that group 1 (no involvement) self-reported higher levels of use of these strategies than their level of awareness. Group 2 (one year of involvement) showed higher marks on both use and awareness than group 1, and the two indi-cators were nearly equal to each other. Group 3 (more than one-year in-volvement) showed the highest rating of use and of awareness, but fac-ulty indicated that they were higher in awareness of the strategies than in their actual use of them with students. These findings are not surprising when one takes a developmental perspective: the more one learns about the complexities of cooperative learning, for example, the more self-critical (or modest) one becomes when claiming a high level of imple-mentation. By the same token, faculty members with little or no faculty development experience, as in the case with Group 1, they tend to over-estimate their skills in an area of low awareness. Indeed, we often see this with student developmental inventories.

Another survey was conducted among all participants in the faculty development program over all five years. Of 200 faculty participants sur-veyed, 60 provided usable responses. Respondents overwhelmingly showed that they had indeed implemented curricular changes, made use of developmental advising techniques within the classroom, and taken steps to foster a more inclusive classroom. Fifty-five of 60 faculty felt that they had a deeper understanding of the content of the program. Based on four years of data collection, including these findings, we are confident that faculty who work within our program to redesign instruction con-tribute to higher levels of student learning.

Few studies focus on the relationship between faculty development programs and student outcomes or retention; even though, ". . . both within and among colleges, faculty lack opportunities to learn from one another at precisely the moment when increasing communication among a diverse faculty has become a necessity" (Gabelnick et al., 1990, p. 7). However, surveys done by Gaff (1991) find that institutions with major faculty development programs did experience success in their stu-dent, faculty, and institutional outcomes.

CONCLUSION

In response to Boyer's (1987) observation that faculties are discouraged by inadequate support for intellectual pursuits at their institutions, he

(1990) and other leaders in education have long called for academic attention to include teaching methods, learning theory, and classroom research. Our work at Valencia Community College shows that a comprehensive faculty development program, based on observable and measurable outcomes, positively affects student achievement and retention. The results demonstrate that this major change has positively affected student academic performance and persistence. Encouraging our faculty at Valencia to create improved learning opportunities for students has been both exciting and rewarding. Our program arose from a deliberate desire to build active, collaborative faculty teams who would, in turn, build active, collaborative classrooms reflecting both the needs and priorities of the college. We are encouraged as we continue this process.

REFERENCES

Belenky, M. F., Clinchy, B. M., Goldberger, N. R., & Tarule, J. M. (1986). *Women's ways of knowing: The development of self, voice, and mind.* New York, NY: Basic Books.

Boyer, E. (1987). *College: The undergraduate experience in America.* New York, NY: Harper & Row.

Boyer, E. (1990). *Scholarship reconsidered: Priorities of the professoriate.* Princeton, NJ: The Carnegie Foundation for the Advancement of Teaching.

CAUCUS. (1995). [Computer software]. Front View, Inc.

Gabelnick, F., MacGregor, J., Mathews, R. S., Smith, B. L.(1990). *Learning communities: Creating connections among students, faculty, and disciplines.* New Directions for Teaching and Learning, No.41. San Francisco, CA: Jossey-Bass.

Gaff, J. G. (1991). *New life for the college curriculum: Assessing achievements and furthering progress in the reform of general education.* San Francisco, CA: Jossey-Bass.

Gianini, P., & Sarantos, S. T. (1995). Academic rhetoric versus business reality. In J. Roueche, K. Taber, & S. Roueche (Eds.), *The company we keep* (pp. 203–206). Washington DC: Community College Press.

Kolb, D. (1984). *Experiential learning.* Englewood Cliffs, NJ: Prentice Hall.

O'Banion, T. (1997). *A learning college for the 21st century.* Phoenix, AZ: American Council on Education & Oryx Press.

WIDS instructional designer. (1997). Waunakee, WI: Wisconsin Technical College System Foundation. [Computer Software].

Contacts:

Patrick Nellis
Coordinator, Faculty Development
East Campus, 5-220, MC 3-21
Valencia Community College
Orlando, FL 32825
(407) 299-5000 x2416
(407) 382-2061 (Fax)
Email: Pnellis@gwmail.valencia.cc.fl.us

Helen Clarke
English Professor
Communications Department
Valencia Community College-East Campus
Orlando, FL 32825
(407) 299-5000 x2273
Email: hclarke@valencia.cc.fl.us

Jacalyn DiMartino
Project Director, Title V Grant
Osceola Branch Campus
Valencia Community College
1800 Denn John Lane
Kissimmee, FL 34744
(407) 299-5000 x4165
Email: jdimartino@gwmail.valencia.cc.fl.us

David K. Hosman, Activity Director
Title III Grant for Faculty Development
Valencia Community College, West
P.O. Box 3028
Orlando, FL 32802
(407) 299-5000 x1303
(407) 299-5000 x1984 (Fax)
Email: Dhosman@valencia.cc.fl.us

Patrick Nellis has been working fulltime on faculty and curriculum develop-ment projects for six years at Valencia Community College. He feels very lucky to be part of an extraordinary team of intelligent, caring, and highly skilled fac-ulty and staff. He studied political science at the University of California, Irvine, and teaches US government as an adjunct professor at Valencia. He remains interested in the connections between education and democracy and is there-fore very pleased to be working in the community college setting where these concerns are a part of everyday life. He loves the ocean and surfs when he gets the chance.

Helen Clarke has been Professor of English at Valencia Community College since 1990 where she has also participated in a wide variety of faculty development efforts. Last year she was an activity coordinator for the College-Level Achievement Initiative and for the last eight years has coordinated Teaching Writing: A Process in Itself, a seminar series focusing on active and collaborative approaches that make teaching and evaluating writing more effective. She also conducts writing across the curriculum workshops for the college. She is currently designing a department-level seminar series for adjunct faculty. She thinks most clearly when gardening and running.

Jacalyn DiMartino was recently selected as Project Director for a Title V grant project. Her experience with faculty and curriculum development at many levels (middle school, high school, and college) spans many years. Also, she has taught mathematics for over 20 years. Her interests include music and travel.

David K. Hosman has been on the management team of three major Title III grants, all supporting faculty development at Valencia Community College. He is the former Director of the Student Success Program at Valencia, and spent 16 years in Student Services. He is a licensed mental health counselor and is a regional consultant/trainer for the Faculty Development Division of the Houghton Mifflin Company. He enjoys golf, cycling, and playing with his grandchildren for relaxation.

APPENDIX 9.1

PERFORMANCE-BASED INSTRUCTION (PBI) IN WISCONSIN INSTRUCTIONAL DESIGN SYSTEM (WIDS) FORMAT FOR THE CRITICAL THINKING COMPONENT

Instructional Level	Professional development
Target Population	Faculty and staff at Valencia Community College
Description	A professional-level development program to understand, design, and implement improved critical thinking models with students at Valencia Community College.

COMPETENCIES AND PERFORMANCE STANDARDS

1) **Redevelop curiosity and self-awareness**
   Domain-affective
   Level-internalization
   Importance-essential
   Difficulty-medium

   Criteria performance will be satisfactory when:
   a) you complete personality assessment: MBTI
   b) you complete learning style assessment: Kolb LSI
   c) you articulate reaction to and implications of self-awareness for intellectual curiosity
   d) you articulate the importance of personality and learning style to student learning

Conditions for assessment:
a) submission of completed assessments (MBTI and Kolb LSI) prior to workshop
b) format for reaction/implications statement from following choices: oral, video, written
c) in-workshop, and/or out-of-workshop assignments
d) group and/or individual activities

Learning objectives:
a) describe your personality style via MBTI
b) describe your learning style via Kolb LSI
c) reflect on where the excitement in learning comes from [intrinsic motivation]

2) **Evaluate selected theories about knowledge acquisition**
Domain-cognitive
Level-evaluation
Importance-essential
Difficultly-high

Criteria performance will be satisfactory when:
a) you explain Bloom's taxonomy, with all six elements present
b) you summarize Kuhn's theories
c) you present an example of a paradigm of knowledge
d) you articulate the importance of a construction of knowledge perspective to student learning

Conditions for assessment:
a) choices of presentation format: oral, video, written
b) in-workshop, and/or out-of-workshop assignments
c) group and/or individual activities

Learning objectives:
a) list and explain Bloom's taxonomy
b) interpret Kuhn's history of science
c) paraphrase the concept of paradigm
d) defend a construction of knowledge perspecti

3) **Identify stages of critical thinking**
Domain-cognitive
Level-analysis
Importance-essential
Difficulty-high

Criteria performance will be satisfactory when:
a) you create a concept map of a critical thinking stage model
b) your concept map has at least four stages and includes transition points
c) you articulate connections among models presented in workshop
d) you discuss relevance of stage models of critical thinking to classroom practices

Conditions for assessment:
a) choices of presentation format: oral, video, written
b) in-workshop, and/or out-of-workshop assignments
c) group and/or individual activities

Learning objectives:
a) describe Perry's stage model
b) contrast Belenky stage model with Perry's
c) paraphrase Nelson's version of stages
d) detail Nelson's guide to transitions
e) describe Novak's concept mapping techniques

4) **Identify ways of knowing (epistemology) within your discipline**
Domain-cognitive
Level-synthesis
Importance-essential
Difficultly-medium

Criteria performance will be satisfactory when:
a) you provide examples of ways of knowing within your discipline
b) you compare/contrast your examples to ways of knowing in other disciplines
c) you relate personality and learning style to the dominant ways of knowing in your discipline
d) you relate knowing how to know in your discipline to course design, student learning, and or development advising

Conditions for assessment:
a) choices of presentation format: oral, video, written
b) in-workshop, and/or out-of-workshop assignments
c) group and/or individual activities

Learning objectives:
a) examine different ways of perceiving understanding
b) identify structure of knowledge in higher education
c) compare/contrast ways of knowing within your discipline to those of other disciplines
d) identify Kolb LSI relationship to academic disciplines

5) **Explain how practitioners "do"**
Domain-cognitive
Level-application
Importance-essential
Difficulty-high

Criteria performance will be satisfactory when:
a) you relate an example of how knowledge is built in your discipline
b) you present a solution to a major problem discipline
c) you describe an area of meaningful ambiguity (where experts disagree and no certain answer exists) in your discipline.
d) you create a concept map of procedures for solving/knowing in your discipline
e) you describe elements of course design that model procedures of your discipline

Conditions for assessment:
a) choices of presentation format: oral, video, written
b) in-workshop, and/or out-of-workshop assignments
c) group and/or individual activities

Learning Objectives:
a) describe prominent contributions to the knowledge base in your discipline
b) tell how to solve a problem in your discipline
c) identify areas of meaningful ambiguity (where experts disagree and no certain answer exists in your discipline
d) justify procedures of knowing in your discipline
e) explain connections between what you do in your discipline and what you do in your class

6) **Create and sell your rationale for critical thinking**

Criteria Performance will be satisfactory when:
a) rationale includes importance of critical thinking to your course and discipline

Domain-cognitive
Level-synthesis
Importance-essential
Difficulty-high

b) rationale includes statement of importance of critical thinking outside of course and school contexts
c) rationale is research-based
d) you communicate rationale to students and colleagues

Conditions for assessment:
a) rationale is clearly reflected in course syllabus assignments, and activities (as verified by peer assessment)
b) rationale is communicated in classrooms, departmental meetings, conferences, etc.

Learning objectives
a) research critical thinking literature related to your discipline
b) defend the role of critical thinking in your course and discipline
c) explain the role of critical thinking skills (general and discipline specific) outside of the academic context
d) internalize and model critical thinking behaviors
e) adjust presentation to audience

7) **Adapt a model of critical thinking to your discipline**
Domain-cognitive
Level-synthesis
Importance-essential
Difficulty-high

Criteria Performance will be satisfactory when:
a) model includes developmental (stage) framework
b) model provides step-by-step process for learners
c) model includes appropriate levels of challenge and support for student progress
d) model includes methods of transition to higher levels of cognition for learners
e) model embodies procedures of your discipline
f) model addresses different learning styles
g) you create a concept map for your model
h) you explain how to integrate model into classroom

Conditions for assessment:
a) model is peer assessed in workshop context by colleagues within your discipline

Learning objectives:
a) identify areas of your course(s) that are challenging to students
b) identify means to support students to meet the challenges of your course
c) choose/develop appropriate materials and activities
d) integrate critical thinking model into course design/curriculum

8) **Assess the effectiveness of your critical thinking model**
Domain-cognitive
Level-evaluation
Importance-essential

Criteria performance will be satisfactory when:
a) you measure student engagement in the learning process
b) measurement indicates level of student thinking, interest, involvement, and understanding
c) you share results (feedback) from the measurement with students at next meeting

Difficulty-high

d) measurement includes student self-assessments
e) results of assessment are used in refinement/redesign of model

Conditions for assessment:
a) using a Classroom Assessment Technique (CAT)
b) CAT designed to capture relevant information about student thinking in relation to model
c) CAT to be used immediately following learning activity
d) data from CAT to be summarized. into a format that can be shared with both students and colleagues

Learning objectives:
a) correlate assessment strategies to goals of the model
b) establish methods to monitor or measure student involvement/participation
c) process assessment results with students
d) develop, select, implement, and process student self-assessment
e) revise critical thinking model as appropriate

9) **Develop an implementation plan for your model of critical thinking**
Domain-cognitive
Level-application
Importance-essential
Difficulty-medium

Criteria performance will be satisfactory when:
a) you apply model to (a) specific course(s)
b) you measure student performance (growth) in critical thinking
c) you report on results of this approach

Conditions for assessment:
a) implementation plan is peer assessed within workshop context

Learning objectives:
a) choose, develop assessment strategies and instruments
b) discuss logistics of implementation
c) employ cycle of classroom experimentation, feedback, evaluation, and revision
d) share findings as appropriate

10

After Twelve Years of Teaching the College-Teaching Course

Michael B. Paulsen
University of New Orleans

This essay provides a detailed presentation of the perspectives, approaches, activities, materials, and evaluative information that characterize and distinguish a formal, credit-earning, semester-long graduate course in college teaching. This report is based on the author's experiences and reflections drawn from, and expressed after, 12 years of teaching the college-teaching course. Based on an intensive study of advances in theory and research related to teaching, learning, learners, and diversity; students engage in 1) actual teaching, in which they integrate learning theory and other pedagogical knowledge with the content knowledge of their own subject-matter areas; 2) extensive theory and research informed observation and analysis of the teaching of others; 3) the giving and receiving of detailed, theory and research informed feedback about the teaching and learning that they have practiced and observed; and 4) the creation of pedagogical content knowledge essential to advancement of the scholarship of teaching.

INTRODUCTION

Programs for the pre-professional preparation of future faculty during graduate school extend from substantial curricular reform efforts, such as the Doctor of Arts degree (Glazer, 1993), on the one hand, to the traditional teaching assistant experience in a largely research focused graduate program, on the other. Most current efforts lie somewhere in between these extremes. For example, extensive and structured teaching assistant training programs chart a path to various forms of certification for teaching at universities such as Colorado, Illinois, and Syracuse (Border, 1993; Lambert, 1993), concentrations of courses in college teaching are available to graduate students at institutions such as Florida State

University (Schuster, 1993), and courses in college teaching are required of all new faculty at some institutions such as Miami-Dade Community College (Jenrette & Napoli, 1994).

Although formal, credit-earning, semester-long graduate courses in college teaching have not played a central or dominant role in the preparation of future faculty across the nation, such course offerings have increased and some of the more recent models of courses in college teaching have emphasized not only the promotion of excellence in teaching but also the development of scholars of teaching (Kreber, 1999a). At many colleges and universities, one course in college teaching constitutes the first, and sometimes the only, substantial investment in the enhancement of teaching and learning. Therefore, the sharing of, experimentation with, and analysis of, our experiences with such courses are especially important.

The purpose of this essay is to describe and present the perspectives, approaches, activities, materials, and evaluative information that characterize and distinguish a formal, credit-earning, semester-long graduate course in college teaching. This report is based on my experiences and reflections drawn from, and expressed after, 12 years of teaching the college-teaching course.

A FULL-SEMESTER, CREDIT-EARNING GRADUATE COURSE ON COLLEGE TEACHING

For the past 12 years, one to three times per year, I have had the opportunity to teach a full-semester, credit-earning graduate course on teaching and learning in the college classroom. I have developed and taught the course at three large, public, doctorate-granting universities. Students in the course have come from the ranks of graduate students, faculty, and administrators at two-year and four-year colleges, universities and professional schools, and from every conceivable disciplinary or subject-matter background. The disciplinary or professional backgrounds of the students have included the arts, humanities, social sciences, math and natural sciences, business, engineering, computer science, architecture, agriculture, medicine, dentistry, law, ministry, nursing, education, counseling, social work, public administration, military science, and more. While some students have little or no college teaching experience, others have 25 or more years of such experience. Although the course has been presented in a variety of delivery formats, the most common is meeting one evening a week for three hours throughout a 16-week semester. This course is designed to help prepare future college professors (graduate students in any discipline) for their roles as teachers, and to help current two-year and four-year college instructors (faculty in any discipline) to continue to increase their effectiveness as teachers.

DISTINCTIVE FEATURES OF THE COURSE

The course has a number of distinctive features that, in combination, have served to make the course unusual in its approach, and according to evaluation data, very effective as well. The following sections describe these features in detail.

The Interaction of Theory and Practice

One of the predominant themes of the course is that all activities, inside and outside the classroom, are designed to provide opportunities for the students to relate existing theory and research on learning and teaching to effective practice in realistic, context- and content-specific settings. For example, each student engages in 1) actual teaching, in which they draw upon the content knowledge of their own subject-matter area; 2) extensive theory and research informed observation of the teaching of others; and 3) the giving and receiving of extensive, theory and research informed feedback about the teaching and learning that they have practiced and observed.

Solid Grounding in Learning Theory and Research

The first quarter of the semester is devoted to the intensive study of advances in theory and research related to teaching, learning, learners, and diversity. In preparation for in-class group activities, students complete an extensive set of reading assignments from Feldman and Paulsen's (1998) book, *Teaching and Learning in the College Classroom*. These readings cover the following topics: 1) behavioral and humanistic theories of learning; 2) advances in research about social and cognitive perspectives on learning; 3) theories of adult learning and development; 4) learning style research; 5) intellectual, psychosocial, moral, epistemological, racial-identity and other theories of student development relevant to learning; 6) gender differences in learning and development; 7) learning in the multicultural classroom; 8) research on teacher behaviors that are particularly effective in terms of their correlations with students' achievement or learning in college; 9) models of traditional approaches to college teaching, and 10) theory and research related to a variety of emerging models of college teaching, such as feminist pedagogy, critical pedagogy, and critically reflective teaching.

A wide variety of in-class group activities provide the students with a range of opportunities to develop their own individualized and meaningful connections between these diverse theoretical perspectives and their applications to teaching practice in personally relevant settings. The students construct their own meanings regarding these theories through peer teaching and collaborative learning activities (Bosworth & Hamilton, 1994). These activities encourage students to analyze and design various features of effective learning environments and articulate effective teacher behaviors and learning activities for learners who are diverse in ways that are explicable in terms of one or more of the theoretical perspectives identified in the readings. The most important feature of all of these assignments and activities is that they result in all of the students being well informed about existing theories about learning, learners, and diversity, in preparation for the remainder of the course that is highly clinical in nature.

Taking Risks, but Feeling Safe

The great majority of classroom time in the course is dedicated to a clinical application of the research and theories of teaching and learning identified in the previous section to actual teaching practice. This occurs through the conduct and observation of teaching, the giving and receiving of detailed feedback about the observed teaching, and the thorough analysis of such teaching. In the clinical part of the course, students are asked to take risks; many of the activities in which students are engaged can be self-revealing. This means that it is absolutely essential that the classroom environment for the college teaching course is one in which students can feel safe when taking such risks.

A variety of classroom activities contribute to the creation of a safe environment for the students. As examples, I will describe two of the techniques that I have found to be very effective in helping the students in the college teaching class feel safe and comfortable with me and with each other. During the first class meeting, I ask each student to prepare a five-minute lesson to be presented in the following class meeting, usually on a nonacademic subject like a hobby or other favorite activity of the student. I ask each student to design a lesson that will address all eight phases of Gagne's (1974) model of the teaching-learning process—motivation, apprehension, acquisition, retention, recall, generalization, performance, feedback—and will be fun to teach and fun for classmates to learn. During the next class, students are assigned to heterogeneous groups of five. Each member of a group explains, with some demonstration, to the other members of their group, how his or her lesson will address each of the eight phases of Gagne's teaching-learning model. As each explains the lesson, the other group members experiment for the first time with the process of giving reinforcing and constructive feedback—an important precursor of things that will be important throughout the rest of the course. The students are well aware, of course, that every member's lesson will be critiqued by the others in the group; therefore, the students quickly become effective at establishing a group norm of expressing all feedback in a constructive manner. After all members have had their turns, each group elects one person to teach their lesson before the whole class, based on the criteria of how well the lesson addresses the eight phases and how fun it would be to teach and learn.

Next, I ask the other four members of each elected "teacher's" group to prepare to role-play the parts of students in their teacher's class. I explain that the teachers have a trick up their sleeve for this exercise, because they remain with their groups and prepare their groupmates to be very good students in their class! In other words, they coach their students on when and how to respond during their lesson. This reduces the perceived risk of teaching a lesson in front of their peers, and also encourages the group members to work together in a mutually supportive manner in preparing for the lesson. After preparation, each group, in turn, moves to the front of the room and constructs a little "fishbowl"— the first of many to follow in the course—of one person role playing the part of teacher and four others role playing the parts of students in their teacher's class. During the lesson, the members of all other groups carefully observe and all student-teacher interactions and record them on an observation and feedback sheet that arranges information according to each of the eight phases of the learning model being applied in the lesson. At the end of each lesson, the observers share their feedback on how the lesson addressed the eight phases of the model. Because all students know that their group will be next to be up there in front of the class— and that everyone will be playing various self-revealing roles in the fishbowl in front of the class throughout the semester—the growing classroom and group norm of always reporting observations and offering feedback in a constructive manner becomes more firmly reinforced and established. In these—and many other ways—the students and I work together to create a learning environment from the beginning of the semester that will help students feel safe enough to be willing to take the self-revealing risks associated with the clinical phases of the course.

Another activity designed to create a safe learning environment is one that the students and I have come to call "Putting the Teacher on the Hot Seat." The purpose of this activity is to get students to really trust me. To accomplish this, it is essential that I place myself in a very vulnerable and self-revealing position. Our in-class study of learning theory and research is accomplished with small groups engaged in collaborative learning. Once the groups understand their tasks and the goals of the activities and are interactively engaged, I alternate between visiting and not visiting the groups. However, as Brookfield (1995) explains in his "fly on the wall" example, the dynamics of power and implicit assumptions in the classroom are likely to influence the meanings that students assign to the teacher's group visiting behavior. To begin the activity, I sit in the one red "hot seat" facing the students who take their seats in an arc of chairs. I ask the students to think about the various group activities in which they have been engaged, and to recall that sometimes I visited or joined their group, while other times I did not visit their group. Next, I ask the students to tell me exactly what they really thought or how they felt when I did or did not visit their group during an activity. Students' first comments are usually very positive, such as "I always like it when you come by and visit our group, because you help clarify the ideas and concepts we are discussing." But soon, the comments become noticeably deeper and mixed in their substance and tone. Examples are "Sometimes when you visit, we are really on a 'roll' and your visit kind of interrupts that," or "When you visit our group, I feel uncomfortable and sometimes even stop participating, because I feel like you're evaluating me," or "When you are nearby, but don't visit our group, we wonder what you're thinking, whether we're doing the assignment 'right,' and whether you're disappointed in what we're doing."

Examples of my responses are "I didn't know you felt that way" and "Why did you feel that way?" Then I tell them what I think my reasons for visiting or not visiting groups are and we discuss how my espoused motives differ from their perceptions. Next, I point out that what I think my purposes are may not be the real truth, so, "Please ask me questions that will help me to discover what my hidden assumptions really are." With the students committed to probing and me to frank introspection, results have revealed that sometimes I visit one group over another because I feel guilty that I gave them the toughest assignment or I assume they can't do the task without my help, or even that I want to show off my expertise on a group's topic. The crucial outcomes of this activity are the construction of a safe environment in which the students and I have already taken personal risks and have responded with complete support for one another. By the time we have completed all aspects (including debriefing) of the activity, the students' capacities to trust me have deepened remarkably. The result is an unusually strong foundation for the cultivation and expression of understanding and support between the students and me, and among the students, for the rest of the course. Of course, I do not encourage the students to try anything like this in their own classrooms; this activity is only intended to build a strong foundation for trust in the college teaching course. Instead, I encourage my students to obtain feedback from students about learning activities in their own classrooms, using straightforward classroom assessment techniques like the "one-minute paper" (Angelo & Cross, 1993).

The clinical part of the course accounts for about two-thirds of our time in the classroom, it is the most distinguishing and dominant feature of the course, and it creates most of the self-revealing aspects of class participation. The following section describes this feature of the class in detail.

THE CLINIC IN THE COURSE

The teaching-learning clinic is the dominant feature of the course and provides opportunities for students to apply extant research and theories about teaching and learning to the actual practice of teaching and learning. Students gain valuable experience in observation and analysis as well as giving and receiving detailed feedback about the observed teaching and learning. The following sections describe the primary features of the clinic in the course.

Theoretical Grounding: Motivational, Cognitive, and Social Theories

For use in the extensive clinical portion of the course, I use a three-dimensional theoretical framework that has proven to be informative, accessible, and productive for students as they actively engage in the observation and analysis of a wide range of teaching and learning behaviors. The framework is solidly grounded in recent advances in cognitive, social, and educational psychology. Research has consistently demonstrated that students' motivational orientations; use of cognitive, metacognitive, and other self-regulated learning strategies; the social environment of the classroom; and teaching behaviors that are moderately to highly correlated with student achievement contribute significantly to student learning in college (Feldman, 1998; Paulsen & Gentry, 1995; Pintrich, 1989; Vahala & Winston, 1994). In class, we examine the many ways in which research and theories about learning, learners, diversity, and effective teacher behaviors are clearly and meaningfully connected to one or more of the research-based, theoretical components—motivational, cognitive, and social—of the three-dimensional model we use to guide our observation and analysis of teaching-learning. The students observe, analyze, and give one another feedback on their use of motivational, cognitive, and social strategies of teaching, as well as on the effectiveness of their teaching skills in the areas of elocution, questioning, responding, discussion leading, and learning style differentiated teaching. Furthermore, they relate teaching skills to their impact on students' motivation, cognition, and perceptions of the social environment of the classroom.

Teaching Strategies: Observation and Analysis

In class, I use the social-cognitive expectancy-value theory of achievement motivation to integrate the various perspectives on student motivation to learn (Pintrich & Schunk, 1996). The practical implications of this framework are that teachers must design learning environments that help students to find affirmative and productive answers to the value question of "Why should I learn this or engage in this activity?" and the expectancy question of "Can I perform this task effectively with a reasonable amount of effort?" (Paulsen & Gentry, 1995; Pintrich, 1989; Pintrich & Schunk, 1996). Then I use Keller's familiar—attention, relevance, confidence, and satisfaction—model (ARCS) to operationalize the underlying theoretical perspectives in the actual analysis of teaching-learning behavior (Keller, 1983). Those students assigned to view the lesson from the perspective of motivational approaches to teaching use a set of 28 specific strategies arranged into the four ARCS categories on an observational checklist that is presented in Table 10.1.

In order to meaningfully organize and present the various categories of learning strategies for application in class, I use the categories of cognitive strategies—rehearsal, organization, and elaboration—articulated by Weinstein and Mayer (1986), in combination with Pintrich's (1989) taxonomy of learning strategies that includes three categories of cognitive and three subcategories of metacognitive strategies. The implications for effective teaching, based on the research underlying this framework, are that teachers must design learning environments that help students discover affirmative and productive answers to the question of "How can I perform this task effectively with a reasonable amount of effort?"

TABLE 10.1
Motivation Strategies

ATTENTION

_____ 1) Use novelty: anecdotes, demonstrations, questions, metaphors, controversies.

_____ 2) Inject personal, emotional element into intellectual material.

_____ 3) Expand on familiar material with doses of the unfamiliar and unexpected.

_____ 4) Pose a problem or issue, and ask students for ideas about how to resolve it.

_____ 5) Use analogies to make the strange familiar and the familiar strange.

_____ 6) Project intensity and enthusiasm.

_____ 7) Induce dissonance or cognitive conflict.

RELEVANCE

_____ 1) Use examples based on current student interests.

_____ 2) Use examples of how content will help students in courses and career.

_____ 3) Explain why course is offered or required.

_____ 4) Use personal experiences or case studies to demonstrate relevance.

_____ 5) Explain why the content is important to you.

_____ 6) Call attention to the instrumental values of academic activities.

CONFIDENCE

_____ 1) Sequence content from simpler to more complex.

_____ 2) Help students connect success to personal effort and ability by providing opportunities for them to figure out examples or solutions on their own.

_____ 3) Help students connect success to personal effort and ability using feedback such as "If you continue practicing this, you can really master it."

_____ 4) Use goals and content organizers to help students see the main parts of new material and how they fit together.

_____ 5) Check for student understanding and find out what and how they need something clarified before going on.

_____ 6) Model and encourage effective use of how to learn (cognitive) strategies.

_____ 7) Maintain appropriate levels of difficulty and challenge.

_____ 8) Allow opportunities for students to make choices and decisions in learning.

SATISFACTION

_____ 1) Use verbal praise and informative feedback more than formal evaluation.

_____ 2) Use positive feedback immediately following performance.

_____ 3) Use corrective feedback just before the next application.

_____ 4) Relate negative feedback clearly to performance and not the person.

_____ 5) Praise performance and effort.

_____ 6) Clarify performance expectations for each grade and adhere to them.

_____ 7) Teach student goal setting, self-appraisal, and self-reinforcement.

Note: Adapted from Brophy (1987), Cashin (1979), and Keller (1983).

(Pintrich, 1989). Students use a set of 28 specific strategies arranged into the categories of rehearsal, organization, elaboration, and three sets of metacognitive strategies on an observational checklist that is presented in Table 10.2. Finally, I organize and present the various social strategies of teaching, based on a variety of social theories of teaching and learning, for the class by adopting a condensed version of the categories of social strategies presented by Billson and Tiberius (1991). The research underlying this framework indicates that teachers should design learning environments that help students discover meaningful and productive answers to the question, "How can I learn this with others?" Students use a set of 26 specific strategies arranged into the categories of mutual respect, responsibility and commitment; communication and feedback; cooperation; and security and trust. The observational checklist that students use is presented in Table 10.3.

Teaching Skills: Observation and Analysis

Research on effective teaching behaviors has consistently shown that a teacher's presentation skills—especially in the areas of clarity and organization, but also in areas such as enthusiasm—are significantly related to student achievement (Feldman, 1998). This means that elocutionary skills are an important focus for the observation, analysis, and improvement of one's teaching. In each class, a small group of students observes the lesson from the perspective of elocutionary skills, watching carefully for indicators of effectiveness in both vocal and nonverbal modes of expression and communication. Students observing the lesson from the perspective of elocutionary skills use an observational checklist, presented in Table 10.4, to guide and record their observations. In class, we also examine a variety of ways in which different aspects of elocutionary skills may contribute to students' motivational orientations, use of cognitive strategies, and perceptions of the social environment of the classroom. This gives students practice in relating these teaching skills to the underlying theoretical framework for our analysis of the nature and effectiveness of the teaching and learning activities that characterize each individualized lesson taught in the class.

Similarly, research has consistently demonstrated that teacher behaviors that encourage questions and opinions of students and demonstrate concern with, sensitivity to, and helpfulness with respect to students' progress in class, are significantly related to students' achievement (Feldman, 1998). Therefore, the teacher's use of effective questioning, responding, and discussion-leading skills constitutes another important set

TABLE 10.2
Cognition Strategies

REHEARSAL

_____ 1) Repetition
_____ 2) Recitation
_____ 3) Verbatim note taking
_____ 4) Shadowing–saying material aloud while writing or reading it
_____ 5) Underlining text
_____ 6) Copying notes

ELABORATION

_____ 1) Comparative organizer: shows similarities/differences between new material and existing knowledge
_____ 2) Summarizing
_____ 3) Paraphrasing
_____ 4) Generative note taking: adding reflections to verbatim notes on how new material relates to existing knowledge, situations, or applications
_____ 5) Questioning and explaining
_____ 6) Analogies and imagery
_____ 7) Mnemonic key words

ORGANIZATION

_____ 1) Expository organizer: presentation of a set of broad concepts to help students organize and relate main parts of forthcoming material
_____ 2) Outlining
_____ 3) Clustering and classifying
_____ 4) Concept-mapping; presents key concepts in ovals and lines connecting the ovals with linking words on lines indicating relationships among concepts
_____ 5) Diagramming or flowcharting

METACOGNITION
Planning

_____ 1) Pre-study skimming to identify main points and general structure of material
_____ 2) Setting learning goals to be achieved
_____ 3) Generating questions to be answered during learning
Monitoring
_____ 4) Comprehension monitoring or self-testing
_____ 5) Monitoring attention during study
_____ 6) Adaptations during test-taking
Regulating
_____ 7) Reviewing unmastered material and self-correction
_____ 8) Adjusting rate of studying or coverage of material according to difficulty
_____ 9) Self-reinforcement
_____ 10) Changing cognitive strategies to maximize meaningful learning

---

Note: Adapted from Lefrancois (1991) and Pintrich (1989).

Table 10.3
Social Strategies

MUTUAL RESPECT, RESPONSIBILITY, AND COMMITMENT
_____ 1) Learn more about your students.
_____ 2) Help your students learn more about you.
_____ 3) Observe students' nonverbal behaviors and become more aware of your own.
_____ 4) Build a climate of egalitarianism, tolerance, and respect for diversity.
_____ 5) Remember that your behavior is a model for student behavior.
_____ 6) Create an environment in which teacher and students share responsibility and commitment to learning.
_____ 7) Collect early and regular feedback from students regarding the effectiveness of your teaching and the course in general.
_____ 8) Create opportunities for informal interaction.

COMMUNICATION AND FEEDBACK
_____ 1) Engage in regular interaction with students in the class.
_____ 2) Encourage regular communication among students.
_____ 3) Provide multiple, regular opportunities for students to receive constructive, informative feedback from both you and other students.
_____ 4) Foster a diversity of ideas and perspectives.
_____ 5) Bring each class to a meaningful and friendly closure.
_____ 6) Check student understanding regularly, making more meaningful communication and feedback possible.

COOPERATION
_____ 1) Use peer learning: students teaching other students.
_____ 2) Promote collaborative activities and teamwork.
_____ 3) Use cooperative learning groups with positive interdependence, individual accountability, and heterogeneous work groups.
_____ 4) Foster even participation levels.
_____ 5) Work toward the exploration and resolution of conflicts by searching for commonalities and respecting diversity and differences of opinion.

SECURITY AND TRUST
_____ 1) Make it safe for both the students and you to take risks and be wrong.
_____ 2) Help students explore differences and find commonalities on difficult or controversial issues.
_____ 3) Create a climate in which less frequent participators feel comfortable expressing themselves.
_____ 4) Ask and answer questions in an open, accepting, and constructive manner.
_____ 5) Reduce any status differentials between you and your students.
_____ 6) Take care to handle disruptive behaviors constructively.
_____ 7) Be aware of the natural development of group or classroom norms and encourage the development of norms that promote effectiveness of motivation, cognition, and social teaching strategies.

Note: Adapted from Billson and Tiberius (1991).

TABLE 10.4
Elocutionary Skills

1. Vocal Expression
   - –natural   –clarity
   - –volume   –silences
   - –pace   –respectful language
2. Nonverbal expression
   - –facial expression   –eye contact
   - –posture   –movement
3. Enthusiasm

Note: Adapted from Davis (1993), Diamond et al. (1983), and Lowman (1995).

of targets for the observation, analysis, and improvement of one's teaching. Students use an observational checklist, presented in Table 10.5, that includes sections on types of questions and the extent to which they promote interaction and discussion in the class (see, for example, Andrews, 1980), questioning and responding techniques, and discussion leader roles, to guide and record their observations. In class, we consistently strive to articulate the many ways in which questioning, responding and discussion-leading skills can affect students' motivation, cognition, and perceptions of the social environment of the classroom. Once again, students work to understand the importance of specific teaching skills by relating them to the underlying theoretical framework used for the clinical part of the course. As additional preparation for the observation and analysis of teaching skills, students complete reading assignments from books that offer valuable and practical suggestions regarding the essential teaching skills (for example Davis, 1993; Lowman, 1995; McKeachie, 1999).

One final perspective from which the students view each lesson taught is based on learning-style-differentiated teaching (LSDT) (Butler, 1987). Both teachers and students are diverse in their learning styles. And research has indicated that student achievement can be enhanced when teachers plan learning activities that are consistent with students' preferred learning styles (Claxton & Murrell, 1987). One way teachers can address the diversity of their students' learning styles is by incorporating a variety of learning activities which in combination are responsive to the needs of students with diverse learning styles. In preparation for their observation and assessment of a teacher's use of LSDT, students read about Kolb's learning style inventory (Kolb, 1998), complete the inventory

TABLE 10.5
Questioning, Responding, and Discussion-Leading Skills

TYPES OF QUESTIONS

Divergent (open-ended) versus convergent (closed-ended)

High-level (application, analysis, synthesis, evaluation) versus low-level (knowledge, comprehension. application)

Structured (clearly focused) versus unstructured (vague)

Consistent (single point, one type of thinking) versus inconsistent (subparts with contradictory expectations)

QUESTIONING AND RESPONDING TECHNIQUES

Question & Wait (3–5 seconds)	Reinforcement (appropriate to situation)
Probe (for justifications. assumptions, relationships)	Redirect (ask another for agreement elaboration)
Refocus (shift direction of thought)	Rephrase (reword, subdivide, give information)

DISCUSSION LEADER ROLES

Initiator (plans and states initial problem, question, experience for discussion)

Gatekeeper (encourages/evenly spreads participation, keeps group on track—both time and content)

Giver/asker for reactions (promotes interpersonal response and interaction instead of just sequential recitation)

Information and problem manager (provides/solicits more information as needed, manages problems)

Clarifier, synthesizer. summarizer (at beginning, ending, and other times as needed)

Recorder (or have student record discussion contributions and points made)

Note: Adapted from Andrews (1980). *Effective classroom questioning.* University of Illinois at Urbana-Champaign, Office of Instructional Resources; and Hill (1977).

themselves, and then read Svinicki and Dixon's (1998) article that presents sets of learning activities that address each of the underlying dimensions of Kolb's four learning styles. Students use an observational chart, based on the various learning activities suggested by Svinicki and Dixon for each dimension—concrete experience, reflective observation, abstract conceptualization, and active experimentation—to guide and record their observations regarding LSDT.

The Clinical Setting for Teaching, Observation, Analysis, and Feedback-Giving

The classroom layout for the teaching-learning clinic is a setting that is both spatially distinctive and, more importantly, analytically meaningful. There are several key features of the setting. Every student is assigned a different role for each class. The categories of roles include a teacher, a student in the teacher's class, an observer of theory-and-research-based teaching strategies, and an observer of teaching skills. These categories of roles can be rearranged into three conceptually distinct aspects of the clinical setting, as illustrated in Figure 10.1. First, those playing the roles of teacher and student sit in the middle of the front of the room and constitute a "fishbowl" in which the activities of a realistic classroom take place. For each three-hour class period, two students are assigned the role of teacher, and are asked to prepare a 15- to 20-minute lesson plan; unlike the five-minute lesson taught earlier in the semester, this lesson must be based on the subject matter of each person's own area of academic specialization. Three individuals are assigned the role of students in the teacher's class, while a fourth student role is filled by those assuming the roles of teacher, who alternate between student and teacher roles between the two lessons. Making sure there are four individuals playing the student role is essential so that small group activities (i.e., two students per group) in a lesson can be meaningfully simulated. Under these conditions, the lessons, including interactions between teacher and students, and among students, are surprisingly, impressively, and usefully realistic. Second, several small groups of students are assigned the roles of observing the teaching-learning lesson before them in terms of the conceptual perspective of either motivational, cognitive, or social strategies; and as described above, each student uses an appropriate checklist to record their observations. Third, several small groups of students are assigned the roles of observing the teaching-learning lesson in terms of several sets of specific teaching skills—elocutionary, questioning and responding, discussion-leading, and learning-style-differentiated teaching.

After each lesson, each individual playing a student role writes a "Dear Teacher" letter to the person who just taught the lesson, providing the teacher with feedback, from the unique perspective of the student, about what it felt like to be a student in their class. At the close of the lesson, the observers complete the written recording of their feedback for the teacher and begin their meeting with others who observed the teaching from a similar theoretical perspective (e.g., cognitive strategies or discussion leading skills). After comparing and discussing observations, each observer-group identifies their most essential observations and divides the responsibility for presenting those observations to the entire class. Even though each observer and each observer group actually witnesses the very same lesson, what they actually observe and report varies greatly according to the theoretical or skills-based perspective from

FIGURE 10.1
The Classroom Layout for the Clinical Format of the Course

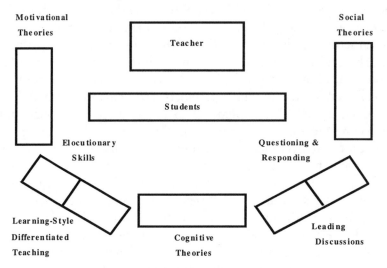

which each individual and group conducts its observation. As observers share their key observations with the whole class and present their feedback orally to the individual who taught the lesson, a very rich, textured, and multidimensional portrayal of the lesson emerges. These data, in turn, provides a detailed and comprehensive basis for an analytic study and discussion of the lesson by all participants in the class.

The observers' reference to what the teacher or students thought or how they felt is a cue to literally ask those who played the role of a student or the teacher to describe in their own words how they really did feel or what they really did think, from their unique perspectives in the lesson. Observers from a particular perspective initiate the discussion with their oral reports of key observations. However, those observing the lesson from alternative theoretical or skills-based perspectives, as well as those who experienced the lesson from the unique perspectives of the student and the teacher, become engaged together as respondents and analysts in the class' social construction of the practical meanings and importance of the teaching and learning behaviors just experienced. All participants join together in a careful consideration of how what they have observed and interpreted relates to existing theory and research on teaching and learning. Throughout the entire observation-sharing, feedback-giving, and analytical aspects of the discussion, the teacher remains in the front of the room, in the very same place as they were during the lesson itself. This approach serves to encourage the observers to direct their observations as feedback to the teacher, which they learn to present in a very constructive tone because they know very well that they too will be, or already have been, in the teacher role. And each member of the class can readily empathize with how vulnerable one can feel when every aspect of the content, words, actions, facial expressions, and so forth that constitute the lesson, are carefully scrutinized by a room full of other people. This approach also helps each person, when they are the one in the teacher role, to become accustomed to being the center of such detailed and, in some ways quite personal, attention and scrutiny; and to realize that taking such risks, with our colleagues and our students, is what gives us opportunities to learn and grow as teachers. Finally, this clinical, interactive setting fosters the norm that indeed, teaching is "community property," something that is, by its very nature, accessible, and appropriate for peer review (Hutchings & Shulman, 1999). And this is a view that clearly has important implications for the value placed on such faculty work in the teaching cultures of colleges and universities (Paulsen & Feldman, 1995) and how such value is manifested in related personnel decision-making processes (Diamond, 1993).

CREATING PEDAGOGICAL CONTENT KNOWLEDGE: A REFLECTIONS PAPER

The general principles of effective pedagogy, grounded in traditional educational research, constitute only one component of the knowledge base for effective teaching. The teaching-learning process, by its very nature, is content-specific. Therefore, another important component of the knowledge base for teaching emerges from a teacher's reflection on the application of general pedagogical knowledge to the unique challenges of teaching in their own content area.

Making Connections: An Act of Creation

The result of such reflective practice—that is, examining the special nature of applying general principles to the teaching of specific content—is the creation of pedagogical content knowledge (PCK) (Shulman, 1987). Recently, researchers and other scholars of teaching have referred to these acts of creation as one of the features of the scholarship of teaching (Kreber, 1999b; Paulsen, 2000). Furthermore, because different teachers—even in the same content area—have unique personalities, learning and teaching styles, and beliefs and assumptions about the teaching-learning process, the act of creating PCK must naturally be, to some extent, teacher-specific as well as content-specific. Based on this perspective, students are asked to think of their PCK as being unique to each of them as individual teachers who teach in a specialized content area.

To promote the creation of PCK, students are encouraged to keep a journal of their reflections on the various ways in which the readings and classroom experiences throughout this course relate to and have practical and meaningful implications for the special challenges of teaching in their own fields. By the end of the course, students are asked to complete a paper based on a reflective and critical analysis of the relationships between the general principles and practices of effective teaching and the unique challenges of facilitating college student learning in their own teaching fields.

Experiential or Hypothetical Courses

Students choose one of two approaches to their PCK papers. If a student has had college teaching experience, their reflections and analyses can be experiential; otherwise, their reflections and analyses can be speculative. Students are very creative in their PCK papers. Those using the experiential approach sometimes actually engage in classroom research during the semester to help them create PCK. And those taking the speculative approach are equally creative. For example, in order to expand the range of PCK created, one student designed a course in African American Women's Literature that would be uniquely cross-listed in the English department, the Women's Studies Program, and the African American Studies Program. In this way, she was able to explore the special challenges of teaching the content to students who would come to the class from three very different sets of background and motivations or reasons for taking the course. My personal view is that the students' creation of PCK is one of the most valuable outcomes of the course. Indeed, some of the students' efforts would merit publication as pedagogical contributions to content-specific journals.

EVALUATION OF THE COURSE

Both quantitative (student ratings) and qualitative (written comments) evaluation data for this course are available for the most recent six years, those being the years I have taught this course at my current university. Because this course is cross-listed between my department and another, evaluation data are available based on two different official course evaluation forms, one of them based on a 4-point Likert scale and the other on a 5-point scale. I have taught the course eight times in the past six years, during which time students' overall ratings of the course have averaged 3.9 on a 4-point scale and 4.8 on a 5-point scale. A number of persistent themes have appeared in students' written comments in their course evaluations. For example, students often identify the clinical portion of the course as especially worthwhile: "The setup of the class, [with] a high level of peer teaching and peer learning is the only way I would want to take a course such as this." Others appreciate the "careful intertwining of theory, practice and experience" and the "clinic format [that is] useful in translating theory into practice." Another theme is based on students' appreciation of the solid research-based theoretical foundation of the course; that is, they like the fact that the approach taken in this course makes it possible "to bring actual theory of teaching and learning into a clinical setting which is hands-on." Students also appreciate the feature of the course that "creates a very safe environment for students to work in the class" and the "trusting atmosphere of inclusively and opportunity for growth" that characterizes the classroom environment. Another persistent theme expressed by students is that the course "should be mandatory for every college teacher no matter what rank."

Students have also offered insightful suggestions for improvement. For example, some would like to see "longer teaching in clinics, perhaps limit[ing] discussion to 30 minutes and letting teaching be for 30 minutes," or "would recommend the use of videotapes to assist teaching. Have students video[tape] their lessons and then do a self-critique." These are potentially valuable enhancements. I support both ideas and have experimented with them over the years, but have always found that although additional assignments, such as videotaping, are clearly of great value to some students they push, for the majority them beyond the limits of what they are willing and able to accomplish within the confines of what is already an intensely demanding set of course requirements. Nevertheless, I strongly encourage ongoing experimentation with variations on what to include or exclude in a one-semester course.

PERSONAL REFLECTIONS: CHALLENGES THE STUDENTS AND I HAVE FACED

The complex role plays that constitute most of the clinical component of the course require a high level of commitment and dedication on the part of the students, especially in terms of attendance and tardiness.

Because classes are typically filled with busy faculty and graduate students, a certain amount of both tardiness and absenteeism has proven to be unavoidable. Therefore, I have found it necessary to have a minimum of two students assigned to each of the observer role categories. Then, when an absence or tardiness does occur, no one perspective for classroom observation is missed entirely. However, if one of those individuals assigned to play the role of student is tardy, the clinic cannot begin until that role is filled. Rather than ask another student to switch roles, I have elected to play the part of student myself in such instances so that the availability of a particular theoretical or skill-based perspective for classroom observation and analysis is not compromised. This has worked quite well. In fact, the students seem to have a good deal of fun watching me struggle—as I invariably do—in the role of student. In fact, I have often been labeled the problem student in the class, which all agree just makes the role-play even more realistic!

I am always amazed at how effectively most students seem to be able to somehow actively attend to quite a large number of motivational, cognitive, social, or skill-based teaching strategies when they observe a lesson. Nevertheless, it is rare that a student can meaningfully attend to all 28 motivational strategies or all 28 cognitive strategies at the same time. Because such an expectation is unrealistic, I typically encourage the two or three students assigned to a particular observational perspective, such as cognitive strategies, to divide up the subcategories in a fair and practical way. This has proven to be quite effective, and increases the observational coverage of the variety of strategies on the checklists.

For some who teach the college-teaching course, departmental requirements to submit a grade for each student based on a summative evaluation may appear problematic. I have faced this challenge over the years and have sometimes felt perplexed by it. Although I still have not resolved all the relevant issues to my own satisfaction, I have elected to do all I can to make summative evaluation a nonissue. I have let the faculty developer in me take charge in the area of evaluation. Students in the college-teaching course are diverse. Each is working on his or her own developmental issues. Some are struggling just to speak clearly and audibly, while others are enjoying the challenges of managing complex cooperative learning structures. For better or worse, I operate on the assumption that each day, each teacher—whether novice or experienced—begins anew their development, and each day a person can only address the challenges that lie immediately before them. I try to evaluate students' in-class work based on evidence of their preparation for class, their active engagement and involvement in class, their efforts to improve as teachers and to support their peers in such efforts.

CONCLUSION

I hope that my presentation of the goals, theoretical foundations, learning activities, evaluative information, and materials developed and used in this course, will be useful to others who teach, or plan to teach, a full-semester, credit-earning graduate course on college teaching. Furthermore, I hope others will share with me, and other interested teachers and faculty developers, their own experiences and experiments with similar courses so that we all might learn more effective ways to design such courses. This is especially important, because at many colleges and universities, one course in college teaching constitutes the first, and sometimes the only, substantial investment in the enhancement of teaching and learning.

REFERENCES

Andrews, J. D.W. (1980). The verbal structure of teacher questions: Its impact on class discussion. *POD Quarterly, 2* (3&4), 129–163.

Angelo, T., & Cross, K. P. (1993). *Classroom assessment techniques.* San Francisco, CA: Jossey-Bass.

Billson, J., & Tiberius, R. (1991). Effective social arrangements for teaching and learning. In R. Menges & M. Svinicki (Eds.), *College teaching: From theory to practice.* (pp. 87–110). New Directions for Teaching and Learning, No. 45. San Francisco, CA: Jossey-Bass.

Border, L. L. (1993). The graduate teacher certification program: Description and assessment after two years. In K. Lewis (Ed.), *The TA experience: Preparing for multiple roles* (pp. 113–121). Stillwater, OK: New Forums.

Bosworth, K., & Hamilton, S. J. (Eds.). (1994). *Collaborative learning: Underlying processes and effective techniques.* New Directions for Teaching and Learning, No. 59. San Francisco, CA: Jossey-Bass.

Brookfield, S. D. (1995). *Becoming a critically reflective teacher.* San Francisco, CA: Jossey-Bass.

Brophy, J. (1987). Synthesis of research on strategies for motivating students to learn. *Educational Leadership, 45* (2), 41–48.

Butler, K. A. (1987). *Learning and teaching style: In theory and practice.* Columbia, CT: The Learner's Dimension.

Cashin, W. (August, 1979). *Motivating students.* IDEA paper no. 1. Manhattan, KS: Kansas State University, Center for Faculty Evaluation and Development.

Claxton, C. S., & Murrell, P. H. (1987). *Learning styles: Implications for improving education practices.* ASHE-ERIC Higher Education Report No. 4. Washington, DC: Association for the Study of Higher Education.

Davis, B. G. (1993). *Tools for teaching.* San Francisco, CA: Jossey-Bass.

Diamond, N., Sharp, G., & Ory, J. (1983). *Improving your lecturing.* Urbana, IL: Office of Instructional Resources, University of Illinois at Urbana-Champaign.

Diamond, R. M. (1993). Changing priorities and the faculty reward system. In R. M. Diamond & B. E. Adam (Eds.), *Recognizing faculty work: Reward systems for the year 2000.* (pp. 5–12). New Directions for Higher Education, No. 81. San Francisco, CA: Jossey-Bass.

Feldman, K. A. (1998). Identifying exemplary teachers and teaching: Evidence from student ratings. In K. Feldman & M. Paulsen (Eds.), *Teaching and learning in the college classroom.* (2nd ed., pp. 391–414). Needham Heights, MA: Simon & Schuster.

Feldman, K. A., & Paulsen, M. B. (Eds.). (1998). *Teaching and learning in the college classroom.* (2nd ed.). Needham Heights, MA: Simon & Schuster.

Gagne, R. M. (1974). *Essentials of learning for instruction.* Hinsdale, IL: Dryden.

Glazer, J. S. (1993). *A teaching doctorate: The doctor of arts degree, then and now.* Washington, DC: American Association for Higher Education.

Hill, W. F. (1977). *Learning through discussion.* Beverly Hills, CA: Sage Publications.

Hutchings, P., & Shulman, L. S. (1999). The scholarship of teaching: New elaborations, new developments. *Change, 31* (5), 11–15.

Jenrette, M. S., & Napoli, V. (1994). *The teaching-learning enterprise.* Bolton, MA: Anker.

Keller, J. (1983). Motivational design of instruction. In C. M. Reigeluth (Ed.), *Instructional design theories and models* (pp. 383–433). Hillsdale NJ: Lawrence Erlbaum.

Kolb, D. W. (1998). Learning styles and disciplinary differences. In K. Feldman

& M. Paulsen (Eds.), *Teaching and learning in the college classroom* (2nd ed.). (pp. 127–138). Needham Heights, MA: Simon & Schuster.

Kreber, C. (1999a). A course-based approach to the development of teaching-scholarship; A case study. *Teaching in Higher Education, 4* (3), 309–325.

Kreber, C. (1999b). *Defining and implementing the scholarship of teaching: The results of a Delphi study.* Paper presented at the annual meeting of the Canadian Society for the Study of Higher Education (CSSHE), Sherbrooke, Quebec.

Lambert, L. M. (1993). Beyond TA orientations: Reconceptualizing the Ph.D. degree in terms of preparation for teaching. In K. G. Lewis (Ed.), *The TA experience: Preparing for multiple roles.* (pp. 107–112). Stillwater, OK: New Forums.

Lefrancois, G. (1991). *Psychology for teaching.* Belmont, CA: Wadsworth.

Lowman, J. (1995). *Mastering the techniques of teaching.* San Francisco, CA: Jossey-Bass.

McKeachie, W. J. (1999). *Teaching tips* (10th ed.). Boston, MA: Houghton Mifflin.

Paulsen, M. B. (2000). The relation between research and the scholarship of teaching. In C. Kreber (Ed.), *Scholarship revisited: Defining and implementing the scholarship of teaching.* New Directions for Teaching and Learning, No. 82. San Francisco, CA: Jossey-Bass.

Paulsen, M. B. & Feldman, K. A. (1995). *Taking teaching seriously: Meeting the challenges of instructional improvement.* ASHE-ERIC Higher Education Report No. 2. Washington, DC: The George Washington University, School of Education and Human Development.

Paulsen, M. B., & Gentry, J. A. (1995). Motivation, learning strategies, and academic performance: A study of the college finance classroom. *Financial Practice and Education, 5* (1), 78–89.

Pintrich, P. R. (1989). The dynamic interplay of student motivation and cognition in the college classroom. In M. Maehr and C. Ames (Eds.), *Advances in motivation and achievement: Goals and self-regulatory processes, 7.* (pp. 371–402). Greenwich, CT: JAI Press.

Pintrich, P. R., & Schunk, D. H. (1996). *Motivation in education.* Englewood Cliffs, NJ: Prentice Hall.

Schuster, J. H. (1993). Preparing the next generation of faculty: The graduate school's opportunity. In L. Richlin (Ed.), *Preparing faculty for the new conceptions of scholarship.* (pp. 27–38). New Directions for Teaching and Learning, No. 54. San Francisco, CA: Jossey-Bass.

Shulman, L. S. (1987). Knowledge and teaching: Foundations of the new reform. *Harvard Educational Review, 57*, 1–22.

Svinicki, M. D., & Dixon, N. (1998). The Kolb model modified for classroom activities. In K. Feldman & M. Paulsen (Eds.), *Teaching and learning in the college classroom* (2nd ed.). (pp. 577–584). Needham Heights, MA: Simon & Schuster.

Vahala, M. E., & Winston, R. B. (1994). College classroom environments: Disciplinary and institutional-type differences and effects on academic achievement in introductory courses. *Innovative Higher Education, 19* (2), 99–122.

Weinstein, C. E., & Mayer, R. (1986). The teaching of learning strategies. In M. Wittrock (Ed.), *Handbook of research on teaching.* (pp. 315–327). New York, NY: Macmillan.

Contact:

Michael B. Paulsen
Department of Educational Leadership, Counseling & Foundations
348 Bicentennial Education Center
University of New Orleans
New Orleans, LA 70148
(504) 280-6661
(504) 280-6453 (Fax)
Email: mpaulsen@uno.edu

Michael B. Paulsen is Professor of Higher Education in the Department of Educational Leadership, Counseling & Foundations at the University of New Orleans. His research and teaching interests are in college teaching, learning, and faculty development; and the economics and finance of higher education. Dr. Paulsen serves as Consulting Editor for *Research in Higher Education* and Associate Editor of *Higher Education: Handbook of Theory and Research*. He and Ken Feldman are coeditors of *Teaching and Learning in the College Classroom*, now in its second edition, and are coauthors of *Taking Teaching Seriously*.

11

Faculty Development that Transforms the Undergraduate Experience at a Research University

Kathleen S. Smith
University of Georgia

Rethinking the undergraduate experience at research universities is a necessary goal for the new millennium according to the Boyer Commission on Educating Undergraduates (1998). Faculty development efforts provide a starting place for a transformation of the traditional teaching-learning model. This essay describes the faculty development support structure included in a FIPSE sponsored program to promote learning by inquiry. The Center for Undergraduate Research Opportunities (CURO) at the University of Georgia meshes teaching and research so that undergraduate students become participants in the strengths of a research university by becoming part of a community of learners.

INTRODUCTION

Research universities have the potential to offer a virtually matchless education because of their wealth of intellectual power and resources, according to the Boyer Commission on Educating Undergraduates in the Research University (1998). However, most undergraduates are not benefiting from the strengths of the research university, including the opportunity to participate in research and to interact with active research faculty and graduate students. This essay describes a FIPSE-sponsored project which affords undergraduates, research faculty, and graduate students a mechanism to become a community of learners sharing their particular expertise and insights with each other.

193

THE CENTER FOR UNDERGRADUATE RESEARCH OPPORTUNITIES

In 1997, the honors program, in cooperation with the Office of Instructional Support and Development and the Office of Sponsored Programs of the Vice President for Research at The University of Georgia, submitted a proposal to the Foundation for Improving Post Secondary Education (FIPSE) entitled "Synergizing Research and Education: A Center for Undergraduate Research Opportunities." The proposal outlined a mechanism to encourage a more learner-centered university by establishing a Center for Undergraduate Research Opportunities (CURO). CURO's purpose is to enhance opportunities for undergraduates to undertake individual research, to support faculty initiatives to make a role for undergraduate students in their research, and to provide graduate students serving as research assistants with training in the mentoring and management of student research personnel. The proposal was funded by FIPSE, and CURO activities began in the fall of 1997.

CURO ACTIVITIES

Faculty Development Efforts

The Office of Instructional Support and Development (OISD) provides the mechanism to communicate with faculty and graduate students who might be interested in working with an undergraduate. Well-established new faculty orientations, teaching assistant (TA) workshops, teaching support seminars, OISD publications, and web pages advertise the CURO opportunity. OISD staff members also coordinate the CURO TA support seminars.

Each fall, new faculty participate in a two-day orientation conducted by the faculty development office which includes an invitation to join the CURO faculty. These faculty agree to accept undergraduate researchers and to provide opportunities for undergraduates to work on a portion of their research or to provide mentoring in research skills for a student who may be working on an independent research project.

Experienced research faculty are also invited to teach one of the courses undergraduates might take to develop their project. These courses provide a forum for experienced research faculty to guide a group of undergraduates in the development of a research question and in setting up a research project. The courses include guidance in writing a project abstract, and in developing a bibliography, an annotated outline of the project, and a hypothesis. The class members work on identifying a methodology for each project and a project time line. Each member has a fully developed research proposal by the end of the class. Once projects are established, research faculty are the teacher of record for an independent credit seminar where individual students work one-on-one with the faculty member and a graduate student on an independent project.

Individual mentoring of undergraduates in this setting is fairly costly in terms of time allocation, so an essential element of the Center for Undergraduate Research Opportunities is a program to develop mentoring skills for graduate students so they may effectively help the faculty member work with the undergraduate. These graduate student scholars constitute the unique strengths of a research university. Those who are awarded assistantships are usually the best and brightest students in their discipline and afford undergraduates a wonderful source of inspiration and expertise. Since graduate teaching and laboratory assistants are very involved in the lower division courses, they can help undergraduates identify areas of interest and faculty members who might have research opportunities. Graduate students can suggest the many avenues to pursue a research project including internship possibilities, credit classes, and individual research interests. In addition, they can guide students in the process of participating in the Center for Undergraduate Research Opportunities (Figure 11.1).

This graduate assistant mentoring is crucial to get projects started and to manage the mechanics of the various stages of the project. Graduate students also act as the liaison to the faculty member of the team and, when necessary, provide opportunities for the undergraduate to interact directly with the faculty member as well as keep all members of the team updated on the progress of the research. Patricia Cross (1998) has documented the value of working in this type of learning community and argues they have a sound philosophical, research, and pragmatic base. The 1998 Boyer Commission report also endorsed learning communities structure with the statement that participants are more experienced than others, some are far along the way toward academic maturity, and some are not. Still, all are committed to the exploration of defined areas of knowledge, and in the university, as envisioned here, they work together. Faculty members, graduate students, and baccalaureate students all bring their particular combinations of energy, imagination, experience, and accumulated knowledge to bear.

TA Development Support Structure

An essential component of the CURO support effort is to provide a mechanism for graduate students to broaden their graduate experience as they mentor undergraduates. During the first two years of the project, the

FIGURE 11.1
Undergraduate Research Opportunities

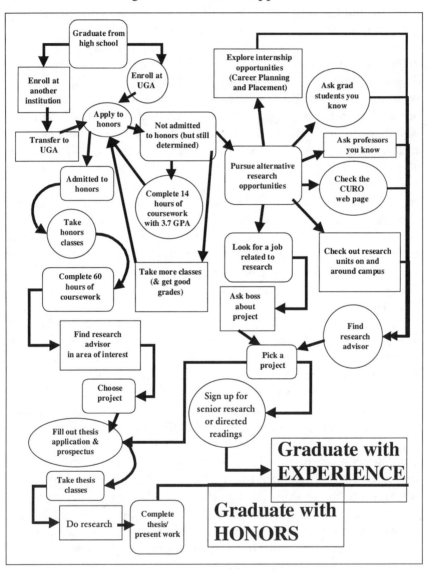

CURO TAs identified a number of reasons graduate students would benefit from the mentoring experience (see Figure 11.2). For graduate students preparing for academic careers, this kind of experience reflects future faculty roles (Gaff & Lambert, 1996). Supervision of projects also provides leadership opportunities, which can prepare graduate students for roles in business and the private sector.

Since the role of graduate students as members of the learning community is so crucial to the feasibility of widespread undergraduate research opportunities, we have focused on providing extensive support for the graduate assistant mentoring role. An annual fall workshop introduces the Center for Undergraduate Research Opportunities, outlines the benefits of developing this aspect of university scholarship, and details mentoring strategies which have proven successful in working with undergraduates. CURO TAs who have successfully mentored undergraduates in the research setting lead this workshop and provide a source of inspiration for new graduate teaching and laboratory assistants as they begin their graduate program.

CURO TA Seminars

The annual fall workshop is followed up by a series of CURO TA-led seminars to address discipline-specific issues. We have made efforts to select CURO TAs in both the sciences and humanities. Early in the fall semester, graduate students are invited to attend seminar sessions led by experienced CURO TAs. These include discussions on teaching undergraduates the techniques and safety issues needed to work in a laboratory, as well as sessions on time management, improving writing and independent thinking skills, and teaching the scientific process. We also address techniques to involve students in research, to start a student on a research project, and to teach library research skills. All sessions include discussions on the importance of technical and scientific preparation before beginning research, the ethics of research, and expectations for accurate documentation. Most important for the graduate students' future careers are discussions with the experienced CURO TAs on the constructive, supportive, and creative management of research that encourages the learning-by-inquiry concept of teaching.

Graduate assistants who complete these seminars and who successfully supervise undergraduates are invited to apply for an additional fractional graduate assistantship of $500. These graduate students also participate in shaping and delivering the CURO TA seminars the following fall.

FIGURE 11.2

**15 Good Reasons for Graduate Students to
Mentor Undergraduate Researchers**

1. Provides a forum for the graduate student to work as a team with an undergraduate and a faculty member

2. Increases graduate student involvement with the research of the discipline

3. Helps the graduate student clarify their own research techniques

4. Provides an opportunity for an undergraduate researcher to explore a topic which could inform the graduate student's research or technique

5. Gives graduate students an opportunity to refine how they teach someone about their discipline

6. Creates an opportunity to work with an undergraduate in a mentoring role

7. Highlights and makes public the graduate student's expertise in the discipline

8. Reflects mentoring roles in future academic positions or the public sector

9. Enlarges the dimension of graduate preparation and provides an opportunity to document a role which might attract future employers

10. Could result in a publication

11. Helps graduate student explore writing strategies and the writing expectations in the discipline

12. Helps graduate student identify time management strategies which aid in meeting deadlines and in project completion

13. Contributes to synergizing research and teaching

14. Capitalizes on the strengths of a research university in having the best and brightest in the discipline (graduate students) interacting with undergraduates

15. Helps future employers identify the graduate student as someone willing to share your knowledge with others

Credit Classes

Regularly scheduled teaching support classes for graduate students have added a session on mentoring undergraduates in the research setting. A class web page provides sample projects, a description of a variety of research methods, and writing resources to help guide students in writing up the results. Other class sessions focus on the benefits of learner-centered approaches to guiding undergraduate learning. Each graduate assistant is asked to identify an aspect of their discipline or research in which undergraduates might be encouraged to conduct independent research.

Publications

The CURO TA opportunities and resources for mentoring undergraduates are also outlined in The teaching assistant newsletter and TA handbook received by every graduate teaching and laboratory assistant. CURO TAs also helped to adapt a mentoring brochure originally developed for mentoring graduate teaching assistants (Smith, 1995). This brochure uses basic mentoring concepts and applies them to the process of effective project management (see Figure 11.3) and effective undergraduate mentoring (Figure 11.4), (Smith & Klaper, 1999).

Effective project management (see Figure 11.3) involves encouraging undergraduates to work on a research project and helping them connect their research interests to existing faculty research or to individuals who can help them develop research skills. TAs are frequently asked to clarify roles, responsibilities, and support services for undergraduates. This kind of pre-project planning is essential to developing a sound project. For example, helping undergraduates to identify library sources, databases, and writing support helps immensely in getting students started on projects. A detailed written project description clarifies, early in the process, expectations and procedures for all members of the team. A list of the faculty, TA, and peer support structure also identifies the key people who can assist with the development of the project. To avoid unnecessary misunderstandings or accidents, policies related to safety and equipment use should also be discussed and posted. Frequent contact with the undergraduate to discuss specific project outcomes and to help resolve any problems is essential. This is where TAs can encourage faculty involvement and expertise.

Effective undergraduate mentoring (see Figure 11.4) encourages the best young scholars in a discipline, represented by an institution's graduate students, to interact with individual undergraduates. Lower-division classes are an ideal introduction to the culture of a discipline as

FIGURE 11.3
Mentoring Undergraduate Academic Projects
Effective Project Management

Pre-project Planning	Detailed Project Description	Frequent Contact
Includes a discussion of: *Ways to identify under-graduates who may be interested in a project and ways to link projects to interests of TAs and faculty in development stage *Supervision of faculty roles, responsibilities, benefits *TA role description, responsibilities, benefits *Undergraduate eligibility, responsibilities, benefits *An orientation to support services for undergraduates developing projects including sample projects, contact phone number, email, and web sites of resources *Details of the process to sign undergraduate up for project *Issues to address with undergraduate to start the project	Includes: *Written project description *Written description of project responsibilities and priorities *A list of project support systems including faculty contact, peer mentors, graduate assistant help *Discussion and written description of university policies that directly affect project and relevant issues of safety and liability *A written explanation of departmental policies on the use of equipment	Includes: *Regular meetings to discuss progress and formulate strategies for —time management —organizational skills —writing skills *Opportunities for peer mentoring to provide undergraduates with peer support in developing their project *Access to faculty and TAs to discuss specific project issues

undergraduates interact with their graduate assistants and faculty. Effective involvement in the discipline is crucial in encouraging their interest in a particular field. As interests develop, graduate assistants and faculty must be sensitive to the diverse needs of undergraduates as they help develop a project. Professional roles must be clearly outlined and a mechanism to communicate accomplishments and help in trouble shooting problems is essential to an atmosphere of mentoring, collaborating with, and challenging undergraduates in their intellectual development.

FIGURE 11.4
Mentoring Undergraduate Academic Projects
Effective Undergraduate Mentoring

Academic Socialization	Departmental Support	Developmental Support
Includes:	Includes:	Includes:
*Commitment and sensitivity to the diversity of undergraduates in terms of cultural, racial, gender, and ethnic backgrounds *Clearly stated professional roles for faculty, graduate assistants, and undergraduates (power relationships, dating, project responsibilities, etc.) *A mechanism to publicize accomplishments (web page, bulletin board, or library) *Constructive criticism and help in troubleshooting problems *Atmosphere of mentoring, collaborating with, and challenging undergraduates *Opportunities to guide students' intellectual development *Discussions with undergraduates on the culture of the discipline	*Posted departmental resources for undergraduate projects including contact people and technology use *Posted departmental information about skill development workshops *A mechanism for networking within the department to link resources with interests	*Project development workshops, credit classes, internships *Opportunities to learn about past projects *Close monitoring by faculty or supervising TA for formative purposes *Clearly stated project requirements and opportunities for revisions *Opportunities for self-reflection and growth in describing project *A variety of experiences linked to individual interests and project goals *Intellectually challenging and interesting projects that reflect future goals *Help in writing up the project experience

Graduate students provide the link to departmental support of the project and help model the culture of the discipline as they work with the undergraduate. Graduate assistants can also help the undergraduate identify experiences that will provide developmental support for their project. For example, they can identify past projects which may be helpful, and the classes and seminars an undergraduate can take to help develop their project. Graduate students also monitor the progress and help to identify aspects of the project that may need to be developed. Finally, graduate assistants can provide the structure for writing up the project in a format that reflects the style of the discipline.

EVALUATION

Before the establishment of the CURO effort, less than 20 honors theses were normally completed each year. An indication of the effectiveness of the CURO initiative is the increase in the number of students who attempt to complete a research project and write an honor's thesis. Currently there are 151 undergraduates enrolled for independent research credit. Forty-eight undergraduates completed their theses in the spring of 1999. More than 350 faculty have joined the CURO faculty willing to take on an undergraduate research student, and faculty are increasingly involving undergraduates in their funded research efforts. In addition, graduate students are actively seeking an opportunity to work with undergraduate students, which is another indicator of the effectiveness of the program because it provides an added dimension to graduate preparation. Graduate students completing the CURO TA program and successfully participating in the supervision of an undergraduate research project are provided with certification that enhances their professional portfolio. We will continue to assess the value of the preparation we provide for graduate students in supervising undergraduates.

Through the supervision of an outside evaluation consultant, we are also tracking participants to determine the subjective impact of work in faculty research programs and objective changes of undergraduate thinking about early career trajectories. In addition, we are tracking the number of undergraduates involved in extramurally supported research.

CONCLUSION

Adding the elements of managing and mentoring undergraduates in the research setting to the workshops, credit classes, and seminars has added an important dimension to faculty development and graduate preparation which has the potential to transform the undergraduate experience at a research university. The CURO initiative has made it possible to dramatically increase the number of undergraduates working on research projects, so funding for CURO will continue from the university beyond the initial FIPSE-sponsored program in order to further the success of the first three years of the project. The Office of Instructional Support and Development will continue to include the concept of undergraduate research and learning communities in its faculty and TA development efforts.

To implement this type of faculty development effort on other campuses, it is important to focus on the early inclusion of new faculty, the involvement of experienced research faculty, and the training of graduate assistants in the concept of learning communities. New faculty orientations and seminars can introduce undergraduate research as part of the campus culture. Senior faculty can be included by special invitation in a list of faculty willing to mentor a project. Capitalizing on the strengths of a research university, graduate assistants can be encouraged to provide the mechanism for large numbers of research faculty to work as a team with undergraduates. Universities might also work closely with departments that already conduct some undergraduate research to identify graduate students who might help other graduate students in mentoring individual undergraduates and in creating materials which faculty and TAs might find helpful. By making public the advantages of including this type of activity as part of graduate preparation, departments may be more willing to encourage all of their faculty and graduate students to participate in research teams. It can also be used as a recruitment incentive because undergraduates have better access to faculty via the graduate student and have an opportunity to work with the best young scholars in their disciplines. Including departments that have not been involved in this type of research by special invitation and recognition if they participate also involves more of the university. Supporting this kind of learning community (Cross, 1998) provides an effective means of managing projects and mentoring undergraduates and has the potential to transform the undergraduate experience at a research university.

REFERENCES

Boyer Commission on Educating Undergraduates in the Research University. (1998). *Reinventing undergraduate education: A blueprint for America's research universities*. Lawrenceville, NJ: The Carnegie Foundation for the Advancement of Teaching.

Cross, P. K. (1998). Why learning communities? Why now? *About Campus, 3* (3), 4–11.

Gaff, J. G., & Lambert, L. M. (1996, July/August). Socializing future faculty to the values of undergraduate education. *Change*, 38–45.

Smith, K. S. (1995). Managing and mentoring graduate teaching assistants at the

University of Georgia. In T. A. Heenan (Ed.), *Teaching graduate students to teach: Engaging the disciplines* (pp. 101–106). University of Illinois at Urbana-Champaign, Office of Conferences and Institutes.

Smith, K. S., & Klaper R. D. (1999). Graduate assistant involvement in transforming the undergraduate experience at research universities. *The Journal of Graduate Teaching Assistant Development, 6* (2), 95–102.

Contact:

Kathleen S. Smith
Senior Academic Professional
Office of Instructional Support & Development
Instructional Plaza
University of Georgia
Athens, GA 30602
(706) 542-1355
(706) 542-6587 (Fax)

Kathleen S. Smith has directed the TA Program for the Office of Instructional Support and Development at the University of Georgia since 1990 and the International Fellows Program since 1997. In collaboration with the honor's program, she directs the FIPSE-sponsored CURO TA program to encourage graduate students to mentor undergraduate research projects. Her research includes a longitudinal study of the career path of participants in the ten-year-old TA mentor program. The decade-old study includes data documenting the influence of graduate preparation on career choices and the transition into a faculty position. She gardens and sails for relaxation and is working on a novel about life in academia which parallels her research interests.

12

The Case for Sophisticated Course Syllabi

Michael J. Strada
West Virginia University and West Liberty State College

Just as the last thing a fish would notice is water, academics tend to overlook the value of a comprehensive course syllabus. It seems too prosaic for some instructors to take seriously. Despite operating largely in obscurity, a nascent body of literature appreciative of the syllabus' latent potential is emerging. The distinguishing features of model syllabi are traced here, and their respective benefits analyzed. First and foremost, good syllabi enhance student learning by improving the way courses are taught. But the potential of syllabi can also be tapped by using them more prominently in the faculty evaluation process. Much slower to develop has been an awareness of how exemplary syllabi can forge substantive links among three curricular levels of the academy often proceeding randomly: individual courses, programs of study at the departmental level, and general studies requirements at the institutional level. The assessment movement now sweeping American higher education can broaden its analytical base by recognizing the exemplary syllabus as a rare fulcrum uniting each of the three academic levels pursuing institutional mission statements.

SCOPE OF THE PROBLEM

Robert Diamond, a widely quoted analyst of American higher education, surveys the literature relating individual courses and institutional curricula and arrives at some unsettling conclusions. Specifically, Diamond decries the prevalence of courses designed with little or no relationship to the curriculum that is in place or to the critical skills students need to acquire, courses of study that are more serendipitous than planned, and higher education curricula that do not produce the results we intend (Diamond, 1998, p. 2).

I believe that one of the tools vital for attacking the problems cited by Diamond is a rigorous course syllabus. But just as the last thing a fish would notice is water, academics often overlook the value of a comprehensive syllabus. Indicative of the low status accorded to the syllabus in academe, no substantial body of literature exists on the subject because it seems too prosaic for sustained inquiry. However, students, professors, and curricular integrity would all benefit if institutions decided to uncork the latent potential of the syllabus, since the bloodless course outline sometimes passing as a syllabus is no more than a caricature of the genuine article.

The inadequacy of some course syllabi received considerable attention in a 1985 article that appeared in the *Chronicle of Higher Education*. Sharon Rubin's report on the findings of a course approval committee at the University of Maryland shed light on this nearly invisible phenomenon. Her faculty committee found a series of pivotal questions unanswered by most of the course syllabi that students received from their professors, such as Why should a student want to take this course? Why do the parts of the course come in this particular order? Will it consist mostly of lecture, discussion, or group work? What skills or knowledge will the tests test? Why have these specific books been chosen? Rubin paints a bleak portrait of her exposure to scores of weak course syllabi. She says that the worst ones fell into two groups: the listers—those whose bare-bones outlines tell what is to be read and done, but without any hint of the principles behind the course; and the scolders—those who read more like caveats from a defense lawyer than heuristic tips from a professor, by detailing the consequences of myriad misbehaviors. The scolders seem intent on practicing defensive pedagogy in a litigious age. Overall, Rubin concludes that the pervasiveness of inadequate syllabi symbolizes an unhealthy deterioration of communication between teachers and students. Such poor communication must seem worrisome to Howard Altman and William Cashin, who write elsewhere that the primary purpose of a syllabus is to communicate to one's students what the course is about, why it is taught, where it's going, and what will be required of them to complete it successfully (Altman & Cashin, 1992, p. 3).

The good things accompanying the metamorphosis from weak two-pagers to dense, thoughtful ten-pagers, are well-kept secrets. Faculty seldom champion the value of the course syllabus—a document considered destined for student eyes only. The time-honored principle of academic freedom also exacerbates the problem of the underachieving syllabus by shielding against unsolicited interference into the sanctity of the professor's classroom space. When this happens, faculty isolation and resistance to change naturally result. Another contributing factor is psychological denial on the part of some professors. I have heard colleagues remark that a ten-page syllabus qualifies as an exercise in futility. Why? Because such a tome is supposedly too long for students to read, even though the same instructors may routinely assign students more than 1,000 pages to read during a semester. Many students are savvy enough to recognize the syllabus ten pages as the most important ten pages of the course; those less savvy students we can enlighten didactically by explaining how milking the syllabus for all it's worth serves their best interests. In my introductory social science course, I give a syllabus quiz on the second day of class to highlight the status of the syllabus (I will send a copy of this 23-pager to anyone requesting it). Other ideas for making students conversant with the syllabus include placing them periodically in small groups to discuss certain parts of it; asking them to write brief reaction papers that analyze sections of the syllabus; and having them evaluate the syllabus by specifying what they like, dislike, and recommend for revision.

ESSENTIAL ELEMENTS OF SOPHISTICATED SYLLABI

In the most comprehensive work to date on syllabi, Judith Grunert (1997) offers many useful suggestions, all of which advise that professors think through the content, as well as the process, before constructing their syllabi. Grunert envisions a reflective exercise powerful enough to improve courses by clarifying hidden beliefs and assumptions as part of a well-developed philosophical rationale for the course. The professor's unique academic soul should shine through in an elegant syllabus. Students benefit when they can glean from the syllabus exactly what it is that professors want them to be able to do and exactly how they will be assessed when they do it. Only by carefully planning a course can these lofty objectives come to fruition. What Grunert advocates might more ambitiously be called a course manual rather than a standard course syllabus. She looks with disfavor on documents skimmed over during the first class meeting and then filed away. Rather, she prefers dog-earred learning tools, use frequently as reference documents, that give more than mere information. Students should develop the habit of using these tools. Stripped to bare essentials, Grunert's ideal syllabus seeks to:

- Describe the course content, including its goals and objectives

- Describe the structure of the course and its significance within the general program of study

- Discuss what mutual obligation students and instructors share

- Provide logistical as well as procedural information about what will happen, when, and where

Another useful model providing the nuts and bolts required to construct exemplary syllabi comes from Howard Altman and William Cashin (1992). They advocate building 11 components into the very architecture of the serious syllabus:

1) **Course information**: title, number, credits, prerequisites, location, meeting time

2) **Instructor information**: name, title, office number, hours, phone, email

3) **Readings**: textbook author, publisher, cost, why it was chosen, and how extensively it will be used, supplementary readings, and whether required or recommended

4) **Course goals** (more general) and **student learning outcomes** (more specific)

5) **Course description**: content of the course and how it fits into the broader curriculum

6) **Instructional methods**: the relative weight of respective pedagogical techniques (e.g., lecture, case study, small group discussion, values clarification, games, journal writing) should be explicated

7) **Course calendar**: a schedule (daily or weekly) of time structuring that identifies substance as well as dates for all assignments

8) **Course policies**: specific rules of the game concerning issues like attendance, tardiness, class participation, make-up exams, and plagiarism

9) **Grading**: how students will be evaluated, what factors will be included, their relative value, and how they will be tabulated into grades all resonate in the student psyche

10) **Checklist**: a listing of all course assignments at the end of document helps students keep track of what must be done and when

11) **Support services**: in what ways can the library, learning center, tutoring service, advising center, or computer center help students to succeed in this course? (Altman & Cashin, 1992, pp. 3-4)

HEURISTIC BENEFITS OF SOPHISTICATED SYLLABI

First and foremost, fine syllabi serve to enhance student learning. Since college courses vary greatly, and since professors bring their uniqueness with them when they enter the classroom door, students don't really know what to expect during the pivotal first class session. Marie Birdsall (1989) cites research suggesting that the fear of the unknown produces anxious students on the first day of class. She argues that a thorough syllabus represents the best means of reducing student anxiety, thus launching the course in the right direction.

A thoughtful syllabus also works in a variety of more subtle ways: as a window revealing the philosophical disposition of the instructor; as a cognitive map showing why the intellectual terrain covered is important; as a model conveying to students the belief that planning has pedagogical value; as a contract binding the parties together; as a message that good teaching is important, and is facilitated by a model syllabus; as an antidote to the deterioration of communication between professor and student criticized above by Rubin; as testimony that excellent teachers have high expectations for themselves, as well as for their students; as a resource germane to the faculty evaluation process; and as the only substantive link between individual courses and the mission pursued by the wider curriculum. Diamond's book (1998) includes quotations taken from various professors who have reflected on the benefits flowing from their shift to a comprehensive syllabus. In the words of one instructor: "It helped a great deal. Faculty colleagues from other institutions have been able to easily adapt and adopt the course with limited guidance. In addition, I have very few requests for clarification of course requirements, time lines, grading criteria, or weekly assignments. Perhaps some faculty look forward to such repeated discussions—I prefer to teach" (Diamond, 1998, p. 195).

How the course syllabus can be used to improve teaching and to reduce time spent on housekeeping chores is easy to envision. But how the syllabus can aid in the evaluation of teaching remains somewhat opaque to many academic eyes. Too seldom do academic administrators conceptualize the syllabus as germane to assessing faculty performance. No department head would consider evaluating an untenured instructor without a class visit, and rightly so. But sometimes a sole visit becomes a pivotal event in evaluating an instructor, even though that session is not necessarily representative of the rest of the course. Administrators also ought to identify model syllabi and encourage faculty to emulate such documents. An elegant one operates as a nexus linking a class visit to the instructor's course objectives, readings, exams, and pedagogical techniques (which may differ from those of the evaluator). By discussing atypical techniques—such as group inquiry activities, writing across the curriculum or peer grading—the instructor can use the syllabus to explain why these methods make sense for this course.

Most experienced professors sense intuitively that when they plan ahead, organize their work well, and inform students exactly what they want, better teaching produces better learning. These hunches are confirmed in a recent study examining commonalties found among Carnegie Professors of the Year recognized by the Council for Advancement and Support of Education (CASE). University of Georgia management professor John Lough, who spawned the idea of dissecting the behavior of Carnegie Professors of the Year to see what makes them tick, set out to discover what in business studies is referred to as best practices benchmarking: in this context, behaviors associated with superior teaching.

One universal characteristic cited by Lough is that great teachers are very well organized, and their syllabi reflect this fact. The syllabi are written with rather detailed precision. Clearly stated course objectives and requirements are a hallmark. Typically, there is a precisely laid out day-by-day schedule showing specific reading assignments as well as other significant requirements and due dates (Roth, 1996, p. 220). The editor of this fine volume, John Roth, Professor of Holocaust Studies at Claremont McKenna College, reinforces Lough's conclusion that great teachers are organized: they focus their concentration. Roth also notes that a broad, interdisciplinary curiosity characterizes Carnegie Professors of the Year, as does a love of research, dispelling the persistent myth that teaching and research are mutually exclusive. Outstanding teachers do not regard teaching and research as two separate activities. One informs the other (Roth, 1996, p. 227).

The solid planning endemic to exemplary syllabi can also yield dividends for both departmental and institutional curricula. This insight is driven home in one of the articles contributed to the Roth volume by 1994 Carnegie Professor of the Year Anthony Lisska, Professor of Philosophy and Director of the Honors Program at Denison University. Lisska emphasizes that curricular structures matter because they impact the learning process in profound ways. While neither as overt, nor as exciting, as the performance dimension to teaching, a rigorous syllabus enhances the academic structure which in turn enhances pedagogical success, and Lisska cites the honors program at Dension as illustrative. We don't immediately see the connections among curriculum, what curriculum structures enable us to do pedagogically, and how these structures assist in the development of the craft of teaching (Roth, 1996, p. 90). Professor Lisska's intriguing admonition that curricular structures (including fine syllabi) matter, should not be dismissed as too abstract to operationalize.

The potential exists for the course syllabus to forge substantive links between the three curricular levels of the academy that Diamond suggests often proceed in random directions: 1) the demonstration of quality teaching and learning in specific courses, 2) coherent and consistent programs of integrity at the departmental level, and, 3) institution-wide general studies requirements—all of which should contribute to the general mission statements of colleges and universities. Only by institutionalizing the sophisticated course syllabus can we aspire to connect individual courses to departmental programs to general studies to mission statements. Only comprehensive course syllabi provide detailed snapshots of what actually transpires inside the four walls of college classrooms. Only substantial course syllabi enable us to link intelligently the three different levels of curricular modernization now taking place in US higher education. And only dense course syllabi provide soft data to augment the hard data typically generated to satisfy contemporary demands for curricular accountability emanating from oversight bodies.

MODEL SYLLABI AND OTHER RESOURCES

The West Virginia Consortium for Faculty and Course Development in International Studies (FACDIS) consists of 375 faculty members representing more than 15 disciplines and coming from all 20 institutions of higher education in West Virginia—public- and private-sector colleges, community colleges, and universities. For the past 20 years, the FACDIS statewide consortium has conducted numerous projects internationalizing the content of extant courses and creating new courses. FACDIS believes that solid course syllabi not only improve specific courses but also energize innovation in the general curriculum, and provide the mechanisms to make curricular reform accountable. Consequently, the consortium has overseen the transformation of hundreds of modest two-pagers into far more ambitious documents. While length alone may not constitute a sufficient condition for a dynamic course syllabus, it is nevertheless a necessary condition.

Similarly committed to rigorous course syllabi is the Semester at Sea program (SAS). Funded in part by the Institute for Shipboard Education, and based since 1980 at the University of Pittsburgh, SAS circles the globe twice annually with 600 students and 50 faculty and administrators aboard this sailing university. Academic courses in many disciplines are taught during 50 days at sea, and course-relevant field trips occur while visiting port cities. When I taught on the SAS faculty in 1990, professors had to submit detailed and defensible syllabi, since this unique program is routinely challenged to demonstrate the academic rigor of a floating campus visiting a dozen countries in four months. All syllabi required the approval of the relevant host department at the University of Pittsburgh before professors' courses were accepted into that semester's academic program. I read all course syllabi accepted for our voyage and found them to contain both depth and complexity.

Another organization that recognizes how excellent syllabi improve the curriculum is the Fund for the Improvement of Post-Secondary Education (FIPSE). From 1990–92, FIPSE funded a model syllabus program with the American Political Science Association (APSA), resulting in 11 monographs of 100-plus pages covering the discipline's key courses. Exemplary syllabi are solicited, veteran scholars select a few of the best ones, the editor writes a synthesis citing common themes among the elite syllabi, and the top syllabi are described and analyzed. The collection of syllabi for international relations, edited by Emory University's Linda Brady (1991), observes that those selected all present alternative theoretical perspectives, make theories concrete by using historical examples or case studies, keep students informed about contemporary affairs, and treat the course as a vehicle to develop research or writing skills. All of these APSA model syllabi collections can be found on the APSA website. Similarly, the American Sociological Association's website makes model syllabi readily available to interested faculty. Countless syllabi spanning both the humanities and social sciences can be easily accessed at Humanities-Net, and college and university syllabi from around the world are provided at Global Syllabi. Operating under the name of world lecture hall, an extensive site based at the University of Texas, Austin includes syllabi covering all academic disciplines (websites cited below).

A few creative syllabi caught my eye in one look around the Internet (see URL resources in endnotes). The syllabus for US Diplomatic History taught by Ernest Bolt at the University of Richmond is clear, concise, includes detailed assignments, encourages students to schedule conferences with him, and introduces each topic with pithy questions like: Why was Billy Joel interested in this subject? Did Harry Truman overreact in the Truman Doctrine speech? Would John Kennedy have pulled out of Vietnam had he lived longer? A rigorous, innovative, interdisciplinary undergraduate seminar is traced in Alix Cooper's Harvard University syllabus for Nature in Early Modern Europe and America. It begins by asking this intriguing question: What connection exists between the ways people have thought about nature and the way they have actually behaved towards it? An impressive reading list is given for each class period; activities for the last class are chosen by the students themselves.

While I have heard about courses taught completely online, I had no idea how one would be organized, until I read the syllabus for Charles Keyes' introductory philosophy course at Duquesne University. I was impressed by the inductive methodology allowing students to formulate their own answers to philosophical questions. Handwritten notebooks (substance) and journals (reactions) are submitted electronically, along with a term paper. Students have a chat-line to communicate with each other, and technical computer assistance is provided by trained course monitors. The final syllabus I selected because it illustrates something that administrators everywhere are now nudging faculty to introduce: capstone courses intended to tie together the experiences of an academic major. The capstone sociology course at Duke University taught by Kenneth Spenner explains the rationale behind the capstone concept, employs an engaging case study project for student participation, places students in teams for other projects, and uses current events as a way to relate engagingly concepts learned in prior courses to contemporary real world occurrences.

CONCLUSION

An authority on American higher education, Robert Diamond, points to cracks in the curricular foundation at three levels of the academy (individual course, departmental major, institutional general studies program). It is suggested here that the sophisticated course syllabus, often overlooked in academia, can assist efforts to restore curricular integrity. Not only do model syllabi improve teaching and learning in individual courses, they can also enlist all three levels of the curriculum in furthering the mission statements that constitute higher education's blueprint. If conceptualized more complexly, the course syllabus has the potential to broaden the base of curricular accountability called for by the assessment movement which currently occupies center stage in higher education.

REFERENCES

Altman H., & Cashin, W. C. (1992, September). *Writing a syllabus.* Manhattan, KS: Kansas State University, Center for Faculty Evaluation and Development.

Birdsall, M. (1989). *Writing, designing, and using a course syllabus.* Boston, MA: Northeastern University, Office for Effective Teaching.

Brady, L. (1991). *Political science course syllabi collection: International Relations.* Washington, DC: American Political Science Association.

Diamond, R. (1998). *Designing and assessing courses and curricula: A practical guide.* San Francisco, CA: Jossey-Bass.

Grunert, J. (1997). *The course syllabus: A learning-centered approach.* Bolton, MA: Anker.

Roth, J. K. (Ed.) (1996). *Inspiring teaching: Carnegie professors of the year speak.* Bolton, MA: Anker.

Rubin, S. (1985, August). Professors, students, and the syllabus. *Chronicle of Higher Education, 7,* p. 56.

INTERNET ENDNOTES

The following URLs carry examples of outstanding syllabi representing various disciplines:

The Humanities (H-net)
http://www.h-net2.msu.edu/~aseh/syllabi/

World Lecture Hall
http://www.vcu.edu/mdcweb/english/

American Political Science Association Model Syllabi Project
http://www.apsanet.org/teaching/syllabi/APSA/

Global Syllabi
http://www.ecnet.net/users/bigOama/syllabi/syllabi.html

American Sociological Association
http://www.asanet.org/pubs/tchgres.htm

EdWeb
http://www.edweb.cnidr.org:90/

Virtual Classroom
http://www.enmu.edu/virtual/virt.html

Developing Educational Standards: Overview
http://www.putwest.boces.org/standards.html

The Global Campus
http://www.csulb.edu/gc/

WebEd Curriculum Links
http://www.badger.state.wi.us/agencies/dpi/www/WebEd.html

Courseware for Higher Education on the World Wide Web
http://www.philae.sas.upenn.edu

AskERIC
http://www.erieir.syr.edu

Syllabus Web
http://www.syllabus.com

Ernest Bolt Syllabus
http://www.richmond.edu/~ebolt/syll327.html

Alix Cooper Syllabus
http://www.h-net2.msu.edu/~aseh/syllabi/cooper.htm

Charles Keyes Syllabus
http://www.duq.edu/~keyes/bpq/syllabus.html

Kenneth Spenner Syllabus
http://www.soc.duke.edu/courses/soc190_syl_f96.html

Contact:

Michael J. Strada, Professor of Political Science
West Liberty State College
Visiting Professor and FACDIS Co-Director,
Department of Political Science, P.O. Box 6317
West Virginia University
Morgantown, WV 26506-6317
(304) 293-7140
Email: mjstrada@cs.com

Michael Strada has taught international studies courses at West Liberty State College since 1969 and at West Virginia University since 1985. At WVU he serves as co-director of the statewide international studies consortium known as FACDIS. Strada's recent publications include an *Through the Global Lens: An introduction to the social sciences* (Prentice Hall, 1999), a scholarly book on Russians in American film and foreign policy, and an article in *USA Today* on political movies. The subject of his current research is Americanadians: draft evaders who moved to Canada during the Vietnam War. In 2000 he won the West Liberty State Excellence in Professional Activity award for the third time and was selected a spring commencement speaker. In the preface to his textbook, he says that he "is actively involved in his grandsons' athletic teams because he believes that sports teach a work ethic, and that the extended Strada family's rituals of choice revolve around sports." His grandsons compete in baseball, soccer, and hockey and he tries in vain to keep up with them.

13

The Role of a Teaching Center in Curricular Reform

Constance Ewing Cook
University of Michigan

Instructional consultants can play a crucial role in curricular reform. They gather evaluation and assessment data about the current curriculum so that faculty decisions about improvements are based on empirical evidence. They organize and facilitate meetings and retreats at which faculty make curricular decisions, and they provide pedagogical expertise and resources to help with course design and enhancement. They also provide ongoing data for formative evaluation of the new curriculum. Examples from the University of Michigan's Center for Research on Learning and Teaching illustrate instructional consultants' contributions to the curricular reform process.

INTRODUCTION

The dean invited us to a faculty meeting to talk about the services that the Center for Research on Learning and Teaching (CRLT) could provide to her school. CRLT is the University of Michigan's teaching center, and it offers a wide array of services to all 19 schools and colleges on the Ann Arbor campus, including the professional school led by this dean. In preparation for the faculty meeting, the CRLT colleagues and I gathered examples of our work in UM's other schools and prepared handouts for the presentation.

At the meeting, we made our pitch, but the faculty expressed no interest in our services. The dean, who is a strong proponent of teaching and learning improvement, was clearly disappointed. She tried to engage her faculty by mentioning that the school could use our assistance with its new curricular reform effort. A senior professor expressed amazement, saying: "How can CRLT possibly help with curricular reform when no one there is familiar with our discipline?"

Unfortunately, faculty often assume that a teaching center cannot be of assistance with curricular reform. Survey data show that only 6.1% of faculty on campuses with teaching centers report that they consider the center helpful with course planning, and only a handful of faculty consider it a strong influence or a helpful source of assistance and feedback (Stark & Lattuca, 1997, pp. 225, 229, and 272).

With occasional exceptions (e.g., Diamond; 1989, and Gaff, 1983), the literature on curricular reform rarely mentions that instructional consultants can play a useful role in the design and planning process (see Gardiner, 1992, for an overview of the curricular reform literature). Furthermore, most literature about teaching center programs and services does not mention curricular reform. That is true in spite of the fact that the mission of the Professional and Organizational Development Network in Higher Education (POD), the association of instructional consultants (also called faculty developers), is to foster professional development in three areas: faculty development, instructional development, and organizational development; and all three are integral to curricular reform (Diamond, 1988). As used here, the term curricular reform refers to the review and revision of existing sets of courses or the creation of new sets of courses that a program, department, or school/college offers to its students.

The purpose of this article is to present how instructional consultants can be useful in the curricular reform process. Since their contributions are often labor intensive, instructional consultants at a teaching center are more likely to be helpful than those unaffiliated with a center since centers usually provide professional colleagues and support staff to augment and facilitate individual consultants' efforts.

Typically, there are several obstacles to curricular reform, all of which instructional consultants can help overcome. First, curricular reform often flounders because faculty views about the current curriculum are based only on anecdotal information and hypothetical conjectures. There is no consensus about shortcomings or strengths in the current curriculum because there is no empirical data. In the absence of data showing otherwise, it is easy for colleagues opposed to change to contend that the current curriculum is adequate or for those who are eager for change to insist that change is essential. Even if everyone wants a change, the absence of commonly shared evaluation data makes it difficult to come to consensus about the direction the changes should take. Instructional consultants can help by providing evaluation and assessment data for the current curriculum so that faculty decision making is empirically based.

Second, once faculty have the evaluation data in hand, curricular design and enhancement may not occur because of faculty time constraints. Faculty may be reluctant to come together to review the curriculum because it is such a lengthy and potentially contentious process. Instructional consultants can provide assistance with many aspects of faculty meetings and retreats so that faculty have less responsibility for planning and logistics, and meetings are more likely to be substantive, flow smoothly, and prove useful.

Once faculty have decided to craft new courses or enhance existing ones, they need resources and expertise to do it effectively. Otherwise, the efforts may fall short of the objectives. Instructional consultants can supply expertise on pedagogical issues to enhance student learning, and they can sometimes offer grants themselves or help make the case to other funders.

Finally, faculty frequently agree on revising a curriculum but then do no evaluation to make sure the new courses actually achieve the student learning goals they had agreed upon. Instructional consultants can help with ongoing data collection for formative evaluation.

EVALUATION OF THE CURRICULUM

Evaluation of the curriculum typically begins with a request for help from an academic administrator, usually a dean, program director, or department chair. They come to CRLT with a problem, such as low enrollments or poor student retention. Instructional consultants often respond by asking that they engage a small group of faculty, perhaps a steering committee, who can help decide how to gather evaluative information about the current curriculum, including assessment of student learning.

Many consultants have expertise in survey research, so they may work with faculty and administrators to design a questionnaire that can be used for a broad review of curricular issues. Sometimes, they facilitate focus groups or interviews in order to gather enough information to design a good survey. Other times, the survey comes first, and when it is clear what the big picture is, they use focus groups or interviews to do in-depth research on specific issues that the survey data identified as problematic. Instructional consultants can organize and facilitate data collection, transcribe the data, and then analyze and report on it.

As part of their general evaluation of the curriculum, many faculty want to know what it is their students are actually learning. Accrediting agencies, state governments, and academic administrators also want to know. Therefore, instructional consultants at many teaching centers play a role in gathering outcomes assessment data for both internal and external curricular review.

CASES FROM THE UNIVERSITY OF MICHIGAN

Some stories from CRLT's work at the University of Michigan illustrate the many roles that instructional consultants can play.

Department of Biology

The Department of Biology in the College of Literature, Science, and the Arts requested CRLT assistance to evaluate its two key introductory courses. A faculty committee started by determining the specific learning goals it wanted the introductory course sequence to meet, and then the committee gathered data from a variety of sources to evaluate the extent to which the introductory courses were succeeding. CRLT helped the faculty review student ratings forms from previous years in order to identify areas of student dissatisfaction and then shape a questionnaire that was distributed to students in upper-level courses. Finally, CRLT conducted focus groups separately with undergraduate students, graduate student instructors (GSIs), and faculty members, for the purpose of exploring in depth some issues that the survey had shown to be problematic.

By the time the faculty convened to consider alternative curricular options, they had a shared understanding of the strengths and weaknesses of the current course sequence. Their students had said they wanted a course with more active learning and more connection between the lecture and lab. As one of the faculty leaders noted, these comments did not reveal anything new but helped prioritize the biggest problems and justify the expenditure of resources to solve one problem instead of another. As he put it, "After the CRLT report came out and it was in black and white . . . to not do anything would have been unthinkable because there it was: 500 students, 30 GSIs, and several professors saying that this format was very unsatisfying . . ." (M. Amerlaan, personal communication with E. Brady, November 2, 1999).

After reviewing the results of the evaluation, the biology faculty created a single course to replace the former two-course sequence. They also added a discussion section in order to tie together the lecture and lab and provide more opportunity for students to take an active role in the learning process (University of Michigan Department of Biology, 1998). Now that the new introductory course is in place, student evaluations of the course are much more positive, on average, than for the courses they replaced (M. Amerlaan, personal communication with E. Brady, November 2, 1999).

After the conclusion of the curricular reform process, a biology faculty leader highlighted CRLT's importance in the change process: "What made it really work was having some people from CRLT come in who were neutral and who weren't seen to have any biases. It just cloaked the whole thing in a more true research aura as opposed to an attempt to forward individual interests" (M. Amerlaan, personal communication with E. Brady, November 2, 1999).

A School that Wishes to Remain Anonymous

The dean of this school was concerned about dissatisfaction expressed by some students of color, but he was unsure about what actions to encourage the faculty to take. He called in CRLT consultants, and they worked with a small faculty steering committee to develop a protocol of focus group questions. The focus groups included students of color, white students, and faculty—each meeting separately with CRLT facilitators of the same race or ethnicity. The focus group topics included both multicultural issues and other student concerns.

After completing the focus groups, CRLT sent the school a report summarizing the students' comments. Among them were insufficient multicultural content in the curriculum, faculty who did not know how to handle sensitive topics in class, and an absence of enough sense of community in the school.

In response to the report, the school invited CRLT consultants to design and facilitate a faculty retreat on multicultural teaching. At the retreat, faculty shared and discussed strategies for infusing multiculturalism into the curriculum and leading controversial discussions. Through role plays, CRLT's instructional consultants offered suggestions and gave faculty the opportunity to practice new approaches.

Since the retreat, there have been several changes at the school, including routine inclusion of more students on the curriculum committee and frequent discussion of ethics and values as part of regular faculty meetings. An accrediting team that recently visited the school rated it outstanding in its inclusion of multicultural materials in the curriculum and attention to issues of diversity. As one faculty member said, "The school works hard on multicultural issues pretty consistently now" (Personal communication, January 12, 2000).

Landscape Architecture Program

The faculty in the landscape architecture program of the School of Natural Resources and Environment wanted to gain an understanding of the reasons why incoming students had chosen the program and the skills and knowledge they hoped to acquire. They also wanted students' impressions of the current course sequencing and scheduling.

A CRLT instructional consultant worked with the faculty to design and conduct focus groups and surveys. She then provided the faculty with a report on student backgrounds and interests, as well as recommendations for change. The recommendations included better distribution of the workload from one semester to the next; making more connections among the courses, with each course building on the one before; and responding to the needs of nontraditional students whose schedules made them unable to take courses in a specific sequence.

At the conclusion of the curricular reform process, the program chair noted CRLT's value. He said it was the initial focus group and survey data that made it clear that curricular restructuring was necessary. He also cited the importance of the instructional consultant's role as a more objective observer: "By having someone outside the faculty come in and do this assessment, we likely got more honest responses. We were able to identify both small issues that we could address by simple fine tuning and better communication and the larger issues that required major restructuring." Finally, he commented on the value of involving students in curricular reform through surveys and focus groups: "Rather than students feeling left out or becoming worried that the program they were experiencing was somehow 'broken,' they felt like they were very much a part of the process and partners with faculty in making improvements" (R. Grese, personal communication, January 9, 2000).

LESSONS LEARNED

In each of the stories, faculty and administrators realized it was important to collect data about the current curriculum before rushing to judgment about making improvements. In each case, the data collection process (surveys, focus groups, and interviews) brought student voices into the decision-making process. The student data convinced skeptical faculty that change was really necessary, and it also offered information for priority setting by highlighting the biggest issues and pointing to directions for change. The involvement in data gathering by a neutral CRLT consultant lent credibility to the process and helped convince faculty of the veracity of the evidence.

COURSE DESIGN AND ENHANCEMENT

Facilitation of Meetings and Retreats

Collection of evaluation data about the curriculum often goes hand-in-hand with retreat facilitation. Instructional consultants try to make sure that the former leads to the latter, as was the case in the biology, anonymous school, and landscape architecture examples above. It sometimes seems that the hardest part of curricular reform is getting faculty together to make decisions. Faculty time is at a premium, so it is important to make the decision-making process go smoothly. CRLT often helps achieve that objective.

An instructional consultant used the Delphi method to minimize the amount of time that history of art department faculty spent revising their curriculum. The Delphi method involves a decision tree, with a series of questionnaires, each building on the consensus developed by the one before (Stritter, Tresolini, & Reeb, 1994; Tiberius, 1997). In the case of art history, the consultant summarized the responses after each round of the questionnaire and crafted new questions that slowly narrowed the options.

Initial questionnaires asked about competencies and knowledge that faculty consider integral to an art history major. By the time they arrived at the retreat, the faculty had already developed a consensus, and the retreat became an opportunity to brainstorm about ways to implement the objectives they had agreed upon. One issue that came up at the retreat was differentiation among 100-, 200-, 300-, and 400-level courses, so after the retreat, the consultant followed up by sending questionnaires about the competencies and knowledge faculty thought students should be expected to acquire at each course level.

Using grants competitions, CRLT also provided funding for the retreat, thereby giving the event more sense of importance. As one history of art professor noted, "There's kind of an impetus that is given to the project outside of the department—recognition and acknowledgment of its importance . . . It says that what you're interested in doing strikes other people as being important too. To have some of those 'dangling hooks'—outside visitors, meals—all of those things can help" (P. Simons, personal communication with E. Brady, November 17, 1999).

Over the years, CRLT has organized and facilitated a great number of faculty retreats for curriculum review. Instructional consultants have also reduced the amount of time that faculty have had to spend on the decision-making process by summarizing the retreat conversations and providing follow-up documents, as was done for history of art.

CONSULTATION ON PEDAGOGY

Some faculty object to curricular reform because they do not want to do course revisions and retooling. Instructional consultants can ease their workload by helping with pedagogical aspects of course design. Pedagogy is critical to the delivery of new courses and new curricula. Most faculty do not consider themselves pedagogical experts, but without attention to pedagogy, curricular reform may not accomplish the faculty's student learning goals.

Instructional consultants often give faculty advice about how to integrate critical thinking and active learning into new subject matter. For example, in the University of Michigan's extensive calculus reform project, the math department chair credited CRLT with helping the department incorporate cooperative learning into the curriculum. He said, "We had a consultant from CRLT . . . whose cooperative learning got students to talk to each other and explain their difficulties. Students come out with much more appreciation of mathematics as a useful discipline" (A. Taylor, personal communication, March 5, 1997).

Instructional consultants can also provide assistance with multicultural teaching and learning, such as fostering an inclusive classroom climate, teaching students with a variety of learning preferences or needs, and handling sensitive topics and emotional discussions in the classroom (e.g., Border & Chism, 1992; Cook & Sorcinelli, 1999; Kardia, 1998; Ouellett & Sorcinelli, 1998). CRLT often provides assistance of this nature, as indicated in the anonymous school example above. Additionally, consultants can help with syllabus construction, research paper and examination design, grading practices, and a variety of other aspects of the instructional process. Many provide assistance with the use of instructional technology to foster student learning. As a result, it is common for academic units to call on CRLT consultants when they develop a new curriculum. For example, when the School of Nursing completed its curricular reform process and targeted specific faculty members to teach the new courses, it contracted with CRLT to help the faculty develop pedagogy that would best enhance student learning.

Beyond these generic pedagogy issues that can apply to any course or set of courses, many instructional consultants offer pedagogical expertise of a specialized nature. For example, they may have expertise on inter-disciplinary course pedagogy or writing across the curriculum. With living-learning programs and community service-learning programs so popular on our campuses, instructional consultants often contribute ex-pertise regarding course design for these programs as well.

FUNDING FOR CURRICULAR REFORM

CRLT administers several grant competitions, some of which fund broad curricular reform efforts involving large numbers of faculty in depart-ments or programs. For instructional consultants without such resources, it is nonetheless possible to bolster the requests that faculty make to aca-demic administrators.

Sometimes grants provide the equipment that faculty need in order to create new courses or new learning in existing courses. For example, when the School of Art and Design decided to add a computing curricu-lum, a CRLT grant funded a workroom where faculty could receive in-struction on using computers, grade computer-based assignments, hone their computer skills, and develop course assignments and materials.

Grants can be used for faculty to collect their own data about curric-ular improvements. For example, a grant to a mathematics professor bought him out of some teaching so he could attend science and engi-neering classes to determine what mathematics the students needed for those classes. He then reported to departmental colleagues about how to provide better math service courses. Another grant funded faculty in psy-chology and social work to conduct a quasi-experimental study to evalu-ate the short- and long-term impact of community service courses in De-troit on their students' multicultural learning.

Grants sometimes fund faculty in several academic units to work to-gether to develop interdisciplinary curricula for their students. For exam-ple, a CRLT grant to the School of Nursing provided funding to a faculty member who organized planning meetings for her colleagues, as well as faculty in the Schools of Social Work, Public Health, Dentistry, and Phar-macy. These units jointly developed opportunities for their students to learn about community-based health care.

Sometimes grants are used to bring in new expertise and help a de-partment or program develop new courses or new components of exist-ing courses. For example, a grant to a social work faculty member funded a project involving infusion of material about Asian Pacific islanders into the curriculum. The grant paid for stipends and travel to Ann Arbor for several Pan Asian experts, who then gave presentations and consulted individually with faculty to help them consider how they might incorporate new learning into their courses.

Finally, grants may be used to fund the development of new curricular modules that can be used in many courses. For example, a grant to an engineering professor helped him develop a website with ethics case studies to serve as a resource for all engineering faculty who incorporated ethics instruction into their courses. He offered a workshop to faculty colleagues to generate interactive cases that would add substance and new ethics topics to the website.

Faculty report that CRLT funding is especially useful in giving projects more importance than they would otherwise have. For example, CRLT gave a grant to a faculty member in the Medical School for creation of a videotape about cross-cultural communication, to be used for a required orientation program for first-year students. The project director commented:

> When you are awarded external funding in the Medical School, people sit up and take notice. In the case of my project, CRLT funding gave it both visibility and import. I think the fact that the dean has to sign off on the application is critical. I don't believe the program would have received the visible support it did or have been as successful as it was had I just strung together funds from [internal] sources . . . It was important for me to be able to tap technical expertise. I couldn't have done that without the legitimacy that CRLT lent to my project (L. Robins, personal communication, January 14, 2000).

Thus, CRLT funding for curricular improvements has importance far beyond its dollar value.

FORMATIVE EVALUATION OF THE NEW CURRICULUM

There is not a single fix that solves all problems. Especially when there is a dramatic change in instructional goals and methods, it is wise to collect data over an extended period—both for the purpose of making continual course improvements and also for determining the extent to which individual courses continue to incorporate the new student learning goals. A teaching center can be helpful with ongoing data collection.

Department of Mathematics

The Department of Mathematics began its process of revising introductory calculus instruction nearly a decade ago. Among the new instructional goals were incorporation of cooperative learning both in the classroom and in homework teams; realistic, open-ended problems that encourage analysis and problem solving skills; and the use of writing as a learning tool.

CRLT has worked with math over a period of many years to evaluate the extent to which the new courses are achieving their goals. For this purpose, CRLT has used midterm student feedback (MSF), also called Small Group Instructional Diagnosis (SGID). In an MSF, a CRLT consultant asks students what is going well in the course and what would help them learn more. The consultant synthesizes student comments and provides them confidentially to the instructor—in the middle of the term when it is still possible to make improvements.

Ordinarily, it is individual instructors who utilize MSFs for teaching improvement, but in calculus, course coordinators have used them term after term for most sections of the multi-sectioned courses in order to get a general sense of student satisfaction and self-reports of learning. The MSF data have led to frequent course revisions. For example, MSFs indicated that students did not understand the new learning goals, so the coordinators urged instructors to keep students informed about goals throughout the term. They also incorporated explicit learning goals into course reading assignments in order to maximize student understanding of the new approach to calculus instruction (Black, 1998). The math experience shows that curricular reform is not a one-time process, and faculty continue to need assistance from instructional consultants.

College of Engineering

The College of Engineering decided to assess the extent to which its students were mastering 11 types of knowledge and competencies that a curriculum committee had determined to be essential elements of the undergraduate curriculum. Since most of the eleven were taught in a wide variety of courses, not just one, the college wondered which courses were teaching what. The faculty decided to include in the end-of-course student ratings forms questions about self-reports of learning in all 11 areas. CRLT provided assistance with development of the instrument and with data analysis and reporting. CRLT also aided the college in creating survey instruments for graduating seniors and alumni in order to further assess students' perceptions of their learning.

The college presented a summary of this data to the team from the Accreditation Board for Engineering and Technology (ABET) as it conducted its site visit for reaccreditation. The associate dean later sent a positive report to CRLT, saying, "The evaluators seemed impressed with the assessment plans . . . and they very much liked the way the course evaluations were revamped" (J.W. Jones, personal communication, November 23, 1999). Long term, it will be helpful for the college to have the course-by-course data, as well as the seniors and alumni data, to make sure that the knowledge and competencies the faculty agreed to incorporate into the curriculum continue to be taught.

SOME CHALLENGES FOR INSTRUCTIONAL CONSULTANTS

It is clear that instructional consultants add value to the curricular reform process, and for those of us in the business of improving teaching and learning, there is a lot of satisfaction to be gained. However, involvement in curricular reform carries its own challenges.

Workload

One of the challenges is workload. Curricular reform services, such as focus groups and retreats, are labor intensive. Teaching centers require considerable staffing, both professional and support staff, to supply significant amounts of assistance. However, even with considerable staffing, it is still impossible for a relatively large center like CRLT to satisfy all the demands for its services. It is necessary, therefore, to pick one's clients carefully—perhaps by choosing projects that impact large numbers of students, or perhaps by choosing high visibility projects that will create more of a culture of teaching on campus.

Unused Data

A second, and related, challenge is that of unused data. For example, the interim director of an important campus program asked CRLT to evaluate the academic rigor of his program and determine how to improve student learning. Many surveys and focus groups later, we completed the project and delivered the data to the interim director so he could present it to the permanent director as he came on board. Two years later, the new director admitted that he never used the CRLT data at all. As a result, we now realize that perhaps we should not agree to do evaluations for interim administrators. It might be better to wait until someone is in place that can implement changes—if, indeed, the data indicates that change is necessary. Furthermore, it is problematic to do evaluations for units where faculty are split into factions because the chance of effecting real change are so slim. Sometimes, intelligence gathering about the academic unit can help to determine whether that unit is one that should have priority in the teaching center's list of projects.

Communication about Consultant Role

A third challenge is the one mentioned at the start of this article, namely, the challenge of communicating to faculty about the role of instructional consultants in curricular reform. Word about a center's contribution to one department's curricular reform spreads slowly to other departments because there is a Catch-22 to instructional consulting services: A teaching center can only succeed if its contribution occurs behind the scenes, with faculty taking credit for their own success. If consultants claim credit for curricular and other improvements, faculty may be reluctant to use their services in the future. The Catch-22 occurs because a teaching center needs to have visibility in order to capture enough university resources to do the work that is requested and in order to stimulate enough faculty interest to have a ready market for its services.

Instructional consultants bring considerable value to the reform process and should find ways to inform deans, department chairs, and faculty about the contributions they can make. Consultants make reform more likely and more fruitful by structuring the process and supplying the labor, resources, and pedagogical expertise that busy faculty and administrators may be unable or unwilling to supply themselves. Instructional consultants make it possible for students to learn what the faculty really want them to know.

ACKNOWLEDGMENTS

The author wishes to acknowledge the work of Elizabeth Brady, graduate student in the Center for the Study of Higher and Postsecondary Education, University of Michigan. As part of her independent student project, she conducted interviews of selected faculty who received CRLT grants for curricular reform.

REFERENCES

Black, B. (1998). Using the SGID method for a variety of purposes. In M. Kaplan & D. Lieberman (Eds.), *To improve the academy, 17*, 245–262. Bolton, MA: Anker.

Border, L..B. & Chism, N.V.N. (1992). *Teaching for diversity.* New Directions for Teaching and Learning, No. 49. San Francisco, CA: Jossey- Bass.

Cook, C. E., & Sorcinelli, M. D. (1999). Building multiculturalism into teaching development programs. *AAHE Bulletin, 51* (7) 3-6.

Diamond, R. M. (1988). Faculty development, instructional development, and organizational development: Options and choices. In E. C. Wadsworth (Ed.), *A handbook for new practitioners* (pp. 9-11). Stillwater, OK: New Forums Press.

Diamond, R. M. (1989). *Designing and improving courses and curricula in higher education: A systematic approach.* San Francisco, CA: Jossey-Bass.

Gaff, J. (1983). *General education today: A critical analysis of controversies, practices, and reforms.* San Francisco, CA: Jossey-Bass.

Gardiner, L. F. (1992). *Designing a college curriculum: Overview, planning aids, and selected resources.* Professional Resource No. 4 (copyright by Gardiner).

Kardia, D. (1998). Becoming a multicultural faculty developer: Reflections from the field. In M. Kaplan & D. Lieberman (Eds.), *To improve the academy, 17,* (15-34). Bolton, MA: Anker.

Ouellett, M. L., & Sorcinelli, M. D. (1998). TA training: Strategies for responding to diversity in the classroom. In M. Marincovich, H. Prostko, & F. Stout (Eds.), *The professional development of graduate teaching assistants.* Bolton, MA: Anker.

Stark, J. S., & Lattuca, L. R. (1997*). Shaping the college curriculum: Academic plans in action.* Needham Heights, MA: Allyn & Bacon.

Stritter, F. T., Tresolini, C. P., & Reeb, K. G. (1994). The Delphi technique in curriculum development. *Teaching and Learning in Medicine, 6* (2), 136-141.

Tiberius, R. (1997). Small group methods for collecting information from students. In K. T. Brinko & R. J. Menges (Eds.), *Practically speaking: A sourcebook for instructional consultants in higher education* (pp. 53-63). Stillwater, OK: New Forums Press.

University of Michigan Department of Biology. (1998). *Alumni Newsletter,* p. 5.

Contact:

Constance Ewing Cook
Director, Center for Research on Learning and Teaching
Associate Professor of Higher Education
Adjunct Associate Professor of Political Science
University of Michigan
3300 SEB
Ann Arbor, MI 48109-1259
(734) 763-0159
(734) 647-3600 (Fax)
http://www.umich.edu/~crltmich
Email: Cecook@umich.edu

Constance Ewing Cook is Director of the Center for Research on Learning and Teaching (CRLT) at the University of Michigan–Ann Arbor campus. She is also Associate Professor in the Center for the Study of Higher and Postsecondary Education (CSHPE), the higher education program at Michigan, and teaches a graduate course on improving teaching and learning in higher education. Additionally, as a political scientist, she teaches a course on public policy in higher education and is the author of a recent book on the topic: *Lobbying for higher education: How colleges and universities influence federal policy* (Vanderbilt University Press, 1998).

14

Technology and the Culture of Teaching and Learning

Sean Courtney
University of Nebraska-Lincoln

Faculty development professionals in postsecondary institutions face many challenges helping faculty adapt to the new forms of information technology. Chief among them is understanding how technology is forcing us to rethink current classroom practices. To aid this effort, this essay identifies and analyzes six key dimensions of traditional cultures of teaching and learning and attempts to show how technology, particularly computer-mediated forms, is transforming their meaning and potential impact.

> *"[The] professor . . . sits alone in his office, concentrating as he hunches over the computer. He is busy teaching."*
> *Lincoln Journal Star, June 8, 1997*

INTRODUCTION

Against a varied background of social forces (such as the revolution in microchip technology, institutional trends, diminishing budgets, increasing numbers of nontraditional students) there is almost no university or college in the US today that is not grappling with the question of technology and its role in augmenting or even transforming traditional, classroom-based teaching practices.[1] Even as presidents and CEOs of postsecondary institutions establish technology roundtables and faculty groups consider what stance is most appropriate (University of Illinois, 1999), individual instructors find themselves caught in a difficult quandary: How does one respond to the new winds of change blowing across their profession? Various reactions are produced, as depicted in Figure 14.1.

FIGURE 14.1
Faculty Response to Technology

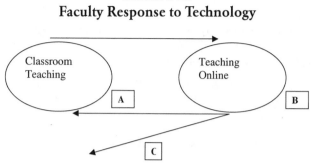

Initially, faculty may be tempted to take current curricula and transfer them directly to the web with little effort to modify them.[2] The straight arrow between A and B in Figure 14.1 represents this set of actions. For example, if we mainly see teaching as transmission of information and view the preferred method of transmission as the lecture, then we may see computers primarily as tools to aid the task of broadcasting our message (Fox, 1983). Indeed, there is a strong feeling in the academy, shared by many faculty members, that all computers, even when they are the main modality of teaching, are really no more than tools. The view being argued here, however, is that new forms of information technology, principally the computer, are more than tools: Used to their full capacity they are capable of transforming pedagogical practices. The arrow curving back from B to A represents the idea that once one teaches online, he or she may come to realize that old ways of doing things no longer seem to work, if they ever really did. Thus, teachers who value transmission may find that their notes can easily be posted in a virtual library, leaving them wondering what else is involved in teaching their subject. This kind of experience may lead some faculty to question what about their teaching is critical to the success of learning and what was simply conventional and convenient in the traditional face-to-face format. They may begin to isolate the different parts of the integrated whole, to segment the apparently seamless fabric of the current culture. Now, armed with insights, they begin afresh (depicted in Figure 14.1 as the curve from A back to B), prepared to discard that which no longer serves a purpose in the new milieu. But, in doing so, they are in the exhilarating stages of creating a new culture of teaching and learning. (Other faculty may, of course, conclude that these bells and whistles are not why they got into teaching in the first place. The curved line renders their consequent dismissal of the new technology from B to C.)

The purpose of this essay is to explore what happens to our teaching as we embrace new forms of information technology. Is technology, as some have claimed, merely a tool that will reproduce bad teaching as well as good? Or is it something more dynamic and fundamental, compelling us to rethink the manner of our pedagogy in exciting new ways?

TEACHING AND LEARNING AS CULTURAL SYSTEMS

Classroom-based teaching and learning, for all its warts, is an integrated system. The actions of teachers and the corresponding reactions of their students are symbiotically interconnected. They occur within a context that gives them meaning. In this culture of pedagogy, the teacher engages in certain kinds of actions; e.g. lecturing, which the teacher believes are designed to facilitate learning of a subject matter and which, crucially, students recognize as being teaching. Likewise, for their part, teachers expect students to perform certain actions which traditionally they, the teachers, recognize as learning; e.g., taking notes and writing term papers. Any departures from these solidified—even atrophied—norms are likely to evoke protest, and clearly the move online represents a departure of potentially major proportions.

What defines this culture of pedagogy? And how might it change under the impact of the new technologies? Images can provide clues as to where we should look for answers. First is a typical bare-bones classroom housing tables and chairs in a rough rectangle. Around the rectangle sit the students and the teacher. The period together will be spent mainly in discussion, with the teacher posing questions and, in so doing, facilitating a process of engagement with the text. This picture represents the traditional culture of pedagogy. Now imagine a second image involving "between ten and 20 students [ranging] from mature adults to primary school children [are] seated in a circle in a way that when the students all turn outwards with their backs towards one another, they face a computer. For about 45 minutes they . . . work with the computer in a computer-assisted instruction mode. At the end of that time, they . . . [turn to face each other and over the same period of time are] involved, with the teacher, in a discussion of the subject they had studied with the computer" (Tiffin & Rajasingham, 1995, p. 5).

There is a final image, that of a class of students who never meet except online, via the computer and a modem, because all are scattered in time and space. For this group, the class meeting consists of messages that they post to a server, a machine that brings them together in no particular time or space, but nevertheless in mediated conversation. They discuss of the text, as does the group that meets face-to-face. All three images are examples of a culture of pedagogy, capable of explication, analysis, and critique. That culture can be described in terms of the following fundamental categories:

- Space and time
- Embodiment and identity
- Power and control
- Knowledge and text
- Work and interaction
- Tools and technology

In sum, teaching is an orchestration of goal-directed activities located in a particular space and time. Occupying those coordinates are actors who have identities and express themselves in various roles. The purpose of the activities centers on a text which represents desired knowledge. The teacher manages the activities, thereby exercising power and control. The activities constitute the work of the group and may call for various interactions among the actors involved. Finally, the work of the group is advanced by means of various tools and technologies. This defines the culture of pedagogy in the abstract. How does this culture appear in reality and how does it change under the impact of technology?

SPACE AND TIME

Learning is organized in time and space. Classrooms and the class period are living embodiments of that organization, without which learning would appear to be impossible. As a student in one of my classes noted, "I actually thought that to earn a degree, you must be present in a classroom."[3] Historically, classrooms have been synonymous with learning. "The idea of people gathering together in some special site for learning goes back well before the industrial revolution, and the classroom by itself has proved a remarkably resilient and endurable place for learning" (Tiffin & Rajasingham, 1995, p. 3). Clearly, many professors find it hard to imagine a class without four walls and a set time for meeting. These dimensions more than any other probably accounts for the status of the classroom as a "pedagogical isomorphism," according to Jaffee (1998), meaning a form of practice that continues to exist long after it may have outlived its usefulness.

In the traditional classroom, represented by the first image described above, place and time, space and duration invoke rituals of participation. Though often unexplored as pedagogic points of interest, classes have significant time dimensions: beginnings, middles, and ends. There is an entering of the classroom and a leave-taking (Courtney, Jha, & Babchuk, 1995). On entering the class, the student sizes up her fellow students: What are they like? Will I like them? Will they like me? Leaving the class evokes its own ritual of departure. Will this particular group of peers ever meet this way again? And in between, there are the rhythms of the semester (Duffy & Jones, 1995), those peculiar ebbs and flows, when the urge to learn wars with the urge to relax and take it easy.

What happens to time and place when we teach online? How much are beginnings, endings, and meetings between teacher and student so ingrained in our psyche and how much do we depend on them to give us a sense of the class, to be part of the defining structure of the class, that if they appear absent we find it hard to function? What happens when there is no formal identified beginning or ending? What happens when we do not meet face-to-face with our students? A few years back, I taught my first distance learning course (with Lotus Notes as the web management system). As the planning team met to discuss course design options, it soon became clear that the faculty, myself included, were uncomfortable with never seeing their students. How could they interact and ultimately evaluate learners if they never saw them? To alleviate our discomfort, we arranged for a meeting of the students and faculty in the early part of the semester. When we met for a one-day get-acquainted workshop, I experienced a culture shock, a curious sense of disorientation. I thought "These men and women sitting scattered around the technology lab were not my students; they belong (sic) to all of the faculty present." Nor did the feeling of not belonging dissipate over the semester. While from time to time I attempted to converse with students in the designated "chat room," with few exceptions, there was none of the usual interaction associated with a face-to-face encounter. And the contrast was made all the more stark by the fact that I also happened to be teaching a small-group seminar during the same semester, where sitting around a square of tables, talking and joking about the subject had become the relaxed norm.

Clearly, once the classroom moves online there are no four walls common to all the participants. Instead, students have their own four walls, which happen to be wherever they decide is convenient for study: home, office, study, hotel room. Timewise, a class can be as short as five minutes or as long as two hours, just the length of time it takes to download and read the postings of your class companions and to respond if you want. What does that do to your sense of the class and the discipline it takes to learn and be a student? This is not just about the physical dimensions of a learning environment. There is a psychological dimension of even greater significance. For if you have to drive out into the night to get to class, that calls forth its own routine and planning effort, even if the inconvenience if palpable. But when the classroom moves into your home office, and all it takes is a hand motion to enter and be in class, what then of discipline and commitment to learning? Does the breaking down of boundaries serve as a distraction from the difficult task of learning? Do you learn just as well, sitting in your study in your pajamas, noshing on a bagel, as you appraise the images and symbols on the glowing screen in front of you?

At the same time, the computer-as-educator also makes previously intractable issues now much more salient. Just-in-time learning now seems very doable. New potential pockets of learners emerge, including those who previously considered further study inaccessible. Students take courses based on their needs relative to their proximity to the campus and on constantly changing schedules. The primary benefit is that more adults are going back to school or considering the option of extending their education. There is now even the possibility for an amazing individualization of learning with the potential invention of the PAD or personal access device (Downes, 1998). With new opportunities come new challenges. Separated asynchronously in cyberspace, how do learners interact? How are faculty to recreate a sense of community among learners who may not even share domicile in the same hemisphere (Palloff & Pratt, 1999)?

EMBODIMENT AND IDENTITY

Increasingly, the educational literature has begun to take seriously what has fast become a major topic of interest among sociologists, anthropologists, and feminist scholars (Weiss & Haber, 1999). This is the notion that the teachers embody as well as model what they are teaching; that they are an embodiment, a physical "code," who carry certain messages to their students, messages that go beyond what is to constitute knowledge, learning, and successful performance, extending even to what it is appropriate to say or do within the confines of a norm-dominated environment like the classroom (Chapman, 1998). As learners, we are similarly embodiments of multiple roles and identities (as mothers, fathers, sons, daughters, employees, etc.), which transcend the classroom.

By way of illustration, in a study of adult basic education classrooms (Courtney et al., 1995), we asked students to give us their impressions of fellow class members. In one notable case, one student admitted his shock and considerable discomfort at discovering that most of the people he was sharing a class with were prisoners from the local correctional facility. Even though, for the most part, the students pursuing basic literacy skills or the GED in this study, were young men and women from backgrounds not unlike those of the local prison population, their expectations were very different. It appears, though research is needed to support a stronger conclusion, that students expect other students to be like them in significant ways, both in terms of intelligence and ability, if not in terms of looks, income, or other factors of cultural value.

Though ostensibly in class to learn or to teach, teachers and students alike are more than mere ciphers or cognitive roles. They are persons who occupy bodies, about which it is easy to form judgments, often mistaken, based solely upon impressions. The teacher appears first and foremost as a living person, a body, with all of the qualities that go with that entity: clothes, appearance, mannerisms, and so forth. All of these weave into the culture of learning. Teachers, like learners, are members of social, economic, and cultural groups. They can be expected to react to the people in front of them. You might say, by way of example, that teaching accountancy is the same regardless of the identities of your students. But is this the case? As teachers, don't we have certain expectations about what our students will look like, and if those expectations are not met, won't we react accordingly?

Now, if you move all of this visible body stuff to the web, what happens? If the class could be anywhere in the world, and students could be from anywhere in the world, if you might never see them, won't you react differently than if they were all sitting there in front of you? Some might say that anonymity might cut down on possible discrimination based on perceptions. But invisibility is a double-edged sword. If the teacher cannot experience the multiple embodiments of his or her learners, is the commitment to helping them learn lessened? These are dimensions of the culture of learning that we have only begun to explore.

Another way to address this is through the concept of identity, captured in the various roles we take on as teachers and learners. The teacher, who enjoys the role of stand-up dispenser of wisdom before a large audience that gives him energy, may drift in cyberspace, unable to find a psychological anchor to tether him. Correspondingly, the learner who is accustomed to a certain battle for attention in that same traditional academic environment, and thrives on the cut-and-thrust of classroom discussion, may feel curiously unmotivated in the ethereal world of cyberspace. Research is beginning to uncover the role of the computer in shaping the social interactions and community building of the online classroom (Palloff & Pratt, 1999). Some learners it causes to come out of their self-imposed isolation and to shine on the web. Others it alienates, even frightens. In this respect, as with all of the other cultural dimensions being discussed here, it is no exaggeration to say that technology is more than a mere tool of convenience. Its power to transform human interactions, as well as to critically mold the teaching and learning exchange cannot be underestimated.

Knowledge and Text

In the traditional classroom, the teacher-as-expert distributes her knowledge to the student body by way of the text, which includes syllabus, notes, and various handouts, along with the actual textbook. They in turn recognize the teacher as expert or the holder of the knowledge which they seek. While the text is separate from the teacher in the traditional paradigm, nevertheless the teacher embodies the text and becomes the mouthpiece through which its difficulties are mediated. In such an environment, it is not hard to see how the teacher remains at the center of all pedagogic activity—figuratively if not literally—and how student activity in the pursuit of learning must always refer back to the teacher's actions. Correspondingly, all would-be interactions between teacher and student or among students themselves will be limited to what is task-related, tasks that have to do with understanding and internalizing "descriptions of the world" (Laurillard, 1993), the official subject of the course.

Movies like "Ferris Bueller's Day Off," "Dead Poets' Society," and "Stand and Deliver," even given their very different sympathies, all convey the timeless impression of the teacher at the center of all that matters. In the typical university classroom, the teacher is at the heart of the classroom's geography. While occasionally she steps to the side, this is mostly the exception that proves the rule. She dominates the discourse. Occasionally, students resist this domination and talk to each other in sidebar conversations. But the teacher finds this mostly distracting and will discourage it.

Teaching online, however, does something funny to the text and to the teacher's role in the creation of knowledge. Again, let me illustrate. In my own teaching online, I have noticed an interesting thing happen as we begin to discuss the text (Courtney, 1997). In one case, when students had responded to the main questions, once they had finished the work I had set before them, they turned naturally, or so it appeared to me, to discussions of how the theory applied to their own practice. From there it was a simple transition to where the focus became their expertise and interests. As the focus changed so did the discourse; from the artificial talking about that characterizes most academic discourse—that which describes a world theorized by others—the asynchronous dialogue became a talking within (Lave & Wenger, 1991), that which characterizes the discourse of people working on a joint task and attempting to help each other in the process. In the process, what I had to say became less relevant, mainly because I was not a K–12 teacher like them. They could learn from me, benefit from my expertise, and respect my command of the theory. But when it came to the everyday dimensions of their work worlds and the putting into practice of what I had taught them, they needed each other more than they needed me.

My point here is that this is also true of the traditional classroom: Students need each other and can benefit from each other's experiences as they tackle common problems of the profession. However, in the typical classroom, the likelihood of this happening is seriously diminished mainly because the teacher's—rather than the learner's—curriculum dominates the pedagogic discourse. It is the problems of the text—the teacher's problems—which get worked on rather than the learner's. This experience captures for me the essence of the argument that moving teaching online means more than using a computer as a tool. Working in an asynchronous environment that carries expectations of students constantly interacting and reflecting, it seems natural for the teaching—the direct instruction part—to become decentered, for the students to join the inner circle of learning so that, at some moments, there appears to be no distinction between the teacher and the taught, the teaching and the learning.

Finally, knowledge must be current, so the text must be new. In the past such newness was guaranteed by bringing out new editions of the text. Today, particularly with the existence of the web, currency may be more associated with finding the most up-to-date information on the Internet. Likewise, with the extension of the classroom beyond the traditional four walls—with its literal movement diffused in cyberspace—expertise and currency should be sought where it exists: at other sites and among those who are in the midst of new knowledge-generation.

Power and Leadership

Issues of power, control, authority, and leadership are often hard to detect, even in the traditional classroom setting and may be the deepest aspects of the culture of teaching and learning. Who has the power in the classroom? Ostensibly and mainly it belongs to the teacher, who acquires it through the institution for which he or she works. How is it used? Presumably, it is used fairly. Many syllabi now carry what might be termed a pedagogical disclaimer, a clause that says that all students will be treated equitably and reasonably regardless of various biological and social attributes; e.g., religion, gender, and sexual orientation. Some aspects of power seem obvious, even if many of the actors involved would disclaim any such quality. Feminist scholars like Tisdell (1993) and others have written about the interlocking systems of privilege both students as well as teachers can draw on in order to make their point, argue their case, or otherwise win position within the rigors of the modern graduate classroom. As has been pointed out, teaching is a rhetorical enterprise (Laurillard, 1993), and learners often exhibit resistance to the text. Mechanisms and attributes of the teacher as the embodiment of more than knowledge; e.g., that he is a white upper-middle-class male, are all brought to bear in an effort to convince the student that he or she is the expert and that the knowledge being dispensed is worth having.

Nonetheless, power rarely appears as such, and how we find evidence of it in the classroom is a tricky business, complicated by the reality that teachers as a group exhibit different fundamental approaches to the teaching act and therefore embrace issues of power and privilege in different ways. For the transmission style of teaching, for example, power is never on the table, according to Pratt (1998). Rather, there are clear lines drawn between teacher and student, and the roles and functions of each within the class setting. The syllabus and its language, even the bearing of this category of teacher, make it clear who has the power. Little is negotiated.

With the nurturing instructor, on the other hand, issues of power may at least be on the table. This type of instructor wants to know his or her students, will want to elicit and discuss their academic goals and personal interests, with a view to incorporating them into the weekly workings out of the syllabus. Here, students are given some say in the proceedings, with resultant feelings of power. Of course, in keeping with the subtlety of the subject, this granting of power may be more apparent then real. Teachers may cede control over various aspects of the curriculum without ceding the power (Herron, 1996). For example, in insisting that the class negotiate with the teacher about such things as assignments and their evaluation, the teacher may be sending a message that students are not free not to negotiate the curriculum or to decide that they would prefer a top-down approach of teaching style rather than the more informal, discussion-oriented approach.

What happens to power and control in cyberspace? Anecdotal evidence from a variety of sources (Snyder, 1995) suggest that faculty experience a more democratizing effect as they begin to teach online. They start seeing students willing to take greater responsibility for their own learning. And they start to realize that the success of the course ultimately depends on the students' willingness and ability to initiate and maintain a community of common interest in within the broad confines of the virtual classroom (Palloff & Pratt, 1999). Similarly, with greater use of collaborative models of instruction (Koshman, 1996), when a group is given a range of tasks pursuant to the goals of the course, it is natural that they begin to assume greater control over the proceedings. As one of my students noted: "Power . . . is controlled at various levels: The instructor has the power to create the course and its interactions; the student has the power to interact and learn at his or her own pace. As larger models of education are devised (i.e., open universities, etc.) and traditional models disappear or are modified away this will be a greater issue" (personal communication, December, 1999).

Power also comes from the fact that the move to the web essentially introduces all players into a world of dynamic information over which they have little say or control. The teacher who controls the text is also sending a message about what is permissible as knowledge and discourse within the four walls of his or her class. A class in cyberspace has no walls and no such artificial constraints. The teacher may begin the virtual library, for example, filling it with the support material that he or she deems fit. But such sites have permeable walls. And, in theory, students could fill them with whatever they think relevant to their goals and the aims of the course. From here it is but a short walk to recasting the purpose of the classroom as knowledge building (Scardamalia & Bereiter, 1996), rather than knowledge dissemination as has traditionally been the case. In such a world, the guest presenter may no longer be the person that the teacher thinks may fit the bill, but whomever the students can link up with and draw into the class through the new and open spaces of the virtual classroom.

Work and Interaction

The classroom is a pedagogical system framed within permeable, manipulable dimensions of space and time. It contains actors embodying various roles and identities, goals and ambitions. Ostensibly, it is about the dissemination and construction of knowledge, activities accomplished within norms and constraints that are slowly and inevitably changing. In the traditional classroom, the main work performed is that of the professor. Students work too: taking notes, occasionally asking questions, but this work is really marginal to the main work, that of the professor expressing his knowledge of the subject. Students' main work belongs elsewhere; that is why they study at home or write research papers in their dorms. Classrooms are centers where the expertise of the teacher is on display; students listen in on the performance, mainly as spectators. A session I once attended at a Lilly Conference on college teaching makes this point about the pedagogic division of labor beautifully. The paper was titled, "Solving homework in class and receiving lectures at home: Reversing the situation." The presenter was making the point that if students were having a lot of difficulty solving the problems that he had set in the classroom, did it not make more sense to use classroom time to work on these problems (in a sense the work of the classroom became the students' home work) and to do the presentation somewhere else; that somewhere else being the web, where the professor subsequently began to post his lectures.

That this particular engineering professor was making use of the computer to help reconfigure the work of his classroom is no coincidence. His reversal of the situation—his redesign of the curriculum so that the work of his students became the work of the classroom—captures dramatically what is at issue as our teaching moves online and technology continues to impact what we consider to be patterns of work and interaction that are acceptable as teaching and learning. If more and more the computer can be used to do things such as post our lecture notes, create and grade tests, and do a host of management-oriented activities once considered essential aspects of classroom life, then more and more time is freed up for something else. What is that something else? Could it be the opportunity, at last, to truly facilitate student learning, to do the hard work of getting students to think, and to focus on motivational factors such as the creation of community among learners individually isolated by the traditional norms of the classroom? That clearly is the hope of those who are championing the revolution in information technology.

As the work of classroom is increasingly distributed among the various actors involved, it is natural to start seeing collaboration as a preferred mode of interaction among learners. For this reason, more than any other, educators and researchers have become interested in computer-mediated forms of learning and in ways in which learners can be brought together to accomplish complex tasks, what has come to be termed computer-supported collaborative learning (CSCL) (Koshman, 1996). Research is beginning to document the ways in which computer-mediated forms of collaboration are having their impact, both in terms of bringing learners together in the synergistic accomplishment of joint tasks—what researchers refer to as effects with technology (Kolodner & Guzdial, 1996) and of documenting the ways in which overall learning performance can be enhanced through CSCL (effects of technology). At the same time, researchers are also beginning to realize how improvements in performance, while appearing to be the effects of technology, may turn out on closer examination to be the result of students coming together to learn almost despite the technology.

Schutte (1997), in a paper which first circulated on the web, interestingly enough, compared the performances of two groups of students, those taking his class via the traditional classroom versus those taking it on the web. He found the performance of the latter to be significantly better than that of the former but concluded that much of the performance differences can be attributed to student collaboration as to the technology itself. In fact, the highest performing students (in both classes) reported the most peer interaction. Therefore, it is important that faculty contemplating the use of the virtual format pay attention to the issue of real-time collaboration, whether carried from within the traditional classroom or in the context of virtual space (Schutte, p. 3).

It is inevitable that the teacher's role will be transformed from that of transmitter of information to that of facilitator of the learner process. Becoming a facilitator will mean the decentering of teaching in favor of learning, thus hastening the move from the instructional paradigm to the learning paradigm, (Barr & Tagg, 1995). At the same time, the work of the classroom will become more authentic, real, real-time, just-in-time, problem- and project-based (Courtney, Vasa, Luo, & Muggy, 1999). Certainly, with responsibilities being distributed across teachers, the work of planning becomes much more crucial. The spontaneity of the teacher, his or her situated actions, will remain as crucial as ever. However, what these actions will look like will change. Inevitably, too, students will want to engage with knowledge on their own terms and will want a greater say in what goes on in the classroom. And there are models for how this might look. Goldman (1996) has described mediating worlds in which work is organized along both social as well as a task dimensions. Groups organized into computer-supported, collaborative work groups are going to do what work groups do all over the world: integrate their social, emotional selves into their work lives, which of course will impact their identities and power as learners. If I am able to bring myself as a whole person into the classroom, then this affects how I see the relevance of learning to my life. It also affects my sense of agency or empowerment in my dealings with the world.

Tools and Technology

In a sense, everything that has been discussed in this essay up to now has been about technology, either directly or indirectly. Each of the dimensions of culture analyzed here has been touched in one way or another by the far-reaching impact of new informational forms. The traditional limitations of pedagogic space and time, for example, have been mitigated if not entirely swept away by the mere motion of a device called a mouse. Students from the other side of the globe can attend a classroom here at the University of Nebraska without ever leaving home. A teacher can attend a conference in Asia and still be available to teach a class back in the US (Palloff & Pratt, 1999).

At the same time, as technology gains in power and sophistication, more and more is possible in the transaction between learner and instructor. A century ago, learning at a distance meant contact by letter correspondence: Student and tutor experienced each other only as written forms. Today, with the right add-on or plug-in, I can send my image a 1,000 miles and obtain that of my student over the same distance. We are present to each other, visually, aurally, and orally through the use of technology.

If technology has shattered time and distance, created new spaces for interaction, and made possible virtual encounters between learner and teacher, its impact on the pedagogic text may be the most far-reaching yet. For now, we appear to be witnessing the true democratization of knowledge, as the formerly bounded world of the student and the teacher is permeated by a pervasive all-encompassing web of information and meaning. Within the traditional classroom, technology and tools are add-ons, for the most part. A presentation using slides may admit in a little of the outside world. A movie displays the intricacies and passions of that world more fully. For the most part, however, the manner in which the world of the content is to be explored is handled by the medium of language, infrequently supported by sound or image, technology or tool. Not so with many of the new forms of computer-mediated communication for whom skilled tool use is an integral aspect of the teaching and learning environment. The computer opens a window to expertise wherever it exists. Both student and teacher can access it, instantly. Computers do more than access and organize information, however. They are capable of packaging it in ways that promise more long-lasting impact, a key element in the definition of learning.

Which brings us full circle back to the question of learning itself. The traditional view of the learning process, one that fits easily with many of the traditional practices of teaching at our institutions of higher learning, defines it as the acquisition of conceptual knowledge by an individual learner, knowledge that is found represented by schematic structures in the brain or consciousness (Sfard, 1998). Schools and universities, for the most part, still support an interpretation of learning as an abstracted manipulation of symbols in an environment that is largely individualistic and competitive (Resnick, 1987). Given a view of learning as mere cognitive information processing, it is but short step to seeing teaching as the transmission of that information and of the lecture as the preferred mode of transmission. Finally, learning that emphasizes acquisition and transmission will call for a technology that merely facilitates information retrieval and storage.

But new cultures of pedagogy require new theories of learning. Competing with the traditional model is one that sees learning as the construction of new knowledge based on prior experiences (Courtney et al., 1999; Pratt, 1998). That construction takes place in a context of use, a community of practice in which authentic knowledge is manipulable through tool use and capable of immediate application in real-world settings. While traditional classroom-based learning can certainly accommodate the pedagogical implications of this new analytic perspective (Lave & Wenger, 1991), it may well be the world of computer-mediated pedagogy that sees the coming into fruition of the exciting implications of new theories of learning, particularly those that tie learning to context and tool use (Rogers, 1997).

Discussion
In the long run, the pendulum is likely to swing too far in the direction of technology at all costs. It seems inevitable. From the statistics on distance education cited at the beginning of this report to the cautionary example of what happened with educational television in the 1950s and

1960s (Tiffin & Rajasingham, 1995), we must expect the sentiment to prevail that if something can be done on the Internet, it ought to be, and that if it can't, it is probably not worth doing at all. However, when the pendulum does swing back, and many smaller swings are already occurring, the result I feel sure will be an enormous enriching of our educational discourse, an extraordinary enlarging of our pedagogic vocabulary, and a much needed redefinition and revitalizing of our roles as teachers. As faculty and faculty developers, that future really is in our hands.

References

Barr, R., & Tagg, J. (1995, November/December). From teaching to learning: A new paradigm for undergraduate education. *Change, 27* (6), 13–26.

Chapman, V. L. (1998). Adult education and the body: Changing performances of teaching and learning. *Proceedings of the 39th Annual Adult Education Conference* (pp. 301–306). San Antonio, TX: University of the Incarnate Word.

Courtney, S. (1997). "The class started without me": Toward a new culture of learning and teaching. *Proceedings of the 17th Lilly Conference on College Teaching* (pp. 63–66). Oxford, OH: Miami University.

Courtney, S., Vasa, S., Luo, J., & Muggy, V. (1999). *Characteristics of adults as learners and implications for computer-based systems for information and instruction.* Minneapolis, MN: America's Learning Exchange, Minnesota Department of Economic Security.

Courtney, S., Jha, L., & Babchuk, W. (1995). "Like school": A grounded theory of life in an ABE/GED classroom. *Adult Basic Education: An Interdisciplinary Journal, 4* (3), 172–195.

Downes, S. (1998). *The future of online learning.* Unpublished manuscript, Assiniboine Community College.

Duffy, D. K., & Jones, J. W. (1995). *Teaching within the rhythms of the semester.* San Francisco, CA: Jossey-Bass.

Fox, D. (1983). Personal theories of teaching. *Studies in Higher Education, 8* (3), 151–163.

Goldman, S.V. (1996). Mediating micro worlds: Collaboration on high school science activities. In T. Koschman (Ed.), *CSCL: Theory and practice of an emerging paradigm* (pp. 45–92). Hillsdale, NJ: Lawrence Erlbaum.

Herron, J. (1996). Helping whole people learn. In D. Boud & N. Miller (Eds.), *Working with experience.* (75–94). London, England: Routledge.

Jaffee, D. (1998, November). *Pedagogical isomorphisms and resistance to change in higher education.* Paper presented at the 8th Annual Conference, Creating Alternative Learning Cultures, SUNY, New Paltz.

Kolodner, J., & Guzdial, M. (1996). Effects *with* and *of* CSCL: Tracking learning in a new paradigm. In T. Koschman (Ed.), *CSCL: Theory and practice of an emerging paradigm* (pp. 307–320). Hillsdale, NJ: Lawrence Erlbaum.

Koshman, T. (1996). *CSCL: Theory and practice of an emerging paradigm.* Hillsdale, NJ: Lawrence Erlbaum.

Laurillard, D. (1993). *Rethinking university teaching: A framework for the effective use of educational technology.* London, England: Routledge.

Lave, J., & Wenger, E. (1991). *Situated learning: Legitimate peripheral participation.* New York, NY: Cambridge University Press.

National Center for Education Statistics. *Distance education at postsecondary institutions: 1997–98.* [online]. Available: http://nces.ed.gov/pubsearch/pubsinfo.asp?pubid=2000013.

Palloff, R.M., & Pratt, K. (1999). *Building learning communities in cyberspace.* San Francisco, CA: Jossey-Bass.

Pratt, D., & Associates (1998). *Five perspectives on teaching in adult and higher education.* Malabar, FL: Krieger.

Resnick, L. (1987, December). Learning in school and out. *Educational Researcher, 16* (9), 13–20.

Rogers, Y.(1997). *A brief introduction to distributed cognition.* Available: http://www.cogs. susx.ac.uk/users/ yvonne/dcog.html.

Scardamalia, M., & Bereiter, C. (1996). Computer support for knowledge-building communities. In T. Koschman (Ed.), *CSCL: Theory and practice of an emerging paradigm* (pp. 249–268). Hillsdale, NJ: Lawrence Erlbaum.

Schutte, J. (1997). *Virtual teaching in higher education: The new intellectual superhighway or just another traffic jam?* [online] Available http://csun.edu/sociology/virexp.htm

Sfard, A. (1998). On two metaphors for learning and the dangers of choosing just one. *Educational Researcher, 27* (2), 4–13.

Snyder, M. (1995). *An investigation into the factors that encourage university faculty to use information technologies in their teaching.* Unpublished doctoral dissertation, University of Nebraska, Lincoln.

Tiffin, J., & Rajasingham, L. (1995). *In search of the virtual class.* London, England: Routledge.

Tisdell, E. (1993). Interlocking systems of power, privilege, and oppression in adult higher education. *Adult Education Quarterly, 43* (4), 203–226.

University of Illinois (1999). *Teaching at an Internet distance: The pedagogy of online teaching and learning. The report of a 1998–1999 University of Illinois Faculty Seminar.*

Weiss, G., & Haber, H. F. (1999). *Perspectives on embodiment: The intersection of nature and culture.* New York, NY: Routledge.

ENDNOTES

1. According to the federal government, 79% of publix four-year institutions, as of 1997–98, were offering distance education classes. While the number of courses and enrollments nearly doubled between 1994 and 1998, the fastest growth occured with the use of the Internet to offer education, jumping from 28% of institutions in 1995 to 60% in 1998 (National Center for Education Statistics, Distance Education at Postsecondary Institutions: 1997–98).

2. Currently, the range and complexity of the various technologically mediated formats for educational purposes is considerable. For present purposes, when I speak of technology transforming postsecondary teaching, I am mainly referring to the use of computer-based formats, such as the Internet.

3. Quotes generally are taken from students participating in a course taught using Lotus Notes, an enhanced email communication system, in the fall of 1996 and 1999.

Contact:

Sean Courtney, Associate Professor
Department of Educational Psychology
University of Nebraska
Lincoln, NE 68588-0345
(402) 472-5927   FAX: (402) 472-8319

Sean Courtney has been at the University of Nebraska since 1989. Originally trained in the areas of adult education and human resource development, his current work focuses on improving college teaching and assessing the impact of technology on teaching and learning. He has a strong interest in facilitation and collaborative forms of inquiry, and in working with faculty to integrate complex models of teaching into their practice. Recent publications include "Characteristics of adults as learners and implications for computer-based systems for information and instruction" (p. 79), America's Learning eXchange, Minnesota Department of Economic Security. (January 1999). He is currently an Associate Professor in the Department of Educational Psychology, at the University of Nebraska-Lincoln.

Section III

Focus on Faculty Development and Professional Support

15

Developing New Faculty: An Evolving Program

Gloria Pierce
Montclair State University

This essay describes the evolution of a program for the development of new faculty at a public teaching university. The year-long process of orienting the newest professors to the campus and assisting them with their scholarship and teaching results in additional (albeit unplanned and unexpected) benefits, such as professional renewal of senior faculty who serve as advisors and enhanced functioning of the university itself. Vital to the program's success is the productive involvement of key campus constituencies and responsiveness to feedback.

INTRODUCTION

"**I** wish this program existed when I joined the faculty at MSU!" Senior professors at a public university often repeat this refrain when they begin to realize the nature of the new faculty program that was instituted there six years ago. Their wistful remarks testify to the success of a faculty development program mandated for all newly hired tenure track faculty since 1994 at Montclair State University (MSU). At that time, the University embraced the expanded definition of scholarship advanced by Ernest Boyer (1990) by creating the Faculty Scholarship Incentive Program (FSIP) that offers all faculty the opportunity to engage in a scholarly project as an alternative to a full teaching assignment. Newly hired faculty participate by attending a two-hour session each week of their first academic year at MSU. Five senior faculty members (one from each college or school of the university) serve as advisors to the incoming cohort, helping them to become oriented to the university, establish a research agenda, and develop excellent teaching skills.

RATIONALE

The rationale for the New Faculty Program (NFP) is strongly rooted in an organization development perspective that values human talent and considers its nurturance to be a major role of management (Gibb, 1978). The program itself demonstrates the commitment of the university's administration and professoriate to several principles that undergird a strong academic institution. First, a university's greatest strength resides in the quality of its faculty which is reflected in the quality of education delivered to students and in productive scholarship, as broadly defined by Boyer (1990). Second, it makes organizational sense to assist the newest faculty with the daunting tasks of acclimating to a new institution (and sometimes a new geographical area, as well), preparing courses, teaching effectively, and maintaining their scholarly activities (Boice, 1992). Third, constructive retention of faculty is mutually beneficial. Alignment of individual needs and values with organizational goals and culture produces high levels of faculty performance and satisfaction as well as institutional excellence (Rausch, 1984). If a good fit cannot be made, however, it is better for both to find out sooner rather than later.

STRUCTURE

The New Faculty Program operates under the auspices of the provost/vice president for academic affairs and is administered directly by the office of the assistant vice president for academic affairs. As chief administrative officer of the division of academic affairs, the provost/VPAA oversees its three colleges, three schools, and several other academic centers and programs. The NFP Director, who reports to the assistant VPAA, is a professor with a background in organizational development, counseling, and adult education. She is responsible for recruiting and managing the five advisors (also referred to as mentors or resource faculty), for designing and developing the program, and for facilitating the weekly sessions. Because the resource faculty play such a vital role, their selection is a crucial responsibility of the director, in consultation with the assistant VPAA.

Resource Faculty

The resource faculty agree to serve for one year and receive a stipend equal to the compensation for a three-credit course each semester. Several have continued for more than one year, however, because there is no restriction on length of service, and some continuity is desirable. Advisors attend and help to facilitate the weekly group sessions and may spend another hour each week providing guidance on an individual basis. For these duties, they need excellent group process and interpersonal skills and a willingness to share their wealth of experience and knowledge about academic life and the culture of the university. Members of past cohorts appreciate the individual attention given to them, although not all junior faculty are receptive to the greater intensity of a one-on-one relationship. Some seek the counseling and psychological support of a mentor, while others require and request support that is more instrumental in nature, such as assistance in locating funding sources for research, grant-writing, or guidance about committee service. Hence, advisors are a resource for new faculty, providing assistance across the spectrum of developmental relationships (Kram, 1985). Originally, each mentor was assigned several proteges, a feature of the program that felt inauthentic. New faculty now have the opportunity to request various kinds of help from any of the advisors, as needed—a much more fluid process that seems to be more natural and comfortable for both.

Weekly Sessions
The first semester is front-loaded with nuts and bolts information about various support services that new faculty are likely to use (see Appendix 15.1). Recently, this orientation has taken the form of a poster session where new faculty can meet and speak with representatives from units such as the academic success center, which provides services related to student advisement, psychological counseling, service learning, students with disabilities, career development, tutorials, basic skills, etc. The poster session is another example of a modification made in response to previous cohorts' requests for an alternative to what they experienced as a parade of presenters each week. The new format has proven to be a more casual and lively occasion where faculty can choose to spend as much time as they wish at any particular display. Similarly, feedback from participants led to an expansion of the library orientation, which now provides more assistance in the use of library resources for research projects.

During the second semester, the focus shifts to more substantive considerations. At this point, the cohort has learned the essentials of the university environment and turns its attention to teaching and learning issues and further planning of research agendas (see Appendix 15.2). Representatives from the office of research and sponsored programs join the resource faculty in conducting seminars on preparing grant proposals both for external funding sources and for internally sponsored programs. The weekly sessions become more seminar-like in character and address matters of curriculum development, instructional methods, assessment and grading, and diversity. New faculty are pleased to take a more active role, preparing and presenting sessions on topics of their choice.

KEY ELEMENTS

The NFP was developed in the context of a university with established resources and the administrative leadership to use them wisely. Five major components form the foundation of the program: 1) effective lateral and vertical feedback and communication processes; 2) administrative vision, commitment, and cooperation; 3) senior faculty's ability to provide mentorship and advisement to junior faculty; 4) senior faculty's skill and experience with professional development and effective educational practices; and 5) two specialized units created to assist faculty with all aspects of their teaching role—the Institute for Critical Thinking and the Center of Pedagogy.

Feedback Loops

Effective communication processes have been a hallmark of the New Faculty Program and are essential to its success. Continuous quality improvement (Deming, 1982, 1986, 1993) is achieved in several ways: 1) by soliciting written formative evaluations from the cohort of new faculty at the end of the first semester; 2) by written summative evaluations from them at the end of their academic year; 3) by informal feedback at the weekly seminars; 4) by regular assessment and consultation among the NFP director, the resource faculty, the assistant vice president for academic affairs and the provost/vice president for academic affairs; and 5) by an open line of communication between the director and other stakeholder constituencies on campus, such as deans, department chairs or other administrative divisions. The open flow of information and ideas allows problems to be encountered and remedied quickly. Yearly improvement results in a dynamic, evolving program that is highly responsive to the needs of new faculty and the campus community.

Administrative Support

The involvement of several levels of administration affects the NFP in various ways. Foremost is the leadership of the provost and staff in the office of academic affairs in providing the resources and attention necessary to operate the program. Administrative support is shown financially at a cost of approximately $350,000 per year for a cohort of 20 new hires. This figure accounts for 25% of their salary, the stipend paid to resource faculty, release time for the director, refreshments, books, duplicating costs, and secretarial/clerical services.

Academic deans play an important role in several ways. First, they enlist the cooperation of department chairs who must schedule new professors' classes to allow them to attend NFP seminars. The two deans who co-authored the FSIP agreement with the faculty union remain especially committed to the NFP, each of them spending one full session with every incoming cohort to address contractual matters and FSIP procedures.

The attitude of department chairs and deans can have a chilling or salubrious effect on how new faculty view the NFP. Their support is needed, therefore, to point out the value of the program and to encourage the new members of their department to participate. The cooperation of other divisions on campus is necessary to inform new faculty about their services and how to access them. To sum up, the involvement of administrative personnel—deans, chairs, and division heads—is an integral part of the program.

Role of Senior Faculty

The five tenured professors who act as mentors are, unquestionably, the lifeblood of the program, developing the closest relationships with the cohort because of their active presence throughout the year. In the public forum of the weekly sessions, the five advisors work as a team to guide new faculty through the wide range of tasks they must perform, from academic advisement of students to preparation of reappointment applications and FSIP proposals.

In addition to facilitating plenary group discussions, advisors work with self-selected sub-groups as they develop sessions to be presented during the second semester. Cohorts decide upon presentation topics according to their concerns and their perceptions of current problems and issues in teaching and learning: "Teaching with sensitivity to diversity," "Using technology in instruction," "Teaching graduate students," and "The teacher-scholar in the teaching university."

University politics (i.e., the operation of the informal or hidden organization) is another area where senior faculty deal with the concerns of new faculty. Advisors find it can be difficult to give candid assessments about certain issues without causing undue consternation about reappointment, tenure, and promotion. Most senior faculty prefer to accentuate the positive aspects of campus culture lest they ignite negative expectations or fuel undue fears. Junior faculty, however, urge their mentors to be brutally honest about any pitfalls they may encounter. For example, participants from past cohorts have commented that they wanted the resource faculty to guide them through the rocks and shoals of institutional politics and to interpret for them the meaning of seemingly trivial issues that are laden with significance because of past events.

Advisors also act as moderators of a board game (Bollin & Hill, 1996) played by teams of new faculty in which they are challenged to reflect on various aspects of teaching and learning and to share their experiences and insights with the group. The lively discussions stimulated by the game's questions require the advisors to use their skills in group work to keep the discussion on track, to keep the process moving, and to encourage reticent members of the group to participate.

Resource faculty must model effective group facilitation and instructional methods for two important reasons. First, the success of the cohort itself depends largely upon on the development of a healthy group. Second, modeling is important because of its transferability to the classrooms of new faculty. Many sessions of the NFP advocate best practices in teaching and learning such as student engagement, caring pedagogy, a safe learning environment, etc. If the content of the sessions becomes incongruent with the process (what individuals are actually experiencing), however, dissonance is created that contaminates the message and compromises learning goals (Argyris & Schon, 1974). Unfortunately, the first cohort suffered from these discrepancies and from insufficient processing of their learning experience. Subsequently, the director made certain to choose advisors who would model best practices, who are attuned to the affective and maintenance needs of the group (Gladding, 1995) and who are capable of facilitating productive interactions. Increased attention to group process, therefore, is another significant change in the NFP since its inception.

Support from Special Units

The NFP draws heavily on the services of two special units that are well established at the university. The mission of the Institute for Critical Thinking is to foster critical thinking across the disciplines. Institute fellows are faculty from academic departments throughout the university who are committed to fostering critical thinking skills and dispositions in their students. As seminar leaders, they show new faculty how to infuse critical thinking into the curriculum and demonstrate instructional methods that foster critical thinking (Meyers, 1988). Practica in areas as diverse as music, broadcasting and the media, writing, philosophy for children, history, chemistry, biology, art, economics, marketing, and computer technology have enriched the program immensely.

Initially delivered during the fall semester, the critical thinking seminars became a source of stress for the first cohort of new faculty who felt overwhelmed by their breadth and depth and suggested that they be scheduled later in the year. Thus, the emphasis on critical thinking now occurs during the spring semester, after the new faculty have had a chance to get their bearings.

The Center of Pedagogy is another source of assistance from within the institution. The philosophy of the center is based on the work of John Goodlad (1990, 1994) and other prominent educators (Giroux, 1983, 1988; Noddings,1995; Paul,1990; Greene, 1986, 1988; Freire, 1973, 1985; Brookfield, 1988, 1990). Its mission is to prepare students for participation in a social and political democracy and to encourage the use of best practices in pedagogy. Faculty affiliated with the center design activities to introduce new professors to principles such as caring pedagogy (Noddings 1995), and innovative methods to enhance their teaching, such as peer observation and coaching (Showers, 1984).

RESULTS

The NFP has produced unintended positive outcomes as well as met its stated objectives. Benefits accrue to three groups—junior faculty, senior faculty, and the university itself—and occur in three arenas—the classroom, the campus, and careers (gains in academe). These intersect with one another, producing nine categories of results, as shown in Table 15.1.

New Faculty

Because of the emphasis on teaching and learning, one would expect the NFP to have a substantial impact on curriculum, classroom climate, and delivery of instruction. New faculty attest to the aphorism "confidence breeds competence" (Fullan, 1993, p. 113) when they report feeling more self-assured about preparing syllabi, learning activities, tests, and assessing student work. Also, they are secure in the knowledge that help is available should questions or problems arise. Furthermore, junior faculty believe that the care shown to them by their advisors has made them more caring toward their students and more able to create a classroom climate conducive to learning. Thus, effects of the program extend to the students of new faculty.

TABLE 15.1
Outcomes of New Faculty Program

	Classroom	Campus	Career
New faculty	• Caring pedagogy • Critical thinking • Student engagement	• Integrated into university • Knowledge of services • Stress reduction	• Plan research agenda • Continue scholarship • Professional development
Senior faculty	• New instructional methods • Reflective of practice • Deepened knowledge of pedagogy	• More appreciated • More influential • More isolated	• Rejuvenation as scholars • Impetus to resume research • Professional development
University	• Reputation for teaching excellence • High achieving students • Better retention rates	• Increased productivity of junior and senior faculty • Enhanced lateral and vertical communication • Improved procedures • Humanization of culture	• Recognition for leadership in higher education

NFP participants also gain a sense of connection and importance to the campus community. As a member of one cohort put it, "I never expected to feel so much a part of the university so quickly. Our group likes to joke about having our own hybrid theme song: 'You've got a friend . . . here, there, and everywhere.'" In general, comments made by new faculty indicate that they perceive the campus environment as welcoming and friendly, although there are pockets where friction exists. Thus, the program achieves a major goal—integration of new faculty into the university community.

By the time the program ends, the cohort has begun to plan and implement a scholarly agenda. They have learned how to access funding sources for their research and professional development. Many NFP participants already have received external grants and most are taking part in the FSIP or another internally sponsored research program.

Senior Faculty

Professional development of the seasoned faculty who were asked to become mentors was not an explicit goal of the NFP. Nevertheless, professors who became involved found it an enriching experience and were rejuvenated in significant ways. Some reported that the NFP supplied the impetus to resume research projects that had been languishing. Others felt fortunate to have the opportunity to reflect on their teaching (Schon, 1983) and became enthusiastic about new approaches to learning in their classrooms. "It's so seldom that we actually get the chance to contemplate our teaching practices and to discuss what we do and how we feel about things in a safe environment. This year with the new people has been a real blessing," remarked one of the resource people.

The experience of veteran faculty parallels that of their protégés in that they too feel more included in university life and more able to function effectively within it. Some claim to be energized by their ability to make a significant contribution and to influence the university culture in positive directions (Wunsch, 1994), as this comment reveals: "The best part (of the NFP) for me was getting close to what's going on here. The idea of being influential is pretty compelling. Plus, it's really invigorating to know I'm doing something so worthwhile and that it's truly appreciated and valued."

Other instances further illustrate the convergence of individual with institutional renewal. Because of linkages made in the course of NFP events, several advisors formed collaborative relationships with colleagues. One such partnership resulted in a highly respected program in the School of the Arts. Such scholarly projects bring prestige to the university and help to alleviate the isolation that threatens to become an occupational hazard of the professorate (Fullan, 1993, p. 34).

The University

From an organizational development perspective, potential advantages to the university as a whole are consequential (Wunsch, 1994). Although a comprehensive study is yet to be undertaken, anecdotal evidence and patterns observed by administrators point to definite improvements in organizational processes and climate. For instance, there is increased productivity by junior and senior faculty alike, as evidenced by their contributions to conference proceedings, publications, new programs, and revised courses. Such accomplishments enhance the university's reputation as a respected academic institution.

Internally, organizational functioning has been enhanced by the feedback loops and linkages created by the proliferation of lateral and vertical communication—between academic departments, between the professoriate and professional staff, between faculty and administration, and across professorial ranks. For example, the vice president for academic affairs and assistant VPAA signal their interest and accessibility by leading a discussion of the shifting paradigm in higher education (Barr & Tagg, 1995; Boyer, 1990; Glassick et al., 1997; Plater, 1995) and its relevance to faculty careers at MSU. Additionally, feedback from faculty has led to policy and procedural changes in the library and in the employee benefits and student advisement offices. In general, greater personal contact among people has tended to humanize the university and improve its functioning.

Perhaps the most significant institutional impact remains to be evaluated—what students gain from better teaching. Administration and faculty expect that improved classroom instruction will lead to higher student achievement levels and more meaningful learning. This hypothesis has yet to be tested, however, as the full effect of the NFP becomes apparent over time.

RECOMMENDATIONS

Enact Change Expeditiously
More than any other factor, the key to effective new faculty development is to be vigilant about its shortcomings and to make necessary modifications as quickly as possible. This ensures a continually evolving program that is responsive to the needs of new faculty and others upon whose support the program depends. Such responsiveness is accomplished through ongoing feedback and evaluation by the new faculty and by using a preference indicator at the end of the first semester which gives them a voice in the following semester's activities. Receptivity to feedback from other parts of the university, as well, can help to establish a win-win situation that builds optimum support for the program. Flexibility should not compromise the program's integrity, however, nor interfere with its goals. Program directors should resist pressure from those who would forward their own agenda without regard for program objectives.

Choose and Use Resource Faculty Well
It is critical to select capable advisors and to use their talents wisely and to structure the program to make use of their time and expertise. If advi-

sors feel underutilized, they may lose interest and become disengaged. Selection processes must insure that advisors are powerful teacher-scholars who are eager to share their wealth of experience in a positive way. The ideal adviser is a learner-centered, skilled facilitator who encourages the observance of group boundaries such as attendance and punctuality, keeps the group on task, and fosters productive norms and group cohesion (Gladding, 1995). At best, new faculty should experience a fully functioning group that can serve as a model for their own classrooms.

Follow Developmental Guidelines

Program design should follow fundamental principles of curriculum development and need satisfaction. A basic orientation to university structures and services should precede sessions that focus on educational theory and skill building. New faculty need to become sufficiently grounded in their new workplace before they can fully attend to complex pedagogical concepts or career planning. Instructional methods should involve the participants as actively as possible, with new faculty taking responsibility for conducting sessions themselves in later stages of the program.

Attend to Amenities

Various social and celebratory events reinforce the impression that new faculty are valued and accepted into the university community. These might include coffee service for the weekly sessions; an orientation dinner with the president, vice presidents, and deans; and socials/ receptions at the end of each semester for presenters. Such events send a message of appreciation for all those who contributed to the program throughout the year and provide another opportunity for interaction in a cordial atmosphere. Although they represent a small portion of the total cost of the program, amenities such as these help to form the bonds between people that tend to enhance the overall functioning of the university.

CONCLUSION

Although the particular configuration of resources and talents will vary from one institution to another, capable administrators can draw upon the unique set of assets that exist on their campuses. A well-planned program for the development of new faculty can yield rich rewards far beyond its primary purpose. Although efforts focus on the newest members of the professoriate, the synergistic effects of a successful program extend to many other campus constituencies, including students, and ultimately the academic institution itself.

REFERENCES

Argyris, C., & Schon, D. A. (1974). *Theory and practice: Increasing professional effectiveness.* San Francisco, CA: Jossey-Bass.

Barr, R., & Tagg, J. (1995). From teaching to learning: A new paradigm for undergraduate education, *Change, 27* (6), 113–25.

Boice, R. (1992). *The new faculty member.* San Francisco, CA: Jossey-Bass.

Bollin, G., & Hill, P. (1996). *Reflections on practice.* Board game developed for the Pennsylvania Society of Teaching Scholars (PASTS).

Boyer, E. L. (1990). *Scholarship reconsidered: Prioritizing the professoriate.* Princeton, NJ: Carnegie Foundation.

Brookfield, S. D. (1988). *Developing critical thinkers.* San Francisco, CA: Jossey-Bass.

Brookfield, S. D. (1990). *The skillful teacher.* San Francisco, CA: Jossey-Bass.

Deming, W. E. (1982). *Quality, productivity, and competitive position.* Cambridge, MA: MIT Press.

Deming, W. E. (1986). *Out of the crisis.* Cambridge, MA: MIT Press.

Deming, W. E. (1993). *The new economics for business, government, and education.* Cambridge, MA: MIT Press.

Freire, P. (1973). *Education for critical consciousness.* New York, NY: Continuum.

Freire, P. (1985). *The politics of education: Culture, power, and liberation.* South Hadley, MA: Bergin & Garvey.

Fullan, M. (1993). *Change forces: Probing the depths of educational reform.* Bristol, PA: Falmer Press.

Gibb, J. R. (1978). *Trust: A new view of personal and organizational development.* Los Angeles, CA: The Guild of Tutors Press.

Giroux, H. A. (1983). *Theory and resistance in education.* New York, NY: Bergin and Garvey.

Giroux, H. A. (1988). *Schooling and the struggle for public life.* Minneapolis, MN: University of Minnesota Press.

Gladding, S. T. (1995). *Group work: A counseling specialty* (2nd ed.). Englewood Cliffs, NJ: Prentice-Hall.

Glassick, C. E., Huber, M. T., & Maeroff, G. I. (1997). *Scholarship assessed: Evaluation of the professoriate.* San Francisco, CA: Jossey-Bass.

Goodlad, J. I. (1990). *Teachers for our nation's schools*. San Francisco, CA: Jossey-Bass.

Goodlad, J. I. (1994). *Educational renewal*. San Francisco, CA: Jossey-Bass.

Greene, M. (1986). In search of a critical pedagogy. *Harvard Educational Review, 56* (4), 427–441.

Greene, M. (1988). *The dialectic of freedom*. New York, NY: Teachers College Press.

Kram, K. E. (1985). *Mentoring at work*. Glenview, IL: Scott, Foresman.

Meyers, C. (1988). *Teaching students to think critically*. San Francisco, CA: Jossey-Bass.

Noddings, N. (1995). Teaching themes of care, *Phi Delta Kappan, 76* (9), 675–679.

Paul. R. (1990). *Critical thinking*. Rohnert Park, CA: Center for Critical Thinking and Moral Critique.

Plater, W. M. (1995). Future work: Faculty time in the 21st century. *Change, 27* (3), 23–33.

Rausch, E. E. (1984). *Balancing needs of people and organizations: The linking elements concept*. Cranford, NJ: Didactic Systems, Inc.

Schon, D. A. (1983). *The reflective practitioner: How professionals think in action*. New York, NY: Basic Books, Inc.

Showers, B. (1984). *Peer coaching: A strategy for facilitating transfer of training*. Eugene, OR: Center for Educational Policy and Management.

Wunsch, M. (Ed.). (1994). *Mentoring revisited: Making an impact on individuals and institutions*. San Francisco, CA: Jossey-Bass.

Contact:

Gloria Pierce
Montclair State University
College of Education and Human Services
Upper Montclair, NJ 07043
Email: PierceG@mail.montclair.edu

Gloria Pierce is Professor in the College of Education and Human Services at Montclair State University where she has been Director of the New Faculty Program since its inception in 1994. In addition to her staff development activities, she teaches courses she developed to incorporate principles of feminist therapy into the graduate program of the Department of Counseling, Human Development, and Educational Leadership.

APPENDIX 15.1

SAMPLE SCHEDULE
NEW FACULTY PROGRAM
FALL SEMESTER

September   x   Introductions and needs assessment:
Resource faculty meet with new faculty

xx   Orientation tour of library services:
Library director and staff specialists

xx   Poster session to introduce support services on campus, such as the Academic Success Center

xx   Overview of the reappointment process: Advisement by resource faculty and recently reappointed junior faculty

October   x   Planning a scholarly agenda: Strategies for research and publication

xx   Addressing issues of diversity on campus: Interactive discussion led by the dean of students

xx   Local Selected Procedures Agreement and the State contract: Discussion with the dean of CEHS and a faculty union representative

xx   Academic advising from a faculty perspective: Seminar led by resources faculty

November   x   Reflections on practice: Teams of new faculty play a board game to stimulate discussion of teaching and learning

xx   Faculty Scholarship Incentive Program: Discussion with the dean of SAM and a union representative

xx   Securing external funding and internal grants other than FSIP: director of the office of research and sponsored programs

xx   "New directions for higher education: Implications for MSU" Discussion with the VPAA and assistant VPAA

December   x   Formative evaluation of the fall semester and planning for the spring semester

xx   Holiday celebration with president and presenters

APPENDIX 15.2

SAMPLE SCHEDULE
NEW FACULTY PROGRAM
SPRING SCHEDULE

January	x	Peer observation and coaching project (Part I): Introduce concepts and establish guidelines and partnerships
February	x	Teaching and learning session: Infusing critical thinking into the curriculum
	xx	Research and grant opportunities: External and internal sources of assistance
	xx	Teaching and learning session: Nurture and challenge in the classroom
	xx	Peer observation and coaching project (Part II): Intensive work in dyads
March	x	Teaching and learning session: Assessing and grading student work
	xx	Spring break
	xx	Selection of groups and topics for group-developed sessions in April
	xx	Teaching and learning session: The teacher-scholar—a delicate balance
	xx	Processing of peer observation and coaching project (Part III): Partners share learning with cohort
April	x	Group developed session: Teaching graduate students—methods, challenges, rewards
	xx	Group developed session: Teaching for equity—sensitivity to diversity in the classroom
	xx	Group developed session: Teaching with technology—computer applications to instruction
	xx	Final processing of the year's experience: Summative evaluation and recommendations for future cohorts
May	x	Farewell social and reception for presenters and president

16

Publish, Don't Perish: A Program to Help Scholars Flourish

Tara Gray
New Mexico State University

Jane Birch
Brigham Young University

Faculty often believe that if they do not publish, they will perish. Faculty developers can respond to this need by helping faculty increase their scholarly productivity. Research shows that faculty are more productive if they write for 15–30 minutes daily, organize their writing around key sentences, and get extensive feedback on drafts. This article evaluates a program hosted on two campuses that aimed at supporting 115 faculty achieve these goals. Throughout the program, participants kept records of time they spent writing and the number of pages they wrote and at the end of the program, they were surveyed. These data reveal that if participants continued to write and revise prose at the rate they did during the program, they would produce 75 polished pages per year. According to survey results, 83% of participants would participate in the program again, and 95% would recommend it to their colleagues.

INTRODUCTION

This essay evaluates the extent to which "Publish, Don't Perish," a program designed to help faculty flourish as writers, enabled participants to achieve the following three program goals: 1) Improve time management by developing the discipline to write daily for at least 15–30 minutes; 2) improve writing by learning to organize each paragraph, section, and paper around a key sentence; and 3) improve writing by seeking feedback within a community of scholars. These outcomes were measured by records faculty participants kept of their time spent writing, and their subsequent levels of productivity, and by a participant survey administered at the conclusion of the program.

For many faculty, scholarship is an important coin of the realm, with both short- and long-term purchasing power. The phrase "publish or perish" refers to the impact scholarly productivity may exert in faculty hiring and firing, promotion, and access to resources. Scholarly productivity is typically measured by the number of articles published in peer-reviewed journals, with those published in the top-tier journals receiving the strongest weighting. While much criticism has been justly targeted at measures that reduce productivity to a simple head count of articles published in peer-reviewed journals, this measure has become the de facto standard at many institutions and is unlikely to change in the near future (Bellas & Toutkoushian, 1999). Given the importance of scholarly productivity, faculty developers can play an important role in assisting faculty by providing programmatic support for their scholarly efforts. The question becomes, "How can faculty developers help faculty improve their scholarly productivity?"

Some research suggests that patterns of productivity are difficult to change because the more productive scholars have already acquired a cumulative advantage which cannot be matched by their less productive colleagues. According to this school of thought, productive scholars gain an early advantage which leads to positive outcomes (e.g., developing an early interest in research), and increased opportunities (mentoring by a prominent scholar, publishing early, etc.), that compound the early advantage and lead to further advantages (receiving a faculty appointment in research institutions, developing extensive collegial networks, and so forth) (Creamer & McGuire, 1998). Indeed, although many factors affect scholarly productivity, relatively few can be readily altered by the faculty member. Table 16.1 illustrates the variety of factors that affect productivity. Note that many are either fixed or beyond the faculty member's ability to change. Gender, for example, is fixed, and once a terminal degree is acquired, so is much of one's educational background.

However, other researchers point out that attitudes and behaviors are within a scholar's ability to change and may be among the strongest and most persistent factors affecting productivity (Blackburn & Lawrence, 1995). Because attitudes and behavior can be changed, they are of particular interest to faculty developers who work in the area of scholarly productivity. Boice (1987, 1989, 1991, 1992, 1994, 1996) is one faculty developer whose pioneer research in scholarly productivity has led to

TABLE 16.1
Factors Affecting Scholarly Productivity

Personal Factors	Examples of Factors	Relevant Citations
Innate personal characteristics	Age Gender Race IQ	Astin & Davis, 1985 Bellas & Toutkoushian, 1999
Personal and family background	Socioeconomic origins Marital status Size of family	Bellas & Toutkoushian, 1999
Educational background and opportunities	Type of degree acquired Time spent acquiring the degree Quality of the institution Academic field	Bentley & Blackburn, 1990
Professional experience and opportunities	Postdoctoral fellowship Employment in research institution Extensive collegial networks Mentoring by a prominent scholar Academic rank Years of experience Number of grants Tenure	Blackburn, Behymer & Hall, 1978 Creamer & McGuire, 1998
Current professional context	Academic discipline and milieu Quality of the institution Geographical location Publication norms Social support Work stress Workload and schedule	Blackburn & Lawrence, 1995 Neumann & Finaly-Neumann, 1990 Ramsden, 1994 Wanner, Lewis, & Gregorio, 1981
Attitudes and behaviors	Disposition Commitment to research Percentage of time spent on research Number of journal subscriptions Number of hours worked Time management	Creamer & McGuire, 1998 Bellas & Toutkoushian, 1999 Boice, 1992 Blackburn & Lawrence, 1995

helping faculty address the specific attitudes and behaviors that lead to greater scholarly productivity.

Boice observed that some faculty publish far more than others and that these faculty differ in both their attitudes and behavior. These faculty complain little about busyness; they seem more positive and less stressed about their jobs. As teachers, they set limits on the time they spend on lecture preparation, limiting it to about half what other faculty spend, and yet students consider them *more* effective teachers. As scholars, they write during more weeks of the semester, including the busiest weeks. They rarely write in binges (except for grant writing). They actively solicit advice about both teaching and research. And they receive feedback on their writing when it is still in its formative stages.

Boice also studied factors that inhibit scholarly productivity, including the perception among faculty that they are too busy to publish. When he asked 108 new faculty at a regional university whether or not this was the busiest year of their lives, 55% of the faculty surveyed answered, "yes". After faculty were asked to keep careful records of their workweeks, however, most were "forthright with admissions that they were not nearly as busy as they had supposed" (Boice, 1992, p. 17). They discovered that they rarely had days without some free period, which they usually used for a low-priority activity such as reading mail or talking on the phone.

In addition to feeling too busy, Boice found that many faculty believed they could not write unless they could isolate big blocks of time (Boice, 1987, 1989). However, "big" blocks of time are precisely what most faculty do not have. When faculty wait for big blocks of time, first they wait for summer, then sabbatical, then retirement (Boice, 1992, p. 18). Boice's research led him to propose that faculty can be productive if they find ways to write daily for at least 15–30 minutes. By writing daily, researchers keep the flame of their research alive because their writing becomes part of their daily thinking, which means they are ready to write when their next writing session arrives.

The faculty development programs Boice piloted confirmed that faculty could greatly increase their scholarly productivity by writing daily and by being held accountable for doing so. In his studies, a control group wrote as they always had, but an experimental group wrote daily for 30 minutes. In one study, only 19% of the controls completed a paper in a year, but 75% of the experimentals did (Boice, 1996, p. 90). In another study, faculty who set aside 30 minutes a day to write drafted or revised almost 64 pages in a year, which was almost four times the productivity (17 pages) of the control group (Boice, 1989, p. 609). In the same study, Boice had a second experimental group who agreed to write daily and accept biweekly visits from him during the blocks of time that they had agreed to write. This group wrote or revised 157 pages per year, which was more than twice as much as those who agreed to write daily but were not visited (64 pages) (Boice, 1989, p. 609).

Working in the tradition of Boice, Gray developed a semester-long faculty development program aimed at helping faculty increase their scholarly productivity. Like the programs directed by Boice, faculty were held accountable for writing 15–30 minutes a day. Faculty were also encouraged to take other steps aimed at improving their attitudes and behavior regarding writing. These 12 steps to scholarly productivity, which are published elsewhere (Gray, 1999), focus on having faith in oneself as a writer, and then taking steps to improve time management, writing strategies, and seeking regular help from others (see Table 16.2).

These 12 steps serve as the subject of the first half of the six-hour opening workshop for participants in the semester-long program: "Publish, Don't Perish—A Program to Help Scholars Flourish." The second half of the opening workshop is aimed at helping faculty improve their writing, especially in terms of organizing paragraphs around key sentences and seeking feedback from others in a community of scholars.

METHODS

In the spring of 1998, the program was founded under the direction of Gray at New Mexico State University; the following year, it was repeated there and also piloted at Brigham Young University, under the direction of both Gray and Birch. In the three versions of "Publish, Don't Perish," a total of 115 faculty completed the semester-long program, with an average retention rate of 75%. Table 16.3 describes demographic characteristics of the participants.

At New Mexico State University, participants were recruited by means of a flier that was sent to all 750 faculty. This flier invited faculty to enroll as a participant and a research subject for a stipend of $100. Initially, 63 faculty responded to the flier and enrolled. Because this was twice the expected number, separate sections were held for technical and nontechnical writers. In the first year at New Mexico State University, 38 faculty completed the program, for a 60% completion rate.

The semester-long program had several components, including opening and closing workshops as well as roundtables every other week. During these roundtables, participants met in small groups to give and receive feedback on their writing. Participants seemed to work in groups that were only loosely clustered by discipline; i.e., some groups seemed to have mostly scientists or engineers, but if those groups were full, participants moved to other groups. In the first year, no leadership was provided for the groups. Some of the groups were enormously successful, but others were not. The program director believed that if leadership were provided

TABLE 16.2
Twelve Steps to Scholarly Productivity

1) Believe you have something to say.

Time Management Strategies
2) Become a manager of your time, not a victim of it.
3) Differentiate between the urgent and the important.
4) Write at least 15–30 minutes daily.

Writing Strategies
5) Work on one project at a time—until you gain some momentum.
6) Don't finish the literature review first: read as you write, and write as you read.
7) Organize each paragraph, section, and paper around a key sentence.

Get Help From Colleagues
8) Hold yourself accountable to others.
9) Share early drafts with trusted colleagues.
10) Listen carefully to criticism, repeat it back, and suggest a change you might make in response.
11) Develop thick skin—really thick.
12) Kick it out the door and make 'em say "no."

to give focus and direction to the groups, participants would have a better experience, and the completion rate would improve. Therefore, in the second year, eight successful alumni of the program were enlisted to serve as group leaders and these leaders received extra training before the program opened. Under the direction of group leaders, groups seemed more focused, and the completion rate for the second year at New Mexico State University improved from 60 to 70% (28 out of 40).

Brigham Young University is twice the size of New Mexico State University, so invitations were extended only to junior faculty. An over-enrollment was expected, so the tone of the invitation was stern: Please do not enroll unless you are committed to meeting the full requirements of the semester-long program. Faculty members were not paid but, as expected, the program was popular as soon as it was advertised. Two hundred junior faculty were invited to participate, and over 25% wanted to enroll. Due to space limitations, only 43 were admitted. Forty-one of these participants persisted throughout the semester at Brigham Young University, for a completion rate of 95%.

Data from all three versions of the program are presented here, which include data from records participants kept regarding when and how much they wrote and a survey of the participants at the end of the program (the completion rate for the survey varied between 93% and 100%).

TABLE 16.3
Characteristics of Participants

	Average	NMSU 1998	NMSU 1999	BYU 1999
Participants	*38*	38	36	41
Gender				
Male	*46%*	45%	39%	54%
Female	*54%*	55%	61%	46%
Tenured				
Yes	*19%*	32%	25%	0%
No	*81%*	68%	75%	100%
Time as college professor				
1–6 years	*72%*	55%	72%	90%
7–15 years	*21%*	34%	22%	8%
20–30 years	*6%*	10%	6%	2%
Research Area				
Arts/Humanities	*24%*	24%	12%	37%
Science/Engineering	*22%*	18%	22%	27%
Agriculture	*13%*	21%	17%	0%
Education	*9%*	5%	6%	15%
Social Sciences	*9%*	8%	14%	5%
Health/Social Services	*7%*	5%	3%	12%
Business	*4%*	0%	11%	2%
Other	*12%*	18%	17%	2%

An important limitation of the study is that all the data come from participants, and no attempt was made to compare the scholarship produced by participants to nonparticipants. This limitation could be corrected in future studies by comparing the productivity of participants to nonparticipants. However, if the study were to compare the number of publications resulting from the writing during the program period, both groups would have to be studied for a period extending after the program ended.

PUBLISH, DON'T PERISH: GOALS AND GOAL ATTAINMENT

The "Publish, Don't Perish" program helps faculty:

1) Improve time management by developing the discipline to write daily for at least 15 to 30 minutes

2) Improve writing by learning to organize each paragraph, section, and paper around a key sentence

3) Improve writing by seeking feedback within a community of scholars

Results for Goal #1

Improve time management by writing daily for at least 15 to 30 minutes. Based on Boice's research, as discussed earlier, participants in "Publish, Don't Perish" were encouraged to use two techniques: 1) Write daily for at least 15 to 30 minutes, and 2) hold themselves accountable for doing so. In the program orientation, participants were exposed to research about the effectiveness of both techniques. Participants were then required to keep records on the time of day and number of minutes they spent writing. These records were submitted every other week to their group leaders at the roundtables. By keeping records of their time spent writing, participants were held accountable, especially to themselves.

By self report, participants wrote an average of two days a week and averaged 27 minutes a day for each day in the workweek. At this rate, participants were able to produce 1.5 new pages per week and to revise another 1.5 pages. If participants continued this pace of writing and revising for a year, they could produce 75 pages, or about three journal articles a year (see Table 16.4).

At the end of the semester, participants were asked to agree or disagree with statements that asserted the program had helped them improve their time management. For each statement about time management, at least 63% of participants agreed (see Table 16.5). Their comments indicated that the program helped them because it prompted them to write daily, and to be accountable to other members of their group:

> *"The most important skill I learned was the habit of writing for a half-hour first thing when I get to work. I completed two papers (both accepted) and the rough draft of a paper that has been hanging over my head for years. And much of this was accomplished in a half-hour per day."*

> *"I personally needed the direction to come each week and be asked, 'How'd it go?' 'What did you do?' 'Why didn't you do as planned?' Just having to tell someone the silly excuses I have for not working on my research would help me quit allowing it to happen."*

> *"What helped me the most was just the accountability to other people. I submitted two manuscripts this semester, and I never could have done that without the aid of the workshop."*

More faculty, however, commented on another form of accountability that helped them—recording the time they spent writing on writing worksheets:

TABLE 16.4

Achievement of Goal #1—Writing Daily for at Least 15 to 30 Minutes:
Data from Records Kept by Participants

Goal	*Average*	NMSU 1998	NMSU 1999	BYU 1999
Writing five days/week				
Mean (days/week)	*2.1*	1.4	2.1	2.9
Range* (days/week)	*5.2*	4.5	4.5	6.5
Writing 15–30 minutes/day				
Mean (minutes/day)	*27*	15	27	40
Range* (minutes/day)	*201*	72	87	444
Writing 1–3 new pages/week				
Mean (new pages/week)	*1.5*	1.4	.9	2.1
Range* (new pages/week)	*10.8*	11.5	4.0	17.0

*The minimum reported for each range was always zero, so only the upper value of the range is shown.

TABLE 16.5

Achievement of Goal #1—Improving Time Management:
Percent Agreeing on the Survey of Participants

Statement	*Average*	NMSU 1998	NMSU 1999	BYU 1999
I feel less victimized by my busy schedule.	*63%*	53%	69%	68%
I am more realistic about how I spend my time and where it goes.	*84%*	74%	97%	81%
My scholarship was aided by the process of filling out and turning in writing worksheets.	*63%*	42%	61%	86%
I am a better time manager.	*67%*	55%	67%	78%

"The writing worksheets were like a silent sentinel!!"

"They gave me a weapon to combat procrastination."

"They reminded me to write. And reminded me that I had written."

"I liked having it taped above my desk. It motivated me to sit down for a few minutes so I could reward myself by noting the time."

The majority view was that productivity was improved by writing daily, keeping daily records, and being accountable to one's group. However, a few participants disagreed about the value of writing worksheets, especially in the first year of the program. These comments included,

> *"Writing worksheets were not at all helpful. It was paperwork and had the same onus as the Federal Income Tax!"*

> *"I had some writing periods and some nonwriting periods this semester. During the writing periods, the worksheets helped keep me going and reminded me of my commitment. During the nonwriting periods, they were an irritation* and *induced guilt."*

Results for Goal #2: Improve Writing by Learning to Organize Each Paragraph, Section, and Paper around a Key Sentence.

"Publish, Don't Perish" helped participants improve their writing by learning to organize each paragraph, section, and paper around a key sentence. This technique can be taught in a few hours, and half of the six-hour opening workshop for the program is devoted to learning how to apply the technique to one's own prose, as well as that of other participants. Then, participants use the technique throughout the semester at the roundtables that occur every other week.

In the orientation, participants learn how to check the coherence of a paragraph by identifying the key sentence. The key sentence is the sentence that could be sent as a telegraph if needed in place of the part of the text for which it serves as a key (Williams & Colomb, 1990, pp. 97–103). First, the author reads the paragraph, looking for the key sentence. If the author cannot find the key sentence, the reader will not be able to find it either and may judge the paragraph as unclear or poorly organized. If the author finds two different key sentences, two paragraphs are probably in order.

Once each paragraph has a key sentence, the author checks to ensure that each section has a key sentence and that the paper as a whole has one key sentence. Next, the author makes a list of these sentences (Booth, Colomb, & Williams 1995, pp. 205–206). This list does not have to sound elegant because it was not written to be read this way. However, the list should be logical and coherent if the paper is well-organized. Once it is, the intent of the paper will be much clearer to the audience.

Most "Publish, Don't Perish" participants agreed that the program helped their organization, with at least 70% agreeing with each survey question aimed at assessing this goal (see Table 16.6). Many participants commented,

TABLE 16.6
Achievement of Goal #2—Improve Writing by Learning to Organize
Each Paragraph, Section, and Paper around a Key Sentence
Percent Agreeing on the Survey of Participants

Statement	*Average*	NMSU 1998	NMSU 1999	BYU 1999
I organize paragraphs around one key sentence.	*71%*	*55%*	*83%*	*75%*
I write better organized paragraphs and papers.	*70%*	*55%*	*78%*	*78%*
This program improved my writing.	*83%*	*71%*	*86%*	*93%*

> *"What helped me most in this program was the information on organizing paragraphs. The program brought about some much needed changes in my writing style."*
>
> *"Looking for key sentences in others' writing every two weeks gave me a 'booster shot' of skills to use on my own writing."*

When other groups have requested the one-hour version of this program, they invariably ask for just "the key sentence idea."

Results for Goal #3: Improve Writing by Seeking Feedback from Others within a Community of Scholars

Most faculty realize it is important to seek feedback on scholarly writing; however, they do not seek this help as often as they should for a variety of reasons. First, faculty may think of writing as a solitary endeavor that results in something cast in stone, rather than a social activity that more nearly results in a conversation in print. In addition, faculty may not realize that feedback from readers can save them the most time on early drafts, rather than on a nearly polished product. They may even think that seeking help on drafts is time-consuming rather than time-saving. Faculty may believe that colleagues in their discipline are the only appropriate audience for their work, and they may feel it is more important to impress these colleagues than to get help from them on early drafts. Or, they may not want to impose on their busy colleagues by asking them to read drafts. And finally, they may not know how to seek help from others effectively, and as a result, they may receive help only at the sentence-level, rather than at the organizational level, which is more likely to transform prose.

In "Publish, Don't Perish," we challenge these myths and encourage faculty to experiment for themselves and discover the benefits of seeking early feedback from colleagues. As discussed in the last section, we teach faculty a way of looking at text in terms of paragraphs, sections, and whole papers rather than as a collection of sentences. We point out that publication can be usefully viewed as a social activity resulting in conversations in print. Viewed in this light, it is clear that one of the biggest challenges faced by writers is to clearly communicate their intent to an audience. When writers read their own writing, they are not really reading, but simply reviewing their thoughts at the time they were writing (Booth, Colomb, & Williams 1995, p. 202).

We argue and then demonstrate that receiving feedback on early drafts is a time-saving rather than a time-consuming measure. Early drafts are more likely to elicit comments and to benefit from them (Boice, 1992, p. 29). As a result, getting help on early drafts can save writers enormous amounts of time. That is, writers can receive criticism on organization before they have spent hours perfecting the wording of each sentence, including sentences that will be deleted when the organization improves.

We also teach and then demonstrate that colleagues in one's own discipline are not the only source of good feedback. The program provides a time and place for scholars to exchange drafts across disciplines. Participants learn through experience that some of the best criticism comes from readers in other disciplines. These readers are prone to focus more on the organization and clarity of the paper since they are not familiar with the subject matter. This program provides an ideal opportunity for scholars to exchange criticism on early drafts with colleagues in other disciplines, which helps create a community of critical, yet caring scholars.

Of the three goals of the program, the survey results suggest the program was the most successful in helping participants get feedback from their colleagues, with at least 76% agreeing with each related statement (see Table 16.7). On open-ended questions, some participants commented on how other readers can see problems that the author cannot:

> *"Sometimes you read your paper over and over, and you think everybody will understand it just because it becomes really familiar to you but as soon as you have somebody else reading your work you know the things that are missing."*

> *"Feedback helps me evaluate my own writing more critically. My temptation is to fall in love with my own choice of words and phrases."*

Other participants commented on the sense of community that developed, as well as how participants felt less alone in the process of writing:

TABLE 16.7

**Achievement of Goal #3—Improve Writing by Seeking
Feedback from Others within a Community of Scholars:
Percent Agreeing on the Survey of Participants**

Statement	Average	NMSU 1998	NMSU 1999	BYU 1999
I learned how to get better feedback (by asking questions and repeating criticisms, etc.).	76%	68%	83%	76%
I received supportive feedback.	85%	82%	89%	83%
I received constructive criticism.	83%	84%	89%	77%
I received support and accountability from others.	76%	68%	83%	76%

"My group was always super supportive, so they kept me very pumped."

"The best part of the program was the camaraderie with my group."

"Now I feel like a real member of the faculty here—my research is important."

"I had expected professoring to be a very lonely endeavor."

Other participants commented on how helpful it was to have readers who were outside one's own discipline:

"The feedback was quite beneficial. This is the first time in my career that someone from outside my field had read any of my work, let alone a working copy of a paper. It was very instructive."

"I liked receiving feedback from people alien to my field. Now, I actively seek such feedback. And, I encourage my graduate students to do the same."

"I was amazed that people outside my discipline could offer such incredibly insightful feedback on the organization and clarity of my writing."

"The reviews of my writing by non-scientists are FANTASTIC!"

In fairness, however, a few participants complained about readers: specifically, that readers outside of one's discipline were not effective:

"Though we were counseled to have readers outside of our discipline read our work, I did not feel it worked in this setting. Many of the criticisms were as misguided as my word processor's grammar checker."

"Many of the comments were not completely relevant because they related to how the paper could be more approachable for a 'lay' audience, when in fact it is written for specialists."

Still others felt that participants were not critical enough:

"Most of the feedback was not extremely useful; maybe they [participants] were too nice at times."

"After the first round of readings, the feedback was not as helpful as I had anticipated—much of 'this looks great' and 'I really like this.'"

In response to these criticisms, future versions of the program will differ in two ways: 1) They will encourage participants to join groups in which all participants have similar—but not the same—disciplines (i.e., humanities or science), and 2) they will direct more training at the importance of being critical as well as supportive. Scientists and engineers in particular want to work in groups with each other, and perhaps their writing is different enough that they should. And although faculty are prone to be harsh when they act as anonymous reviewers, they are equally prone to being too nice when placed face-to-face with a colleague. Therefore, future training will focus on providing constructive criticism.

PROGRAM ASSESSMENT

Every faculty development program is a work in progress, and this program is no exception. Nonetheless, the program was rated very highly by participants: 83% would participate in the program again, and 95% would recommend it to their colleagues (see Table 16.8). Participants commented,

"I have much more courage to send things out because of this program. It should definitely be offered every year."

"I think [the program] should be for everybody that is new . . . and not just an option."

CONCLUSION

Our experience on two very different campuses suggests that faculty are highly motivated to improve their scholarly productivity and are willing to participate in faculty development efforts designed to do so. Faculty

TABLE 16.8
Overall Success of Program:
Percent Saying "Yes" on a Survey of Participants

Statement	Average	NMSU 1998	NMSU 1999	BYU 1999
The director facilitated the program well.	95%	*	100%	90%
My group leader facilitated my group well.	78%	**	91%	64%
I will recommend this program to my colleagues.	95%	95%	100%	91%
I would participate in this program again.	83%	82%	89%	78%
The Faculty Center should sponsor this program again.	92%	***	***	92%

*In 1998, this question was not asked.
**In 1998, this question was not asked because there were no group leaders.
***This question was not asked at New Mexico State University.

developers can assist faculty with their scholarly productivity by developing programs based on research-based principles. The data from "Publish, Don't Perish" suggest that participants using the suggested techniques produced 1.5 new pages per week and revised another 1.5 pages. If scholarship were produced and revised at this pace for a year, it could potentially lead to more frequent and better quality written products.

As a result of increased productivity, successful scholarship programs generate praise and gratitude from faculty, as well as departmental, college, and university administrators who have a vested interest in scholarship. Due to the very positive response of both faculty and administrators at the two institutions discussed in this paper, both institutions plan to offer the program on an ongoing basis. Scholarship workshops can be hosted on other campuses as well. Although faculty developers traditionally focus on helping faculty improve as teachers, the time may be right to begin helping faculty more systematically with their scholarship. This valuable service to the faculty can bring added prestige to the faculty development center and thus encourage faculty to take advantage of the multitude of other services available there.

REFERENCES

Astin, H. S., & Davis, D. E. (1985). Research productivity across the life and career cycles: Facilitators and barriers for women. In M. F. Fox (Ed.), *Scholarly writing and publishing: Issues, problems, and solutions* (pp. 147–160). Boulder, CO: Westview.

Bellas, M. L., & Toutkoushian, R. K. (1999). Faculty time allocations and research productivity: Gender, race, and family effects. *The Review of Higher Education, 22* (4), 367–390.

Bentley, R., & Blackburn, R. T. (1990). Changes in academic research performance over time: A study of institutional accumulative advantage. *Research in Higher Education, 31* (4), 327–353.

Blackburn, R. T., Behymer, C. E., & Hall, D. E. (1978, April). Research note: Correlates of faculty publications. *Sociology of Education, 51*, 132–141.

Blackburn, R. T., & Lawrence, J. H. (1995). *Faculty at work: Motivation, expectation, satisfaction.* Baltimore, MD: Johns Hopkins University.

Boice, R. (1987). Is released time an effective component of faculty development programs? *Research in Higher Education, 26* (3), 311–326.

Boice, R. (1989). Procrastination, busyness, and bingeing. *Behavior Research Therapy, 27* (6), 605–611.

Boice, R. (1991). *Quick starters: New faculty who succeed.* New Directions for Teaching and Learning, No. 48. San Francisco, CA: Jossey-Bass.

Boice, R. (1992). Strategies for enhancing scholarly productivity. In J. F. Moxley (Ed.), *Writing and publishing for academic authors* (pp. 15–32). New York, NY: University Press of America.

Boice, R. (1994). *How writers journey to comfort and fluency.* Westport, CT: Praeger.

Boice, R. (1996). *Procrastination and blocking: A novel, practical approach.* Westport, CT: Praeger.

Booth, W. C., Colomb, G. G., & Williams, J. M. (1995). *The craft of research.* Chicago, IL: University of Chicago Press.

Creamer, E. G., & McGuire, S. P. (1998). Applying the cumulative advantage perspective to scholarly writers in higher education. *The Review of Higher Education, 22* (1), 73–82.

Gray, T. (1999). Publish, don't perish: Twelve steps to help scholars flourish. *Journal of Staff, Program, and Organization Development, 16* (3), 135–142.

Moxley, J. M. (1992). *Publish, don't perish: Scholar's guide to academic writing and publishing.* Westport, CT: Praeger.

Neumann, Y., & Finaly-Neumann, E. (1990). The support-stress paradigm and faculty research publication. *Journal of Higher Education, 61* (5), 565–578.

Ramsden, P. (1994). Describing and explaining research productivity. *Higher Education, 28*, 207–226.

Wanner, R. A., Lewis, L. S., & Gregorio, D. I. (1981, October). Research productivity in academia: A comparative study of the sciences, social sciences and humanities. *Sociology of Education, 54,* 238–253.

Williams, J., & Colomb, G. (1990). *Style: Toward clarity and grace.* Chicago, IL: University of Chicago Press.

Contacts:

Tara Gray
Associate Professor
Department of Criminal Justice
New Mexico State University
Las Cruces, NM 88003-8001
(505) 646-1013
(505) 646-2827 (Fax)
Email: tgray@nmsu.edu

Tara Gray serves as Associate Professor of Criminal Justice at New Mexico State University. She has a strong interest in helping faculty collaborate as teachers and scholars. To this end, she regularly gives workshops at universities across the country.

Jane Birch
Program Coordinator
Faculty Center
Brigham Young University
Provo, UT 84602
(801) 378-4008
(801) 378-7467 (Fax)
Email: jane_birch@byu.edu

Jane Birch is Program Coordinator at the Brigham Young University Faculty Center. Among her responsibilities, she directs the BYU Faculty Development Series, an intensive 18-month new faculty program. Her main interest and passion lies in helping faculty make connections between their religious faith and their work as teachers and scholars.

17

Designing Teaching Portfolios Based on a Formal Model of the Scholarship of Teaching

Carolin Kreber
University of Alberta, Edmonton

Many universities now encourage, and some even require, faculty to submit a teaching portfolio as part of their tenure application package. How to evaluate these portfolios, however, remains an unresolved issue, particularly if the task is to make a judgment about whether what is demonstrated in the portfolio reflects engagement in the scholarship of teaching. The thesis of this chapter is that judgments regarding the validity and truthfulness of a teaching portfolio can be made by assessing the extent to which the author has attended to an agreed-upon process of knowledge construction and validation in teaching. A model of the scholarship of teaching is proposed that could guide the design and evaluation of portfolios and an illustration of the process is given.

INTRODUCTION

The 1990s have witnessed a strong interest in the scholarship of teaching, a concept first introduced by Boyer (1990) and Rice (1991, 1992) with the purpose of broadening the widely spread but narrowly conceived interpretation of scholarship as discovery research, but since then further developed by those who advocate not only greater recognition of college and university teaching but also its advancement (for example, Edgerton, Hutchings, & Quinlan, 1991; Glassick, Huber, & Maeroff, 1997; Kreber, in press; Kreber & Cranton, in press; Menges & Weimer, 1996; Paulsen & Feldman, 1995; Richlin, 1993; Shulman, 1998). Whether the interest lies primarily in the recognition of teaching, or its advancement, or both, the observation that teaching is largely a private activity happening behind closed classrooms doors while research is public, and, therefore, open to peer review, has been made by all proponents of the scholarship of teaching. This fundamental difference between the activities of research and teaching resulted in the formulation of the problem of how teaching could become more public and thereby open to a process of peer review, similar to that used for research.

In response to this question, many universities now encourage, and some even require, faculty to submit a teaching portfolio as part of their tenure application package. A teaching portfolio is essentially an instructor's self-portrait of his or her approaches and accomplishments in teaching; this means that the instructor chooses how to present him- or herself, just as a researcher chooses how to present a study in a scholarly article. However, a teaching portfolio is not just a snapshot illustration and analysis of an instructor's teaching but rather a series of snapshots taken over time to demonstrate his or her evolution as a teacher.

The objective of this essay is threefold: first, to review literature on the purpose and content of the teaching portfolio and address the still unresolved issue of assessment. Second, to introduce a formal model of the scholarship of teaching (Kreber, 1999; Kreber & Cranton, in press). As part of this second objective, an attempt will be made to define the apparently rather elusive concept of the scholarship of teaching in clear and accessible terms. In doing so, the author will draw on the results of a recent Delphi study conducted with a panel of international experts in this field (Kreber, in press). The third goal is to demonstrate how the proposed model could guide the design and evaluation of teaching portfolios, particularly if the purpose of the assessment is to identify whether what is reported in the portfolio demonstrates a faculty member's engagement in the scholarship of teaching. The model of the scholarship of teaching described in this chapter is considered formal as it is derived through deductive analysis of Jack Mezirow's (1991) theory of transformative learning, a notion developed in the adult education literature and informed by both critical social theory (Habermas, 1971, 1984) and constructivist psychology (Kelly, 1955). It also appears to be consistent, overall, with the results of the recent Delphi survey (Kreber, in press).

THE TEACHING PORTFOLIO

The idea of the teaching portfolio originated in Canada in the early 1970s (Knapper, McFarlane, & Scanlon, 1972) and later resulted in a publication sponsored by the Canadian Association of University Teachers

(CAUT) titled "The teaching dossier: A guide to its preparation and use" (Shore et al., 1980, 1986). Teaching portfolios have both formative and summative purposes. By keeping a record of their teaching over time, faculty have the opportunity to reflect on the data they collect, make changes as a result, and compare the data and evidence gathered after the change has been implemented to those of the previous year. As a result of this cyclical process, they demonstrate responsibility for their professional development in teaching. More problematic is the use of teaching portfolios for summative purposes. In case a teaching portfolio is required as part of the tenure application, for example, an evaluation committee will be charged with the task of making a decision about the faculty member's teaching prowess. The various documents and sources compiled in the teaching portfolio, among them a philosophy statement, outlines of courses taught, unsolicited comments from students, written feedback from colleagues, examples of course work completed by students, summary of teaching evaluation from students, and so forth, certainly provide a broader and perhaps more objective picture of teaching than student ratings of instruction alone. Furthermore, teaching portfolios allow faculty to gain greater responsibility for (and control over) the evaluation of their teaching (Shore et al., 1986). Notwithstanding these significant benefits, some unresolved issues remain. To date, the following problems have been addressed insufficiently:

- How can teaching portfolios be assessed without a definite set of criteria that guide such an evaluation (Knapper, 1995)?

- How can teaching portfolios be assessed without the assessors being trained in such evaluation?

- Who is in a position to decide what is a good teaching philosophy statement—the basis of one's teaching—and what is not?

With respect to the third problem consider a well-articulated statement that reflects a general philosophy that is not shared by the majority of committee members. To what extent does it make sense to argue that one philosophy is better than another? To what extent does a philosophy statement fall under the auspices of academic freedom? Put differently, to what extent should it be accepted (as scholarly) without questioning the validity and truthfulness of the statement—or in other words—the process by which results (beliefs about teaching) have been achieved?

The thesis of this essay is that judgments regarding the validity and truthfulness of a teaching philosophy statement—and, for that matter, all sections of a teaching portfolio—can be made by assessing the extent to which the author of the statement has attended to an agreed upon process of knowledge construction and validation in teaching. A formal model of the scholarship of teaching that purports to explain these processes will be introduced next.

A FORMAL MODEL OF THE SCHOLARSHIP OF TEACHING

The scholarship of teaching means different things to different people; yet a recent Delphi study (Kreber, in press) showed that there is consensus among those studying the subject that not every person that teaches practices the scholarship of teaching, but that the scholarship of teaching requires sound knowledge of how students learn. Faculty acquire this knowledge as they explore the relationships between teaching and learning.

Menges and Weimer (1996) demonstrated how formal or research-based knowledge on teaching and learning can inform our teaching practice. Faculty reading about relevant educational research enhance their knowledge of how students learn. At the same time, the authors encourage the development and dissemination of the wisdom of practice; that is, the insights faculty gain from their personal teaching practices and their own informal or formal study of teaching and learning. Recently, Weimer (in press) suggests that the "wisdom of practice" itself needs to be improved so as to rely not only on experiential knowledge but to be informed by, and perhaps extend, what we have come to understand about teaching and learning. According to these authors, it is both existing formal or research-based knowledge, as well as faculty's experience-based knowledge of teaching and learning, which contribute to the scholarship of teaching. Participants in the Delphi study agreed on a series of statements that define the scholarship of teaching. The five that seem most relevant to the argument presented in this chapter are reported here (for a more comprehensive report and discussion of this study please see Kreber, in press):

1) Those that practice the scholarship of teaching carefully design ways to examine, interpret, and share learning about teaching. Thereby they *contribute* to the scholarly community of their discipline.

2) The scholarship of teaching entails a public account of some or all of the following aspects of teaching: vision, design, interaction, outcomes, and analysis, in a manner that can be peer reviewed and used by members of one's community

3) The conduct of research on teaching and learning (less formal and formal) contributes to the advancement of pedagogical content knowledge, and presents forms of the scholarship of discovery that overlap with, and are part of, the scholarship of teaching.

4) The scholarship of teaching is an activity that, in the context of promoting student learning, meets each of the following criteria:

   - it requires high levels of discipline-related expertise

   - it breaks new ground and is innovative

   - can be replicated and elaborated

   - can be documented

   - can be peer reviewed

   - has significance or impact

5) A person practicing the scholarship of teaching is aware of, experiences, and can express an underpinning conceptual framework for their teaching; a framework that is strongly related to students learning outcomes.

Kreber and Cranton (in press) introduced a model of the scholarship of teaching that is intended to both explain and guide the development of the scholarship of teaching. Furthermore, the model conceives of scholarship not only in terms of outcomes—that is the knowledge faculty have gained—but gives equal emphasis to the process of acquiring this knowledge. Two basic assumptions underlying the model are:

1) Faculty learn about teaching through reflection on both research-based and experience-based knowledge about teaching; thereby they develop pedagogical knowledge in a broad sense as well as pedagogical content knowledge.

2) Faculty can demonstrate their learning in the form of a teaching portfolio.

REFLECTION ON TEACHING

Following George Kelly's (1955) notion of "constructive alternativism," Mezirow (1991) argues that people construct their own realities on the basis of their interpretation of events and that these interpretations, in turn, function as perceptual filters in how they go about understanding their environment. These perceptual filters or meaning perspectives determine the expectations they have for the outcome of events. Sometimes the expected outcome does not take place; in this case, the individual has the choice to reflect on the experience and to revise the original expectation, and his or her perspective. With respect to faculty learning about teaching, an example might be a faculty member who expects students to abuse an opportunity to self-evaluate their learning but finds that the majority of students evaluate themselves quite accurately and some even lower than he or she would have done. The faculty member may revise his or her assumption that incorporating self-evaluation in college classes leads to grade inflation.

Reflection can occur on three different levels. Mezirow (1991) distinguishes content, process, and premise reflection. An individual engaging in content reflection describes the problem and asks, "What do I know should be done in this situation?" A person engaging in process reflection asks, "How do I know that?" This second form of reflection addresses the process of problem solving. Finally, a person engaging in premise reflection asks, "Why is it important that I address this problem in the first place?" Mezirow (1991), who bases his theory of transformative learning also largely on Jürgen Habermas' (1971, 1984) work of a critique of ideology, argues that only premise reflection is critical reflection and can lead to emancipatory learning. Emancipatory learning is the kind of learning whereby individuals come to question the origins and validity of the presuppositions that guide their beliefs and actions (Cranton, 1994, 1996; Mezirow, 1991). Content and process reflection are not insignificant, however, and can lead to important instrumental learning (identifying cause-effect relationships through the empirical-analytical method) and communicative learning (achieving deeper understanding of the meaning of experience through the hermeneutic cycle).

Following this theory, Kreber and Cranton (in press) and Kreber (1999) argued that faculty develop scholarship in teaching as they engage in content, process, and premise reflection on research-based and experience-based knowledge about teaching. The scholarship of teaching, therefore, comes about as a result of various combinations of instrumental, communicative, and emancipatory learning processes, resulting in knowledge about instruction, pedagogy (including pedagogical content knowledge), and the larger curriculum. Following this model, faculty can provide evidence of their scholarship of teaching by demonstrating that they have reflected on research-based and experience-based knowledge of teaching on any of the three levels (content, process, and premise), and acted on the results of their reflection. As faculty's learning and knowing about teaching can be demonstrated, it follows that, given appropriate criteria, it can be assessed through a process of peer review (Kreber, 1998). How this model can facilitate the design and evaluation of teaching portfolios will be discussed below.

USING THE MODEL TO DESIGN TEACHING PORTFOLIOS

The notions of content, process, and premise reflection provide meaningful guidance for the design and evaluation of teaching portfolios. When faculty engage in the "what," "how," and "why" questions posed by the model of the scholarship of teaching, they develop a self-portrait of their approaches and achievements in teaching. Content reflection asks "What do I presently do?" and "What have I accomplished?" Process reflection asks, "How do I know that what I do is effective?" and premise reflection asks, "Why does it matter that I address this problem in the first place?" When individuals engage in premise reflection they question the presupposition that the problem is in fact relevant.

One important part of the teaching portfolio is the teaching philosophy statement. Interestingly, it is this section that most faculty have considerable difficulty expressing (Richlin, 1995); and yet it is this philosophy that is the basis for how they approach their teaching. Identifying the reasons behind the approaches they take is not something faculty engage in routinely. Examples of such statements exist in the teaching and learning literature (for example, Brookfield, 1990, 1995; Cranton, 1992, 1996; Goodyear & Allchin, 1998); however, few faculty are familiar with these texts, and many feel somewhat at a loss when it comes to articulating their beliefs about teaching.

Generally speaking, philosophies provide a rationale for educational practice (Lawson, 1991; Ozmon & Graver, 1990). Goodyear and Allchin (1998) suggest that "articulating an individual teaching philosophy provides the foundation by which to clarify goals, to guide behavior, to seed scholarly dialogue on teaching, and to organize evaluation" (p. 103). Weimer (1987) defines a theory of practice as "the collection of assumptions and beliefs that form the bedrock beneath the more visible activities of teaching. It's the rationale behind what we do in the classroom" (p. 1). Similarly, Brookfield (1990) encourages us to "develop a philosophy of practice, a critical rationale for why you are doing what you are doing" (p. 195). Apps (1973) suggests that educators should undergo a systematic analysis of the philosophy they are working from. Beliefs should be identified in terms of at least five categories: the overall purpose of education, beliefs about the educator, beliefs about the learner, beliefs about the subject area, and those related to the learning process. A study exploring the teaching philosophies espoused by faculty from different disciplines at a large research university in Canada (Scott, Chovanec, & Young, 1994) found that faculty view their teaching in terms of six dimensions. These show considerable resemblance to Apps' categories. Faculty hold assumptions regarding:

1) the purpose of university teaching and learning

2) the role of the teacher

3) the role of the learner

4) the methods and strategies used

5) evaluation and assessment

6) constraints

In order to show how the notions of content, process, and premise reflection on formal educational research and personal teaching experience can be helpful to faculty in articulating their beliefs within these six dimensions, this section concludes with an example drawn from the author's own teaching philosophy statement. Within each dimension, content reflection encourages individuals to make their beliefs explicit. This is where most teaching philosophy statements end. The thesis of this essay is that articulating one's beliefs, while necessary, is not sufficient if the goal is to demonstrate one's engagement in the scholarship of teaching. To reiterate, the scholarship of teaching requires demonstration of knowledge about teaching, the application of this knowledge, as well as its advancement through pedagogical content knowledge (Paulsen, in press), in a way that can be peer reviewed. It is process reflection that leads faculty to provide evidence for their beliefs. Such evidence is grounded in the existing educational literature and personal teaching experience. Finally, when individuals engage in premise reflection, they both gain and show awareness of why it is meaningful to attend to the problem in the first place.

For reasons of limited space and the purpose of illustration, the example that follows will focus on four dimensions of the teaching philosophy statement: 1) the purpose of higher education, 2) the role of students, 3) the strategies used, 4) and the assessment of learning. It should be noted that the philosophy statement, typically, is considered a one-page articulation of one's beliefs. As such, it is conceived of more as an introduction to the portfolio rather than the essence of the portfolio. The argument here is that the philosophy statement determines and guides everything we do in teaching. As such, all aspects of the teaching portfolio can be—and perhaps should be—integrated within this statement. A good teaching philosophy statement explains why certain approaches were taken and makes reference to supporting material in the appendix section. The philosophy statement is therefore not an introduction to but is the teaching portfolio. To be complete, it should address all six dimensions discussed earlier.

EXAMPLE OF A TEACHING PHILOSOPHY STATEMENT BASED ON CONTENT, PROCESS, AND PREMISE REFLECTION ON RESEARCH-BASED AND EXPERIENCE-BASED KNOWLEDGE

THE PURPOSE OF HIGHER EDUCATION
(IN MY FIELD OF STUDY—ADULT LEARNING)

Content Reflection

I see the purpose of university education as helping learners recognize the links between research in the field and their practice and how both inform each other. I think that universities are places where people need to learn to take responsibility for their learning, to argue reasonably, and to respect different viewpoints, cultures, and ways of living. In short, I think that universities are places where people grow professionally, intellectually, and personally. I also think that universities are places that can stimulate a love for learning.

Process Reflection

Research on university student development in university (for example Astin, 1993; Baxtor-Magolda, 1992, King & Kitchener, 1994; Perry, 1970; Pascarella & Terenzini, 1991) indicates that higher education has positive effects on students on all three levels. A couple of years ago when facilitating a discussion group among colleagues on the goals of higher education and the development of critical thinking skills in students, I was stunned by how differently the concept of critical thinking and development is construed (for example, as problem-solving and advancement in the discipline on the one hand versus as development as a person and reflective citizen, on the other). Participating in electronic discussion forums such as the STLHE or POD listservs further contributed to my thinking in this area.

My experience as a university student and junior faculty member further supports this assumption. It is not the exception when students comment after a course that assumptions were challenged and they want to make changes to their practice, that they are motivated to learn more about the subject, or that they want to become an academic (see appendix for comments from students).

Premise Reflection

Brookfield in his book *The Skillful Teacher* (1990) offers four reasons for why it is important to be clear on one's goals and purposes. Personally, I find that it provides structure and consistency to my teaching. Sometimes students do not want to be challenged—they are tired after a day of work, and their major reason to come to class that night is to get credit for the course. They then are quick to challenge the educator who tries to foster critical thinking, collaborative work, and self-direction. Without a rationale that justifies my approach, I think I would have to give in to their felt needs without any meaningful discussion.

THE ROLE OF STUDENTS

Content Reflection

I see the student's role as one of co-learner, co-planner, and to some extent expert (many of my students have many more years of teaching experience than I do, and some hold professional degrees). I think that students' reasons for participation vary considerably: Some do it because they need the degree, some do it because they want to learn about the subject in order to either enhance their practice or embark on an academic career, and others do it primarily to interact with others and be a little challenged (Houle, 1961). I realize that my expectations of them (with respect to the nature of the assignments) vary with their reasons for participation—this is a critical issue that I have not quite resolved for myself. Not surprisingly perhaps, I prefer working with those that are academically inclined. Across all students, however, I expect them to come to class well-prepared, be willing to engage in class discussions and activities, to assume some responsibility for their learning in the course, justify their point of view, listen to and reflect on other people's points of view, and demonstrate respect toward all other members of the group.

Process Reflection

How do I know that these expectations are reasonable? I have noticed that most of the students I work with have a wealth of relevant professional or life experience that can contribute in very positive ways to the course. I also observe that once learners have identified their goals and had input into how they can achieve those, they are more highly motivated to succeed. I realize that once students have noticed how much more they get of out of the class if they prepare for it, they also see the value of it. On a theoretical level, some of the literature on self-directed learning suggests that adequate degrees of learner control enhance motivation to learn (for example Candy, 1991; Garrison, 1997). The literature on inclusive classrooms raises our awareness that all voices should be respected (Brownlie & Feniak, 1998).

Premise Reflection

Being aware of the roles that I expect of the students allows me to articulate these expectations clearly at the beginning of the course. It seems to me that I owe course participants this information and disclosure. It is then up to them to decide whether they want to stay in the course or leave. If they stay, I take this as their consent/agreement with what I proposed.

THE TEACHING STRATEGIES I USE

Content Reflection

I use a combination of lecture, discussion, and many forms of group work. I often have different groups review a text that was assigned for the particular class and ask them to identify what, in their view, were the key points of the reading. Then I have them articulate how these points relate to, or inform, their practice. I also ask them to reflect on what is not yet known about the topic, and what they would suggest as an important step in future research. After 30–45 minutes of group work, I have each group report back to the other members of the class. In case I think that certain important issues have been neglected, I raise them. I also provide further information drawn from my own reading or research. With the goal of making students aware of the assumptions or knowledge they hold, I also use role play, debates, short case studies, and critical incidents. Research on collaborative learning suggests such approaches have positive effects on students learning (e.g., Matthews, 1996).

Process Reflection
My experience with following a very interactive approach in my classes and to varying the instructional methods has been very positive. Many students comment that a particular activity helped them to better see the link between theory and practice, or the difference between certain theories, or some simply comment after class that they can't believe that three hours have gone by and they had so much fun. Surely, having fun in class isn't everything but I think it's good when it happens. On a more theoretical level, the educational literature encourages teachers to use a variety of instructional methods in order to sustain students' attention, to not teach exclusively to one particular type of learner, and to make sure that the methods chosen are appropriate in relation to the learning task defined by the learning objective (Cranton, 1992; Fuhrman & Grasha, 1983; Svinicki & Dixon, 1987). Higher-order learning, in particular, tends to be fostered in a learning environment characterized by dialogue, collaboration, mutual respect, and constructive criticism (Donald, 1997).

Premise Reflection
I think knowledge about teaching strategies and when to use them is critical because as a professional educator I want to be able to justify my practice. For example, it would be very hard for me to justify the exclusive use of the lecture method in my course with a group of 16 students of diverse cultural backgrounds, prior knowledge, learning styles, and personality types, when the majority of learning objectives are aimed at students' ability to explain and discuss critical issues.

HOW I ASSESS LEARNING

Content Reflection

At the undergraduate level, my intent is to have learners not only absorb primarily instrumental knowledge (e.g., how to design instructional interventions; how to conduct program reviews and assessments of learning) but to become critically reflective professionals. With this purpose in mind, I have them keep a reflective learning journal on their experiences as learners and educators and analyze it, just like any other piece of qualitative data, for underlying themes and assumptions. I also ask them to identify and discuss the relationships they see between their educational philosophy, values, learning style, teaching style, and psychological type; to develop not only technically sound but meaningful learning objectives; to select appropriate strategies; and to provide a rationale for their choice. Finally, I ask them to articulate their theory of practice. As simplistic as this may sound, many students have tremendous difficulty identifying their assumptions and often uncritically assimilate information. Furthermore, these assignments require students to synthesize the material covered in class. Students do not earn grades for quantity but quality; arguments need to be backed up by sound reasons, and evidence for critical engagement with the material.

At the graduate level, reflection on one's practice is just as important, but I also evaluate students' research ability and knowledge of the field. Weekly insight cards (one-page [reflective] annotations based on the readings) ensure that learners have actively engaged with the material. I do not ask them to summarize the text but to identify just one or two issues they found interesting and articulate why. The second assignment is to identify a research question, conduct a literature search, and write an annotated bibliography on the selected readings. Here I expect to see good understanding of content as well as critical engagement. The third assignment is a discussion paper based on the books and articles reviewed for the annotated bibliography. Here I expect an ability to synthesize research material, recognize strengths and weaknesses, and draw plausible conclusions. In both undergraduate and graduate courses I encourage students to submit their work any time for formative evaluation. On an informal level, I evaluate learning by asking questions in class. Listening to students' group presentations and observing individual students during activities, also allows for a fairly accurate assessment of their learning. Many students also offer unsolicited comments.

Process Reflection

Students have conducted excellent work this way, as demonstrated by the high quality of their assignments at both the graduate and undergraduate levels. Furthermore, the educational literature (for example Bloom & Krathwohl, 1956) suggests that higher-order learning is encouraged when students have to analyze, synthesize, and evaluate information and process it on a deep level (Biggs, 1987; Entwistle & Ramsden, 1983). It seems to me also that students' self-direction and motivation is enhanced when there is some choice regarding assignments. In the graduate course, students choose the topic for their annotated bibliography and term paper. In the undergraduate course, students have a choice with respect to at least one of the assignments.

In one instance, I conducted a classroom research project on students' conceptualization of course content before and after the class. The study was later published (see *Teaching in Higher Education*).

Premise Reflection

I think it is important that I evaluate the learning of students in my courses so that they receive feedback on their learning process. With some students, the feedback I provide is more supportive; with others it is more challenging—it all depends on the individual student. At any rate, I think it is important to help students self-regulate their learning, including monitoring the objectives they set, the learning strategies they choose, and the beliefs they hold about themselves as learners. I also think it is important that students receive feedback on whether their conceptualization of course content is appropriate.

EVALUATING THE TEACHING PORTFOLIO

So how would or could such a statement be peer reviewed? Whether or not the various assumptions and beliefs articulated in the philosophy statement are actually practiced can be demonstrated in the appendix section of the teaching portfolio. Course outlines, results from formative and summative evaluations of teaching, examples of classroom research projects, criteria used for assessing student learning, excerpts from the literature on learning that struck a chord, own published work on teaching and learning, to mention just a few examples, provide evidence regarding the truthfulness of the statement. Members of faculty evaluation committees who understand the notions of content, process, and premise reflection on research-based and experience-based knowledge could make a judgment of the extent to which a philosophy statement is plausible by looking for evidence of the faculty member's engagement in the three forms of reflection, his or her awareness of educational research relevant to teaching and learning, and the degree to which he or she has made an effort to learn from personal teaching experience. In making a decision regarding the validity of a teaching philosophy statement, the defining criterion is therefore not whether or not other members of the academy espouse the same beliefs, but whether what is suggested in the statement seems plausible if evaluated against the proposed model of the scholarship of teaching.

As part of their model, Kreber and Cranton (in press) provide a list of indicators of engagement in the scholarship of teaching which could guide such peer review. Indicators are seen as the concrete action faculty take from which active engagement in the scholarship of teaching can be inferred. Some suggestions for such indicators follow (for a more comprehensive list sees Kreber & Cranton, in press):

1) asking for peer review of course outline

2) collecting data on students' perceptions of methods and materials

3) experimenting with alternative teaching approaches and checking out results

4) writing critiques on "how-to" books

5) administering learning styles or other inventories to students

6) writing an article on how to facilitate learning in the discipline

7) gathering feedback from students on their learning the concepts of the discipline

8) reading articles or books on learning theory

9) conducting an action research project on student learning

10) comparing classroom experience to formal research results on student learning

11) participating in philosophical discussions on student learning on, for example, a listserv or with colleagues

12) reading books on the goals of higher education and comparing goals to those underlying the programs offered in the department

Clearly, other indicators are possible, and the development of further indicators by those who practice the scholarship of teaching is both necessary and encouraged. Note that these indicators are not meant to be used as a checklist in a sense that if all indicators are checked off then we have an example of the scholarship of teaching. It seems more meaningful to take the indicators as what they are, a list of suggestions, and become comfortable with the idea that the scholarship of teaching can probably be demonstrated in many different ways (see for example, Theall & Centra, in press). At the same time, however, not every teaching portfolio will be an example of the scholarship of teaching. The Delphi panel in the above mentioned study also raised the question whether and how excellence in teaching versus the scholarship of teaching could be valued. A discussion of this question can be found in Kreber (in press). The focus in this essay is the teaching portfolio as a way of demonstrating the scholarship of teaching, not excellence in teaching. Clearly, teaching portfolios are very appropriate for demonstrating teaching excellence also.

The most difficult problem to be tackled in the process of peer review is to make the critical discrimination between excellent teaching and the scholarship of teaching. Addressing the following three questions will be paramount: 1) Did the individual engage in content, process, and premise reflection on experience-based and research-based knowledge about teaching and learning? 2) In doing so, did the individual contribute to the development of pedagogical content knowledge? 3) Was this pedagogical content knowledge shared with other members of one's discipline?

The degree to which this was done, I would suspect, is an indication to the degree to which the person demonstrates the scholarship of teaching. To complicate matters further, it would follow that faculty can demonstrate the scholarship of teaching not only in different ways but most likely also to varying degrees.

If the model of the scholarship of teaching were accepted by the larger academic community, it could also be conceptualized as a set of agreed-upon norms. When members of a faculty evaluation committee engage in dialogue around the plausibility of a teaching philosophy based upon these norms, they construct communicative knowledge (Cranton, 1994; Habermas, 1984; Kreber & Cranton, in press; Mezirow, 1991), where the rightness or plausibility of an argument is determined by consensus within a community of peers.

SUMMARY

The purpose of this essay was to demonstrate that a formal model of the scholarship of teaching could be effectively used for the design and evaluation of teaching portfolios. As the teaching philosophy section of the teaching portfolio was shown to be difficult to write for many faculty, the chapter offered an example to illustrate how the notions of content, process, and premise reflection on research-based and experience-based knowledge can guide the articulation of one's teaching philosophy. At the same time, suggested that the format provides a way of assessing the extent to which the teaching portfolio demonstrates engagement in the scholarship of teaching, a process inadequately addressed to date.

REFERENCES

Apps, J. W. (1973). *Towards a working philosophy for adult education.* (ERIC Document Reproduction Service No. ED 078 229).

Astin, A. W. (1993). *What matters in college? Four critical years revisited.* San Francisco, CA: Jossey-Bass.

Baxter Magolda, M. (1992). *Knowing and reasoning in college: Gender-related patterns in students' intellectual development.* San Francisco, CA: Jossey-Bass.

Biggs, J. R. (1987). *Students' approaches to learning and studying.* Melbourne, Australia: ACER Press.

Bloom, B. S., & Krathwohl, D. R. (1956). *Taxonomy of educational objectives: The classification of educational goals.* New York, NY: Longmans.

Boyer, E. L. (1990). *Scholarship reconsidered: Priorities of the professoriate.* Princeton, NJ: Carnegie Foundation for the Advancement of Teaching.

Brookfield, S. (1990). *The skillful teacher.* San Francisco, CA: Jossey-Bass.

Brookfield, S. (1995). *Becoming a critically reflective teacher.* San Francisco, CA: Jossey-Bass.

Brownlie, F., & Feniak, C. (1998). *Student diversity: Addressing the needs of all learners in inclusive classrooms.* Markham, Canada: Pembroke.

Candy, P. (1991). *Self-direction for lifelong learning.* San Francisco, CA: Jossey-Bass.

Cranton, P. (1992). *Working with adult learners.* Toronto, Canada: Wall and Emerson.

Cranton, P. (1994). *Understanding and promoting transformative learning.* San Francisco, CA: Jossey-Bass.

Cranton, P. (1996). *Professional development as transformative learning.* San Francisco, CA: Jossey-Bass.

Donald, J. G. (1997). *Improving the environment for learning.* San Francisco, CA: Jossey-Bass.

Gross Davis, B. (1993). *Tools for teaching.* San Francisco, CA: Jossey-Bass.

Edgerton, R., Hutchings, P., & Quinlan, K. (1991). *The teaching portfolio: Capturing the scholarship of teaching.* Washington, DC: American Association for Higher Education.

Entwistle, N., & Ramsden, P. (1983). *Understanding student learning.* London, England: Croom Helm.

Fuhrman, B., & Grasha, T. (1983). *A practical handbook for college teachers.* Boston, MA: Little, Brown.

Garrison, D. R. (1997). Self-directed learning: Toward a comprehensive model. *Adult Education Quarterly, 48* (1), 18–34.

Glassick, C. E., Huber, M. T., & Maeroff, G. I. (1997). *Scholarship assessed. Evaluation of the professoriate.* San Francisco, CA: Jossey-Bass.

Goodyear, G. E., & Allchin, D. (1998). Statements of teaching philosophy. In M. Kaplan & D. Lieberman (Eds.), *To improve the academy, 17,* 103–122, Stillwater, OK: New Forums.

Habermas, J. (1971). *Knowledge and human interests.* Boston, MA: Beacon Press.

Habermas, J. (1984). *The theory of communicative action.* Boston, MA: Beacon Press.

Houle, C. (1961). *The inquiring mind.* Madison, WI: University of Wisconsin Press.

Kelly, G. A. (1955). *The psychology of personal constructs. Vol 1. A theory of personality.* New York, NY: Norton.

King, P. M., & Kitchener, K. S. (1994). *Developing reflective judgment.* San Francisco, CA: Jossey-Bass.

Knapper, C. K. (1995). The origins of teaching portfolios. *Journal of Excellence in College Teaching, 6* (1), 45–56.

Knapper, C. K., McFarlane, B., & Scanlon, J. (1972). Student evaluation: An aspect of teaching effectiveness. *CAUT Bulletin, 21* (2), 26–34.

Kreber, C. (1998). Perfection through reflection: The teaching portfolio to evaluate and professionalize university teaching *(in German)*. In *Handreichungen zur hochschuldidaktik* (section 18, pp. 1–24), Handbuch Hochschullehre. Bonn, Germany: Raabe Verlag.

Kreber, C. (1999). A course-based approach to the development of teaching-scholarship: A case study. *Teaching in Higher Education, 4* (3), 309–325.

Kreber, C. (Ed). (in press). *Revisiting scholarship: Identifying and implementing the scholarship of teaching* (tentative title). New Directions for Teaching and Learning. San Francisco, CA: Jossey-Bass.

Kreber, C. (in press). Observations, reflections, and speculations: What we have learned about the scholarship of teaching and where it might lead. In C. Kreber (Ed.), *Revisiting scholarship: Identifying and implementing the scholarship of teaching* (tentative title). New Directions for Teaching and Learning. San Francisco, CA: Jossey-Bass.

Kreber, C., & Cranton, P. A. (in press). Exploring the scholarship of teaching. *Journal of Higher Education, 71* .

Lawson, K. H. (1991). Philosophical foundations. In P. Jarvis & J. M. Peters (Eds.), *Adult education* (pp. 282–301). San Francisco, CA: Jossey-Bass.

Matthews, R. (1996). Collaborative learning: Creating knowledge with students. In R. Menges & M. Weimer (Eds.), *Teaching on solid ground* (pp. 101–124). San Francisco, CA: Jossey-Bass.

Menges, R., & Weimer, M. (Eds.). (1996). *Teaching on solid ground.* San Francisco, CA: Jossey-Bass.

Mezirow, J. (1991). *Transformative dimensions of adult learning.* San Francisco, CA: Jossey-Bass.

Ozmon, H., & Graver, S. (1990). *Philosophical foundations of education* (4th edition). Toronto, Canada: Merrill.

Pascarella, E. T., & Terenzini, P. T. (1991). *How college affects students : Findings and insights from twenty years of study.* San Francisco, CA: Jossey-Bass.

Paulsen, M. B. (in press). The relation between research and the scholarship of teaching. In C. Kreber (Ed.), *Revisiting scholarship: Identifying and implement-*

ing the scholarship of teaching (tentative title). New Directions for Teaching and Learning. San Francisco, CA: Jossey-Bass.

Paulsen, M. B., & Feldman, K. A. (1995). Toward a reconceptualization of scholarship: A human action system with functional imperatives. *Journal of Higher Education, 66*, 615–641.

Perry, W. G. (1970). *Forms of intellectual and ethical development in the college years: A scheme.* Troy, MO: Holt, Rinehart, & Winston.

Rice, R. E. (1991). The new American scholar: Scholarship and the purposes of the university. *Metropolitan Universities, 1*, 7–18.

Rice, R. E. (1992). Toward a broader conception of scholarship: The American context. In T. G. Whiston, & R. L. Geiger (Eds.), *Research and higher education: The United States and the United Kingdom* (pp. 117–129). Buckingham, England: The Society for Research into Higher Education and Open University Press.

Richlin, L. (1995). A different view on developing teaching portfolios: Ensuring safety while honouring practice. *Journal of Excellence in College Teaching, 6* (1), 161–178.

Richlin, L. (Ed.). (1993). *Preparing faculty for new conceptions of scholarship.* New Directions for Teaching and Learning, No. 54. San Francisco, CA: Jossey-Bass.

Scott, S. M., Chovanec, D. M. & Young, B. (1994). Philosophy-in-action in university teaching. *The Canadian Journal of Higher Education. XXIV* (3), 1–25.

Shore, B. M., Foster, S. F., Knapper, C. K, Nadeau, G. G., Neill, N., & Sim, V. (1980, 1986) *The teaching dossier: A guide to its preparation and use.* (Rev. ed.). Montreal, Canada: Canadian Association of University Teachers.

Shulman, L. S. (1998). Course anatomy: The dissection and analysis of knowledge through teaching. In P. Hutchings (Ed.), *The course portfolio.* Washington, DC: American Association for Higher Education.

Smith, R. A. (1995). Creating a culture of teaching through the teaching portfolio. *Journal of Excellence in College Teaching, 6* (1), 75–100.

Svinicki, M. D., & Dixon, N. (1987). The Kolb model modified for classroom activities. *College Teaching, 35* (4), 141–146.

Theall, M., & Centra, J. A. (in press). Assessing the scholarship of teaching: Valid decisions from valid evidence. In C. Kreber (Ed.), *Revisiting scholarship: Identifying and implementing the scholarship of teaching* (tentative title). New Directions for Teaching and Learning. San Francisco, CA: Jossey-Bass.

Weimer, M. (1987). Theories of teaching. *The Teaching Professor, 1*(3), 1–2.

Contact:

Carolin Kreber
Adult and Higher Education
Department of Educational Policy Studies
7-151 Education North
University of Alberta
Edmonton, ABT6G 2G5
Canada
(780) 492-7623
(780) 492-2024 (Fax)
Email: carolin.kreber@ualberta.ca

Carolin Kreber has been a faculty member in the Department of Educational Policy Studies at the University of Alberta since 1997. She teaches undergraduate and graduate courses on the psychology of adult learning, adult development, and instructional design. From 1993 to 1997 she worked as an educational development consultant at the Instructional Development Office at Brock University in Southern Ontario. Her present research focuses on faculty's integration of their professorial roles, the development and assessment of the scholarship of teaching, and student learning in science.

18

Strengthening Collegiality to Enhance Teaching, Research, and Scholarly Practice: An Untapped Resource for Faculty Development

Gerlese S. Åkerlind
Australian National University

Kathleen M. Quinlan
Cornell University

Collegiality lies at the intersection of various aspects of academic practice, including teaching as well as research. As such, assisting junior faculty in learning to build their collegial networks becomes a powerful point of intervention for faculty developers, even for those who focus on teaching development. Data from interviews with faculty engaged in both teaching and research, plus our experiences in conducting a series of career building initiatives are analyzed to identify junior faculty perceptions of the role of collegiality and barriers to establishing collegial ties. Two main barriers are identified: 1) knowing that collegiality and networking is important, and 2) knowing how to go about establishing oneself as a colleague. Recommendations are then offered to faculty developers for working with junior faculty to help address each of those barriers, drawing on the authors' experiments with various workshops and forums.

INTRODUCTION

Collegiality plays a pivotal role in academia, lying at the intersection of different aspects of academic practice. The significance of collegiality in scholarly communities is taken for granted in the realm of academic research, in which the entire system of peer review, conference attendance, and publication is structured to promote the sharing of work to critique and build upon. Although the role of scholarly community and collegiality is less recognized than other aspects of academic work, academic leadership and community service assume that there is a network of scholars and a community that is being served. Furthermore, the literature on teaching improvement over the past decade has given increasing recognition to the significance of community and collegiality.

The concept of the scholarship of teaching (Boyer, 1990; Glassick, Huber, & Maeroff, 1997) has contributed to international attention to peer review and peer collaboration in teaching (Cosser, 1998; Hutchings, 1996; Ramsden, Margetson, Martin & Clarke, 1995; Palmer, 1995; Trow & Clark, 1994; Valimaa, 1994). Viewing peer review as the heart of scholarship, the peer review of teaching movement strives to elevate the status of teaching by invoking the academic convention of peer review. According to Hutchings and Shulman (1999) the scholarship of teaching has four main requirements: 1) being public, 2) open to critique and evaluation, 3) in a form that others can build on, 4) and inquiry-oriented. These criteria put scholarly communities at the center of scholarship in teaching in the same way as they are for scholarship in research.

Given the significance of collegiality to scholarly teaching, academic leadership, service to the community, and research productivity, working with faculty to help enhance their skills in building collegial networks is a particularly effective point of intervention for faculty developers. Yet there has been relatively little attention paid in the literature to faculty development strategies and activities for building skills in collegial networking, or to the challenges that individual faculty face as they learn how to network effectively.

Where the issue of collegial networking has been addressed, it is commonly conceived of narrowly. The most commonly presented purpose of collegiality is to enhance career progression and build research contacts. Mentoring programs are one of the most commonly implemented developmental interventions (Quinlan, 1999) to address this purpose.

This relatively narrow vision and approach restricts the potential of collegial networking as a form of faculty development. When collegiality is primarily seen as a part of developing as a researcher, instructional developers whose primary focus is on enhancing teaching and learning may regard it as outside of their mission. In addition, relying solely on structured mentoring programs for junior faculty leaves those faculty in schools or institutions without such programs with little support in developing networking skills and strategies. Even where mentoring programs are in place, they have the potential to undermine the importance of faculty taking individual responsibility for and being proactive about building their own networks.

Robert Boice's (1992) comprehensive, longitudinal study of new faculty members in two American universities provides strong support for our arguments about the importance of working with junior faculty to assist the development of collegial networking skills. He stresses that the development of collegiality is one of the key tasks or challenges facing new faculty and emphasizes the significance of collegiality for both teaching and research development. He found that collegiality does not typically develop instantly or spontaneously, but must be explicitly worked on and learned. He also found the desire for collegial contacts in teaching to be as significant a need as the desire for contacts in research. However, his suggestions for faculty development initiatives to help develop collegial skills for new faculty were limited to the typical recommendation of developing a mentoring program.

The aim of this essay is to further explore the nature of collegiality in academia and how junior faculty can be assisted in building collegial networks. We consider a broad range of ways that faculty developers can support junior faculty with the task of building collegial networks and scholarly communities. To do so, we first look more closely at how faculty view the development of collegiality, in order to inform faculty development efforts in this area. This essay draws on data and insights gained from a study of conceptions of academic growth and development among junior and mid-career faculty at a research-intensive university in Australia. In addition, we build on the outcomes of a series of career development initiatives undertaken over a number of years at the same university. Analyzing those sources and reflecting on our own experiences as faculty development professionals working with members of faculty, we present several potential barriers to developing collegiality. We also suggest strategies that faculty developers may use to help overcome these barriers, in order to support faculty effectiveness in a variety of forms of scholarly work.

DATA SOURCES AND METHODS

Interviews with Faculty

As stated above, a significant source of information for the issues addressed in this paper come from a series of interviews conducted with faculty about their professional growth and development. All of the interviews were with faculty engaged in both teaching and research at the Australian National University. The Australian National University is a traditional, research-intensive university located in the capital of Australia. Interviews were semi-structured, asking faculty what growth and development meant to them, how they went about it, what they were trying to achieve, and why they did it that way, working from examples of development activities volunteered by the interviewees.

The interviews were conducted during the calendar years 1997 and 1998. The faculty interviewed included two groups: 15 junior faculty in entry-level appointments in their first year of appointment to the Australian National University, and ten mid-career faculty. The interviewees were all employed full-time, but on varying terms of appointment and from varied disciplines, cultural backgrounds, and gender. It is important to note that the interviews were conducted as part of a larger study of academic growth and development (Åkerlind, 1999a,b), and thus designed with other purposes and questions in mind than those addressed in this paper. Nonetheless, the views of collegiality that emerged during the interviews provide a useful source of information to help inform the issues raised here.

Career Development Initiatives
Over a similar period as the interviews (1996–1998), several career development initiatives for junior faculty began, with a varying focus on teaching and research faculty, research-only faculty, and women faculty. Again, the goals of these initiatives were broader than developing skills in collegiality, but this issue emerged (either deliberately or spontaneously) as a common theme across the activities, providing further experience to draw on for this paper. The initiatives included:

- a two-day conference for junior women faculty on "Advancing our Careers"

- a one-day workshop for junior faculty on "Building a Career in Academia"

- a half-day workshop for PhD students and postdoctoral fellows on "Planning Life after a PhD"

- a one-week "Academic Women's Writing Retreat" on scholarly writing and publication

- regular half-day workshops on "Developing a Teaching Portfolio"

- support for a series of flexible mentoring initiatives, designed to suit individual schools

As well as the lessons we learned in designing these activities, we draw on written evaluation responses from participants, comments made during panel presentations by experienced faculty, notes from semistructured discussions among participants at different points during the activities, and our experiences with other faculty development activities. Our joint reflection on these data helped to elucidate issues and potential barriers to forming collegial networks and informed the strategies proposed later in the paper for working with junior faculty on enhancing collegiality and networking.

Types of Collegial Networks and Barriers to Effective Networking

In addressing the question of how we as faculty developers can best assist junior faculty in successfully networking to build collegial contacts, an important starting point is gaining a sense of the ways in which faculty view collegiality. The interviews described above provided a useful source of data in this regard, showing the existence of a variety of different types of networking plus common barriers to being proactive about developing collegial contacts.

As a group, the faculty interviewed referred to a large range of types of collegial contacts that they had formed or needed to form as part of their growth and development. Not all of these were academic contacts, but all involved networks that are essential for achieving the full range of academic work and scholarly practice:

- teaching networks with fellow teachers in one's discipline

- student networks, leading to potential PhD students and postdoctoral fellows

- community networks, particularly to facilitate field work

- research networks, facilitating collaborative research, grant applications, publications, etc.

- media networks, especially to enable greater impact of research findings on the community or broader society

- consultancy networks in private firms and industrial organizations, to increase opportunities for applied research and associated funding

- collegial networks of any type to reduce a sense of academic isolation

This broad range of types and goals of collegial networking both supports and extends Boice's (1992) findings on collegial needs of new faculty. Although Boice limited his discussion of collegial contacts to campus-based colleagues, it is clear that potential colleagues need to be viewed more broadly, including off-campus and significant nonacademic networks. These findings also raise the potential for faculty developers to use the concept of collegiality when working with faculty on a variety of fronts, including instructional development.

As well as considering the range of collegial needs experienced by faculty, it is important to elucidate the range of prior knowledge, strategies, and expectations about collegiality held by junior faculty which help or hinder them in building collegial networks. This understanding aids us in identifying perceptions and strategies junior faculty already have that we can build on and barriers that get in the way of further developing collegial ties. We identify two primary barriers to successful networking among junior faculty, each with several variations. The two barriers can be loosely described as the problem of knowing *that* versus the problem of knowing *how*. The existence of these barriers is supported by the interviews with faculty and our experience with participants in the career development initiatives described above.

Knowing that Proactive Networking Is Important

The first potential barrier to developing collegiality is simply not being fully aware of its importance in faculty life. Evidence of the prevalence of this lack of awareness comes indirectly from the interviews with faculty described above. As the interviews were designed to elicit faculty conceptions of their own growth and development, including their approaches and strategies for developing themselves, the interviewees were encouraged to mention a variety of personally meaningful ways of thinking about and actualizing their development as faculty. Yet only seven of the 15 junior faculty interviewed spontaneously talked about activities that could broadly be called networking or developing collegiality.

Seemingly, for more than half of the junior faculty interviewed the task of developing collegiality as an aspect of faculty development was not important enough to them to raise spontaneously in the context of a discussion about professional growth and development. While several of the experienced faculty interviewed also did not mention this aspect of their professional development, the percentage was substantially smaller than for the junior faculty, with only three of the ten mid-career interviewees *not* raising collegiality issues.

An associated form of naiveté involves not realizing the degree to which one must take the lead and be proactive about building these contacts, even though the importance of developing collegial networks per se is recognized. Some junior faculty may be aware of the importance of becoming a member of scholarly communities but believe that such contacts will occur naturally as an automatic consequence of the normal process of publication and conference presentations, with no additional, focused effort required on their part. One of the junior faculty interviewed, a mathematician in his first year at the Australian National University, illustrates this view in relation to his reputation as a researcher:

> *"The research side I don't really worry about much. I think that as long as one is doing good research, your work [. . .] will be accumulating. They may not like you in the first place, but after a long time they know that you are doing good research, they will accept you. Once you have done that, you are totally validated in the world environment. Not only for myself, but also for the department and for the Australian National University and for the country. They are all connected. That is my strategy for developing myself. I'm not really worried about that."*

This new academic seems to think that to become recognized, he simply has to produce good research and wait to be discovered. He does not seem to attend to his role in promoting his work and himself.

Finally, there are faculty who may be aware of the importance of networking for *some* purposes—to help them in publishing or in building consultancies, for example—but may not have thought about the role of collegiality in other aspects of their academic work, for instance, in improving their teaching.

Knowing How to Network Effectively
The barrier described above does not exist for all junior faculty; many are both aware of the importance of networking and realize that they must be proactive in the process of building collegial ties and establishing themselves in scholarly communities. However, at this point another barrier can arise, in that they may not feel capable or confident in their abilities to go about networking.

For these faculty, the challenge is not in learning *that* they need to develop collegial networks, but in learning *how* to develop collegiality. Their needs are illustrated in workshop evaluation comments like, "[I now have a] much more thorough idea of the kinds of strategies I'll be using in working towards my career goals." In workshops, these individuals value the opportunity to widen their repertoire of strategies for initiating collegial contacts. They express appreciation for the new strategies that are introduced, and are often relieved to discover that sustaining contact with colleagues is a common difficulty, shared by many of their peers.

However, there is often more involved in learning how to be active in networking than simply learning appropriate skills and strategies. For some, there are psychological or psychosocial barriers related to an individual's shyness, self-confidence, or socialization. Thus, learning how to build collegial contacts has two levels: lack of knowledge or skill with particular strategies and approaches to networking, and difficulty feeling personally comfortable with engaging in the recommended strategies and approaches once they are known.

This latter type of barrier brings up complex issues of self-confidence and personal identity. Some faculty explained that it required considerable confidence and courage to introduce oneself to senior (or indeed junior) colleagues or to share one's work with them. There were several variations on this theme, though what is common to the variations is that achieving success in building a scholarly community can mean confronting oneself in a personal way. Rather than simply needing more techniques or strategies for networking, some faculty need to address personal and emotional aspects of becoming a colleague.

For example, a number of participants in the "Advancing our Careers" conference requested courses on assertiveness as a follow-up to the event. In addition, experienced faculty who were panelists at the conference also emphasized the need to overcome difficulties with the assertive, self-promotional dimension of networking. To be successful in academia, one of them put it succinctly, "I need to be the sort of person that I'm not." Related issues identified by participants in the other workshops on career development include difficulties with risk-taking, negotiation skills, procrastination and the imposter syndrome.

One of the junior faculty interviewed, a recent PhD graduate and new faculty member in Women's Studies, spoke at length about the process of re-envisioning herself as a faculty member:

> *"You are all the time trying to work out how you might be, being employed as an academic . . . And it's interesting when you have friends who are still in the student category. There is something that's happened that makes you different."*

She goes on to cite several instances and examples which she sees as part of being an academic, including:

> *"I think one of the things I've done is that I haven't been bashful about trying to make contact with established people in my area of study around the world. That's a really good thing to do, and to follow that up. Because that's also part of rethinking yourself as a colleague of theirs. Most people are really responsive."*

In another example, she refers to an invitation to present at an international conference:

> *"I suppose that it was an achievement that I was invited to go by [. . .] who was a very warm and encouraging person. But that's what being comfortable about being an academic is, because there is no insecurity about whether the work is going to be appropriate or whether it will link up well with a whole series of what other people, who have also been invited, are doing. It worked extremely well because . . . the people at the conference were more or less at the same level . . . That was a really happy experience for me. An affirming one."*

Envisioning herself as a member of a community of colleagues—all at an equivalent level—rather than as a junior colleague at a lower level, was a crucial part of her relative comfort about developing collegial ties, compared to the experiences of many junior faculty.

Along the same vein, one of the experienced faculty interviewed, from the College of Forestry, explained that it has been his growing self-confidence that allows him to more comfortably seek out the input of a wider circle of colleagues on his work:

> *"I think it's recognition that there are no limits; that the limits are imposed only by yourself, really—which comes with confidence . . . I think I just feel totally confident, first with my own abilities, but second, because of that, I have absolutely no problem in getting other input from a lot of other people. I suppose what I tend to do more now than I ever have done is to solicit input into project design and implementation. I mean I've always done that to some extent, but probably more now than ever, I think, for a few reasons. One is that I've realized that you can do quantum jumps a hell of a lot easier with other people involved—if they're good people, obviously. I think, also, it's a matter of confidence in your own stature, or whatever you want to call it."*

What comes through in these and other comments is the need for junior faculty to develop strategies to help them feel comfortable and confident about networking, as a separate issue from the need to become aware of a wider range of possible networking strategies per se.

IMPLICATIONS FOR FACULTY DEVELOPMENT

The two types of barriers described above require different types of assistance to promote the successful formation of collegial contacts. In the sections below, we address each type of barrier separately, suggesting ways that faculty developers can address them.

How Faculty Developers Can Address Barriers of Knowing that Proactive Networking Is Important

This first type of barrier represents a lack of awareness of the importance of collegiality to all forms of scholarly work, or of the importance of one's own proactive role in developing collegiality. What is needed is consciousness-raising among such faculty.

However, the biggest challenge faculty developers face in initiating consciousness-raising activities is simply reaching the faculty concerned. Without an awareness of their own role in promoting and managing their careers, these faculty are unlikely to seek out or spontaneously avail themselves of workshops, consultations, books, or other guidance in these areas.

As a first suggestion, faculty developers may need to rethink their marketing strategies for forums addressing issues of collegiality in order to better appeal to those faculty who are not already seeking to develop themselves in this area. For instance, a workshop entitled "Advancing Your Research Career" may be more appealing to the interests of faculty like the new mathematician quoted earlier than one entitled "Building Research Networks," even if they address similar issues. It is our experience that designing programs to meet the needs of faculty is a somewhat separate exercise from designing the marketing of these programs so that faculty perceive them as addressing their needs. The latter aspect requires as careful attention as the former.

In a similar way, faculty developers may take advantage of a range of agendas and forums on various other topics to introduce and reinforce the theme of collegiality. At an orientation session for new appointees, for example, the importance of collegial networking might be a key topic addressed. A newsletter on teaching enhancement could include suggestions for developing collegiality, testimonials from senior faculty on its importance for them, and examples of their personal strategies for building scholarly communities to support their academic productivity in a variety of ways. Actively searching for opportunities to reinforce the message that the best ideas are often developed with the input of others—whether those ideas become the subject of a paper or a theme in a course or lecture—may heighten awareness within the university community of the importance of collegiality.

If junior faculty are not coming to us directly, it behooves us as faculty developers to think creatively about ways of reaching them indirectly. Senior faculty, course coordinators, heads of research labs, and department chairs have occasions to interact with junior faculty that we do not. Consequently, searching for ways to educate senior colleagues about the career development needs of their less experienced colleagues may be a fruitful avenue to pursue. Senior faculty can be invited to attend or play a role in orientations or other activities that are mainly geared towards junior faculty. Programs on academic leadership can include attention to senior faculty roles in supporting less experienced colleagues. Faculty developers might also consider occasional letters or electronic mailings to department chairs in which this type of issue is raised.

Formal mentoring programs in which the mentors participate in an orientation or training program also come to mind. As we noted earlier, mentoring programs are a common response to these concerns. Even in the absence of a formal program, however, senior colleagues could be encouraged to play a more active role in educating and guiding junior staff in achieving success in their scholarly work, simply in the course of their everyday activities.

However, it is important to be prepared for the fact that senior faculty are not always aware of the needs of their less experienced colleagues or aware that these needs are not necessarily being spontaneously addressed within normal departmental or school processes. For instance, during a seminar we presented on mentoring needs of junior faculty held within one of the Australian National University's science schools, senior members of the audience claimed that these needs were spontaneously addressed by the lab-based, collaborative nature of the discipline. Junior members of the audience, helping to convince the more senior members otherwise to the contrary courageously offered comments.

Such comments are more persuasive when they come from junior faculty themselves rather than from faculty developers. Using workshops and programs to collect comments from new faculty can be useful in this regard. For instance, during one of our workshops, participants generated two pages of career development suggestions which we typed up for distribution after the event. Such documents can act as a convincing aid when approaching more senior faculty about the needs of more junior faculty, as well as forming a useful resource to distribute at future workshops, in newsletters or orientation programs, and during individual consultations with new faculty.

As a final suggestion, faculty development centers might work with schools or departments in creating faculty development liaison people located within particular subject areas. Such liaisons provide opportunities for sympathetic faculty within the discipline to champion these issues. They may even be explicitly charged with responsibility for organizing initiatives to promote collegiality in the local culture.

How Faculty Developers Can Address Barriers of Knowing How to Network Effectively

A key consideration in addressing this type of barrier is the need for faculty development programs to place as much emphasis on strategies for feeling comfortable about networking as on strategies for networking per se. Otherwise, personal or self-perceptual barriers can interfere with putting good networking strategies into practice.

We have experimented with a number of ways of approaching these barriers. One successful approach is the use of panels of faculty who share their personal experiences of networking. Panels made up of either senior or junior faculty can both be effective, appealing to different needs of junior staff. On the one hand, senior faculty can present a long-term perspective, reflecting on their experiences and changing perceptions over time. Furthermore, as they have reached a position of some success, the strategies they describe carry weight. On the other hand, it is easier for junior faculty to identify more closely with their peers or near peers, making suggestions which arise from panels of junior or mid-career faculty potentially more convincing and easier to imagine emulating— especially when there are psychosocial barriers to overcome.

In some of our programs we have chosen to include panels of both junior and senior faculty. Subsequent feedback from participants in these programs showed equal appreciation for both types of panels. Mixed panels of faculty with different levels of experience is also an option we have used with success.

Even more important is the process of selecting and briefing members of such panels, whatever their makeup. To be effective, it is essential that panel members have a positive attitude toward the issues at hand, are sensitive to the needs of junior faculty, and are willing to speak frankly from their own personal experience. For instance, a member of one of our panels, a senior academic and chair in his department, read aloud from a harsh manuscript rejection letter received in response to the first publication attempt of his career. He then read aloud a recent letter of rejection, explaining that such critiques were a standard experience for faculty at all levels, whether they talked about it or not. You can imagine the effect that this kind of frankness had in opening up discussion. It legitimized the fact that written work does not have to be perfect before it can be shown to one's colleagues and assured the audience that rejection letters are normal experience that can be used to improve one's work. Participants and the panelists went on to discuss the value of seeking feedback from colleagues when preparing and improving papers.

As in most settings, fellow participants in workshops or other events are a wonderful resource for each other. Small group discussion, where participants feel less exposed, is a fruitful arena for generating networking strategies, acknowledging personal barriers and sharing ways of overcoming such barriers. For instance, many participants in our programs have expressed difficulty with feeling comfortable sharing their work and introducing themselves to new colleagues at conferences. Through small group discussion, participants in our programs have shared the following strategies for making the process more comfortable: Attend smaller rather than larger conferences, as they tend to be friendlier and less anonymous; select a conference for regular attendance, as you tend to accumulate contacts over a number of years with other regular attendees; take part in organized sightseeing side trips to make contacts within a smaller, informal group.

Another illustration of the experience and wisdom that new faculty can contribute comes from the following excerpt of an interview with a new member of faculty, several months into his first appointment following graduate school. He describes how he sits in on the classes of faculty in his department (cultural studies) who have a strong word-of-mouth reputation as outstanding teachers, in order to develop his own teaching:

"I approached them directly. I said, 'Look, I understand that you're a great lecturer,' joking but serious as well. So they appreciate that because everyone has an ego. And to have a colleague come to you and say that—they love it and they accept you as well. So they don't feel intimi-

dated by you or anything. So, you go along to their class and they love it . . . Two of them whom I thought were really brilliant in the way they teach—I mean they've been teaching for about 15 years, and both of them are very, very competent—they also felt the need to ask me what I thought! And I thought that was nice, too, because of the modesty . . . So that's one way of approaching colleagues . . .

Usually I took notes. I'm not passive, so I'm actually writing notes and suddenly I find myself, while taking notes and observing, comparing myself and thinking, 'Ah, I can't do that; and I don't do that; I've never done this.' So it's really alerted me to my weaknesses basically, so I really appreciate that . . . So that's what colleagues are, human resources. I think that's the best resource you have, and the most available one as well. Something you can tap into by just picking up the phone or just talking to them. So I value that a lot . . ."

In addition to discussions about networking, fellow junior faculty can also be used to provide initial positive experiences in collegiality; for instance in seeking feedback on one's work. Mutual feedback sessions among participants can be organized as part of a program, or as an optional follow-up. We have successfully conducted small group feedback sessions focusing on sharing draft grant proposals, paper publications, and in-class teaching.

As a final suggestion, it is also possible to explicitly focus on personal barriers to networking as a specific part of a workshop, by bringing in outside expertise. We have invited counselors from the Australian National University's Counseling Center to address this issue as part of workshop programs, under titles such as, "What Gets in the Way—Identifying and Overcoming Personal Barriers to Putting your Plans in Place." This is usually done following a segment on setting goals and making plans, and has been well received.

CONCLUSION

To summarize, this essay argues first for a broad conceptualization of collegiality as a common theme underpinning and unifying academic scholarship in all areas, including teaching, research, and service. This view suggests that helping individual faculty to build a variety of collegial networks and helping to create forums in which collegiality is promoted may be a particularly effective point of intervention for faculty developers. This intervention may be useful even for those developers who interested solely in instructional enhancement because as we come to see teaching as a community activity that requires opening up teaching activities for collegial review and collaboration. Thus, helping faculty establish collegiality and colleagueship becomes a key task in teaching development, as well as other aspects of academic development.

Viewing collegiality as lying at the intersection of various aspects of academic work offers us a fresh perspective on our roles as faculty developers. While existing literature on cultures of teaching and peer review of teaching, for example, makes arguments about the centrality of collegiality and collaboration for teaching enhancement, it falls short on proposals for how collegiality is manifested and promoted more generally, across various types of work. This essay analyzes several barriers to developing collegiality and offers examples of activities that might address those barriers at the level of individual faculty. In doing so, it also provides a framework that could be extended further. One could apply the same analysis at the level of schools and departments—analyzing both aids and barriers to collegiality and suggesting strategies to facilitate collegiality. Similarly, the concept could be applied more broadly at the level of universities, disciplines, or professional conferences, identifying aids and barriers to networking successfully within these contexts.

Thus, while this essay offers practical suggestions for faculty developers working with individual faculty, it also offers a new conceptual framework for analyzing the context of academic work based on an understanding of the key role played by collegiality and its potential for faculty development interventions and programs.

References

Åkerlind, G. S. (1999a, July). *Growing and developing as an academic: What does it mean?* Paper presented at the annual conference of the Higher Education Research and Development Society of Australia (HERDSA), Melbourne, Australia.

Åkerlind, G. S. (1999b, August). *Improving university teaching: How academics approach their growth and development.* Paper presented at the biennial conference of the European Association for Research in Learning and Instruction (EARLI), Gothenburg, Sweden.

Boice, R. (1992). *The new faculty member.* San Francisco, CA: Jossey-Bass.

Boyer, E. L. (1990). *Scholarship reconsidered: Priorities of the professoriate.* Princeton, NJ: Carnegie Foundation for the Advancement of Teaching.

Cosser, M. (1998). Towards the design of a system of peer review of teaching for the advancement of the individual within the university. *Higher Education, 35,* 143–162.

Glassick, C. E., Huber, M. T., & Maeroff, G. I. (1997). *Scholarship assessed: Evaluation of the professoriate.* San Francisco, CA: Jossey-Bass.

Hutchings, P. (1996). *Making teaching community property: A menu for peer collaboration and peer review.* Washington, DC: American Association for Higher Education.

Hutchings, P., & Shulman, L. (1999). The scholarship of teaching: New elaborations, new developments. *Change, 31* (5), 11–15.

Palmer, B. H. (1995). *Lesjes van de Nederlanders: Little lessons from the Dutch to promote educational quality.* Palo Alto, CA: American Institute of Research.

Ramsden, P., Margetson, D., Martin, E., & Clarke, S. (1995). *Recognizing and rewarding good teaching in Australian universities.* Canberra, Australia: Australian Government Publishing Service.

Quinlan, K. M. (1999). Enhancing mentoring and networking of junior academic women: What, why, and how? *Journal of Higher Education Policy and Management, 21* (1), 31–42.

Trow, M., & Clark, P. (1994). *Managerialism and the academic profession: Quality and control.* Higher Education Report No. 2. London, England: Open University, Quality Support Centre.

Valimaa, J. (1994). Faculty on assessment and peer review—Finnish experience. *Higher Education Management, 6* (3), 391–408.

Contacts:

Gerlese S. Akerlind
Centre for Educational Development and Academic Methods
The Australian National University
Canberra ACT 0200 Australia
61 2 6249 0056
61 2 6249 4023 (Fax)
Email: Gerlese.Akerlind@anu.edu.au

Gerlese S. Akerlind is a lecturer in the Centre for Educational Development and Academic Methods at the Australian National University in Canberra, Australia. She convenes the centre's programs of sustained study and scholarship in teaching and learning, and coordinates programs of career management for early career academics and those newly appointed to the University. She is also a PhD candidate at La Trobe University, researching conceptions of academic work and growth and development as an academic.

Kathleen M. Quinlan
Director, Office of Educational Development
S2 014 Schurman Hall
College of Veterinary Medicine
Cornell University
Ithaca, NY 14853-6401
Email: Kmq1@cornell.edu

Kathleen M. Quinlan is Director of the Office of Educational Development in the College of Veterinary Medicine at Cornell University where she works closely with faculty in support of teaching and learning. Her primary interests are in problem-based learning and learning in the clinical setting. Formerly, she was a lecturer in the Centre for Educational Development and Academic Methods at the Australian National University in Canberra, Australia.

19

Faculty Quality of Life

Sally S. Atkins
Kathleen T. Brinko
Jeffrey A. Butts
Charles S. Claxton
Glenda T. Hubbard
Appalachian State University

An interdisciplinary research team conducted a formal assessment of campus culture and faculty quality of life at Appalachian State University. Interviews with a stratified random sample of full-time, tenure-track faculty revealed five themes: 1) the importance of human relationships, 2) the deep commitment of faculty to student learning, 3) general satisfaction with academic life, 4) the personal sacrifice of faculty members for their work, and 5) perceptions of incongruence between institutional rhetoric and action. Recommendations are offered for readers to apply to their own universities to help faculty, staff, students, and administrators work together toward becoming an institution that is a true community of learners.

INTRODUCTION

Many of the difficult issues facing higher education today involve the erosion of some key values of faculty life: commitment to students, collegiality, intellectual integrity, professional autonomy, an ethic of public service, and a sense of connectedness to the mission of the institution. External demands for accountability, loss of public trust, and financial constraints have placed pressures on academic institutions. For faculty members, these pressures—along with decreasing mobility, increasingly stringent requirements for promotion and tenure, multiple role expectations, mandates for post-tenure review, and erosion faculty governance—have a great impact on faculty satisfaction, self-esteem, and quality of life (Austin, Brocato, & Rohrer, 1997; Bowen & Schuster, 1986; Rice & Austin, 1988; Smith, 1990). Because of the central role of the faculty in the work of the academy—especially their influence on students—faculty vitality and well being are crucial. In our quest for greater accountability and productivity, it is imperative that we recognize the critical importance of promoting professional and personal growth for faculty.

FACULTY QUALITY OF LIFE AT APPALACHIAN

Appalachian State University is a comprehensive university of approximately 12,500 students, and one of the 16 institutions that comprise the University of North Carolina system. Because teaching excellence is our primary mission, and because strong faculty-student relationships are our tradition, faculty quality of life is an important priority at Appalachian. The present study is part of a long-term effort of the university to understand and address issues of individual and collective well being and organizational effectiveness. Over a period of 14 years the university has systematically studied the quality of life of several groups, including faculty (Hageseth & Atkins, 1988), staff (Hageseth & Atkins, 1989), new faculty (Branch, 1995), and chairpersons (Atkins & Hageseth, 1991). The university has also engaged in an ongoing examination of the philosophical underpinnings of faculty and staff well being (Hubbard & Atkins, 1995; Hubbard, Atkins, & Brinko, 1998; van der Bogert, Brinko, Atkins, & Arnold, 1990). These studies have influenced a number of programmatic and structural changes at Appalachian.

KEY INFLUENCES ON OUR WORK

Our ongoing efforts in reflective organizational change have been influenced by a number of current thinkers in higher education and organizational development. One stream of research that has greatly contributed to our thinking is Peter Senge's (1990) work on the learning organization. Senge sees learning organizations as places "where people continually expand their capacity to create the results they truly desire, where new and expansive patterns of thinking are nurtured, where collective aspiration is set free, and where people are continually learning how to learn together" (1990, p. 3). In Senge's model, members of a group work toward becoming a learning organization by practicing five disciplines: 1) personal mastery (intentionally learning and growing), 2) team learning (helping one another learn and grow), 3) mental models (uncovering deeply ingrained assumptions), 4) shared vision (working toward a collective purpose), and 5) systems thinking (understanding the whole as a system of interrelated, interacting parts).

Additionally, our thinking and our process are greatly indebted to Parker Palmer's (1992, 1997, 1998) ideas on community and epistemology, Robert Kegan's (1994) work on meaning making and stages of adult development, Nevitt Sanford's (1980) seminal thinking on faculty development, and Margaret Wheatley's (1992) conceptualization of self-organizing systems as applied to human organizations.

Our work builds on the research of numerous colleagues in faculty development who have focused on broad issues of faculty vitality and quality of life. Our themes echo many of those found in Robert Boice's (1991) studies of new faculty, Mary Deane Sorcinelli's (1992) studies of new junior faculty stress associated with the tenure process, Irene Karpiak's (1997) studies of midlife faculty, and Arthur Crawley's (1995) studies of senior faculty. Our work is also consistent with the findings of the most recent survey of faculty members at 38 colleges and universities (Magner, 1999).

METHODS

Our research team was interdisciplinary in nature and consisted of three faculty members and two administrators working under the auspices of the Hubbard Center for Faculty and Staff Support. Our disciplinary backgrounds included biology, faculty and instructional development, higher education, psychotherapy, and counseling and human development. The chairperson of the Institutional Review Board approved the study, assuring that it conformed to the regulations stated in Appalachian State University's Policy and Procedures on Human Subjects Research.

Instrument
The 90-minute structured interview protocol was partially based on the instrument used in the previous study of faculty (Hageseth & Atkins, 1988). The instrument also included some items from a staff quality of life survey that was being conducted simultaneously at Appalachian (Langdon, in preparation) and additional questions based on Senge's (1990) five disciplines. The instrument addressed three general areas of faculty perceptions: individual quality of life, organizational culture, and mission and vision (see Appendix 19.1).

Sample

Subjects consisted of a stratified random sample of full-time, tenure-track faculty members. The Office of Institutional Research and Planning generated a list of all full-time, tenure-track faculty members sorted by department, with the order of faculty names randomized within departments. We selected ten percent from each department, contacting each person by phone to secure his/her assent for participation in the study. Similarly, in departments that had 14 or fewer full-time, tenure-track faculty, the first person on each departmental list was contacted. Likewise, in departments that had between 15 and 24 full-time, tenure-track faculty, the first and second persons were contacted, and so forth. If a selected faculty member was serving in an administrative role (such as chair or assistant dean), he or she was excluded from the study, and the next faculty member on the list was contacted. If a faculty member declined to participate (one individual) or was unavailable (two individuals), the next person on the list was substituted.

The subjects reflected the demographic parameters of our institution: The mean age was 49.2, the average number of years at the university was 13.1, and 29% of the sample were women. The sample included 24 full professors, ten associate professors, and 14 assistant professors. The identity of the subjects and their individual comments were kept confidential. After constructing a draft of the instrument and securing Institutional Review Board approval, we reviewed the purposes and methods of qualitative research and the procedures for structured interviewing (Bernard, 1995; Ely, 1991). We then conducted a pilot study of selected upper-level administrators (the chancellor and the four vice chancellors) to hone the interview questionnaire, to practice our interviewing skills, and to inform these individuals of the exact nature of the study.

Individual subjects were interviewed by a pair of interviewers (one male and one female) randomly assigned from our research team. Both members of the interviewing pair hand-recorded or keyboarded responses during each interview and compared notes immediately after the interview. During the interview, the two sought to create an atmosphere of empathy and respect and attended to nonverbal and verbal cues. While the interview questionnaire served as a guide for thorough and systematic collection of all data relative to the topics studied, we sought to go beyond mere descriptions of events and opinion to understand respondents' meanings in relation to the topics. We focused on understanding how each person was constructing her or his experience at Appalachian.

After all interviews were completed, the entire research team *by* consensus analyzed and tabulated responses to each question. We attempted to honor each interviewee's specific words as well as the research team's collective discernment of meaning. By consensus we developed categories from the responses themselves. Both the frequency of specific categories of responses and the emergence of general themes were considered in the analysis. The type of question, the content of the response, and the context of the response helped us determine which themes were most important.

RESULTS

In the process of analyzing the data, we found that faculty responses to the different questions clustered into several categories. The research team reviewed each category of response for each question and by consensus grouped the categories into themes. In reporting the findings of this study, we wish to highlight the five themes that emerged and to explore the relationship of the themes with each other. A copy of the detailed results analyzed question by question is available from the authors. (see http://www.hubbard.appstate.edu/od/qols.html)

Theme #1: The Centrality of Relationships
The most important factor in faculty quality of life is the quality of interpersonal relationships. For faculty, relationships with students are a high priority, a source of deep satisfaction, and a crucial aspect of creating an environment for learning. The images faculty use to describe their work, their sources of satisfaction, and their best experiences involve collegial relationships with students. However, many faculty feel increasingly less able to allocate time for such relationships. One subject stated, "We need to make sure that people with power understand that the essence of teaching is in relationships, and relationships take time." Relationships with colleagues are another important element of faculty life, one that can be deeply rewarding or profoundly hurtful. One subject echoed the sentiment of many when referring to positive relationships with colleagues: "The greatest satisfaction in my work environment has been the people I've worked with over the years." Another said, "I cherish their contribution to my growth." We also heard stories about negative collegial relationships: "I'd like a less rancid, hostile, negative, mean atmosphere in my department." Many faculty say the next step in their personal growth is to improve relationships, and many believe the university

needs to strive to create an environment of community, with more mutual respect, civility, and dialogue among faculty, staff, students, and administrators. As one faculty member said,

> *"If scientists only talk to scientists, then the scientific method is the only way to get anything done. If historians only talk to historians, then history is the only reality. Not knowing each other is destructive to the community as a whole. It allows us to build up images of each other based on half-truths. We need each other desperately."*

Relationships with family and friends also play an important role in faculty quality of life. Family responsibilities and personal relationships are regarded both positively—as supporting and enhancing professional work. For example, one subject said, "I have a very supportive husband. He appreciates what I do and goes out of his way to help me pursue professional opportunities important to me." The flip side, however, is that the demands of personal responsibilities can increase the amount of stress faculty feel in their professional work. One interviewee said,

> *"My parents are both in their 70s. They have enough money, but are unable to keep their affairs in order. Dad [is disabled] and Mom is recovering from cancer. It is a strain to be here and have them live in [another state]."*

Theme #2: Commitment to Student Learning

Most faculty members are deeply committed to providing meaningful and life-changing learning experiences for students. They often see their work as a calling, requiring strong commitment and sense of purpose. One subject stated, "I put students ahead of other things. This is a service profession. It is a privilege." Faculty members believe their primary mission is to foster student learning and to help students become lifelong learners and good citizens with appropriate values and interpersonal skills. As one interviewee said, "I want to impart to my students an excitement for learning and an excitement about their field. I want to give them marketable skills. I want them to have strong problem solving skills and a sense of ethics." Further, Appalachian faculty envision education as a process that is much deeper and more transforming than job training. One subject stated, "I'm concerned about students being prepared to write and speak, not just for a good job, but for a good life." Another said, "One place where colleges have gotten in trouble is seeing themselves as training schools. College should be about opening minds and eyes." Faculty believe that maintaining and improving the quality of the educational experience offered to students should be a high priority for future changes in the university. One subject observed, "Educating for the next century is the most important thing."

With the goal of enhancing the quality of educational opportunities for students, many faculty believe we need to limit enrollment and to increase resources for departments and the library. One subject expressed concern for shrinking resources: "I'm troubled when I hear people talk about delivering instruction more efficiently in larger classes. I don't deliver instruction." Faculty desire changes that will enable them to spend more time with students, such as reduced number of classes, reduced class sizes, less paperwork, and fewer committee assignments. As one faculty eloquently stated, "I'd like to teach less so I can teach better."

Appalachian faculty are also troubled by the pressures for accountability, not because they are afraid to be found out as poor teachers, but because they fear that inappropriate measures may be used. For example, one said, "Education is valuable, and the most valuable aspects are difficult to measure. Our product is not like soybeans." Another expressed a concomitant concern: "So much of what we do doesn't count on paper."

Theme #3: Satisfaction with Academic Life
Regarding general satisfaction with academic life, our findings correlate with a recent study (Sanderson, Phua, & Herda, 2000) showing that 90% of American faculty find deep satisfaction in "the academic life." Most enjoy learning in their field and delight in sharing that joy of learning with others. One interviewee articulated the sentiment of many: "I feel fortunate to be in a profession in which I really like what I'm doing." Professional satisfaction in academic life is also related to a number of other factors, such as professional autonomy, self-direction, and opportunities for further professional growth and learning. One subject said, "The university is a central part of my life. I have always felt supported, recognized, and free to go in the directions important to me." Many find deep satisfaction in making an important contribution to the lives of students, the discipline, and society. As one interviewee said, "My status in the field is less important to me than my influence on students."

Theme #4: Personal Sacrifice
The large majority of faculty members believe the professorial workload is difficult—if not impossible—without making very costly personal sacrifices. As noted previously (Sanderson, Phua, & Herda, 2000; Karpiak,

1997; Sorcinelli, 1992) most find it very difficult to balance their professional workload of teaching, scholarship, and service effectively, and they find it almost impossible to balance their personal and professional lives. One faculty member said, "My personal life gets put on hold so that I can balance the professional. It gets put on hold a lot." Another observed, "Last weekend I had one and one-half hours—that was my personal life last week." In deciding which area to sacrifice, most choose to devote more time to the profession and their students at the expense of family and personal life. One interviewee lamented, "I wish I had more time for family." Another subject recounted, "My wife and I are separated; my workaholism probably caused the separation. It is difficult to balance. I am trying hard to make my family my first priority, but my workload interferes."

Others say that their lives are somewhat balanced, but their descriptions suggest that they simply accept the assumption that their personal life must be sacrificed. One subject observed, "Work just eats up your life." Previous studies have noted the perceived demands of faculty life as contributing to the potential for faculty "burn out" (Bowen & Schuster, 1985; Freedman, 1986; Jacobson, 1984; Schuster & Bowen, 1985; Karpiak, 1997; Altbach & Lewis, 1995). Of the few who feel that they are able to balance the demands of both their personal and professional lives, most do so by combining the two, such as by working side-by-side on projects with a spouse who is also a faculty member. Others mentioned socializing with colleagues. For example, one subject observed, "My work life overlaps with my personal life. Many of the same people I see socially I see on committees."

Theme #5: Incongruence between Rhetoric and Action

Some faculty question the integrity of institutional rhetoric and leadership, doubting the effectiveness and honesty of administrators, a phenomenon also noted by Altbach and Lewis (1995) in an international study of faculty attitudes. Some appear to mistrust administrators in general, with the intensity of distrust generally stronger at the dean and upper levels of administration. One example is that the stated mission of Appalachian places primary emphasis on teaching and learning. One faculty member stated, "The emphasis on teaching does not reduce the expectations of the traditional things. I get irritated with the mixed messages." Another said, "I think the administration needs to sit down and decide what the mission is and go after it. They can't have one department or college going one way and another going another. We need consistency and continuity." Many faculty see the mission as changing or unclear. For example, one subject said, "I don't know if I know what our university really does; we're not actually doing anything to help the area or the nation; the stuff from administrators is money and 'cover your ass,' not vision." Others believe the institution is hypocritical, with actual policies, procedures, and budget allocations reflecting a mission quite different from the stated mission. One subject captured a common sentiment: "People look at what is really rewarded, not what the administration says is rewarded." Another faculty member wished for a change in our collective perspective: "We should recapture a vision where administrators see themselves as serving faculty and staff, to enable faculty and staff to serve students."

Other faculty also worry about an increasing lack of substance, meaning, and integrity. One subject said, "We need less stress on procedure and more on substance. A common joke about Appalachian is that it seems to emphasize procedure over substance. It's a public relations approach now." Another stated the sentiment more positively: "We're trying to grow horizontally, more people, more buildings, etc. It's time to grow by deepening our definition of identity and purpose."

DISCUSSION

The stories of the 48 individuals interviewed in this project give us meaningful information about current faculty life and the climate of the university. The findings of the present study reaffirm those of other recent studies in noting the strong commitment of faculty to their work, the general satisfaction with academic life (Sanderson, Phua, & Herda, 2000; Sorcinelli, 1992), and the critical importance of relationships in faculty perceptions of quality of life (Gablenik, 1997; Karpiak, 1997; Palmer, 1997). Among these diverse faculty members, there is a strong sense of responsibility and a high level of professionalism despite their dissatisfactions, frustrations, and disappointments. There is also a yearning, individually and collectively, for real human community with colleagues and with students, and for learning that goes beyond the superficial—learning that is deepening and life-changing for themselves and their students. Faculty morale varies greatly from department to department; some departments are characterized by a sense of mutuality with colleagues and administrators. In contrast, other departments have a toxic environment that withholds support and undermines emotional and professional growth. As noted in previous studies (Massy & Wilger, 1995; Atkins &

Hageseth, 1991; Hagaseth & Atkins, 1988), the department chairperson plays a critical role in setting the cultural tone of the department.

Many critics of higher education argue that the professoriate is not committed to teaching. State legislatures, boards of trustees, and accrediting agencies now insist on accountability and assessment of outcomes in ways never experienced by higher education before. Within institutions themselves, many faculty feel attacked and see a loss of public esteem that in the past was one of the intangible rewards for academic life. However, examination of the five themes emerging from the data convinces us that the faculty interviewed in this study are unselfishly committed to influencing their students and the world in positive ways, with little thought of personal gain.

INTERRELATIONSHIPS AMONG THE FIVE THEMES: A SYSTEMS PERSPECTIVE

Peter Senge (1990) suggests that the problems facing organizations are in direct proportion to our ability—or inability—to see the organization as a whole. Senge's notion of systems thinking is a framework for seeing interrelationships rather than individual parts and can help us become aware of the subtle interconnections among apparently disparate pieces. Thus, systems thinking helps us to examine the five themes not as isolated pieces but as different strands of a larger whole. Previously, we articulated the themes separately, but we acknowledge that the separation is artificial. Each theme is intertwined with all the others, affecting each of them and in turn being affected by them. Figure 19.1 suggests a way to think about these interrelationships.

In our examination of the five major themes, it is clear that one, the centrality of relationships, is the matrix holding and shaping the faculty member's expression of the other themes. The quality of the relationships—whether positive or negative—with students, colleagues, administrators, and family appears to function as a lens which focuses the expression of the other themes and acts to reduce or exacerbate the tension between themes. Thus in our visual model, the circle of relationships encompasses and surrounds the circles representing the other themes.

While we recognize there are interactions and potential tensions among all of the themes, there is a dialectical tension between the theme of satisfaction with academic life and the theme of personal sacrifice, and between the theme of commitment to student learning and the theme of incongruity between rhetoric and action. For that reason, we have placed

FIGURE 19.1
The Interrelationship among the Five Themes

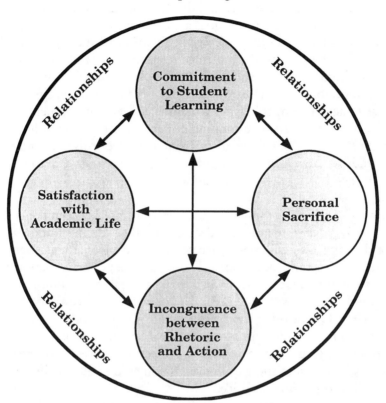

the circles representing those themes as polar opposites upon the background of the theme of the centrality of relationships. At first it would appear that the faculty members' reported satisfaction with academic life is diametrically opposed to the high level of personal sacrifice involved in accomplishing the myriad tasks of faculty work. However, if the quality of relationships between the faculty member and his/her colleagues and students is high and rewarding, the potential opposition of the intense demands of faculty life is ameliorated, and personal sacrifice becomes an accepted aspect of faculty life. Similarly, it seems contradictory that many faculty members perceive an incongruity between institutional rhetoric and action while simultaneously having a high level of commitment to student learning. However, if the quality of relationships between the faculty member and students is positive, the faculty member is more willing to accept and tolerate a perceived incongruity between rhetoric and action. Conversely, if the relationships between the faculty member and students are negative, the tension and dissatisfaction with perceived institutional incongruities are heightened.

Tensions between other pairings of themes and the interaction between those themes and the milieu of relationships, while more subtle, are as intricate and fluid as those discussed previously. For example, the degree of personal sacrifice involved in faculty life would, at first glance, appear to act to dampen a faculty member's deep commitment to student learning since such commitment may entail more time demands, and thus more personal sacrifice. Nonetheless, positive relationships with students can reinforce the faculty member's commitment to student learning and lessen the perceived emotional and personal cost of the personal sacrifices.

In a like manner, positive personal relationships between the faculty member and department chairs, deans, and other administrators can reduce the psychological importance of perceived incongruence between institutional rhetoric and actions. Those positive personal relationships will also tend to increase faculty members' general satisfaction with academic life and their willingness to accept personal sacrifice as a part of life in academe. On the other hand, unpleasant relationships or conflicts between faculty and administrators can heighten the importance of perceived incongruence between rhetoric and action and result in a negative feedback loop, diminishing both satisfaction with academic life and the palatability of personal sacrifice.

A high level of satisfaction with academic life—due in part or in whole to supportive and positive relationships with students, colleagues, and administrators—can increase a faculty member's commitment to student learning. Conversely, difficult relationships with students and colleagues can decrease general satisfaction with academic life and have a concomitant impact on commitment to student learning.

We must reemphasize that all five themes are interconnected and interrelated. The level of satisfaction with academic life is influenced and shaped by the quality of all interpersonal relationships within the sphere of the university community; and the satisfaction with academic life in turn helps to mold the level of commitment to student learning, the acceptability of personal sacrifice, and the perception of incongruence between institutional rhetoric and action. While we recognize that our proposed model is imperfect—as are all models—it has helped us to understand the results and to formulate recommendations.

RECOMMENDATIONS

Several possible directions emerge from this research. Based upon careful consideration of the data, we offer readers the following recommendations. We hope the recommendations will be useful starting points for open conversations at our own university and perhaps at others regarding strategic planning, policy development, programming, resource allocation, and structural change. We hope these recommendations will help faculty, staff, students, and administrators work together toward fulfilling the university's mission and the university's goal of becoming a true community of learners.

Recommendation #1: Recognize and Honor the Centrality of Human Relationships

- Support university, college, departmental, and unit efforts to become more effective working and learning communities involving faculty, staff, students, and administrators.

- Create opportunities for individual and collective learning focused on understanding leadership, group process, interpersonal dynamics, and self-reflection.

- Increase the skills of administrators, faculty, and faculty leaders in these arenas.

- Recognize the pivotal role of department chairpersons in the well being of the institution by providing support for chairperson professional growth and development.

- Provide increased assistance to chairpersons so that they have the time to fulfill their roles as faculty leaders.

- Support formal and informal activities that foster cross-disciplinary and cross-unit interaction.

- Encourage examination of problems and issues from multidimensional perspectives.

Recommendation #2: Support the Deep Commitments of Faculty to Foster Student Learning

- Provide faculty with the clerical support, equipment, time, classrooms, and office space to do their jobs well.

- Ensure that faculty reward systems recognize differing faculty contributions that promote student learning outside as well as inside the classroom.

- Redefine departmental values so they are consistent with the primary purpose and values of the university. Encourage academic departments to move toward a collective responsibility for teaching and learning.

Recommendation #3: Preserve the Traditional Satisfactions of Academic Life for Faculty

- Preserve academic freedom and faculty autonomy—the hallmarks of academic life.

- Provide faculty with strong support for their continued professional and personal growth. Create opportunities for growth within the university, particularly activities that encourage interdisciplinary learning.

- Support and encourage scholarship in all its many forms. Define scholarship broadly, and embrace disciplinary differences in how scholarship is practiced.

Recommendation #4: Encourage Flexibility of Faculty Work and a More Balanced Life

- Support faculty in maintaining quality work while keeping a well-balanced life. Encourage faculty to honor family priorities and spiritual needs, and to nurture physical and emotional well being.

- Respect and reward differing contributions made by individuals during the stages and seasons of academic professional life.

- Create ways to evaluate and reward the quality of work, rather than the quantity of work.

- Reward work that contributes to the good of the whole as a learning community.

- Reduce the increasing paperwork and the subtle pressures that support a culture of workaholism.

Recommendation #5: Uphold the Integrity of the Academic Mission of the University

- Encourage and support efforts for individual units and the university as a whole to be a learning community.

- Work toward a consensus regarding the university's mission, synthesizing the values of a liberal education, the values of applied professional programs, the stated institutional mission, the educational needs of today's students, and the deep commitment of faculty to student learning.

- Make all university decisions regarding resources, space, policies, procedures, and strategic planning consistent with the academic purposes of the university. Allocate resources based on the direct and indirect support of the academic mission.

- Clarify the mission of the university to students, faculty, staff, and administrators at every level of the university.

- Align the reward systems for faculty with the university mission.

- Streamline and make meaningful the annual report process. To encourage shared vision and shared responsibility, create a seamless process that holds individuals and units responsible for implementation of the principles of the mission statement and strategic plan.

- Create opportunities for individual and collective learning focused on understanding systems thinking.

- Open lines of communication across units and up and down the hierarchy.

REFERENCES

Altbach, P. G., & Lewis, L. S. (1995). Professional attitudes—an international survey. *Change, 27*(6), 51–58.

Appalachian State University. (1998). *The strategic plan.* Boone, NC: Appalachian State University.

Atkins, S. S., & Hageseth, J. A. (1991). The academic chairperson: Leading faculty is like herding cats. *Journal of Staff, Program, and Organizational Development, 9*(1), 29–35.

Austin, A. A., Brocato, J. J., & Rohrer, J. D. (1997). Institutional missions, multiple faculty roles: Implications for faculty development. In D. Dezure & M. Kaplan (Eds.), *To improve the academy*, *16*, 3-20. Stillwater, OK: New Forums.

Bernard, H. R. (1995). *Research methods in anthropology*. Walnut Creek, CA: Altamira.

Boice, R. (1991). New faculty as teachers. *Journal of Higher Education*, *62* (2), 150-173.

Bowen, H. R., & Schuster, J. H. (1985). Outlook for the academic profession. *Academe*, *71* (5), 9-17.

Bowen, H. R., & Schuster, J. H. (1986). *American professors: A national resource imperiled*. New York, NY: Oxford.

Branch, V. (1995). Teaching is "job number one": New faculty at a comprehensive university. *Journal of Staff, Program, and Organizational Development*, *12*, 209-218.

Crawley, A. L. (1995). Faculty development programs at research universities: Implications for senior faculty renewal. In E. Neal (Ed.), *To improve the academy*, *14*, 65-90. Stillwater, OK: New Forums.

Ely, M. (1991). *Doing qualitative research: Circles within circles*. Bristol, PA: Falmer.

Freedman, J. (1986). The professor's life, though rarely clear to outsiders, has its rewards and costs. *Chronicle of Higher Education*, *31* (23): 92.

Gablenik, F. (1997 Jan/Feb). Educating a committed citizenry. *Change*, *29* (1), 30-35.

Jacobson, R. L. (1984). AAUP's leaders assays decline in faculty morale, governance. *Chronicle of Higher Education*, *27* (18), 15-17.

Hageseth, J. A., & Atkins, S. S. (1988). Assessing faculty quality of life. In J. G. Kurfiss (Ed.), *To improve the academy*, *7*, 109-120. Stillwater, OK: New Forums.

Hageseth, J. A., & Atkins, S. S. (1989). Building university community: Where's the staff? *Journal of Staff, Program, and Organizational Development*, *7* (4), 173-180.

Hubbard, G. T., & Atkins, S. S. (1995). The professor as a person: The role of faculty well-being in faculty development. *Innovative Higher Education*, *20*, 117-128.

Hubbard, G. T., Atkins, S. S., & Brinko, K. T. (1998). Holistic faculty development: Supporting personal, professional, and organizational well-being. In M. Kaplan & D. Lieberman (Eds.), *To improve the academy*, *17*, 35–49. Stillwater, OK: New Forums.

Karpiak, I. E. (1997). University professors at mid-life: Being a part of—but feeling apart. In D. Dezure & M. Kaplan (Eds.), *To improve the academy*, *16*, 21–40. Stillwater, OK: New Forums.

Kegan, R. (1994). *In over our heads: The mental demands of modern life*. Cambridge, MA: Harvard University Press.

Langdon, H. H. (in preparation). *Staff quality of life study*. Boone, NC: Appalachian State University.

Magner, D. K. (1999, September 3). The graying professorate. *The Chronicle of Higher Education*, A18–19.

Massy, W. F., & Wilger, A. K. (1995). Improving productivity. *Change*, *27* (4), 10–21.

Palmer, P. J. (1992). Divided no more: A movement approach to educational reform. *Change*, *24* (2), 12–17.

Palmer, P. J. (1997). The renewal of community in higher education. In W. E. Campbell & K. A. Smith (Eds.), *New paradigms for college teaching* (pp. 1–18). Edina, MN: Interaction Book Co.

Palmer, P. J. (1998). *The courage to teach: Exploring the inner landscape of a teacher's life*. San Francisco, CA: Jossey-Bass.

Perry, W. G. (1970, 1999). *Forms of intellectual and ethical development in the college years: A scheme*. New York, NY: Holt, Rinehart & Winston.

Rice, R. E., & Austin, A. (1988). High faculty morale: What exemplary colleges do right. *Change*, *20* (2), 50–58.

Sanderson, A., Phua, V. C., & Herda, D. (2000). *The American faculty poll*. Chicago, IL: National Opinion Research Center.

Sanford, N. (1980). *Learning after college*. Orinda, CA: Montaigne.

Schuster, J. H., & Bowen, H.R. (1985). The faculty at risk. *Change*, *17* (4), 13–21.

Senge, P. M. (1990). *The fifth discipline: The art and practice of the learning organization*. New York, NY: Doubleday.

Sorcinelli, M. D. (1992). New and junior faculty stress: Research and responses. In M. D. Sorcinelli & A. E. Austin (Eds.), *Developing new and junior faculty* (pp. 27–37). San Francisco, CA: Jossey-Bass.

Smith, P. (1990). *Killing the spirit: Higher education in America.* New York, NY: Viking.

van der Bogert, V., Brinko, K. T., Atkins, S. S., & Arnold, E. L. (1990). Transformational faculty development: Integrating the feminine and the masculine. In L. Hilsen. (Ed.), *To improve the academy, 9,* 89–98. Stillwater, OK: New Forums.

Wheatley, M. J. (1992). *Leadership and the new science.* San Francisco, CA: Berrett-Koehler.

Contacts:

Sally S. Atkins
Professor, Human Development & Psychological Counseling
Faculty/staff psychologist, The Hubbard Center
Appalachian State University
Boone, NC 286808
Email: Atkinsss@appstate.edu

Kate T. Brinko
Director, Faculty and Academic Development
Hubbard Center for Faculty and Staff Support
Appalachian State University
P.O. Box 32074
Boone, NC 28608-2074
(828) 262-6152
(828) 262-6159 (Fax)
Email: Brinkokt@appstate.edu

Jeffrey Butts
Director, Hubbard Center for Faculty and Staff Support
Appalachian State University
P.O. Box 32074
Boone, NC 28608-2074
Email: Buttsja@appstate.edu

Chuck Claxton
Professor Higher Education
Appalachian State University
Boone, NC 28608
(828) 262-2875
(828) 262-6035 (Fax)
Email: Claxtoncs@appstate.edu

Sally Atkins coordinates the organizational development efforts of the Hubbard Center for Faculty and Staff Support at Appalachian. Recently this effort has included research on quality of life issues, chairperson development, administrative internships, and other initiatives for organizational change. She is a full-time faculty member, teaching courses in expressive arts therapy.

Kate Brinko has been Director of Faculty and Academic Development at Appalachian State University since 1988. As her career matures, she finds her interests moving from traditional faculty development efforts—working with individuals in a one contact, short-term, content-based activity—to working with groups in deeper, long-term, self-awareness and community-building efforts. Participating in this interdisciplinary research team researching faculty quality of life over a two-year period of time was one of her most professionally rewarding activities.

Jeffrey A. Butts has been Director of the Hubbard Center for Faculty and Staff Support at Appalachian State University since 1995. Previously he served as chairperson of the Department of Biology where he continues to teach general zoology, comparative anatomy, and vertebrate evolution.

Chuck Claxton is Professor in the Higher Education Program at Appalachian State University. He served on the faculty of the Summer Institute for the Management of Lifelong Education at Harvard University from 1986–1995. His major research interests are institutional change, adult development, and the learning organization. He and his family live in the small mountain town of Blowing Rock, NC.

Glenda Hubbard has been Director of Counseling for Faculty and Staff for four years, after serving as part-time counselor in the office while serving as a program coordinator and professor in counselor education for 25 years. After participating in the ASU Quality of Life research project, she is committed to the development of programs that improve the quality of life for faculty, staff, and students on the campus.

APPENDIX 19.1
APPALACHIAN STATE UNIVERSITY
1997 FACULTY QUALITY OF LIFE STUDY

Purpose
By request of the provost, the Hubbard Center is conducting a follow-up study to the one done ten years ago. Its purpose is to ascertain the views of faculty about the organizational climate of Appalachian and the quality of faculty life as they see it. These findings will become the basis for recommendations to the Division of Academic Affairs.

Confidentiality and Hand Recording
1) The identity of all interviewees will be held in strict confidence. Information will be recorded by us and analyzed by the team of five interviewers. We have 20 questions, which take approximately one and one-half hours.

2) Are you willing to participate?   Yes   No

3) Do you have any questions before we begin?   Yes   No

Demographic Data
1) Department

2) Rank

3) Years at rank

4) Years at Appalachian

5) Gender

6) Age

7) Marital/Relationship Status

8) Do you have responsibility for the care or support of children? Please explain.

9) Do you have responsibility for the care or support of parents? Please explain.

NB: An asterisk denotes that this question appeared on the previous faculty quality of life survey. Italics denote that this question is drawn from Senge's five disciplines.

Quality of Life

*1) On a scale of 1–10 (1 being the most negative, 10 being the most positive) rate your overall quality of life. Please comment on your rating. How does this compare with your quality of life ten years ago? (If person was here ten years ago.)

*2) a. What are the major factors that contribute to your satisfaction in your life?

   b. What are the major factors that contribute to your dissatisfaction in your life?

*3) On a day-to-day basis, what in your work setting has the greatest impact on your morale?

4) a. How do you balance your professional responsibilities of teaching, research, and service?

   b. How do you balance your professional and personal life?

*5) a. Describe your best experience working at Appalachian.

   b. Describe your worst experience working at Appalachian.

6) How do you balance your individual/professional needs on the one hand, with your sense of collective responsibility, on the other hand?

*7) a. In your own development as a professional and as person, what is the next step in your professional growth?

   b. What is the next step in your personal growth? (i.e., your growing edge; or What are the questions you are working on?) (personal mastery)

*8) Give a word or phrase that comes to mind when you hear each of the following words:

Health	Spirituality	Parents
Aging	Retirement	Children
Leisure		

Organizational Culture

*9) Give us a word or phrase that comes to mind when you hear each of the following words:

Appalachian	Committees	Dean
Teaching	Department	Administration
Scholarship	College	Students
Service	Chairperson	Colleagues

10) a. On a scale of 1–10 (10 being most positive and being most negative), rank the climate of your department as to how well it supports the professional and personal growth of all of its members. Please comment on your rating. (learning organization)

b. Rank the climate of your college (school or administrative unit). Please comment on your rating. (learning organization)

c. Rank the climate of Appalachian. Please comment on your rating. (learning organization)

11) a. Think about the two or three persons in your department who are most respected. What qualities do they embody?

b. Think about the persons in your department who are least respected. What qualities do they embody?

12) a. Where in your work at Appalachian do you experience being part of a team effort?

b. What is this experience like for you? (team building)

Mission/Vision

13) At a very basic level, what is it you are trying to do in your work at Appalachian? (vision)

14) What in your view is the mission of Appalachian? (vision)

*15) How well does the mission of Appalachian fit with what you are trying to do? (vision)

16) What should we be trying to create at Appalachian in the future? (vision)

17) What particular changes would you like to see at Appalachian in the next ten years? (vision)

18) a. What do you think are the major issues facing Appalachian today?

b. What do you think Appalachian should do to address these issues?

19) If you could change one thing that would have the most impact on your overall quality of life at Appalachian, what would that be?

20) In summary,

a. Would you share an image that describes Appalachian?

b. Would you share an image that describes your professional life here?

Other Comments:

20

Getting Administrative Support for Your Project

Joan Middendorf
Indiana University

For faculty development professionals to succeed with projects, we need the help of key administrators. More than anyone else, they can link our efforts to campus priorities, help us understand the decision-making system, and facilitate our efforts. This essay describes six steps for gaining and maintaining administrative support for projects. The steps entail 1) knowing administrator needs, 2) identifying likely supporters, 3) maintaining good working relationships, 4) involving the sponsors, 5) evaluating the sponsors' commitment, and 6) recognizing the support of sponsors. Collaboration with administrators and application of the stages is illustrated with a case study of Indiana University's Freshman Learning Project.

INTRODUCTION

For faculty development professionals to succeed with projects—whether in getting faculty to accept new teaching approaches or any other change—we need the help of key administrators. More than anyone else, they can link our efforts to campus priorities and help us understand the decision-making system. Through their knowledge, influence, and resources, they can provide support for our project. But, how do we get administrators to provide this kind of support? We need to clarify for ourselves what we need from them and identify which of them can best give what our project needs. Then, we focus—with understanding, respect, and recognition—on their concerns, needs, and goals.

While we usually can clarify what we need and who we should involve, we often fail to truly understand the viewpoints of those we ask for help. Loaded down with project meetings, seminars, materials development, and other details, we often ask for administrative support without recognizing the administrators' perspectives, responding to their concerns, or providing recognition for their contributions. Only by getting in the other person's shoes—even when he or she is an administrator—can we move toward a truly collaborative and successful project. Several administrators give their advice on how to make a program successful.

ADMINISTRATORS ON GETTING SUPPORT

At the 1999 POD Conference session, "Getting Administrative Support for Your Project," three POD leaders gave their advice for getting administrative support.

- Steve Richardson, Vice President for Academic Affairs, Winona State University:

  "If you make the administrators look good, they will give you additional support." "You have to make your program have visibility and credibility."

- Joan North, Dean, College of Professional Studies, University of Wisconsin-Stevens Point:

  "The closer in rank you are to the person you want support from, the more likely you will get the support you need."

- Mary Deane Sorcinelli, Associate Provost for Faculty Development, University of Massachusetts at Amherst:

  "Your programs should be viewed by faculty as enrichment rather than remedial. Listen to the faculty and administrators, be responsive, and make connections."

Moreover, by aligning our work with the higher-level perspective of administrators, our efforts can become more strategic. If we assume that we know the goals of administrators or that we know what is best for the faculty, our efforts may be off target. We may not spell out our expectations, or we may fail to fit them in with the university planning process.

This essay is the third in a series that draws useful principles from the literature on planned change to enhance the work of faculty developers. For a thorough understanding of the literature on planned change, see Rogers (1995), Havelock (1995), and Dormant (1999). Also, Guskin (1994, 1996) discusses the kinds of changes universities face and the restructuring that will be necessitated. The first essay in this three-part series explains the stages faculty move through in accepting a change, and the strategies we can use to enhance adoption (Middendorf, 1998). The second essay explains the different rates at which faculty accept change and then identifies the faculty most likely to lead their colleagues to accepting new approaches (Middendorf, 1999). This, the third essay, begins with a case study of Indiana University's Freshman Learning Project, and describes six steps for enhancing collaboration between faculty developers and administrators. It is followed by a worksheet for planning ways to get administrative support for your project. This can be used by a planning team before potential sponsors are contacted to increase chances for success.

A Case Study—The Freshman Learning Project

The Indiana University Freshman Learning Project (FLP) supports faculty to find new ways to help students learn more in large introductory courses. The program rests on the assumption that the process of rethinking approaches to teaching is best done within a community of teachers and is best disseminated within that same community. Each year FLP develops a cohort of faculty leaders committed to student learning. The program began with a three-year grant of $379,233 from the president of Indiana University. The grant was awarded as the result of a competitive proposal process. It includes a $5,000 stipend for each faculty participant, as well as an annual course release for the faculty member who co-directs the project.

Annual activities commence with interviews to determine the basic skills and knowledge the faculty teach. This is followed by team building and an informal assessment of roadblocks to learning. In a two-week summer session, faculty study the literature on successful developments in teaching and learning, and they design innovative lessons which they present to the group. The FLP coordinates the activities of these fellows in subsequent years as they meet to discuss the implementation of new teaching strategies in their classes and bring new ideas about pedagogy to the attention of their colleagues.

The positive impact of the program has been manifested in specific innovations in the fellows' classrooms and in their efforts to influence both their colleagues and the institution. For example, one fellow has subsequently become the Associate Dean for Undergraduate Education in the College of Arts and Sciences, a second has become the first faculty member ever to sit on the campus Classroom Design Committee and has taken a more active role on the Bloomington faculty council, and a third played an important role in the College Committee for Undergraduate

Education. Another fellow has created an internet network of instructors in his field and is organizing a seminar for his department to discuss the ideas raised by the FLP. Three of the second-year fellows have already presented innovative model lessons to diverse faculty groups, such as the new faculty orientation. Additionally, Indiana University's president met with the fellows and, after hearing their praise for the transformative experience, provided significant additional funds.

The FLP model thrives because of three key aspects: 1) careful selection of participants, 2) exposure to the scholarship of teaching and learning, and 3) the creation of a tightly linked cohort of fellows who translate new ideas into practice. But to get to this success, the support of administrators was critical. Following are six steps for gaining and maintaining administrative support for a change project such as FLP.

Step 1: Know What the Administrators Need

For all the leaders involved in a project to pull toward the same goals, they must be clear about the concerns of administrators. In interviews, the author asked six university administrators what they looked for in a project they were likely to support. Three themes emerged: compatibility with priorities, buy-in, and widespread influence. Administrators wanted to know the answers to these questions.

Compatibility with institutional priorities

- How does this project fit in with the institutional mission?
- Is the project's goal compatible with the priorities of the institution?
- How much will it cost?

Buy-in from faculty and staff

- How will the faculty and staff be involved in planning?
- How will faculty and staff be involved in implementation?

Widespread impact

- Is this project worthwhile? How many people will it affect?
- Will the results be suitable for journal publication?
- Does it involve credible people whom others will follow?

Projects are more likely to be successful if they are aligned with campus priorities, have buy-in from those involved in implementation, and influence more than a few people. Each of these can be specifically planned for (see Appendix 20.1, Question 4).

Step 2: Identify Likely Supporters

An important step in a project's success is identifying administrators who will support it. The literature calls such a person a "sponsor: a person (or group) with the power and influence to legitimize your project and provide ongoing support" (Dormant, Middendorf, & Marker, 1997). In the university, the ideal sponsor should be high enough in the administration to have power and resources, but not so high up that he or she would not have time to devote to the project. Depending on the size of the organization, we can recruit several layers of sponsors: low-level administrators who will help implement the project, mid-level administrators who will set policy and approve funds, and high-level administrators who will provide symbolic leadership. (In small schools the symbolic and policy levels may be combined.) In general, the lower level administrators are more actively engaged with the project, involving their high profile superiors as needed for impact.

University administrators tend to be extremely busy people whose efforts can be diluted by the sheer number of initiatives and committees they are involved in. How can we get from them the time and effort our new project requires? If we recruit sponsors whose priorities are aligned with the project or if we develop projects that are aligned with sponsor needs, we are more likely to get strong support for our projects.

To find our sponsors, the co-director of the FLP, Professor David Pace (Department of History), and I considered whose needs this project could serve. The Associate Dean for Undergraduate Education of the College of Arts and Sciences was responsible for implementing a new curriculum that involved large enrollment, introductory courses. We aimed the program at the many faculty who would teach the new curriculum. The Director of Instructional Support Services was interested in improving teaching at IU in general. We needed the resources he could provide (staff and computers) as much as he needed our project. So the FLP was mutually beneficial to both of these active sponsors. In turn, these two administrators kept their bosses (a dean and a vice chancellor) informed of the project, calling on them for specific help as needed.

Step 3: Maintain Good Working Relationships

Once the sponsors get on board, we must establish and maintain effective working relationships with them and other administrators in the university hierarchy. In this area, John Kotter's (1985) work on managing bosses can be translated into relations with sponsors and key administrators. Kotter recommends taking the time and effort to nurture relations with superiors by doing the following:

- Learn the administrator's preferred work style.

- Try to understand the administrator's strengths and weaknesses.

- Keep in mind our own personalities, strengths, and weaknesses (especially any sensitivities to supervision).

- Be absolutely clear about mutual expectations.

- Maintain the relationship by being straightforward and keeping the administrator informed.

In managing a project, instructional support personnel will work closely with sponsors and will also interact more tangentially with other administrators who are not directly involved in the project. These may be department chairs of faculty or the supervisors of staff who will implement the project. Depending on how closely tied they are to the program, they need to either be kept well informed or treated as sponsors.

Being sensitive to administrators' work style smoothes the working relationship. For instance, do they prefer to be briefed about the project via memo or through a face-to-face meeting? Do they prefer formal or informal meetings? Do they regard conflict as something to be avoided or as a source for additional ideas? Do they tend to delegate or micromanage? One sponsor of the FLP perceived some unintended criticisms of his staff in a few email messages. His perceptions changed for the better when we discussed the project in person and I then occasionally lunched with him to ensure the message received was the one intended.

As instructional consultants, we face different pressures than administrators do. We can help each other succeed by knowing each others' strengths and weaknesses. For example, if sponsors are quick to criticize and slow to praise, consultants can know not to take negative comments personally. Or if a consultant acknowledges he needs more background, a sponsor can provide it.

Knowing ourselves, particularly our temperament regarding authority figures, can facilitate interactions. Some people habitually resent or are frustrated by those in authority, while others become dependent on authority or compliant with supervisors. Knowing our potential reactions to collaborators in a position of higher authority can help us avoid unthinking reactions. Knowing our weaknesses and strengths can help us avoid our personal pitfalls and play to our strengths.

Ambiguity in expectations for anyone involved in a project can create conflict. By taking the time to put the project goals and individual responsibilities in writing, we provide a chance to clarify and negotiate differences of opinion. This then provides a framework to be sure people complete tasks as agreed. A sponsor can sour on a project if project directors are not dependable about deadlines and other commitments.

Understanding sponsors' work styles, strengths, and weaknesses is essential; having clear expectations of them is not enough. It takes ongoing effort to maintain the relationship. On a few occasions, we made the mistake of assuming our sponsors knew more about what was going on than they did. Keeping them up-to-date on project activities required regular injections of information. We managed this with weekly or biweekly meetings. We tried to keep these meetings brief and to the point. Sponsors also like to be kept informed about any problems or difficulties that may arise.

Some people resent consideration of such issues and complain about campus politics. Politics can indeed be troublesome, but if we view it as a function of how people function in a social system, it is a necessary consideration. Sensitivity to our own and others' work styles fosters optimal cooperation on the project.

Step 4: Involve the Sponsor
The more effort the sponsors put into a project, the more committed they will be to seeing it through. Thus, the project can be strengthened when administrators play a visible role.

Some of the possible ways the sponsors can support a project follow:

- Make a presentation to a funding agency.

- Add their names to a funding proposal.

- Send letters with their signature inviting faculty to become involved.

- Send letters with their signature to department chairs of faculty who will be involved.

- Attend a kick-off meeting and make a brief speech.

- Author a bylined short newsletter article.

- Assign help (such as clerical or graduate assistants) that the project was unable to fund.

These are busy people, and their time is limited. One way to encourage their assistance is by helping them help us. We consider this homework an important part of collaborating with administrators. One sponsor provided letters inviting faculty to participate in the project. Another sponsor gave the brief opening speech setting out the challenge for the faculty in the two-week FLP seminar. We drafted the letter and outlined talking points the sponsors could adapt. While we could have sent the invitation under our own names and also given the kick-off speech, our sponsors had a much greater impact than we would have had. Also, sponsor involvement caused them to be more committed to the project. Since we had input regarding their messages, we were able to raise the probability that the right message was given at the right time. (See Middendorf, 1998, for how to send appropriate messages at the right time.)

Step 5: Evaluate Sponsors' Commitment

When we want to find out how sponsors view a particular change, we need to interview them. We can ask them what is good and what is weak about the project. We use the interview not to talk ourselves, but to listen and learn. (See Appendix 20.1 for a sponsor rating form.) Do the sponsors view the project as useful, understand it fully, empathize with those targeted for a change? Will the sponsors commit resources as well as their own power and influence?

What do we do once we have rated the sponsors? Sponsors can be treated as change projects themselves. (See Middendorf, 1998, for facilitating the acceptance of change.) Sometimes it is necessary to find another sponsor, change the project based on input from the sponsor, or distance yourself from the project if failure seems certain (see Figure 20.1).

Step 6: Recognize the Support of Sponsors

Because the FLP is an ongoing development project, we wanted to ensure the continued collaboration and support of our sponsors. We have found three ways to reinforce their support: creating a culture of documentation, attracting media attention, and thanking them publicly.

Our sponsors have asked us several times for documentation and we have learned to make it a habit as part of furthering the successful relationship. Possible kinds of data include:

FIGURE 20.1
Evaluate Sponsor Commitment

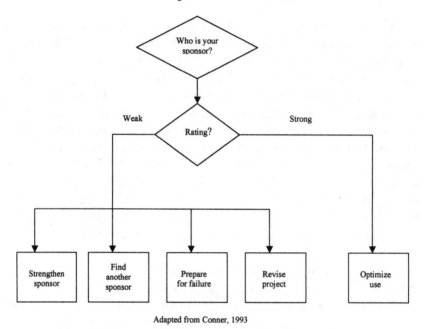

Adapted from Conner, 1993

- numbers of instructors successfully assisted
- numbers of projects completed
- continued use of services (repeat clients)
- numbers of undergraduates affected
- student retention rates
- student satisfaction with courses

We reported, for example, that over the first two years of FLP, 3,784 students were affected in classes the fellows were teaching. We provided sponsors with anecdotal evidence which they used in reports to their deans and the Board of Trustees. For example, one fellow said that the FLP experience "was the most intellectually stimulating two weeks of my 15-year career at Indiana University. I am very excited about introducing innovative teaching techniques to my classes. I learned that I can be a much better teacher than I am now."

To attract media attention, we solicited coverage of public FLP events by the local and campus newspapers and suggested that reporters interview sponsors. In a front page article of the local newspaper—"Faculty Seminar Produces Ideas Focused on Learning"—one sponsor was quoted, "This is part of a very big effort to think about learning on our campus." In the same article, a member of the Board of Trustees endorsed the FLP (Wright, 1998). Helping administrators get recognition in the media has proven beneficial to the project and reinforcing for the sponsors.

Finally, we thanked each sponsor at our end-of-year-celebration of our 1998 and 1999 seminars, by recognizing them and describing what each had contributed.

SUMMARY

Administrative support is crucial to the success of faculty development projects. The Freshman Learning Project was enhanced through strong sponsorship, which reinforced the importance of close administrator involvement. Our six-step model can help organizational and faculty developers manage administrative collaboration.

1) Know what the administrators need.

2) Identify likely supporters.

3) Maintain good working relationships.

4) Involve the sponsor.

5) Evaluate sponsors' commitment.

6) Recognize the support of sponsors.

By fostering collaboration with sponsors and other administrators, faculty development professionals can benefit from the knowledge, influence, and resources which link our efforts to campus priorities and decisions, thus improving the chances that our projects will be well-regarded and have greater chance for success.

REFERENCES

Conner, D. R. (1993). *Managing at the speed of change: How resilient managers succeed and prosper where others fail.* New York, NY: Villard.

Dormant, D. (1999). Implementing human performance technology in organizations. In H. Stolovitch & E. Keeps (Eds.), *Handbook of human performance technology* (pp. 237–259). San Francisco, CA: Jossey-Bass.

Dormant, D., Middendorf, J. K., and Marker, A. W. (1997). *Change mapping*[SM] *participant guide*. Bloomington, IN: Dormant and Associates.

Guskin, A. E. (1994). Restructuring the role of the faculty. *Change, 26* (5), 16–25.

Guskin, A. E. (1996). Facing the future. *Change, 28* (4), 27–37.

Havelock, R. G., & Zlotolow, S. (1995). *The change agent's guide* (2nd ed.). Englewood Cliffs, NJ: Educational Technology Publications.

Kotter, J. P. (1985). *Power and influence: Beyond formal authority*. New York, NY: The Free Press.

Middendorf, J. K. (1998) A case study in getting faculty to change. In M. Kaplan & D. Lieberman (Eds.), *To improve the academy, 17*, 203–224. Stillwater, OK: New Forums.

Middendorf, J. K. (2000). Finding key faculty to influence change. In M. Kaplan & D. Lieberman (Eds.), *To improve the academy, 18*, 83–93. Bolton, MA: Anker.

Rogers, E. M. (1995). *Diffusion of innovations* (4th ed.). New York, NY: The Free Press.

Wright, M. (1998, May 27). Faculty seminar produces ideas focused on learning. *Herald Times*, (A1, A7).

Contact:

Joan K. Middendorf
Director, Teaching Resources Center
Ballantine Hall, room 132
Indiana University
Bloomington, IN 47405-7701
(812) 855-2635
(812) 855-6410 (Fax)
Email: middendo@indiana.edu

Joan K. Middendorf has been Director of the Teaching Resources Center of the College of Arts and Sciences at Indiana University for over a decade. She collaborates with faculty, instructors, and administrators to diffuse pedagogical innovations. In addition, she co-directs the Freshman Learning Project. As the designer of The Change Mappings Workshop, she has presented on leading change at more than 20 corporations. She publishes about college teaching and change in higher education. She studies T'ai Chi for relaxation and as an exercise in learning.

APPENDIX 20.1
GETTING ADMINISTRATIVE SUPPORT FOR A PROJECT

1) **What is your project?** _____

2) **Who might be appropriate sponsors?** _____

3) **How strong are your sponsors?**

    a. Does the sponsor believe this change will be useful?

      Not at all 1 2 3 4 5 Strongly believes

    b. Does the sponsor understand the change?

      Not at all 1 2 3 4 5 Fully understands

    c. Does the sponsor empathize with those who will have to make the change?

      Not at all 1 2 3 4 5 Strongly empathizes

    d. Will the sponsor commit resources?

      Not at all 1 2 3 4 5 Fully commits

    e. Will the sponsor support the change with power and influence?

      Not at all 1 2 3 4 5 Strongly supports

If your total is **20** or above, you probably have a strong sponsor. If your total is below **15**, you may have a weak sponsor. If your total is **10** or below, and this is your major sponsor, you are likely to fail.

4) **How well does the project meet sponsor needs?**

    a. How compatible is the project with institutional priorities? How much will it cost?

    _____

    _____

    b. How will faculty and/or staff be involved with project planning?

    How will faculty and/or staff be involved with project implementation?

    _____

    _____

c. In what ways will the project have an impact?

_____

_____

5) What do you need the sponsors to do?

Some of the possible ways the sponsors can support a project follow:

- Make a presentation to a funding agency.

- Add their names to a funding proposal.

- Send letters with their signature inviting faculty to become involved.

- Send letters with their signature to department chairs of faculty who will be involved.

- Attend a kick-off meeting and make a brief speech.

- Author a bylined short newsletter article.

- Assign help (such as clerical or graduate assistants) that the project was unable to fund.

_____

_____

6) How can you help the sponsors meet the needs of the project?

_____

_____

7) How will you reinforce and recognize their support so they are likely to collaborate again?

_____

_____

8) What documentation of project results can you provide?

_____

_____

9) How will you gain media attention?

_____

_____

10) Where/when will you acknowledge their support?

_____

_____

Bibliography

AAC (Association of American Colleges). (1985). *Integrity in the college curriculum: A report to the academic community.* Washington, DC: Association of American Colleges.

ABET (Accreditation Board for Engineering and Technology). (1998). *Criteria 2000,* (3rd). Baltimore, MD: Accreditation Board for Engineering and Technology.

Adams, A., Bell, L., & Griffin, P. (Eds.). (1997). *Teaching for diversity and social justice: A sourcebook.* New York, NY: Routledge.

Åkerlind, G. S. (1999a, July). *Growing and developing as an academic: What does it mean?* Paper presented at the annual conference of the Higher Education Research and Development Society of Australia (HERDSA), Melbourne, Australia.

Åkerlind, G. S. (1999b, August). *Improving university teaching: How academics approach their growth and development.* Paper presented at the biennial conference of the European Association for Research in Learning and Instruction (EARLI), Gothenburg, Sweden.

Altbach, P. G., & Lewis, L. S. (1995). Professional attitudes—an international survey. *Change, 27* (6), 51–58.

Altman H., & Cashin, W. C. (1992, September). *Writing a syllabus.* Manhattan, KS: Kansas State University, Center for Faculty Evaluation and Development.

Angelo, T. A. (1997). The campus as learning community: Seven promising shifts and seven powerful levers. *AAHE Bulletin, 49* (9), 3–6.

Andrews, J. D.W. (1980). The verbal structure of teacher questions: Its impact on class discussion. *POD Quarterly, 2* (3&4), 129–163.

Angelo, T. A., & Cross, K. P. (1993). *Classroom assessment techniques: A handbook for college teachers* (2nd ed.). San Francisco, CA: Jossey-Bass.

Appalachian State University. (1998). *The strategic plan.* Boone, NC: Appalachian State University.

Apps, J. W. (1973). *Towards a working philosophy for adult education* (ERIC Document Reproduction Service No. ED 078 229).

Argyris, C., & Schon, D. A. (1974). *Theory and practice: Increasing professional effectiveness.* San Francisco, CA: Jossey-Bass.

Astin, H. S., & Davis, D. E. (1985). Research productivity across the life and career cycles: Facilitators and barriers for women. In M. F. Fox (Ed.), *Scholarly writing and publishing: Issues, problems, and solutions* (pp. 147–160). Boulder, CO: Westview.

Astin, A. W. (1993). *What matters in college? Four critical years revisited.* San Francisco, CA: Jossey-Bass.

Atkins, S. S., & Hageseth, J. A. (1991). The academic chairperson: Leading faculty is like herding cats. *Journal of Staff, Program, and Organizational Development, 9* (1), 29–35.

Austin, A. E. (1992). Supporting junior faculty through a teaching fellows program. In M. D. Sorcinelli & A. E. Austin (Eds.), *Developing new and junior faculty* (pp. 73–86). New Directions for Teaching and Learning, No. 50. San Francisco, CA: Jossey-Bass.

Austin, A. A., Brocato, J. J., & Rohrer, J. D. (1997). Institutional missions, multiple faculty roles: Implications for faculty development. In D. Dezure & M. Kaplan (Eds.), *To improve the academy, 16*, 3–20. Stillwater, OK: New Forums.

Ausubel, D. P. (1978). In defense of advanced organizers: A reply to the critics. *Review of Educational Research, 48*, 251–258.

Barber, B. (1992). *An aristocracy of everyone: The politics of education and the future of America.* New York, NY: Ballantine.

Barber, B., & Battistoni, R. (Eds.). (1993). *Education for democracy.* Dubuque, IA: Kendall/Hunt.

Barber, B., & Battistoni, R. (1993). A season of service: Introducing service-learning into the liberal arts curriculum. *PS: Political Science and Politics 26* (pp. 235–262). Dubuque, IA: Kendall/Hunt.

Barr, R. B. (1998, September-October). Obstacles to implementing the learning paradigm. *About Campus, 3* (4), 18–25.

Barr, R. B., & Tagg, J. (1995, November/December). From teaching to learning—A new paradigm for undergraduate education. *Change, 27* (6), 13–25.

Bass, R. (1998). Inventio. www.georgemason.com.

Battistoni, R., & Hudson, W. (Eds.). (1997). *Experiencing citizenship: Concepts and models for service-learning in political science.* Washington, DC: American Association for Higher Education.

Baxter Magolda, M. (1992). *Knowing and reasoning in college: Gender-related patterns in students' intellectual development.* San Francisco, CA: Jossey-Bass.

Bentley, R., & Blackburn, R. T. (1990). Changes in academic research performance over time: A study of institutional accumulative advantage. *Research in Higher Education, 31* (4), 327–353.

Belenky, M. F., Clinchy, B. M., Goldberger, N. R., & Tarule, J. M. (1986). *Women's ways of knowing: The development of self, voice, and mind.* New York, NY: Basic Books.

Bellas, M. L., & Toutkoushian, R. K. (1999). Faculty time allocations and research productivity: Gender, race, and family effects. *The Review of Higher Education, 22* (4), 367–390.

Bennett, J. (1983). *Managing the academic department.* Phoenix, AZ: Oryx.

Benz, C. R., & Blatt, S. J. (1994, April). *Faculty effectiveness as perceived by both students and faculty: A qualitative and quantitative study.* Paper presented at the annual meeting of the American Educational Research Association, New Orleans, LA.

Bernard, H. R. (1995). *Research methods in anthropology.* Walnut Creek, CA: Altamira.

Biggs, J. R. (1987). *Students' approaches to learning and studying.* Melbourne, Australia: ACER Press.

Biggs, J. (1999). What the student does: Teaching for enhanced learning. *Higher Education Research and Development, 18* (l), 55–76.

Billson, J., & Tiberius, R. (1991). Effective social arrangements for teaching and learning. In R. Menges & M. Svinicki (Eds.), *College teaching: From theory to practice.* (pp. 87–110). New Directions for Teaching and Learning, No. 45. San Francisco, CA: Jossey-Bass.

Birdsall, M. (1989). *Writing, designing, and using a course syllabus.* Boston, MA: Northeastern University, Office for Effective Teaching.

Black, B. (1998). Using the SGID method for a variety of purposes. In M. Kaplan & D. Lieberman (Eds.), *To improve the academy, 17,* 245–262. Bolton, MA: Anker.

Blackburn, R. T., Behymer, C. E., & Hall, D. E. (1978, April). Research note: Correlates of faculty publications. *Sociology of Education, 51,* 132–141.

Blackburn, R. T., & Lawrence, J. H. (1995). Faculty at work: Motivation, expectation, satisfaction. Baltimore, MD: Johns Hopkins University.

Bloom, B. S. (Ed.). (1956). *Taxonomy of educational objectives. The classification of educational goals. Handbook I: Cognitive domain.* New York, NY: David McKay.

Boice, R. (1987). Is released time an effective component of faculty development programs? *Research in Higher Education, 26* (3), 311–326.

Boice, R. (1989). Procrastination, busyness, and bingeing. *Behavior Research Therapy, 27* (6), 605–611.

Boice, R. (1991). New faculty as teachers. *Journal of Higher Education, 62* (2), 150–173.

Boice, R. (1991). *Quick starters: New faculty who succeed.* New Directions for Teaching and Learning, No. 48. San Francisco, CA: Jossey-Bass.

Boice, R. (1992). *The new faculty member: Supporting and fostering professional development.* San Francisco, CA: Jossey-Bass.

Boice, R. (1992). Strategies for enhancing scholarly productivity. In J. F. Moxley (Ed.), *Writing and publishing for academic authors* (pp. 15–32). New York, NY: University Press of America.

Boice, R. (1994). *How writers journey to comfort and fluency.* Westport, CT: Praeger.

Boice, R. (1996). *Procrastination and blocking: A novel, practical approach.* Westport, CT: Praeger.

Boix, V. (1997). Of kinds of disciplines and kinds of understanding. *Phi Delta Kappa, 78* (5), 381–386.

Bollin, G., & Hill, P. (1996). *Reflections on practice.* Board game developed for the Pennsylvania Society of Teaching Scholars (PASTS).

Bonilla, J. (1992). *Walking the walk: Towards creating more racially diverse institutions of higher education.* Unpublished doctoral dissertation, University of Massachusetts at Amherst.

Bonwell, C. C., & Eison, J.A. (1991). *Active learning: Creating excitement in the classroom.* ASHE-ERIC Higher Education Report 1. Washington, DC: George Washington University.

Booth, W. C., Colomb, G. G., & Williams, J. M. (1995). *The craft of research.* Chicago, IL: University of Chicago Press.

Border, L. L. (1993). The graduate teacher certification program: Description and assessment after two years. In K. Lewis (Ed.), *The TA experience: Preparing for multiple roles.* (pp. 113–121). Stillwater, OK: New Forums.

Border, L. B. & Chism, N.V.N. (1992). Teaching for diversity. New Directions for Teaching and Learning, No. 49. San Francisco, CA: Jossey-Bass.

Bormann, E.G. (1972). Fantasy and rhetorical vision: The rhetorical criticism of social reality. *Quarterly Journal of Speech, 58*, 396–407.

Bormann, E. G., Cragan, J. F., & Shields, D. C. (1994). In defense of symbolic convergence theory: A look at the theory and its criticisms after two decades. *Communication Theory, 4*, 259–294.

Bormann, E. G., Cragan, J. F., and Shields, D. C. (1996). An expansion of the rhetorical vision component of the symbolic convergence theory: The cold war paradigm case. *Communication Monographs, 63*, 1–28.

Bosworth, K., & Hamilton, S. J. (Eds.). (1994). *Collaborative learning: Underlying processes and effective techniques*. New Directions for Teaching and Learning, No. 59. San Francisco, CA: Jossey-Bass.

Bowen, H. R., & Schuster, J. H. (1985). Outlook for the academic profession. *Academe 71* (5), 9–17.

Bowen, H. R., & Schuster, J. H. (1986). *American professors: A national resource imperiled*. New York, NY: Oxford.

Boyer, E. (1987). *College: The undergraduate experience in America*. New York, NY: Harper & Row.

Boyer, E. (1990). *Scholarship reconsidered: Priorities of the professoriate*. Princeton, NJ: The Carnegie Foundation for the Advancement of Teaching.

Boyer Commission on Educating Undergraduates in the Research University. (1998). *Reinventing undergraduate education: A blueprint for America's research universities*. Lawrenceville, NJ: The Carnegie Foundation for the Advancement of Teaching.

Boyte, H, & Kari, N. (1996). *Building America: The democratic promise of public work*. Philadelphia, PA: Temple University Press.

Brady, L. (1991). *Political science course syllabi collection: International Relations*. Washington, DC: American Political Science Association.

Branch, V. (1995). Teaching is "job number one": New faculty at a comprehensive university. *Journal of Staff, Program, and Organizational Development, 12*, 209–218.

Brew, A., & Boud, D. (1996). Preparing for new academic roles. *The International Journal for Academic Development, 1* (2), 17–26.

Brookfield, S. D. (1988). *Developing critical thinkers*. San Francisco, CA: Jossey-Bass.

Brookfield, S. D. (1990). *The skillful teacher*. San Francisco, CA: Jossey-Bass.

Brookfield, S. D. (1995). *Becoming a critically reflective teacher.* San Francisco, CA: Jossey-Bass.

Brophy, J. (1987). Synthesis of research on strategies for motivating students to learn. *Educational Leadership, 45* (2), 41–48.

Brownlie, F., & Feniak, C. (1998). Student diversity: Addressing the needs.

Bruner, J. S. (1960). *The process of education.* Cambridge, MA: Harvard University Press.

Bush, A. J., Kennedy, J. J., & Cruickshank, D. R. (1977). An empirical investigation of teacher clarity. *Journal of Teacher Education, 28* (2), 53–58.

Butler, K. A. (1987). *Learning and teaching style: In theory and practice.* Columbia, CT: The Learner's Dimension.

Cambridge, B. L. (2000). The scholarship of teaching and learning: A national initiative. In M. Kaplan & D. Lieberman (Eds.), *To improve the academy, 18,* 55–68. Bolton, MA: Anker.

Candy, P. (1991). *Self-direction for lifelong learning.* San Francisco, CA: Jossey-Bass.

Candy, P. C. (1996). Promoting lifelong learning: Faculty developers and the university as a learning organization. *The International Journal for Faculty Development, 1* (1), 7–18.

Cashin, W. (August, 1979). *Motivating students.* IDEA paper no. 1. Manhattan, KS: Kansas State University, Center for Faculty Evaluation and Development.

CAUCUS. (1995). [Computer software]. Front View, Inc.

Chapman, V. L. (1998). Adult education and the body: Changing performances of teaching and learning. *Proceedings of the 39th Annual Adult Education Conference* (pp. 301–306). San Antonio, TX: University of the Incarnate Word.

Chism, N. V. N. (1998). The role of educational developers in institutional change: From basement office to front office. *To improve the academy, 17,* 141–154. Stillwater, OK: New Forums.

Claxton, C. S., & Murrell, P. H. (1987). *Learning styles: Implications for improving education practices.* ASHE-ERIC Higher Education Report No. 4. Washington, DC: Association for the Study of Higher Education.

Cook, C. E. & Sorcinelli, M. D. (1999). Building multiculturalism into teaching development programs. *AAHE Bulletin, 51* (7), 3–6.

Conner, D. R. (1993). *Managing at the speed of change: How resilient managers succeed and prosper where others fail.* New York, NY: Villard.

Cosser, M. (1998). Towards the design of a system of peer review of teaching for the advancement of the individual within the university. *Higher Education, 35,* 143–162.

Courtney, S. (1997). "The class started without me": Toward a new culture of learning and teaching. *Proceedings of the 17ʰ Lilly Conference on College Teaching* (pp. 63–66). Oxford, OH: Miami University.

Courtney, S., Jha, L., & Babchuk, W. (1995). 'Like school': A grounded theory of life in an ABE/GED classroom. *Adult Basic Education: An Interdisciplinary Journal, 4* (3), 172–195.

Courtney, S., Vasa, S., Luo, J., & Muggy, V. (1999). *Characteristics of adults as learners and implications for computer-based systems for information and instruction.* Minneapolis, MN: America's Learning Exchange, Minnesota Department of Economic Security.

Cox, M. D. (1995). The development of new and junior faculty. In W. A. Wright & Associates (Eds.), *Teaching improvement practices: Successful strategies for higher education* (pp. 283–310). Bolton, MA: Anker.

Cox, M. D. (1996). A department-based approach to developing teaching portfolios: Perspectives for faculty developers. *To improve the academy, 15,* 275–302. Stillwater, OK: New Forums.

Cox, M. D. (1997). Long-term patterns in a mentoring program for junior faculty: Recommendations for practice. *To improve the academy, 16,* 225–268. Stillwater, OK: New Forums.

Cox, M. D. (1999a). *Teaching communities, grants, resources, and events, 1999–00.* Oxford, OH: Miami University.

Cox, M. D. (1999b). Peer consultation and faculty learning communities. In C. Knapper & S. Piccinin (Eds.), *Using consultation to improve teaching* (pp. 39–49). New Directions for Teaching and Learning, No. 79. San Francisco, CA: Jossey-Bass.

Cox, M. D., & Blaisdell, M. (1995, October). *Teaching development for senior faculty: Searching for fresh solutions in a salty sea.* Paper presented at the 20th annual Conference of the Professional and Organizational Development Network in Higher Education, North Falmouth, MA.

Cox, M. D., Cottell, P. G., & Stevens, M. P. (1999, October). *Developing and coordinating faculty learning communities: Procedures and materials for practice.* Workshop presented at the 24th annual conference of the Professional and

Organizational Development Network in Higher Education, Lake Harmony, PA.

Cox, M. D., & Sorenson, D. L. (1999). Student collaboration in faculty development: Connecting directly to the learning revolution. *To improve the academy, 18*, 97–127. Stillwater, OK: New Forums.

Cragan, J. F., & Shields, D. C. (Eds.). (1981). *Applied communication theory and research*. Prospect Heights, IL: Waveland.

Cranton, P. (1992). *Working with adult learners*. Toronto, ON: Wall and Emerson.

Cranton, P. (1994). *Understanding and promoting transformative learning*. San Francisco, CA: Jossey-Bass.

Cranton, P. (1996). *Professional development as transformative learning*. San Francisco, CA: Jossey-Bass.

Crawley, A. L. (1995). Faculty development programs at research universities: Implications for senior faculty renewal. In E. Neal (Ed.), *To improve the academy, 14*, 65–90. Stillwater, OK: New Forums Press.

Creamer, E. G., & McGuire, S. P. (1998). Applying the cumulative advantage perspective to scholarly writers in higher education. *The Review of Higher Education, 22* (1), 73–82.

Cross, K. P. (1998, July–August). Why learning communities? Why now? *About Campus*, 4–11.

Cross, K. P., & Steadman, M. H. (1996). *Classroom research: Implementing the scholarship of teaching*. San Francisco: Jossey-Bass.

Cruickshank, D. R., & Kennedy, J. J. (1986). Teacher Clarity. *Teaching and Teacher Education, 2* (1), 43–67.

Cruickshank, D. R., Kennedy, J. J., Bush, A. J., & Meyers, B. (1979). Clear teaching: What is it? *British Journal of Teacher Education, 5* (1), 27–33.

Danzinger, S. H., Sandefur, G. D., & Weinberg D. H. (Eds.). (1994). *Confronting poverty: Prescriptions for change*. Cambridge, MA: Harvard University Press.

Davis, B. G. (1993). *Tools for teaching*. San Francisco, CA: Jossey-Bass.

Deming, W. E. (1982). *Quality, productivity, and competitive position*. Cambridge, MA: MIT Press.

Deming, W. E. (1986). *Out of the crisis* . Cambridge, MA: MIT Press.

Deming, W. E. (1993). *The new economics for business, government, and education*. Cambridge, MA: MIT Press.

Dewey, J. (1916). *Democracy and education.* New York, NY: Macmillan.

Dewey, J. (1938). *Experience and education.* New York, NY: Collier Books

Dewey, J. (1933). *How we think.* Lexington, MA: Heath.

Diamond, N., Sharp, G., & Ory, J. (1983). *Improving your lecturing.* Urbana, IL: Office of Instructional Resources, University of Illinois at Urbana-Champaign.

Diamond, R. M. (1988). Faculty development, instructional development, and organizational development: Options and choices. In E. C. Wadsworth (Ed.), *A handbook for new practitioners* (pp. 9–11). Stillwater, OK: New Forums Press.

Diamond, R. M. (1989). *Designing and improving courses and curricula in higher education: A systematic approach.* San Francisco, CA: Jossey-Bass.

Diamond, R. M. (1993). Changing priorities and the faculty reward system. In R. M. Diamond & B. E. Adam (Eds.), *Recognizing faculty work: Reward systems for the year 2000.* (pp. 5–12). New Directions for Higher Education, No. 81. San Francisco, CA: Jossey-Bass.

Diamond, R.M. (1998). *Designing and assessing courses and curricula: A practical guide.* San Francisco, CA: Jossey-Bass.

Donald, J. G. (1997). *Improving the environment for learning.* San Francisco, CA: Jossey-Bass.

Dormant, D. (1999). Implementing human performance technology in organizations. In H. Stolovitch & E. Keeps (Eds.), *Handbook of human performance technology.* (pp. 237–259). San Francisco, CA: Jossey-Bass.

Dormant, D., Middendorf, J. K., and Marker, A. W. (1997). *Change mapping[SM] participant guide.* Bloomington, IN: Dormant and Associates.

Downes, S. (1998). *The future of online learning.* Unpublished manuscript, Assiniboine Community College.

Duffy, D. K., & Jones, J. W. (1995). *Teaching within the rhythms of the semester.* San Francisco, CA: Jossey-Bass.

Eckel, P., Kezar, A., & Lieberman, D. (1999, November). Learning for organizing: Institutional reading groups as a strategy for change. *AAHE Bulletin, 52* (3), 6–8.

Edgerton, R., Hutchings, P., & Quinlan, K. (1991). *The teaching portfolio: Capturing the scholarship of teaching.* Washington, DC: American Association for Higher Education.

Ely, M. (1991). *Doing qualitative research: Circles within circles.* Bristol, PA: Falmer.

Entwistle, N., & Ramsden, P. (1983). *Understanding student learning.* London, England: Croom Helm.

Evans, W. E., & Guymon, R. E. (1978, March). *Clarity of explanation: A powerful indicator of teacher effectiveness.* Paper presented at the annual meeting of the American Educational Research Association, Toronto, Ontario, Canada.

Ewell, P. T. (1997). Organizing for learning: A new imperative. *AAHE Bulletin, 50* (4), 10–12.

Feldman, K. A. (1989). The association between student ratings of specific instructional dimensions and student achievement: Refining and extending the synthesis of data from multisection validity studies. *Research in Higher Education, 30* (6), 583–645.

Feldman, K. A. (1998). Identifying exemplary teachers and teaching: Evidence from student ratings. In K. Feldman & M. Paulsen (Eds.), *Teaching and learning in the college classroom* (2nd ed.). (pp. 391–414). Needham Heights, MA: Simon & Schuster.

Feldman, K. A., & Paulsen, M. B. (1998). (Eds.), *Teaching and learning in the college classroom.* (2nd ed.). Needham Heights, MA: Simon & Schuster.

Fox, D. (1983). Personal theories of teaching. *Studies in Higher Education, 8* (3), 151–163.

Freedman, J. (1986). The professor's life, though rarely clear to outsiders, has its reqards and costs. *Chronicle of Higher Education, 31* (23), 92.

Freire, P. (1973). *Education for critical consciousness.* New York, NY: Continuum.

Freire, P. (1985). *The politics of education: Culture, power, and liberation.* South Hadley, MA: Bergin & Garvey.

Fuhrman, B., & Grasha, T. (1983). *A practical handbook for college teachers.* Boston, MA: Little, Brown.

Fullan, M. (1993). *Change forces: Probing the depths of educational reform.* Bristol, PA: Falmer Press.

Fulton, C., & Licklider, B. L. (1998). Supporting faculty development in an era of change. *To improve the academy, 19,* 51–66. Stillwater, OK: New Forums.

Gabelnick, F., MacGregor, J., Matthews, R. S., & Smith, B. L. (1990). *Learning communities: Creating connections among students, faculty, and disciplines.* New Directions for Teaching and Learning, No. 41. San Francisco, CA: Jossey-Bass.

Gablenick, F. (1997 Jan/Feb). Educating a committed citizenry. *Change, 29* (1), 30–35.

Gaff, J. (1983). *General education today: A critical analysis of controversies, practices, and reforms.* San Francisco, CA: Jossey-Bass.

Gaff, J. G. (1991). *New life for the college curriculum: Assessing achievements and furthering progress in the reform of general education.* San Francisco, CA: Jossey-Bass.

Gaff, J. G., & Lambert, L. M. (1996, July/August). Socializing future faculty to the values of undergraduate education. *Change,* 38–45.

Gagne, R. M. (1974). *Essentials of learning for instruction.* Hinsdale, IL: Dryden.

Gardiner, L. F. (1992). *Designing a college curriculum: Overview, planning aids, and selected resources.* Professional Resource No. 4 (copyright by Gardiner).

Gardiner, L. (1994). *Redesigning higher education: Producing dramatic gains in student learning.* ASHE-ERIC Higher Education Report 7. Washington, DC: George Washington University.

Gardiner, L. F., Anderson, C., & Cambridge, B. L. (1997). *Learning through assessment: A resource guide for higher education.* Washington, DC: American Association for Higher Education.

Garrison, D. R. (1997). Self-directed learning: Toward a comprehensive model. *Adult Education Quarterly, 48* (1), 18–34.

Gianini, P., & Sarantos, S. T. (1995). Academic rhetoric versus business reality. In J. Roueche, K. Taber, & S. Roueche (Eds.), *The company we keep* (pp. 203–206). Washington DC: Community College Press.

Gibb, J. R. (1978). *Trust: A new view of personal and organizational development.* Los Angeles, CA: The Guild of Tutors Press.

Giroux, H. A. (1983). *Theory and resistance in education.* New York, NY: Bergin and Garvey.

Giroux, H. A. (1988). *Schooling and the struggle for public life.* Minneapolis, MN: University of Minnesota Press.

Gladding, S. T. (1995). *Group work: A counseling specialty* (2nd ed.). Englewood Cliffs, NJ: Prentice-Hall.

Glassick, C., Huber, M., & Maeroff, G. (1997). *Scholarship assessed: Evaluation of the professoriate.* San Francisco, CA: Jossey-Bass.

Glazer, J. S. (1993). *A teaching doctorate: The doctor of arts degree, then and now.* Washington, DC: American Association for Higher Education.

Gmelch, W. H., & Miskin, V. D. (1993). *Leadership skills for department chairs.* Bolton, MA: Anker.

Goldman, S.V. (1996). Mediating micro worlds: Collaboration on high school science activities. In T. Koschman (Ed.), *CSCL: Theory and practice of an emerging paradigm* (pp. 45–92). Hillsdale, NJ: Lawrence Erlbaum.

Goodlad, J. I. (1990). *Teachers for our nation's schools.* San Francisco, CA: Jossey-Bass.

Goodlad, J. I. (1994). *Educational renewal.* San Francisco, CA: Jossey-Bass.

Goodyear, G. E., & Allchin, D. (1998). Statements of teaching philosophy. In M. Kaplan & D. Lieberman (Eds.), *To improve the academy, 17,* 103–122, Stillwater, OK: New Forums Press and the Professional and Organizational Development Network in Higher Education.

Gray, T. (1999). Publish, don't perish: Twelve steps to help scholars flourish. *Journal of Staff, Program, and Organization Development, 16* (3), 135–142.

Greene, M. (1986). In search of a critical pedagogy. *Harvard Educational Review, 56* (4), 427–441.

Greene, M. (1988). *The dialectic of freedom.* New York, NY: Teachers College Press.

Gross Davis, B. (1993). *Tools for teaching.* San Francisco, CA: Jossey-Bass

Grunert, J. (1997). *The course syllabus: A learning-centered approach.* Bolton, MA: Anker.

Guskin, A. E. (1994). Restructuring the role of the faculty. *Change, 26* (5), 16–25.

Guskin, A. E. (1996). Facing the future. *Change, 28* (4), 27–37.

Habermas, J. (1971). *Knowledge and human interests.* Boston, MA: Beacon Press.

Habermas, J. (1984). *The theory of communicative action.* Boston, MA: Beacon Press.

Hageseth, J. A., & Atkins, S. S. (1988). Assessing faculty quality of life. In J. G. Kurfiss (Ed.), *To improve the academy, 7,* 109–120. Stillwater, OK: New Forums Press.

Hageseth, J. A., & Atkins, S. S. (1989). Building university community: Where's the staff? *Journal of Staff, Program, and Organizational Development, 7*(4) 173–180.

Harper, V. (1996). Establishing a community of conversation: Creating a context for self-reflection among teacher-scholars. *To improve the academy, 15,* 251–266. Stillwater, OK: New Forums.

Hativa, N. (1983). What makes mathematics lessons easy to follow, understand, and remember? *Two Year College Mathematics Journal, 14* (5), 398–406.

Hativa, N. (1984). Sources for learning mathematics in undergraduate university courses. *International Journal of Mathematics Education in Science and Technology, 15* (3), 375–380.

Hativa, N. (1985). A study of the organization and clarity of mathematics lessons. *International Journal of Mathematics Education in Science and Technology, 16* (1), 89–99.

Hativa, N. (1995). The department-wide approach to improving faculty instruction in higher education: A qualitative evaluation. *Research in Higher Education, 36* (4), 377–413.

Hativa, N. (1998). Lack of clarity in university teaching: A case study. *Higher Education, 36* (3), 353–381.

Hativa, N. (2000). *Teaching for effective learning in higher education.* Dordrecht, Holland: Kluwer Academic Publishers.

Hativa, N., Barak, R., & Simhi, E. (1998). *Expert university teachers: Thinking, knowledge, and practice regarding effective teaching behaviors.* Paper presented at the conference of the EARLI-SIG on Higher Education, Leiden, Holland.

Hativa, N., & Raviv, A. (1996). University instructors' ratings profiles: Stability over time and disciplinary differences. *Research in Higher Education, 37* (3), 341–365.

Havelock, R. G., & Zlotolow, S. (1995). *The change agent's guide* (2nd ed.). Englewood Cliffs, NJ: Educational Technology Publications.

Hecht, I. W. D. (1999, Fall). Transitions from faculty member to department chair. *The Department Chair: A Newsletter for Academic Administrators, 10* (2), p. 5.

Herron, J. (1996). Helping whole people learn. In D. Boud & N. Miller (Eds.), *Working with experience.* (75–94). London, England: Routledge.

Hill, W. F. (1977). *Learning through discussion.* Beverly Hills, CA: Sage Publications.

Hines, C. V. (1982). *A further investigation of teacher clarity: The observation of teacher clarity and the relationship between clarity and student achievement and satisfaction.* (Doctoral dissertation, The Ohio State University, Dissertation Abstracts International, 42, 3122A.)

Hines, C. V., Cruickshank, D., & Kennedy, J. J. (1985). Teacher clarity and its relationship to student achievement and satisfaction. *American Educational Research Journal, 22* (1), 87–99.

Houle, C. (1961). *The inquiring mind*. Madison, WI: University of Wisconsin Press.

Hubbard, G. T., & Atkins, S. S. (1995). The professor as a person: The role of faculty well-being in faculty development. *Innovative Higher Education, 20*, 117–128.

Hubbard, G. T., Atkins, S. S., & Brinko, K. T. (1998). Holistic faculty development: Supporting personal, professional, and organizational well-being. In M. Kaplan & D. Lieberman (Eds.), *To improve the academy, 17*, 35–49. Stillwater, OK: New Forums Press.

Hutchings, P. (1996). *Making teaching community property: A menu for peer collaboration and peer review*. Washington, DC: American Association for Higher Education.

Hutchings, P. (1999). *1999 Pew Scholars Institute*. Menlo Park, CA.

Hutchings, P., & Shulman, L. S. (1999). The scholarship of teaching: New elaborations, new developments. *Change, 31* (5), 11–15.

Jacobson, R.L. (1984). AAUP's leaders assays decline in faculty morale, governance. *Chronicle of Higher Education, 27* (18), 15–17.

Jackson, K. (Ed). (1994). *Redesigning curricula*. Providence, RI: Campus Compact.

Jaffee, D. (1998, November). *Pedagogical isomorphisms and resistance to change in higher education*. Paper presented at the 8th Annual Conference, Creating Alternative Learning Cultures, SUNY, New Paltz.

Jenrette, M. S., & Napoli, V. (1994). *The teaching-learning enterprise*. Bolton, MA: Anker.

Johnstone, D. B. (1993). Enhancing the productivity of learning. *AAHE Bulletin, 46* (4), 3–5.

Jones, R. (1981). *Experiment at Evergreen*. Cambridge, MA: Shenkman.

Kardia, D. (1998). Becoming a multicultural faculty developer: Reflections from the field. In M. Kaplan & D. Lieberman (Eds.), *To improve the academy, 17*, 15–34. Bolton, MA: Anker.

Karpiak, I. E. (1997). University professors at mid-life: Being a part of . . . but feeling apart. *To improve the academy, 16*, 21–40. Stillwater, OK: New Forums.

Katz, J., & Henry, M. (1993). *Turning professors into teachers: A new approach to faculty development and student learning*. Phoenix, AZ: Oryx.

Kegan, R. (1994). *In over our heads: The mental demands of modern life.* Cambridge, MA: Harvard University Press.

Keller, J. (1983). Motivational design of instruction. In C. M. Reigeluth (Ed.), *Instructional design theories and models* (pp. 383–433). Hillsdale, NJ: Lawrence Erlbaum.

Kelly, G. A. (1955). *The psychology of personal constructs. Vol 1. A theory of personality.* New York, NY: Norton.

Kennedy, J. J., Cruickshank, D. R., Bush, A. J., & Myers, B. (1978). Additional investigations into the nature of teacher clarity. *Journal of Educational Research, 72* (2), 3–10.

King, P. M., & Kitchener, K. S. (1994). *Developing reflective judgement.* San Francisco, CA: Jossey-Bass.

Kloss, R. J. (1994). A nudge is best: Helping students through the Perry Scheme of intellectual development. *College Teaching, 42* (4), 151–158.

Knapper, C. K. (1995). The origins of teaching portfolios. *Journal of Excellence in College Teaching, 6* (1), 45–56.

Knapper, C. K., McFarlane, B., & Scanlon, J. (1972). Student evaluation: An aspect of teaching effectiveness. *CAUT Bulletin, 21*(2), 26–34.

Kolb, D. (1984). *Experiential learning.* Englewood Cliffs, NJ: Prentice Hall.

Kolb, D. W. (1998). Learning styles and disciplinary differences. In K. Feldman & M. Paulsen (Eds.), *Teaching and learning in the college classroom* (2nd ed.). (pp. 127–138). Needham Heights, MA: Simon & Schuster.

Kolodner, J., & Guzdial, M. (1996). Effects *with* and *of* CSCL: Tracking learning in a new paradigm. In T. Koschman (Ed.), *CSCL: Theory and practice of an emerging paradigm* (pp. 307–320). Hillsdale, NJ: Lawrence Erlbaum.

Koshman, T. (1996). *CSCL: Theory and practice of an emerging paradigm.* Hillsdale, NJ: Lawrence Erlbaum.

Kotter, J. P. (1985). *Power and influence: Beyond formal authority.* New York, NY: The Free Press.

Kram, K. E. (1985). *Mentoring at work.* Glenview, IL: Scott, Foresman.

Kreber, C. (1999a). A course-based approach to the development of teaching-scholarship; A case study. *Teaching in Higher Education, 4* (3), 309–325.

Kreber, C. (1999b). *Defining and implementing the scholarship of teaching: The results of a Delphi study.* Paper presented at the annual meeting of the Canadian Society for the Study of Higher Education (CSSHE), Sherbrooke, Quebec.

Kreber, C. (Ed.). (in press). *Revisiting scholarship: Identifying and implementing the scholarship of teaching* (tentative title). New Directions for Teaching and Learning. San Francisco, CA: Jossey-Bass.

Kreber, C. (in press). Observations, reflections, and speculations: What we have learned about the scholarship of teaching and where it might lead. In C. Kreber (Ed.), *Revisiting scholarship: Identifying and implementing the scholarship of teaching* (tentative title). New Directions for Teaching and Learning. San Francisco, CA: Jossey-Bass.

Kreber, C., & Cranton, P. (1999). Fragmentation versus integration of faculty work. *To improve the academy, 18,* 217–231. Stillwater, OK: New Forums.

Kreber, C., & Cranton, P. A. (in press). Exploring the scholarship of teaching. *Journal of Higher Education, 71.*

Kreps, G. (1995). Using focus group discussion to promote organizational reflexivity: Two applied communication field studies. In L. R. Frey (Ed.), *Innovations in group facilitation: Applications in natural settings* (pp. 177–199). Cresskill, NJ: Hampton Press, Inc.

Krieger, S. (1985). Beyond "subjectivity": The use of the self in social science. *Qualitative Sociology, 9* (4), 309–324.

Kurfiss, J., & Boice, R. (1990). Current and desired faculty development practices among POD members. *To improve the academy, 9,* 73–82. Stillwater, OK: New Forums.

Lambert, L. M. (1993). Beyond TA orientations: Reconceptualizing the Ph.D. degree in terms of preparation for teaching. In K. G. Lewis (Ed.), *The TA experience: Preparing for multiple roles.* (pp. 107–112). Stillwater, OK: New Forums.

Langdon, H. H. (in preparation). *Staff quality of life study.* Boone, NC: Appalachian State University.

Laurillard, D. (1993). *Rethinking university teaching: A framework for the effective use of educational technology.* London, England: Routledge.

Lave, J., & Wenger, E. (1991). *Situated learning: Legitimate peripheral participation.* New York, NY: Cambridge University Press.

Lawson, K. H. (1991). Philosophical foundations. In P. Jarvis & J. M. Peters (Eds.), *Adult Education* (pp. 282–301). San Francisco, CA: Jossey-Bass.

Lefrancois, G. (1991). *Psychology for teaching.* Belmont, CA: Wadsworth.

List, K. (1997). A continuing conversation on teaching: An evaluation of a decade-long Lilly Teaching Fellows Program, 1986–1996. *To improve the academy, 16,* 201–224. Stillwater, OK: New Forums.

Lincoln, Y., & Guba, E. (1985). *Naturalistic inquiry.* Newbury Park, CA: Sage.

Lowman, J. (1995). *Mastering the techniques of teaching.* San Francisco, CA: Jossey-Bass.

Lucas, A. F. (1994). *Strengthening departmental leadership: A team-building guide for chairs in colleges and universities.* San Francisco, CA: Jossey-Bass.

Magner, D. K. (1999, September 3). The graying professorate. *The Chronicle of Higher Education,* A18–19.

Marsh, H. W., & Dunkin, M. J. (1997). Students' evaluations of university teaching: A multidimensional perspective. In R. P. Perry & J. C. Smart (Eds.), *Effective teaching in higher education: Research and practice* (pp. 241–313). New York, NY: Agathon.

Massy, W. F., & Wilger, A. K. (1995). Improving productivity. *Change, 27* (4), 10–21.

Matthews, R. (1996). Collaborative learning: Creating knowledge with students. In R. Menges & M. Weimer (Eds.), *Teaching on solid ground* (pp. 101–124). San Francisco, CA: Jossey-Bass.

McKeachie, W. J. (1999). *Teaching tips: Strategies, research, and theory for college and university teachers* (10th ed.). Boston, MA: Houghton Mifflin.

Meiklejohn, A. (1932). *The experimental college.* New York, NY: HarperCollins.

Menges, R., & Weimer, M. (Eds.). (1996). *Teaching on solid ground.* San Francisco, CA: Jossey-Bass.

Merriam, S. B. (1988). *Case study research in education: A qualitative approach.* San Francisco, CA: Jossey-Bass.

Meyers, C. (1988). *Teaching students to think critically.* San Francisco, CA: Jossey-Bass.

Mezirow, J. (1991). *Transformative dimensions of adult learning.* San Francisco, CA: Jossey-Bass.

Middendorf, J. K. (1998) A case study in getting faculty to change. In M. Kaplan & D. Lieberman (Eds.), *To improve the academy, 17,* 203–224. Stillwater, OK: New Forums Press.

Middendorf, J. K. (2000). Finding key faculty to influence change. In M. Kaplan & D. Lieberman (Eds.), *To improve the academy, 18,* 83–93. Bolton, MA: Anker.

Mies, M. (1983). Toward a methodology for feminist research. In G. Bowles & R. Klein (Eds.), *Theories of women's studies* (pp. 117–139). New York, NY: Routledge.

Millis, B. J. (1990). Helping faculty build learning communities through cooperative groups. *To improve the academy, 9,* 43–58. Stillwater, OK: New Forums.

Millis, B. J. & Cottell, P.G. (1998). *Cooperative learning for higher education faculty.* Phoenix, AZ: Oryx.

Morey, A., & Kitano, M. (Eds.). (1997). *Multicultural course transformation in higher education: A broader truth.* Boston, MA: Allyn & Bacon.

Morgan, D., & Spanish, L. (1984). Focus groups: A new tool for qualitative research. *Qualitative Sociology, 7,* 253–270.

Moxley, J. M. (1992). *Publish, don't perish: Scholar's guide to academic writing and publishing.* Westport, CT: Praeger.

Murray, H. G. (1983). Low-inference classroom teaching behaviors and student ratings of college teaching effectiveness. *Journal of Educational Psychology, 75* (1), 138–149.

Murray, H. G. (1985). Classroom teaching behaviors related to college teaching effectiveness. In J. G. Donald & Sullivan (Eds.), *Using teaching to improve* (pp. 21–34). New Directions for Teaching and Learning, No. 23. San Francisco, CA: Jossey-Bass.

Murray, H. G. (1997). Effective teaching behaviors in the college classroom. In R. P. Perry & J. C. Smart (Eds.), *Effective teaching in higher education: Research and practice* (pp. 171–203). New York, NY: Agathon.

NASULGC (National Association of State Universities and Land-Grant Colleges). (1997). *Returning to our roots: The student experience.* Washington, DC: National Association of State Universities and Land Grant Colleges.

National Center for Education Statistics. *Distance education at postsecondary institutions: 1997–98.* [online]. Available: http://nces.ed.gov/pubsearch/pubsinfo.asp?pubid=2000013.

Neumann, Y., & Finaly-Neumann, E. (1990). The support-stress paradigm and faculty research publication. *Journal of Higher Education, 61* (5), 565–578.

Nichols, J. O. (1995). *A practitioner's handbook for institutional effectiveness and student outcomes assessment implementation.* New York, NY: Agathon.

NIE (National Institute of Education). (1984). *Involvement in learning: Realizing the potential of American higher education.* Washington, DC: National Institute of Education.

Noddings, N. (1995). Teaching themes of care, *Phi Delta Kappan, 76* (9), 675–679.

O'Banion, T. (1997). A learning college for the 21st century. Phoenix, AZ: American Council on Education & the Oryx Press.

Orbe, M. P. (1998). *Constructing co-cultural theory: An explication of culture, power, and communication.* Thousand Oaks, CA: Sage.

Ouellett, M. L. & Sorcinelli, M. D. (1998). TA training: Strategies for responding to diversity in the classroom. In M. Marincovich, H. Prostko, & F. Stout (Eds.), *The professional development of graduate teaching assistants.* Bolton, MA: Anker.

Ozmon, H., & Graver, S. (1990). *Philosophical foundations of education* (4th ed.) Toronto, Canada: Merrill.

Palloff, R.M., & Pratt, K. (1999). *Building learning communities in cyberspace.* San Francisco, CA: Jossey-Bass.

Palmer, B. H. (1995). *Lesjes van de Nederlanders: Little lessons from the Dutch to promote educational quality.* Palo Alto, CA: American Institute of Research.

Palmer, P. J. (1992). Divided no more: A movement approach to educational reform. *Change, 24* (2), 12–17.

Palmer, P. J. (1997). The renewal of community in higher education. In W. E. Campbell & K. A. Smith (Eds.), *New paradigms for college teaching* (pp. 1–18). Edina, MN: Interaction Book Co.

Palmer, P. J. (1998). *The courage to teach: Exploring the inner landscape of a teacher's life.* San Francisco, CA: Jossey-Bass.

Pascarella, E. T., & Terenzini, P. T. (1991). *How college affects students : Findings and insights from twenty years of study.* San Francisco, CA: Jossey-Bass.

Patrick, S. K., & Fletcher, J. J. (1998). Faculty developers as change agents: Transforming colleges and universities into learning organizations. *To improve the academy, 17,* 155–170. Stillwater, OK: New Forums.

Paul. R. (1990). *Critical thinking.* Rohnert Park, CA: Center for Critical Thinking and Moral Critique.

Paulsen, M. B. (2000). The relation between research and the scholarship of teaching. In C. Kreber (Ed.), *Scholarship revisited: Defining and implementing the scholarship of teaching.* New Directions for Teaching and Learning, No. 82. San Francisco: Jossey-Bass.

Paulsen, M. B. & Feldman, K. A. (1995a). *Taking teaching seriously: Meeting the challenges of instructional improvement.* ASHE-ERIC Higher Education Report

No. 2. Washington, DC: The George Washington University, School of Education and Human Development.

Paulsen, M. B., & Feldman, K. A. (1995b). Toward a reconceptualization of scholarship: A human action system with functional imperatives. *Journal of Higher Education, 66*, 615–641.

Paulsen, M. B., & Gentry, J. A. (1995). Motivation, learning strategies, and academic performance: A study of the college finance classroom. *Financial Practice and Education, 5* (1), 78–89.

Perry, W. G. (1970). *Forms of intellectual and ethical development in the college years: A scheme.* Troy, MO: Holt, Rinehart, & Winston.

Perkins, D. N. (1992). Understanding performances. In D. N. Perkins (Ed.), *Smart schools: From training memories to educating minds* (pp. 75–79). New York, NY: Free Press.

Perkins, D. N. (1998). What is understanding? In M. S. Wiske (Ed.), *Teaching for understanding: A practical framework.* San Francisco, CA: Jossey-Bass.

Perry, W. J. (1970). *Forms of intellectual and ethical development in the college years.* New York, NY: Holt, Rinehart, and Winston.

Piaget. (1975). *The development of thought: Equilibration of cognitive structures.* New York, NY: Viking.

Pintrich, P. R. (1989). The dynamic interplay of student motivation and cognition in the college classroom. In M. Maehr and C. Ames (Eds.), *Advances in motivation and achievement: Goals and self-regulatory processes, 7.* (pp. 371–402). Greenwich, CT: JAI Press.

Pintrich, P. R., & Schunk, D. H. (1996). *Motivation in education.* Englewood Cliffs, NJ: Prentice Hall.

Plater, W. M. (1995). Future work: Faculty time in the 21st century. *Change, 27* (3), 23–33.

Porter, L. W., & McKibbin, L. E. (1988). *Management education and development: Drift or thrust into the 21ˢᵗ Century?* New York, NY: McGraw-Hill.

Poulsen, S. J. (1995). Describing an elephant: Specialists explore the meaning of learning productivity. *Wingspread Journal, 17* (2), 4–6.

Pratt, D., & Associates. (1998). *Five perspectives on teaching in adult and higher education.* Malabar, FL: Krieger.

Putnam, R. (1995, January). Bowling alone. *Journal of Democracy 6*, pp. 65–78.

Quinlan, K. M. (1999). Enhancing mentoring and networking of junior academic women: What, why, and how? *Journal of Higher Education Policy and Management, 21* (1), 31–42.

Rahn, W. (1998, May 8–9). *Generations and American national identity: A data essay.* Presentation at the Communication in the Future of Democracy Workshop. Washington, DC: Annenberg Center.

Ramsden, P. (1992). *Learning to teach in higher education.* London, England: Routledge.

Ramsden, P. (1998). *Learning to lead in higher education* (2 ed.). London, England: Routledge.

Ramsden, P., Margetson, D., Martin, E., & Clarke, S. (1995). *Recognizing and rewarding good teaching in Australian universities.* Canberra, Australia: Australian Government Publishing Service.

Rausch, E. E. (1984). *Balancing needs of people and organizations: The linking elements concept.* Cranford, NJ: Didactic Systems, Inc.

Resnick, L. (1987, December). Learning in school and out. *Educational Researcher, 16* (9), 13–20.

Rice, E. (1991). The new American scholar: Scholarship and the purposes of the university. *Metropolitan Universities, 1* (4), 7–18.

Rice, R. E. (1992). Toward a broader conception of scholarship: The American context. In T. G. Whiston, & R. L. Geiger (Eds.), *Research and higher education: The United States and the United Kingdom* (pp. 117–129). Buckingham, Great Britain: The Society for Research into Higher Education and Open University Press.

Rice, R. E., & Austin, A. (1988). High faculty morale: What exemplary colleges do right. *Change, 20* (2), 50–58.

Richlin, L. (Ed.). (1993). Preparing faculty for new conceptions of scholarship New Directions for Teaching and Learning, No. 54. San Francisco, CA: Jossey-Bass.

Richlin, L. (1995). A different view on developing teaching portfolios: Ensuring safety while honouring practice. *Journal of Excellence in College Teaching, 6* (1), 161–178.

Richlin, L. (in press). *Teaching excellence, scholarly teaching, and the scholarship of teaching.* New Directions for Teaching and Learning. San Francisco, CA: Jossey-Bass.

Rogers, E.M. (1995). *Diffusion of innovations* (4th ed.). New York, NY: The Free Press.

Rogers, Y. (1997). *A brief introduction to distributed cognition.* Available: http://www.cogs.susx.ac.uk/users/yvonne/dcog.html.

Rosenshine, B., & Furst, N. (1971). The use of direct observation to study teaching. In R. M. W. Travers (Ed.), *Second handbook of research on teaching* (pp. 122–217). Chicago, IL: Rand McNally.

Rossman, G., & Marshal, C. (1989). *Designing qualitative research.* Newbury Park, CA: Sage.

Roth, J. K. (Ed.). (1996). *Inspiring teaching: Carnegie professors of the year speak.* Bolton, MA: Anker.

Rothman, M. (Ed.). (1998). *Service matters.* Providence, RI: Campus Compact.

Rubin, S. (1985, August). Professors, students, and the syllabus. *Chronicle of Higher Education, 7,* p. 56.

Sanderson, A., Phua, V. C., & Herda, D. (2000). *The American faculty poll.* Chicago, IL: National Opinion Research Center.

Sanford, N. (1980). *Learning after college.* Orinda, CA: Montaigne.

Scardamalia, M., & Bereiter, C. (1996). Computer support for knowledge-building communities. In T. Koschman (Ed.), *CSCL: Theory and practice of an emerging paradigm* (pp. 249–268). Hillsdale, NJ: Lawrence Erlbaum.

Schoem, D., Frankel, L., Zuniga, X., & Lewis, E. (Eds.). (1995). *Multicultural teaching in the university.* Westport, CT: Praeger.

Schon, D. A. (1983). *The reflective practitioner: How professionals think in action.* New York, NY: Basic Books, Inc.

Schuster, J. H. (1993). Preparing the next generation of faculty: The graduate school's opportunity. In L. Richlin (Ed.), *Preparing faculty for the new conceptions of scholarship* (pp. 27–38). New Directions for Teaching and Learning, No. 54. San Francisco: Jossey-Bass.

Schuster, J. H., & Bowen, H.R. (1985). The faculty at risk. *Change, 17* (4), 13–21.

Schutte, J. (1997). *Virtual teaching in higher education: The new intellectual superhighway or just another traffic jam?* [online] Available http://csun.edu/sociology/virexp.htm

Scott, S. M., Chovanec, D. M., & Young, B. (1994). Philosophy-in-action in university teaching. *The Canadian Journal of Higher Education, XXIV* (3), 1–25.

Senge, P. M. (1990). *The fifth discipline.* New York, NY: Doubleday.

Sfard, A. (1998). On two metaphors for learning and the dangers of choosing just one. *Educational Researcher, 27* (2), 4–13.

Shapiro, N. S., & Levine, J. H. (1999, November–December). Introducing learning communities to your campus. *About Campus, 4* (5), 2–10.

Shore, B. M., Foster, S. F., Knapper, C. K, Nadeau, G. G., Neill, N., & Sim, V. (1980, 1986) *The teaching dossier: A guide to its preparation and use.* (Rev. ed.). Montreal, Canada: Canadian Association of University Teachers.

Showers, B. (1984). *Peer coaching: A strategy for facilitating transfer of training.* Eugene, OR: Center for Educational Policy and Management.

Shulman, L. S. (1987). Knowledge and teaching: Foundations of the new reform. *Harvard Educational Review, 57,* 1–22.

Shulman, L. S. (1998). Course anatomy: The dissection and analysis of knowledge through teaching. In P. Hutchings (Ed.), *The course portfolio.* Washington, DC: American Association for Higher Education.

Shulman, L. (1999). *1999 Pew Scholars Institute.* Menlo Park, CA.

Shulman, L., & Hutchings, P. (1997). *Fostering a scholarship of teaching and learning: The Carnegie Teaching Academy.* Menlo Park, CA: The Carnegie Foundation for the Advancement of Teaching.

Smith, K. S. (1995). Managing and mentoring graduate teaching assistants at the University of Georgia. In T. A. Heenan (Ed.), *Teaching graduate students to teach: Engaging the disciplines* (pp. 101–106). University of Illinois at Urbana-Champaign, Office of Conferences and Institutes.

Smith, K. S., & Klaper R. D. (1999). Graduate assistant involvement in transforming the undergraduate experience at research universities. *The Journal of Graduate Teaching Assistant Development, 6* (2), 95–102.

Smith, P. (1990). *Killing the spirit: Higher education in America.* New York, NY: Viking.

Smith, R. A. (1995). Creating a culture of teaching through the teaching portfolio. *Journal of Excellence in College Teaching, 6* (1), 75–100.

Smith, S. (1978). *The identification of teaching behaviors descriptive of the construct: Clarity of presentation.* (Doctoral dissertation, Dissertation Abstracts International, 39(06), 3529A.)

Snyder, M. (1995). *An investigation into the factors that encourage university faculty to use information technologies in their teaching.* Unpublished doctoral dissertation, University of Nebraska, Lincoln.

Sorcinelli, M. D. (1992). New and junior faculty stress: Research and responses. In M. D. Sorcinelli & A. E. Austin (Eds.), *Developing new and junior faculty* (pp. 27–37). New Directions for Teaching and Learning, No. 50. San Francisco: Jossey-Bass.

Stark, J. S. & Lattuca, L. R. (1997). *Shaping the college curriculum: Academic plans in action.* Needham Heights, MA: Allyn & Bacon.

Stark, J. S., Shaw, K. M., & Lowther, M. A. (1989). *Student goals for college and courses.* Report No. 6. Washington, DC: School of Education and Human Development, The George Washington University.

Sternberg, R. J. (1989). *The triarchic mind: A new theory of human intelligence.* New York, NY: Penguin.

Stevens, M. P., & Cox, M. D. (1999, October). *Faculty development and the inclusion of diversity in the classroom: A faculty learning community approach.* Paper presented at the 24th annual Conference of the Professional and Organizational Development Network in Higher Education, Lake Harmony, PA.

Stritter, F. T., Tresolini, C. P., & Reeb, K. G. (1994). The Delphi technique in curriculum development. *Teaching and Learning in Medicine, 6* (2), 136–141.

Sullivan, W. M. (2000). Institutional identity and social responsibility. In T. Ehrlich (Ed.), *Civic responsibility and higher education* (pp. 19–36). Phoenix, AZ: Oryx Press.

Svinicki, M. D., & Dixon, N. (1998). The Kolb model modified for classroom activities. In K. Feldman & M. Paulsen (Eds.), *Teaching and learning in the college classroom* (2nd ed.). (pp. 577–584). Needham Heights, MA: Simon & Schuster.

Tatum, B. D. (1997). *Why are all the Black kids sitting together in the cafeteria? And other conversations about race.* New York, NY: Basic Books.

Taylor, P. G. (1997). Creating environments which nurture development: Messages from research into academics' experiences. *The International Journal for Academic Development, 2* (2), 42–49.

Theall, M., & Centra, J. A. (in press). Assessing the scholarship of teaching: Valid decisions from valid evidence. In C. Kreber (Ed.), *Revisiting scholarship: Identifying and implementing the scholarship of teaching* (tentative title). New Directions for Teaching and Learning. San Francisco, CA: Jossey-Bass.

Thomas, T. (1992). Connected teaching: An exploration of the classroom enterprise. *Journal on Excellence in College Teaching, 3,* 101–119.

Tiberius, R. (1997). Small group methods for collecting information from students. In K. T. Brinko & R. J. Menges (Eds.), *Practically speaking: A sourcebook for instructional consultants in higher education* (pp. 53–63). Stillwater, OK: New Forums Press.

Tiffin, J. & Rajasingham, L (1995). *In search of the virtual class.* London, England: Routledge.

Tinto, V. (1995, March). Learning communities, collaborative learning, and the pedagogy of educational citizenship. *AAHE Bulletin, 47* (7), 11–13.

Tinto, V. (1997). Universities as learning organizations. *About Campus, 1* (6), 2–4.

Tisdell, E. (1993). Interlocking systems of power, privilege, and oppression in adult higher education. *Adult Education Quarterly, 43* (4), 203–226

Trow, M., & Clark, P. (1994). *Managerialism and the academic profession: Quality and control.* Higher Education Report No. 2. London, England: Open University, Quality Support Centre.

Tussman, J. (1969). *Experiment at Berkeley.* London: Oxford University Press.

University of Illinois (1999). *Teaching at an Internet distance: The pedagogy of online teaching and learning. The report of a 1998–1999 University of Illinois Faculty Seminar.*

University of Michigan Department of Biology. (1998). *Alumni Newsletter,* p. 5.

Vahala, M. E., & Winston, R. B. (1994). College classroom environments: Disciplinary and institutional-type differences and effects on academic achievement in introductory courses. *Innovative Higher Education, 19* (2), 99–122.

Valimaa, J. (1994). Faculty on assessment and peer review—Finnish experience. *Higher Education Management, 6* (3), 391–408

van der Bogert, V., Brinko, K. T., Atkins, S. S., & Arnold, E. L. (1990). Transformational faculty development: Integrating the feminine and tthe masculine. In L. Hilsen. (Ed.), *To improve the academy, 9,* 89–98. Stillwater, OK: New Forums Press.

Walvoord, B. E., & Anderson, V. J. (1998). *Effective grading: A tool for learning and assessment.* San Francisco, CA: Jossey-Bass.

Wanner, R. A., Lewis, L. S., & Gregorio, D. I. (1981, October). Research productivity in academia: A comparative study of the sciences, social sciences and humanities. *Sociology of Education, 54,* 238–253.

Weimer, M. (1987). Theories of teaching. *The Teaching Professor, 1*(3), 1–2.

Weinstein, C. E., & Mayer, R. (1986). The teaching of learning strategies. In M. Wittrock (Ed.), *Handbook of research on teaching* (pp. 315–327). New York, NY: Macmillan.

Weiss, G. & Haber, H. F. (1999). *Perspectives on embodiment: The intersection of nature and culture.* New York, NY: Routledge.

Wheatley, M. J. (1992). *Leadership and the new science.* San Francisco, CA: Berrett-Koehler.

WIDS instructional designer. (1997). Waunakee, WI: Wisconsin Technical College System Foundation. [Computer Software].

Wiggins, G., & McTighe, J. (1998). *Understanding by design.* Alexandria, VA: Association for Supervision and Curriculum Development.

Williams, J., & Colomb, G. (1990). *Style: Toward clarity and grace.* Chicago, IL: University of Chicago Press.

Wright, M. (1998, May 27). Faculty seminar produces ideas focused on learning. *Herald Times,* (A1, A7).

Wright, W. A., & O'Neil, M. C. (1995). Teaching improvement practices: International perspectives. In W. A. Wright & Associates (Eds.), *Teaching improvement practices: Successful strategies for higher education* (pp. 1–57). Bolton, MA: Anker.

Wunsch, M. (Ed.). (1994). *Mentoring revisited: Making an impact on individuals and institutions.* San Francisco, CA: Jossey-Bass.